FASHION

Barbaralee Diamonstein

FASHION

The Inside Story

RIZZOLI
NEW YORK

For Sally and Carl,
Pamela, Peter, Tommy,
and, of course, Tim

AUTHOR'S ACKNOWLEDGMENTS

These conversations, (a number of which were videotaped as part of the
Van Day Truex Memorial Lecture series at the New School/Parsons School
of Design) were conducted during a two year period, from 1982 through
late 1984. They were an extension of a series of other interviews that I had
conducted with painters, sculptors, architects, photographers, craft-
persons, and interior and fashion designers, which focused on those who
have made significant contributions to contemporary American culture.

For their help in transforming this project into a reality, my thanks to: my
able assistants, Linda Reid, Jill Schaffer, and Jean Zimmerman; to Helene
Curtis, Incorporated, whose support was helpful. My thanks, too, to Pierre
and Fred, who provided a tranquil haven, as well as personal enhancement.

First published in the United States of America in 1985 by
RIZZOLI INTERNATIONAL PUBLICATIONS, INC.
597 Fifth Avenue, New York, NY 10017

Copyright © 1985 Barbaralee Diamonstein

Designed by Massimo Vignelli
Set in type by Roberts/Churcher
Printed and bound in the USA.

Library of Congress Cataloging in Publication Data

Diamonstein, Barbaralee.
    Fashion: the inside story.

    1. Costume designers—United States—Interviews.
I. Title.
TT507.D527   1985   746.9′2′0922 [B]   85–42865
ISBN 0–8478–0610–3 (pbk.)

CONTENTS

FOREWORD

The fashion world for most observers is a mythical kingdom, part Camelot and part Hollywood. The designers are the knights in armor, the movie stars. Attractive in themselves, they possess an intuitive knowledge of the kind of dress that can convert mere mortals into glamorous figures.

There is the excitement of their fashion showings, kin to the extravagant premières of Hollywood's golden age, with Klieg lights flashing, worshipful throngs straining against the silken ropes, and goddesses wrapped in furs and jewels walking down velvet carpets from their limousines to the theater.

How different is that image from reality?

Reality is quite a bit more nerve-wracking. The typical designer puts on a fashion show two to four times a year. He imbues it with as much glamour as possible and, since space is limited, seats are hard to come by. A good show will bring plenty of attention, but the actual selling takes place in the showroom. That's where the salesman has a one-on-one relationship with the buyer. Clothes that look ravishing on the runway can be duds in the showroom.

For fashion is primarily a business and the designer, in addition to being a creative force, is also a business man. He can survive a bad season, or maybe two, but if he loses touch with the clothes people want to wear, he will be looking for another line of work.

What is this combination artist/businessman really like? Is he an arrogant dictator, who raises and lowers hemlines at will, who changes his style periodically so women will have to replace their wardrobes?

In penetrating interviews that allow the designers to speak for themselves, Barbaralee Diamonstein shows us, somewhat surprisingly, that they are reasonably modest souls. They design the clothes they like, but they are quick to praise the work of others. What they have in common is taste—and their taste is varied enough to enable us to pick clothes that we like, too.

They often come from simple backgrounds. James Galanos tells us his father came to the United States from Greece and ran a restaurant. When he found it difficult to get a job designing, he went to California and made his own collection. "I always pursued my ideal of sophistication, or what elegant women should look like," he says, in explaining his success.

They often have a practical stance. Geoffrey Beene stresses "comfort and usefulness" in his designs and brags that "they travel easily and fold—often into the palm of one's hand."

Adolfo, who says "I would dress the whole world in black if I could" also advises women that "with four or five good garments they could travel all over the world."

They are not averse to giving advice on making clothes last longer. "Don't wear them every day," suggests Bill Blass. "Clothes need to breathe and relax too." He and other designers also recommend dry cleaning as rarely as possible—spot clean, brush and air your clothes to cut down on trips to the cleaner, they suggest.

Not the words of prophets and seers?

Quite true.

While many think of fashion designers as proponents of some ethereal kind of chic, they turn out to be pragmatists with their feet squarely on the ground.

The reality factor is far more prevalent in the attitude—and the work—of the American designer than it is for his European counterpart. Design for design's sake, still a prevailing factor in the workrooms and salons of Milan, Paris, and Rome is less predominant in this country, where designers are concerned with Will it Work? as well as Will it Look Beautiful?

Designers here know they make clothes for active women who will not abide an uncomfortable dress no matter how fetching it looks. They know this because they make regular trips to the stores where they actually face the customer. Many of them lead active social lives, mingling with their clients or potential clients. It is no ivory tower existence.

Fashion as an industry is a relatively new phenomenon, dating back to the invention of the sewing machine in the mid-nineteenth century. America took the lead in the production of ready-to-wear, while couture or made-to-order clothes continued to dominate European design.

The couture salons set the pace for hem lengths, colors and the shape of clothes, while America, in terms of design, was regarded as the provinces. As Bill Blass observes, the designer was often hidden away in back rooms and encouraged to take his vacation as soon as the collection was shown, so the manufacturer and the salesmen could make changes in his work. In the last twenty years, this pattern has been broken. More often than not, the designer is also the entrepreneur. His stamp is on the clothes; he runs the show.

In the process, he has grown and matured. His range of interests has grown, along with his powers of observation. Though he is necessarily concerned with function, his aesthetic sense has not atrophied.

Because the designer is aware of women's changing needs, his clothes have a growing pertinence. They are beginning to have an impact in the Far East as well as in Europe. New York is widely recognized as one of the fashion capitals of the world today. So the story of American designers is particularly relevant. They are already beginning to influence the way people look and how they think about clothes on an international scale.

While fashion remains an enigma to many observers, Miss Diamonstein brings us up close and helps us understand how it works. It has its share of glitter and glamour, but it is by no means all froth. By showing us the people who run the show, Barbaralee Diamonstein contributes her bit to piercing the fashion mystique.

Bernadine Morris
August, 1985

INTRODUCTION

Vain trifles as they seem, clothes have, they say, more important offices than merely to keep us warm. They change our view of the world and the world's view of us. . . Thus, there is much to support the view that it is clothes that wear us and not we them; we may make them take the mould of arm or breast, but they mould our hearts, our brains, our tongues to their liking.
—*Virginia Woolf*, Orlando*

In the same way that peacocks grow new plumage each year, human beings attempt to renew themselves with clothing. Our metamorphosis is only superficially comparable to that of the peacock, however, for it is far more than a manifestation of biological needs or physiological processes: it is our uniquely conscious effort to embellish and modify our bodies through the use of materials not inherent to our natural form. Clothing is an all-pervasive and powerful expression of human imagination and spirit; fashion is a refinement, a qualification, of the statement clothing makes. The interviews in this book are based on the premise that fashion comprises all manifestations of body covering which, for a limited time, receive general acceptance.

In the broadest sense, fashion is man's oldest art. It is also one of his greatest examples of collective achievement, for it is culture created by the convergence of individual expression and popular consensus. While some people can never pronounce the word "fashion" without a tone of disparagement—and, regarded superficially, fashion *can* be frivolous—it does reflect the taste, mood, and tone of society more than any other design art. As with architecture, it is a universal symbol through which we define our lives.

Man is the only animal to embellish and modify his natural shape. Anthropologists have long argued that clothing originated not because of the need for warmth and protection, but for the magical powers ascribed to artificially altered appearances. The human body is the basis of all fashion. Sexuality is, logically, a significant influence—it is one of the factors which subconsciously affect the ways in which clothing is used and judged. Indeed, fashion is the most intimate form in the sphere of options in self-expression. Clothing our psyches as much as our bodies, we wear whatever makes us feel better, younger, thinner, richer, prettier, sleeker, sexier, more artistic, intellectual, rebellious, or whatever suits the image we are trying to promote. In her incisive book, *The Language of Clothes*, Pulitzer Prize–winning novelist Alison Lurie comments on fashion's evocative powers: "For thousands of years, human beings have communicated with one another first in the language of dress . . . you announce your sex, age and class . . . through what you are wearing, and very possibly give important information (or misinformation) as to your occupation, origin, personality, opinions, tastes, sexual desires and current mood. Fashion is a language of signs, a nonverbal system of communication."

And it is more. As social commentator Tom Wolfe has written, fashion offers a "sub-rational but instant and very brilliant illumination—of individuals and even entire periods." From headlines to hemlines, in the long sweep of history, public policies and private expressions have always been interrelated. In *Fashion: The Power that Influences the World*, writer George P. Fox reminds us that fashion "has modelled society and shaped empires, and has held in its scales the fates of kingdoms and the destinies of commonwealths. It has entered into the life of all nations and will be identified in its influences on our fortunes forever." Fashion design and clothing styles not only reflect and reveal their time, they offer comment or reaction to the realities of a period. It is now clear how the panache of the '20's, the glamour of the '30's, the slimmer silhouettes and broad-shouldered jackets of the '40's, and the psychedelic rag-tag look of the turbulent '60's demonstrate the relationship between fashion and social attitudes, the economy, technology, moral values, and aesthetic considerations. Yet, because fashion is so thoroughly woven into the fabric of society, its significance as a cultural symbol has often been overlooked.

The field of fashion design has evolved immeasurably from the days when

*Orlando, A Biography by Virginia Woolf; Harcourt Brace Jovanovich, Inc., New York, Copyright © 1928 by Virginia Woolf. Copyright © by Leonard Woolf.

"haute couture" created custom design to serve an elite, wealthy clientele. Over the past fifty years, fashion has emerged from the salon and entered the marketplace, becoming accessible to, and almost as diverse as, its ever growing audience. In the course of his interview, Bill Blass talks of the emergence of this development: "In America, we were the first to make mass-produced clothes, good-looking clothes for the masses." The manufacturers of these clothes became an important force in fashion as they assumed a new role as arbiters of style; their designers, however, long remained unheralded contributors to their success. Blass reminds us that designers "were never allowed out of the back room. Manufacturers didn't want it known that they had even *had* designers."

The anonymity of the designer was also promoted by the department stores and leading boutiques at which fashions were showcased. For decades retailers rarely gave public acknowledgement to designers other than those who were under exclusive contract to them, preferring instead to label clothing with the store's name. It was not until the 1960's that designers such as Bill Blass and Herbert Kasper began to receive recognition and acclaim for their work. The designer as independent fashion force, entrepreneur, and celebrity soon followed.

Today's successful designer is a savvy businessperson, personally involved not only in design, but in production, sales, public relations, and advertising. Enterprising designers have transformed themselves into enthusiastic salespeople for their own clothes. In the 1980's, it is not unusual for designers to promote a season's line through multi-city jaunts which take them across the country as well as abroad. Personal appearances at exclusive stores and at charitable functions add to their allure, resulting in high price tags and bolstered sales. With their charm, salesmanship, and glamour well-packaged, these designers are essentially dressing up America and promoting the growth of the American fashion industry.

And grow it does. The public's insatiable appetite for new fashions keeps the industry booming. Even economic slumps have had little impact on sales. The growth of the fashion industry is evidenced both by its steadily increasing revenues and the broadening scope of what is being marketed by designers. The participation of designers in the merchandising of fashion has enhanced not only the sales of their clothes, but also the marketability of their names. It has become increasingly apparent that the design and successful marketing of apparel serves as the crucial scaffolding on which to hang a full range of licenses. Today's most celebrated designers lend their names and talents to creations as diverse as perfumes, cars, sheets, chocolates, sunglasses, towels, stationery, luggage, and even bullet-proof suits. Ralph Lauren, who is known for the expanse of his design activities, exemplifies the diversity of the contemporary "fashion" designer's domain. He speaks of his range of endeavors that includes cosmetics, fragrance, and home furnishings of all types, and, of course, men's wear. "I have licensees in Japan and Canada, too. I've turned down chocolates; but automobiles I would love to do! I'm a big car fan, but I don't think I'm capable of designing them. I would never put my name on anything I don't do. Whatever I'm not designing, is because I'm not capable of designing it."

The licensing of designers' names is not a recent development. Arnold Scaasi claims that when he licensed his name in 1957, he was the first American designer to do so. Scaasi recalls, "I did children's wear and I did men's ties and men's sweaters, and I did the first Ben Kahn fur collections in 1958. Licensing really meant that you were being given credit for designing what designers had always designed, but had never been credited with before."

The public's response to licensing has been until recently, astonishingly positive. What once was a concern for quality had become an obsession with the designer label. Indeed, the designer label has acquired an extrinsic value independent of the product on which it is placed: a polo pony, a lioness's head, a turtle, or a signature heralds one's fashion sense, awareness of current trends, income, class, social circle, and lifestyle. And the effects of licensing have not yet even been fully realized. The last twenty years have seen the emergence of the designer as head of a business conglomerate, some holding as many as seventy licenses each. Licensing

has precipitated the diversification and expansion of the design activities of a small, but dominant, minority. One result of this development is that it is becoming increasingly difficult for new talent to establish itself. It is entirely possible that licensing has, ironically, diminished the development of the fashion industry's creative potential, and that licensing has replaced the store label as an agent of anonymity for the junior designer. The Oxford American Dictionary defines "style" as "elegance, distinction, the manner of doing something contrasted with the thing done." Every designer distills his style into a particular vision which defines the fashions he creates; this style is further distilled by the interpretation a garment is given by its wearer. Explaining his perception of style, Ronaldus Shamask says, "The Oxford Dictionary explains 'high art' as truth with beauty as a by-product, and 'low art' as beauty with truth as a by-product. And of course, style is neither of those. Style just aims to please."

The elegant, sophisticated woman is central to James Galanos's vision of style. "It has to do with a certain refinement, quality—a paring down—elimination of the superfluous in the clothes that I make. The cut, the line are of the utmost importance; the fit of the dress, and the ultimate components of fabric, color, and proportions are so vital. When you see it all together, on the right person, it's a thing of beauty." In contrast, Pauline Trigère perceives style as the unique achievement not of the fashion designer, but of the fashion wearer. " 'Style' is something that you do yourself. 'Fashion' is what the magazines try to print, or the newspapers try to say, and what women try to copy or capture. 'Style' is something completely individual, something that's *you*. It's an old scarf, an old pin, an old coiffure. It's very hard to describe. Most women don't have it." Oscar de la Renta equates style with good taste, and he believes it is a cultivated characteristic as rare as genius. He explains: "I think good taste comes from appreciation of life, and from learning. No one is born with good taste."

Style is idiosyncratic, and is consequently difficult, if not impossible, to package and market. By focusing on understanding and meeting the particular requirements of their customers, designers help their clientele develop the fashion sense, self-knowledge, and confidence necessary to achieve style. Today's designers are attentive and receptive to cultural and social currents; they have become careful observers and conscientious interpreters of men and women's changing practical and psychological needs. An informed awareness of their audience enables designers to sustain their appeal—and their profits.

According to Albert Nipon, the designer must be accessible to the client in order for the relationship to work successfully. "You can't be in an ivory tower, we learned," he says, referring to himself and his wife, Pearl. "When we create things, we imagine how they are going to work and assume certain things. But when we actually see the clothes in action on the customer, and the customer's reaction to them, it does give us another insight that we then take and translate into our next collection." In creating clothes, the designer's role is simply to please the customer, according to Bill Blass. He explains: "I do think that essentially the role of clothes is to give you some pleasure. I think that in dressing you should please yourself. Mind you, there are occasions when women dress for men, and, certainly, when men dress for women. But essentially it's the way clothes make you feel that makes them right." As the designer for many wealthy, famous women, Blass continues, "The rich have exposure to more in the way of clothes and life and atmosphere in general than the average person does. Their needs *are* different; they go more places, they have more things to do. But today it's less true than it once was because most of these so-called very rich women work. They do something. And I think that probably the biggest influence in the last decade has been that of the working woman." During her career, Mary McFadden has also seen significant changes in the market for which she designs. She describes today's American woman as "more individualistic now than she was in the '60's. The woman of the '70's and '80's has a greater freedom. She's starting to understand herself at a younger age."

The fashion industry's response to women's "greater freedom", and increasingly varied and complex lifestyles, has been to offer a greater variety of goods and styles. As Kasper notes, "What's very important about fashion today is that there is no one look. I think what is fashionable is *versatility*."

Of course, contact with their clients is the most direct way by which designers can assess their market. Norma Kamali rarely allows her photograph to be published so that she can maintain the anonymity which allows her to receive customers' uncensored evaluations of the fashions she sells at her Manhattan boutique.

Pauline Trigère relies on her own experience as a woman in designing womenswear. "Wearing clothes has been an enormous teacher for me," she says. "I have to be at ease with what I wear, and I think that the customer immediately feels the same way."

In being able to design women's clothes with the dual perspective of the designer and the client, Trigère is in the minority, however. One of the greatest ironies of the fashion industry, apparent in all facets of the business, is the fact that most of the designers who create the clothes and images for American women, are men. An inventory of notable designers in the history of fashion reveals that, though women designers have contributed significantly to the advancement of fashion as a design art, males have always well out-numbered their female counterparts. Indeed, as in many other industries, the exclusion of women from positions of importance has until recently been institutionalized in fashion.

Trigère vividly recalls the subordinate role proscribed for women when she began her career in fashion. Soon after her arrival in New York in 1937, she began working as an assistant at Hattie Carnegie, and she still remembers the atmosphere there. "Miss Carnegie used to say that she could not understand a woman designer. She never believed in them. She liked men designers. There *were* no women designers."

In examining the disparity between the number of male and female fashion designers, Trigère, who started her own business under trying conditions during WWII, says, in puzzlement, "Maybe there is something that frightens women to start their own business." As she knows from her own experience, that "something" is a formidable group of difficult and challenging factors: it takes enormous stamina, energy, and courage to raise capital, establish and operate a business, and fulfill marital and familial duties.

That female and male designers bring different, gender-related perspectives to the task of designing womenswear is documented in many of the *Fashion: The Inside Story* conversations; whether the female designer's perspective is *better* is a point on which there is no consensus. Adolfo believes that "men have a very unbiased way of designing clothes for women. I might be completely wrong, but I have a feeling that when a woman designs for another woman, she might think of how the clothes will look on herself. A man has a larger scope in designing clothes for women . . . male designers see women on a pedestal. They don't want to make you look ridiculous."

The personal perspective of the female designer, which Adolfo sees as a limitation, Carolina Herrera perceives as an asset because a woman designer thinks as a woman, can try the dresses on, and knows what looks and feels best.

The men and women interviewed here are among today's most celebrated fashion designers. They have achieved success and fame, but in most instances laurels have been awarded to them only after they've spent years as students of design, apprentices in fashion houses and stores, and struggling independents. These individuals' backgrounds and training are as diverse as their designs. Norma Kamali recalls that she was "creative out of necessity." When her mother could not afford to satisfy her desire to "dress up," Norma would purchase a two dollar dress, remove ugly trimmings, alter and decorate it in her own style. "Then," she declares, "the dress was mine, my own creation. That's how it all started. I just wanted more."

Mollie Parnis also wanted more. In her first summer job, in a showroom of a blouse firm she was occasionally allowed to help the designer, and would tell her to change a collar or shorten the length of a sleeve. She became so involved with the process that she never went back to school in the fall. She wound up being the designer for the firm.

Inventiveness in the showroom also led Perry Ellis into fashion design.

Drawn to the glamour and excitement of retailing he became a buyer for Miller and Rhoads Department Store in Richmond, Virginia. He says he was "strong, aggressive and quite opinionated." Ellis recalls how "almost everything I looked at, that I was coming to buy I wanted to change. I was constantly redesigning other people's clothing. It became very successful for them, and they started asking my opinion." In 1967, one of those manufacturers asked Ellis to come work for him directly. He did, and has worked as a designer ever since.

Donna Karan, who formerly designed for the Anne Klein label, and is now in her own business, remembers being inspired by an idea of the romantic. "I loved dance. I wanted to be a dancer. I loved to illustrate, so I wanted to be a sketcher. . . I love women and I love movement. And I like to watch the whole thing happen. Fashion design wasn't something that I thought I was going to do; it just evolved."

An interest in the human body was also integral to Geoffrey Beene's interest in fashion design. Raised in a large family of doctors, Beene studied three years of a pre-medical curriculum and one year of medicine before switching to fashion design. "Often," he contends, "one has to study in order to know what *not* to do." During anatomy classes, Beene sketched dresses in the margins of his notebook. "Once," he remembers, "it was brought to the attention of the professor and he stopped class to show it to all. Guffaws galore, but I do feel I had the last laugh." In making his career choice, Beene was inspired by the work of Schiaparelli of Paris, and Adrian of Hollywood. Seeing their clothes "kindled the flame that ignited" his decision to become a fashion designer.

Whether on stage or screen or in the theatre of ordinary life, one's dress can create a role; it can sheath us in unexpected drama. It's no wonder that many designers have been influenced by glittering stars and bright lights. Fashion give everyday, earthbound clothes a subtle hint of fire. Louis Dell'Olio, until recently the co-designer with Donna Karan, for the Anne Klein label, recalls that he got "tons of inspiration without even realizing it from the Hollywood designers of the '30's and '40's."

Despite his homespun beginnings as a high school football player in Fort Wayne, Indiana, Bill Blass is another designer riveted as a youth by the world of glamour. "Happily," he says, "I'm one of those people who knew from an early age what I wanted to do. To get the hell out of Indiana was one thing," he jokes now. "Don't forget, this was the legendary time of the depression, when on a Saturday afternoon you could go to the movies for fifteen cents and see Carole Lombard, Marlene Dietrich and Greta Garbo. I knew that making clothes for people of that sort could be the most exciting life in the world for me. So, from that time on—I was very, very young—I started sketching, and selling the sketches to New York manufacturers. When I was eighteen I came to New York to go to school, and eventually to work."

Precisely what makes one become a designer is a story often impossible to tell. James Galanos began sketching dress designs at the age of eight. Today his eye is mature and hones in neatly on its mark, but the sense of childhood wonder remains as an endless reserve. Apart from private, untamed urgings, his designs can be traced directly to influences arising from the past and from foreign cultures.

Adolfo, born in Cuba and known primarily as a milliner early in his career, describes the circumstances which led to a business of designing classically tailored, easy to wear suits, dresses and ballgowns. "I was raised by aunts," he relates, "one of whom was eccentric in her very elegant way of living. She used to tell me that in the 1920's she came from Paris with her hair bobbed, wearing one of those very short dresses, and people used to follow her in the street. Havana was always very fashionable."

Clothing design obviously influenced by other cultures has been used to create an aura of confidence, of being "smart", or well-traveled. We are interested in ravishing silks, rustling taffetas, and intricate ballgowns of the eighteenth century partly because they represent something remote, a bygone age, and partly because designers like Shamask and Mary McFadden cut through a double layer of yesterday and today. Shamask reveals the geometrically classic proportions of the Japanese kimono, while Mary McFadden makes more implicit references to Africa and the Far East.

Contemporary design has as much to do with its own history as with the emotions and, above all, values of the design originator. Perhaps that is why Ralph Lauren's frontier America or prairie-look appeals to such a wide audience. Lauren offers certain personal values which are successfully translated in his creations. His designs express qualities that are simple, but thought to be enduring and, at heart, romantic. It is of little surprise that he uses his wife as a model image of the woman who wears his clothes.

Now, more than in any other time, fashion design is respected as a design art. Clothes from centuries past and from other cultures are being reconsidered: their significance is being captured, or cast off, by new ideas. Fashion, like other arts, can be one man or woman's secret obsession, or it can transcend personality and speak for a large and diverse humanity. Because the shopper has greater choices, and is more informed and adamant about what he or she wants, designers are forced to regard them as tough and exacting critics. Carolina Herrera says, "My greatest success is that women buy my clothes." Arnold Scaasi has been concerned for the customer all along, pointing out, however, that the most relentless critic remains himself: "Maybe that's part of your talent, that you're always striving for something better than you did last time, and hoping that you'll keep it on the same creative level. You don't want to make the clothes look strange, but you want them to look new. So you're working within a framework that doesn't allow you much freedom, and yet you want it to be free and new looking. So, it scares you to death until somebody finally buys that dress."

Fashion design is increasingly a high risk art. There has never been a time when the definition of what is fashionable has been more subject to individual interpretation. With all these factors in mind one would have to agree with Bill Blass when he said, "I would never venture to predict anything beyond next season."

The fashion industry is witnessing and encouraging a new commitment to the design of clothes that can go from the office to an evening out, from taking the children to school to boarding a plane en route to Paris or Peru. Creating built-in versatility is more challenging and necessary than catering to popular, or momentary whims. However, being "in vogue" is hardly a crime. People demand a lot from their clothes. The right dress, or suit, or cut, or weave can make one feel at the center of all they do, or desire. Wild threads can cause us to appear more fascinating then we really think we are. Chic can mean something different to everyone; fashion has become an idiosyncratic response to what we see in our office, during our travels or on the nightly news. High fashion models may slink down a runway paved with graffiti-art, decked out in tennis shoes, T-shirts and billowing break-dance pants—and why not? All of the designers in these interviews reinforce the view that fashion reflects our world.

And what will the next season hold? How will our age be remembered and revealed in its clothing and recorded in its fashion design? Have current designers captured or influenced the emotions and expectations of our society? In an attempt to discover, or at least to glimpse the answers to these and other questions, I decided to go to the source: designers who shape fashion now, and perhaps also in the future. As successful as these designers are, they are all keenly aware that their continued success relies upon endless variety, aimed to please you, their ultimate critic.

Barbaralee Diamonstein

Adolfo, fall, 1985

Below:
Oscar de la Renta, fall, 1982

Opposite:
Perry Ellis, fall, 1985

James Galanos, fall, 1983

Carolina Herrera, fall/winter, 1981

Overleaf:
Norma Kamali, spring, 1985

Below:
Donna Karan, fall, 1985

Opposite:
Herbert Kasper, fall, 1981

Below:
Mary McFadden, fall/winter, 1983

Opposite:
Ralph Lauren, fall, 1982

26

Adolfo

Adolfo, the Cuban born designer of classically tailored, easy to wear suits, dresses, and ballgowns that make women feel comfortable and even glamorous, can be counted on for clothes whose cut, line, and fit are quintessentially American—and permanently in fashion.

BLDD: Recently I heard a well-known designer say that the most important thing to know about fashion design is the selection of fabric. Do you agree?

A: Maybe. Actually I think if you have a feeling for design you can pick up a little piece of any kind of fabric and make just what you want to.

BLDD: What about cut and pattern—isn't it important to understand the difference between the bias and the straight?

A: That's extremely important. Early in my career I realized that to do anything well you have to be very, very sure of how the fabric moves.

BLDD: What's most important to you in choosing a fabric?

A: I like silk to be heavy and exciting to touch because then it drapes much better. And I like velvets, brocades and all kinds of fabrics like that.

BLDD: How do you decide on colors?

A: I would dress the whole world in black, if I could, but that's not possible. So we have to think of white sometimes.

BLDD: On the one hand, women are told that their clothes are now "collectibles." On the other they are told one year that the fit is the most important thing, and another that it is the shorter hemline. How do you decide what silhouette or what hemline to show?

A: I feel the clothes I design should be long-lasting. Because they are quite expensive, they should not be purchased just for one season. You should be able to wear them this year and next year. If you get tired of them, put them in the closet and take them out again and wear them for ten years or longer.

BLDD: How should women decide what style they should wear?

A: That's a rather elastic question. It is very difficult. Sometimes I see clients whom I would like to look one way and they want to look another way. So, sometimes we compromise. Sometimes we don't.

BLDD: Who generally prevails?

A: The mirror, I think! I always insist that they look in the mirror to get a better idea if it's good or bad.

BLDD: Is there such a thing as a classic hemline?

A: No, not really.

BLDD: Is there any length that you especially prefer?

A: Today I like the hem to barely touch the knee. Sometimes I like it a little lower than the knee, but I don't like mid-calf-length skirts. They are old-looking and it doesn't work very well in the sort of designs I do.

BLDD: Let's backtrack for a moment: you spent your childhood in Cuba. Was there a fashion tradition there?

A: Oh yes, very much indeed. I was raised by my aunt, who was eccentric in her very elegant way of living. She would tell me that in the 1920s she came from Paris with her hair bobbed, wearing very short dresses, and people used to follow her in the street. Cuba was very fashionable.

BLDD: When you left Havana for Paris at the age of seventeen, you managed to land a job immediately, at a very well known couture house. For whom did you work, and what did you do there?

A: People say that I worked at Balenciaga, which, of course, I did. But I never saw Balenciaga, and I never even saw the dresses. I used to sweep and pick things up from the floor. It was not a very glamorous job. After that, I was in complete despair, and I came to New York and then went back to Paris where I worked for another house in rue Cambon in back of the Ritz Hotel. That is really my alma mater. In that house, I learned to do all the things that I am experienced in doing today.

BLDD: What brought you to work for the legendary Coco Chanel?

A: I always hoped to be able to make the sort of things she did. In later years I think I have done that. Occasionally people who are indiscreet or misinformed say, "Oh, you copy Chanel." And really, I don't. There is a feeling in what I create that resembles her designs, but actually if you look closely at her's and mine they are not at all the same.

BLDD: What are the major differences?

A: My designs are more contemporary. I like to make them in knits or to combine knits and fabrics.

BLDD: It is clear to anyone who knows your work that you feel a profound professional kinship with Chanel. What did you learn from your apprenticeship with her?

A: I absorbed the things they did there. In France, in the late 1950s, an apprentice was at the bottom of the ladder, and it was not a very easy job. But I learned so many things because I was always doing something. That's how I learned to make hats.

BLDD: How did you get the job at Chanel?

A: My aunt used to be dressed there, and she asked them if I could go there and observe. I was not paid. I was there for six months and then I came back to New York.

BLDD: When one deals with such a classic theme as you do, one redesigns the same suit over and over again. What continues to absorb and interest you about that style?

A: I think that when you create designs like that, there is always a little mystery somewhere, a little secret. Something that you can change. Sometimes it's a new twist so that it no longer looks like the one before, or it's an extension of what you have previously done.

BLDD: I have read that this is going to be the "Year of the Fit." How much of a woman's shape, do you think, should be left to the imagination?

A: First, you have to have a good fit. After that I would say an outfit should not be too fitted, because then it is most uncomfortable. You cannot breathe, you cannot eat, you cannot move, you cannot do anything, and that's no fun at all. I like things fitted, but not overfitted.

BLDD: At one time hats were a necessity for every well-dressed woman or man. In the 1950s you helped make the hat an accessory that was almost indispensable. How did you first become interested in millinery?

A: It was sheer necessity. One has to eat and pay the rent. I was successful making hats, but, you know, I didn't like it. It was like a punishment. In Paris I learned to make hats, and they were very intricate. You have to work with wires, and all kinds of things, and it is a nightmare! Anybody who has ever made a hat knows that it's not the easiest thing in the world.

BLDD: When did you design all those wonderful straw hats?

A: I made the Panama hats when I was at Bergdorf Goodman. When I left, Halston took my job. I moved to another place called Emme. Every time Halston and I meet we commiserate about those not very exciting days.

BLDD: Do you ever design hats to go with your clothes now? Even for a fashion show?

A: No. I like bows better. But to make a bow is not very easy either. I was taught by Chanel: "a bow, is a bow, and it's something very special."

BLDD: What makes your bow more special than the bows we all tie every day?

A: You have to look at them. They are very nice.

BLDD: Is there anything that you learned from designing hats that you applied to your apparel designing career?

A: First, I think, patience; second, maybe patience, and third might be patience, also.

BLDD: How did you progress from the world of Paris couture to be the designer of some of America's most recognized clothing?

A: I am very thankful for my hats, because I met some very exciting ladies in my early career and they switched their interest from hats to clothes when I did. So when I started making clothes I had a complete clientele overnight.

BLDD: There was a Cuban designer, Anna Maria Berrera, who was one of your great teachers. . .

A: She was a marvelous lady who used to work for Vionnet in Paris and then went to live in Cuba. When Castro came, she came to New York. She taught me everything I know about making clothes. She had a very scientific method of making patterns—her system was the best.

BLDD: What in particular did you learn from her that was so important?

A: All the things that are so necessary: planning the fabrics, cutting the patterns. She was so exciting. We used to make dresses out of brown paper, and then we would open up the seams and make our own patterns. I learned to make dresses in a very unorthodox way. It might not be the same for people who study fashion in design school, but we had our own system which worked very well.

BLDD: How did you manage to get the capital to go into business for yourself, especially when you were known primarily as a milliner? Was that something of a problem for you?

A: Not really. Bill Blass gave me $10,000. I went to him and said, "Bill, you know I want to have my own house." By "my own house," I meant my own little room. Even in the '60s you could not go very far with $10,000. But he loaned me $10,000 and another friend loaned me the rest of the money. I was able to pay them back in less than a year. It was very exciting.

BLDD: You said that you started with a ready-made clientele. And you've credited several glamorous and well-known women as your first customers and even your first inspirations as a clothing designer. Who are some of these women and what did you create for them?

A: First, I did hats for the Duchess of Windsor, and I adore her so. She is a marvellous lady and became a wonderful customer of mine. There was also Mrs. William Paley and then Betsy Bloomingdale—tonight I have to dress her up for a ball—and Gloria Vanderbilt, the one for whom I did all the patchwork and fantasy things. They were my teachers.

BLDD: There was a black lace dress that you designed for the Duchess of Windsor that was very well received by her, and, her household as well.

A: Yes, everybody loved that dress. Once I received a lovely note from the Duke of Windsor in Spanish saying, "my wife looked more beautiful than ever." He spoke Spanish very well.

BLDD: How would you describe the style of the clothing that you were designing at the beginning of your career? Was fantasy an important element in those years?

A: Yes, because that was 1962–63, and everyone was making the Indian look and things like that. I could not do that, so I had to go my own way. I did a lot of things with Gloria Vanderbilt then, when she was working on her Elizabethan paintings, and we became very successful.

BLDD: Your clothes have always been very ladylike, a notion that was not very popular in the more freeform, turbulent days of the 1960s. Was your work affected and influenced, eventually, by that period?

A: Not really, I don't think so.

BLDD: What were you designing when everybody was either wearing jeans or dressed as rich gypsies?

A: I did my own patchworks. Gradually I started to make suits that became popular, and I learned to work the knitting machine, which I was very interested in.

BLDD: The use of knit fabrics is one of your innovations, one also that occurred in the mid-60s. Whatever gave you the idea?

A: I wanted to be able to reproduce other kinds of textures in my knits.

BLDD: Are there any artists whose work has inspired your fabric designs, or color combinations, or a certain style or look?

A: Unlike some other designers I am not inspired by museums and what is in them. I am only inspired by my clients. Since I am with so many customers all the time, I'm more inclined to think in terms of what might look well now, or in the future.

BLDD: Let's talk for a moment about everybody's day-to-day clothing concerns. What is a good basic wardrobe?

A: If when you wake up in the morning, you go jogging, you need a jogging suit. After that, I think it is good to have a suit and an afternoon dress, one you can wear in the afternoon and into the night. You can change the blouse and wear the suit until late in the evening. I think that with four or five good garments, you can travel all over the world.

BLDD: If someone had $1000 to spend, how would you suggest they use it?

A: I would say, buy a pair of jeans, a little blazer, a white skirt, and maybe a black knitted dress or a black crepe dress. That would more or less take care of the thousand dollars.

BLDD: Remember how families used to pass clothes on from one generation to the next? Nowadays there are very few people who consider doing that, yet timeless or classic design is a hallmark of your work. What should we do to ensure the long life of the clothes, that you tell us we will be able to wear for at least ten years.

A: You have to be very careful with the dry cleaner. I talk to so many people who seem to spend their whole lives going to the dry cleaner, and I don't know why. It is so expensive, and what they have eventually is a transparent dress.

BLDD: How do you advise people to take care of their clothes, especially your clothes, so that they retain their shape? And if they are soiled, what should they do?

A: They should be placed in a drawer. If you are going to wear a dress at night, it would be nice to lay it on the bed during the day so that when you put it on it is completely flat.

BLDD: How often should they be cleaned?

A: Not too often.

BLDD: Well, how then do you get them to keep their shape?

A: Our's don't lose their shape. When we make the knitted fabric, we iron it for a week so you get the fabric's complete length. It's already stretched. We make the dress by hand so it works out very well.

BLDD: Handwork used to be much more common in Europe than America, and work done on the continent had a reputation for being much finer than any work that was done here. Is that still the case?

A: I think so. In Europe there is still a great deal of handwork done, although we do a great deal of it here, too. Our designs are hand-finished. The buttons of a suit are crocheted into the fabric by hand so you never lose them. The armholes are hand finished and then the suit is all put together by hand.

BLDD: Is it a problem to find people to do that kind of work nowadays?

A: No, not really. There are people who like to do it a lot.

BLDD: You're known—in fact, I'm surprised you don't have one today—to sport a thimble on your thumb even when you are not working.

A: Oh yes, and I feel naked without one!

BLDD: Do you still get a chance to sew?

A: Still get to sew? I never stop sewing! That's my hobby. I enjoy it very much. And I like to cut and sew my samples myself because then I do it the way I like it.

BLDD: Do you have a last name?

A: Yes. My name is Adolfo Sardinia.

BLDD: When did you decide to be known as simply Adolfo?

A: When I first started, I thought it would be easier than to use two names. I thought that one day I would be successful, and that I had better start from the very beginning with a single star-like name.

BLDD: Nancy Reagan's wardrobe includes many Adolfo designs, and your name is often linked with hers in the fashion press. Did you ever expect the media to celebrate your work as it has?

A: No, I didn't really. And, many times I don't like to read the things people write. I already know the story of my life. When I have a fashion show I don't like to read about that either.

BLDD: How do you find out how people react?

A: I know by the audience. If they like it, that is what is important. And I know from my clients, because if they don't like it they will not come back to me. You have a fashion show and everybody is so excited. Then the following day everybody calls you and wants to come. That is most exciting. Why should I destroy my soul over things that might not be quite right?

BLDD: Besides it being a privilege and an opportunity to design for the wife of a head of state, I imagine that sometimes the responsibility can also be a burden.

A: I guess it could be a burden, but the First Lady is charming and I look forward to meeting with her and designing things for her.

BLDD: What are your concerns when you dress someone as highly visible as the wife of a president, such as Mrs. Reagan?

A: Our arrangements are very personal. It is an honor for me and I do more or less what Mrs. Reagan would like. I present things and then she says which ones she wants.

BLDD: If you could dress another leader of your choice, who would it be and what would you create for her?

A: There are so many people I would like to make clothes for. I would like to make dresses for the Queen of England because I think she would look very well in my things. I could do something very different, quite the opposite of the way she dresses.

BLDD: Consider the attention that public figures receive in their choice of clothing. For example, the impact of Lady Diana's wardrobe and jewelry. Diane Keaton's offbeat casual style of dress, and of course, Nancy Reagan's red Adolfo suit. Does that attention really affect the way other women dress?

A: I think it does because of the media. People cannot help being consciously or unconsciously influenced by it.

BLDD: Have you, for example, sold more red suits than you did in the past?

A: No. Sometimes I get irritated when people say, "I suppose your business is going up," because I make things for Mrs. Reagan. It is not like that at all. I don't want to profit from that. If I like to do things for her and she likes me to design for her, I enjoy the work very much, but I am not going to sell a thousand dresses on that account. To tell you the truth, I would not even sell the same designs. I would not go into a store and say, "Oh, I did a dress for the First Lady I now want you to buy." It is not my style.

BLDD: It's been said that taste is almost as rare as genius. How would *you* define good taste and do you agree that it is such a rare commodity?

A: Good taste is very hard to define. There are people who at first seem to have bad taste but in the long run have good taste. Like Barbra Streisand. She has a very odd sort of look, but she can put herself together and look marvelous.

BLDD: Could you name some women who personify good taste for you?

A: I think Mrs. Reagan has great taste, and I love the way Betsy Bloomingdale looks. She is so beautiful and has such spirit. People make me enthusiastic and excited about designing for them. I think Mrs. Onassis has great taste. She has a very special look. Oh, God, I love the way so many people look!

BLDD: How do you design for a client who does have an innovative style of her own?

A: It's communication. We do custom-made clothes. Sometimes people insist on having what somebody else has, and that's not very easy because what looks good on one person might not look good on another.

BLDD: Is it agreeable to you if they adapt a sleeve or a skirt or a blouse that you have designed in a particular way that you think is really right?

A: If the communication is there, between the client and myself, yes. But if it is not, then it's a disaster.

BLDD: Which American woman, or women would you say have had the most impact on the course of American fashion during the last two decades?

A: That's tough. I think Mrs. Onassis has had a lot to do with that.

BLDD: I have heard you describe these times as a "revolving society." What do you mean when you say that?

A: The whole world is *changing*. Through the years, I have met clients who would like to buy something from me and could not afford it. Then, five to seven years later the same person will come back and will be a marvelous client. She will say, "when I first met you, I was not affluent enough to afford your clothes, but life has changed and I am now able to buy them." Society revolves in that way. People who have money now, may not have it in the future, but there is another part of society that revolves and wants to have all the things that the other part has. I think America, especially, is like that. People here are champions. You might be poor at first, but if you try hard, you succeed. Ninety-nine per cent will succeed if they really try.

BLDD: Some fashion designers today extend their ideas to what is described as "total design." They create things such as sheets or cars, as well as clothing and accessories. Are you also involved in licensing products?

A: I do some licensing, but I like to be engaged in what carries my name, so I don't like to get involved in things that don't mean anything at all to me. I am more interested in a few items carrying my name than in producing a thousand things that have nothing at all to do with me.

BLDD: What do you see as the essential difference between fashion and fad?

A: A fad can sometimes pass so quickly that you don't have time to love it or to live with it. In fashion, if things are not so volatile, you come to love them and live with them for a long time.

BLDD: Do you ever design fad clothing?

A: I don't think so, unless they become a fad. But I hope they don't because I wouldn't like that. I like my clothes to be long-lasting and interesting enough to be kept.

BLDD: In your own case, a navy blue jersey or a sweater and a white coat seems to be your uniform.

A: Or a blazer. I don't care about the way I look.

BLDD: But if *you* feel that way, why should *we* feel differently? If you think it's so important for us to look a certain way, why don't you feel that it is equally important for you to do so? Is it different for men than for women?

A: No, I am speaking only for myself. I enjoy seeing women look beautiful, and I also like to see men looking well. That's my temperament. I like to wear white duck pants every day just because I like to wear them, and a pretty sweater—this one which is about to collapse at the elbows any minute—I like it. It is not eccentricity. I feel truly well dressed like this. I design clothes for men, but I have never worn them because they don't look good on me. I like to make them and I am excited to work with beautiful fabrics, but I would never wear them.

BLDD: Are there currently any styles of which you don't approve?

A: I don't like fitted clothes. Clothes should move with you. You should not look like a sausage! I think when you move clothes should adapt to your shape. When you hang clothes on a hanger, I like them to have the shape of your body, the feeling that they are yours. That's a fantasy of mine, I like that. If you wear something very tight, it is not nice at all. Today they make clothes to look very insinuating. I think it is ordinary.

BLDD: How important an element is fantasy in the creation of the clothes that you design for the evening?

A: I think you have to have fantasy. It is most important. You have to believe in something, because if you don't then you cannot manage from day to day.

BLDD: I know you have very strong personal beliefs. . .

A: I do. I'm a Roman Catholic and a good one. I take my religion very seriously. It helps me a great deal from day to day to believe in God and in my religion. It may not work for others, but for me it works very well.

BLDD: Are there any colors or combinations of colors of which you particularly disapprove?

A: There is a color I don't like. It is something they call "periwinkle." I like reds. I like black and red with lots of orange in it, really red-red.

BLDD: What do you see as the most neglected area of fashion design?

A: That is a difficult question. Underwear, I think. Sometimes they make them very fancy, and the detail shows through the clothes. Sometimes what they put inside is more elaborate than what you put on outside. Sometimes women like to wear tightly fitted dresses and the underwear will show through. I think it is just terrible.

BLDD: I think shoes are the most neglected area of fashion design.

A: And they should be so beautiful.

BLDD: And they should be comfortable, too.

A: Yes, but that is something that doesn't go hand-in-hand—to be comfortable and fashionable.

BLDD: How important an element is comfort in your designs?

A: It is important, but with shoes it is especially difficult.

BLDD: If you were to have a retrospective of your work, what would you emphasize?

A: I have a terrible aversion to retrospectives. I don't like to go back. Sometimes the past is difficult and I don't want to think about it. Some people have easier careers and some people have more difficult ones. It's as if somebody told you they want to die and then come back again. I certainly don't want to come back again. Of course I don't like to go, but I don't want to return.

BLDD: You've said that you don't consider yourself an "interesting" designer. Besides your obvious humility, what do you really mean when you say that, and who would you consider an interesting designer?

A: I don't think I am interesting at all. I enjoy my job and I like to oblige. I think Bill Blass, for example, is a more interesting person. Halston is another.

BLDD: Do you mean "interesting person" or "interesting designer?"

A: Both. I think Mary McFadden is absolutely extraordinary. Once I saw a dress of hers and I liked it so much I bought it and took it to my house just to look at. It was so beautiful. It makes me mad when people do not understand something so beautiful as that. I don't only mean her dresses—everyone likes them—but anything.

BLDD: What does that dress look like?

A: It's a piece of Chinese fabric, and a sash. It is so beautiful to look at.

BLDD: Have you ever considered designing costumes for dance, theater or film?

A: Early in my career I met Cecil B. de Mille and he asked me to make hats for a Broadway show. That was a job I would not like to have to do over, because he was difficult. He was nice, but difficult. I did the hats and was absolutely petrified when he came to see them. But Diana Vreeland, who was a great friend of his said, "Oh, Adolfo has made the most beautiful hats for you." I thought I'd die. He liked them. After that I said, no more designing for the theater.

BLDD: Not even clothes?

A: No. In the theater they like to change things, and they change and change until by the time you are finished the design is not yours any more.

BLDD: Would you consider designing any other sort of costume, for example Adolfo jeans?

A: I tried that but it wasn't successful.

BLDD: Did you ever consider doing a children's line?

A: I would like to do that, but I have a feeling one might be inclined to repeat the things for the grown-ups and the clothes would look ridiculous.

BLDD: As a man, do you bring anything special to designing women's clothes that a woman designer might not?

A: I think that men have a very unbiased way of designing clothes for women. I may be wrong, but I have a feeling that when women design clothes for women, they think how those clothes would look on themselves. A man has a wider scope.

BLDD: Then, is the reverse true for women designing men's clothes?

A: Yes, maybe. You've got me there!

Adolfo, fall, 1985

Adolfo, fall, 1985

Geoffrey Beene

Geoffrey Beene is a name synonymous with quality. For twenty years, the Geoffrey Beene label has represented a distinctive style to be reckoned with.

BLDD: How would you characterize the Geoffrey Beene look?

GB: The premise of all my designs is comfort. There is a certain modernity to the clothes—they are lightweight, they are designed for a mobile society. They travel easily and fold—often into the palm of one's hand. They are clothes that move nonconstrictively. At the moment I am concerned with obtaining minimal care of clothing, experimenting with fabrics that have their wrinkles woven in and, for the future, fabrics that thermally adapt to both cold and hot temperatures.

BLDD: Is there any palette that particularly interests you, or that you especially avoid?

GB: I have consistently avoided very bright colors, simply because they overwhelm the individual. I prefer that my clothes frame the person; when they do, they often help to develop a personal style. I much prefer that one comments on a *woman* looking beautiful in one of my dresses as opposed to, say, "She was wearing a beautiful Geoffrey Beene dress."

BLDD: You were born in the South, in Haynesville, Louisiana. How has Southern tradition and a Southern sense of style influenced your work?

GB: Most women in the South are put on pedestals; they are adored. This attitude toward women has never escaped me. I feel it is my duty to enhance their beauty.

BLDD: Was there anyone in your family or close environment that was particularly interested in fashion or tailoring, who influenced you?

GB: No one, whatsoever. On the contrary, I came from a large family of doctors who never encouraged any of my artistic endeavors. In the South, it is generally acknowledged one is a merchant, doctor, lawyer or thief. Anything else is a hobby. I won a scholarship to Tulane University when I was sixteen years old. At that time my parents thought I should continue the family practice of medicine. I studied three years of pre-med, one year of medicine. Often, one has to study something in order to know what not to do. This was true in my case. I had neither the interest nor dedication to be a fine doctor. I had studied fine arts during the summers in the South. Already when I was about eight years old, I was fascinated by fabrics and would often ask an aunt of mine to execute some of my ideas. This practice was looked "down-upon". Oddly enough, my first sketches were shoes, not dresses! My mother says this began when I was about four years old. I am continually trying to discover my early manifestations of loving design. It re-enforces my reply when people ask, "How did you ever go from medicine to fashion?" My answer is, "How did I ever go to medicine in the first place?"

BLDD: Obviously, your interest in anatomy has been long term. Do you see a correlation between your early pre-medical studies and initial interest in the body's interior, and your current involvement in the body's exterior?

GB: I think there's a relevant correlation. Through the study of gross anatomy I'm very conscious of the movements of the body. It has also given me a heightened sense of proportion and body sensuality.

BLDD: Did you do lots of anatomical drawings during your pre-medical studies?

GB: As many as were required, but I fear more sketches of clothes!

BLDD: Even then you were interested in draping bodies. . .

GB: In my Gray's Anatomy Book there were sketches of dresses in the margins. Once it was brought to the attention of the professor and he stopped the class to show it to all. Guffaws galore . . . but I do feel I have had the last laugh.

BLDD: One of your earliest recollections in fashion was as a child playing with fabric. Now an almost painterly use of fabric and collage readily identifies your work. The selection of colors, and the mixing of textures and patterns, seem critical to the evolution of a Geoffrey Beene design.

GB: I work with all the best fabric mills in the world, developing my own fabrics, textures and colors. So, my clothes, and, indeed, any of my collections can only be evolved from the fabric. I have the great fortune to be able to design my own fabrics. I collaborate in France, Italy, Switzerland and England, and now Japan, with the finest mills. In recent years, the French came to me and asked "What can we do for you, Mr. Beene?" I never dreamt of such good fortune for I have respected their techniques all my life. I've been working with Brochier in Lyons and Darquer in Calais and then I've worked with Garigue in London, Zumsteg in Zurich, Gandini and Taroni and Agnona in Milano.

I know when I start a collection what the fabric and colorations are because I have designed most of them. The element of fashion design comes second to this. The fabrics dictate, they are the nucleus of the collection.

BLDD: You use mohair frequently. What quality does it have that has interested you for so long?

GB: It is weightless, effortless, soft and travels well. One can roll it and it fits into any form. It gives the appearance of great bulk and shape, but it's weight is minimal. I'm now trying to combine in mohair very stiff ottoman with very open weaves, the two together. I'll know very shortly if that works! I've been told my sense of coloration is very Oriental, but I don't recall an Oriental in the family, nor did I go to the Orient until 1976 when I went to Japan for the first time.

BLDD: But you read and study . . .

GB: Yes, but it's probably much deeper than that. I am sure it stems from my love of flowers. Most of the flowers that I loved and first became familiar with as a child were oriental in origin. Southern flowers such as magnolias, camellias, azaleas and most bulbs are oriental in origin. It was my first encounter with the glorious subtlety of oriental coloring.

BLDD: Are you still a gardener? And, if so, what sort of garden do you cultivate?

GB: Indeed, I am. I grow all sorts of orchids. The symmetry of orchids is one of the perfections of nature. Nature combines colors in both extraordinary and strange ways. I have many different varieties. The leaves of the plants are ugly, most ungainly, yet they produce blossoms of exquisite beauty. Gardening is the most rewarding hobby in the world, it's always, always beauty. Gardening was my first encounter with nature and it became a passion.

BLDD: Apart from the Oriental influence in your fabric, is there a particular period or a particular person that most influences your design?

GB: The two designers I admired the most when I went into fashion were on totally different pedestals, but both were in a way doing the same thing. One was Schiaparelli in Paris and the other was Adrian in Hollywood. They were so fanciful and imaginative; they kindled the flame that ignited my decision to go into fashion. Chanel and Balenciaga had already perfected their métier in their own personal way. They stuck to it and never changed. Their imagination was not as explosive or as obvious as Schiaparelli's and Adrian's. I was inspired by their wild abandon.

BLDD: Wasn't the use of color by Schiaparelli a dominant force in her designs?

GB: Yes, mad and zany. I went to school in Paris for two years and remember the first couture collection I attended. It was Schiaparelli's. I remember a dress all covered in front, very severe and pure. Then the model turned around and there was a naked halter back with rhinestones forming a 10 to 12 inch explosive spray from her waist. I was startled and thought it was the most enchanting idea. Of course, because the spray was large and heavy, she could not have sat down or moved. But it didn't matter, it unleashed for me the idea that clothing could be both decorative and emotional. As a matter of fact, I think the one thing about clothes that's never really been written about is their emotionalism.

BLDD: What do you mean by the "emotionalism" of clothing?

GB: You must know better than I, because you are a woman and can vent your emotions more than a man. You can change the mood of a woman to please her, or reduce her to tears, by what she wears, or what she feels comfortable in—it's happened a number of times in my career. Women react strongly to what goes next to their skin. Clothes give a clue to a woman's sense of character, of what and who they are! So her emotions can be changed simply by what she's wearing. It's one thing about fashion that's hardly ever discussed—I know emotions are difficult to discuss, but color, for example, can incite so many reactions and women may cry because a neckline may be too high.

BLDD: Are you confirming that clothing is an emotional and political declaration, in addition to body covering?

GB: Yes, I am. It's an individual declaration of how people see themselves, or how they wish other people to see them.

BLDD: Has your style, both in terms of its general spirit and its palette, changed in the more than twenty years that you've been designing under your own label? Or, is there a classical consistency to it from season to season?

GB: Probably most of the colors I employ border on neutrals, drawing other colors into them. I try to embody a friendly, visual look to my clothes, something that is familiar about them, a sense of belonging. And I often think they do look like "old friends."

BLDD: Is it your intent that when one sees your clothes, one should say, "That must be a Geoffrey Beene."

GB: No. I want the wearer to enjoy them and add their own personal style. It is wonderful to see an "idea" perform.

BLDD: How do you feel when you see other designers imitate that Geoffrey Beene look, with varying degrees of success?

GB: It's flattering when it's done well; depressing when it is not. So many people in clothing are so concerned about what other people do. I have always been concerned with what I do. I look at what other people present after a collection, to evaluate my own work. If I think they're doing better than I am, I become most discontent. If they aren't, I feel rather good about it.

BLDD: How would you define a woman of style?

GB: It's very, very personal. A woman who can identify herself, knows what she looks best in, feels the best in, and maintains her look all her life. One of the most rewarding experiences is seeing women wearing part of my clothing in a way I hadn't even dreamt of. That's really inspiring—when it goes beyond the original concept.

BLDD: Do you ever learn anything from the wearer; how the style of your clothes have been adapted?

GB: Many, many times. I remember when I did a group of designs in gabardine about ten or twelve years ago—totally unconstructed as they are today. They were very lightweight and in the most beautiful gabardine. One was a pants suit that had a beautifully tailored blouse with it. I saw a woman wearing it to dinner in Vienna one evening. To my surprise she wore nothing under the jacket, and it became a two-piece tailored suit that suddenly was the most seductive evening dressing in the room. She wore pearls with it, unbuttoned practically to the waist. I became aware of how sexy even an unconstructed tailored jacket could be. There are changes that women make in their own identity that are revelations to me. It makes me very happy when I realize that someone is tuned into my concept of clothing.

BLDD: Is there anything you've seen women do to your clothes that you wish they wouldn't?

GB: Not really.

BLDD: Are there any taboos in fashion, other than the obvious, excessive dressing that marks the so-called "fashion victim?"

GB: Taboos are decided by society, not by a fashion designer.

BLDD: Do you design your own clothes?

GB: I'm very interested in men's clothing emancipation, following the simple theory of comfort that I use in women's wear. Men's working clothes are archaic. One has to break down the establishment a bit, which is quite difficult—no?

BLDD: What do you like to wear?

GB: For me, the ultimate is all-cotton sweatshirts, all-cotton chinos, loafers without any laces at all. That's the essence of pure ease in clothing to me. That's what I change into the minute I get home.

BLDD: What do you enjoy wearing when you're at work, or in climates that do not permit that kind of look?

GB: Sweaters, any clothing that is soft and not rigid. Sweaters as a jacket—wool and linen.

BLDD: What do you wear in the evening if you go to a fancy "dress-up" thing?

GB: Well, many people ask that, because I threw my tuxedo away at the

Geoffrey Beene, spring, 1980

same time I threw away my restrictive or constructed clothing. I have a black cashmere sweater-type jacket, and I wear dark grey flannel pants, a tucked shirt, a black tie and silk stockings, and black patent leather pumps with a grosgrain bow on them.

BLDD: At the moment you're wearing a perfect shirt, perfect tie, perfect trousers, and a wonderful contrasting jacket. However, the "coat" is knit, rather than fabric, and it doesn't match your trousers. Do you think that people in the so-called "non-creative" professions, those in the traditional world of work, could manage to free themselves to look as comfortable as you must be today? You look unencumbered, yet appropriately dressed.

GB: That's the whole theory. It's men at work that I am concerned about. There are enough playclothes and leisure clothes, but there is no clothing in which men could work and be comfortable the entire day. The change would *not* be intimidating to men. It would require re-fabrication and lack of construction, not coloration! Women know change, comfort and liberation of clothing; men do not!

BLDD: Do you think the change is possible in this lifetime?

GB: We're beginning to see breakthroughs. For example, I introduced Beenebag Men in 1971, the concept of men dressing like I do, in soft clothes. American manufacturers did not sense change, but the Japanese picked it up instantly. Now I have thirteen boutiques in Japan. They love their men to dress comfortably at work, so they will perform better. I've made the sweater I'm wearing in exactly the color of grey flannel, and in navy blue, to demonstrate that one could look as proper, as establishment, as one wishes, and be *comfortable* at the same time. It worked! My boutique opened in Japan four months ago, and has already tripled in size. So there is *that* acceptance!

BLDD: You refer to yourself not as a fashion designer, but as a "conceptual" designer. What do you mean?

GB: Clothing, no matter how attractive or bizarre is not valid, if it does not fulfill the needs of a society. My concept of clothing is comfort, and usefulness. That's the reason I don't often use the word "fashion ." Fashion design is not always useful. It's either a designer's ego, or it's fantasy. If clothing is not intended to work, or to be enjoyed, it becomes highly questionable. I'm very serious about clothing and designing within the framework of reality. It is a far greater challenge to me, than working with sheer fantasy. One has to conceptualize about what clothing is and what it does, as well as its visual aspects.

BLDD: Do you do your own sketching and your own drawing?

GB: Only my own "hieroglyphics"—they are not easily read. Fortunately, I have an assistant who's been with me since I began my own business who takes my sketches and deciphers them. I'm too impatient, really, to make pretty sketches. Whenever an idea needs enhancing, I ask one of my talented illustrative assistants to sketch it for me. Most of my concepts are architectural, linear, or they're curves, diamonds, squares, or rectangles, all bordering on geometry. I seem to work best within a geometrical context. At one time in the 60's they called me an architectural designer. Then I switched to soft clothes. My clothes are still essentially architectural, but now they drape.

BLDD: Has architecture been an important influence? Are you particularly interested in the work of architects?

GB: Yes, I am fascinated by it. I was recently in Vienna where there's a lot of neo-classical and art deco architecture which I find superb. There is such clarity to the works of great architects.

BLDD: Your passion for gardening is shared by many architects, some of whom think it is the noblest of work.

GB: I agree. Gardening borders upon TRUTH.

BLDD: Your love of flowers is apparent throughout your offices. Do you use floral patterns in your designs?

GB: Constantly. Usually my flowers are very graphic, either through spacing, or black and white coloration.

BLDD: Have you "dressed" any members of your family?

GB: My mother and my sister. I have loved transforming my mother's thoughts about clothes. Once again, one gets into emotions. Her figure isn't ideal, but it's rather on a "happy" heavier side. She always tended toward rigid more structured clothes, as she says, "because of her size."

Now she knows what I call structural softness, enjoys sensual fabrics, has the joy of wearing them. She is now into pants, which she had never worn before, and tunics in extraordinary fabrics, and fabrics that travel. Chemises! I put her into evening chemises and different gowns in the simplest way, and she looks marvelous and reflects it. She's happy in her clothes, has begun to identify with them—a remarkable change that shows how one is elevated by what one wears.

BLDD: Are there any public personalities that you have "dressed," in which you've seen the same evolution?

GB: Not as many public personalities would turn themselves over totally to me as my mother did. And when one confronts gigantic egos, that is something of another nature. There are many people I think that I have exposed to the glory of the comfort of clothes. The public doesn't read about my clients for they are not trendy people who want their names in the papers; nor do I wish to exploit them.

BLDD: If you had a favorite young niece who could not afford a wonderful wardrobe, and who had more taste than funds, and the wit to know that it was a good time to start her wardrobe over, what would you recommend that she buy?

GB: Probably anything made in wool jersey—a T-shirt top, a pair of pleated trousers, a skirt, and a coat-jacket—all the same color—all the same fabric.

BLDD: And what would that color be?

GB: It would probably be navy, or khaki—those two colors which have endured in men's wear with such versatility.

BLDD: Yves St. Laurent said that after twenty-five years as a designer, his opinion was that the chicest look that a woman could have would be to wear black pants, black sweater, and a black satin raincoat. Is that a view that you share?

GB: Just about, but not exactly. I would prefer a slicker synthetic raincoat instead of satin, better for day and evening, and that would probably be navy, more flattering than black. A sweater might be too warm certain times of the year. I would probably suggest a silk jersey blouse.

BLDD: What do you consider the chic-est look?

GB: I think a simple chemise dinner dress to the floor, accessorized properly, can perform in a million different ways. I've seen so much exaggeration over the years; in the end simplicity is just what chic or style is all about. The road to simplicity, however, is very complex.

BLDD: Does the chemise have to be in an exotic fabric?

GB: No, it could be wool jersey. That's one of my favorite fabrics for evening. I love taking what would be daytime fabrics back into evening, back and forth.

BLDD: What, other than jersey, would qualify?

GB: A heavy silk crepe. I have a new silk and wool charmeuse that is heavy and has a heavy drape; it is heaven! I don't necessarily like fabrics that are confined to evening. A woman changing, say, a black chemise from day to evening shows versatility and style. That individual identifies with herself expressing her own personal taste and style.

BLDD: Have you ever done any interior design, other than the extensive renovation of your own apartment in New York?

GB: Well, I did my home on Long Island, which was in the February 1984 Architectural Digest. And I just bought a new home in Palm Beach, which I am redoing with Phillip Haight. My Long Island home consists mostly of French, Louis XVI furniture, my apartment is modern, and the home in Palm Beach is art deco, built in 1930.

BLDD: Do you get to spend much time in any of these places?

GB: I go to Long Island every weekend, and I hope to go to Palm Beach quite a bit once it's finished.

BLDD: You've designed everything from men's wear to bed linens, to gentlemen's cologne, to eyeglass frames, hosiery, furs, and ladies' shoes. Is there anything that you've always wanted to design that you haven't yet?

GB: I still say, apart from clothes, what I enjoy the most *is* shoes. There is a grace and sensuality to the foot.

BLDD: How many licensees do you have? Are there any offers to which you wouldn't put your name?

GB: I have about thirty licensees. There are many that I've turned down.

Geoffrey Beene, spring, 1983

Things you wouldn't believe—for example, dental floss. It was too difficult to put the label on! Then I turned down dog perfume; I think they smell so good, they don't need any perfume. Those are two of the most ridiculous. But there are loads of others. I try not to design anything unless I can have input, and quality control.

BLDD: Do you really have control over the design and quality of each thing that you license?

GB: Contractually I do, but it is difficult in practice. I will suddenly see something with my name that I had nothing to do with. The trouble with licensees is they take license. The most successful ones are those in which I have the greatest input.

BLDD: Is there any person you think of as epitomizing good taste who could serve as a role model to most women, because of their choice of clothes, or their manner of comporting themselves?

GB: Garbo!

BLDD: How would you describe her clothes and her manner?

GB: She had a casual attitude to her clothes even in the evening. Comfort was always there. I have never seen her look uncomfortable in what she was wearing. I saw an old film of hers in Vienna recently, in some scenes she wore exotic clothes, but they were always loose. They were not skin-tight. They were sometimes highly embellished, but they moved easily. She wore a beautiful skull cap. I realized she had framed herself—even her hair was tucked away, it came right in on the face. Her whole movie life reflected ease and unconcern.

BLDD: How fashionable do you think Princess Diana, the most influential woman on fashion in the world these days is?

GB: I think she is charming, but perhaps not allowed to be influential in her own way. People should assert their own taste. The rigidity of the code of royalty, like that of men's wear, is archaic.

BLDD: Long before it became fashionable, you mixed patterns and textures and color. Where did that idea ever come from?

GB: Because I am fascinated with textures and fabrics—to mix them is simply to compound the fascination.

BLDD: Were you influenced by artists, architects, interior designers?

GB: All.

BLDD: Do you respond to the work of a particular artist? Either in palette or structure?

GB: It changes constantly. At the moment, I am into the energy of the Art Deco period.

BLDD: Do you think of yourself as part of the "fashion crowd"?

GB: Hopefully, though I think of my work as being different. Often my thinking is apart from their's.

BLDD: In what way?

GB: Not their way.

BLDD: What is "their way?"

GB: Not my way.

BLDD: There's the Oriental again!

GB: I'm sort of a loner. I have been most of my life. I am not a joiner—one who always seems committed to a code of behavior. I don't respect that. I respect individuality, and I wish to be an individual. It's that simple.

BLDD: What country do you think has the most significant influence on fashion design today?

GB: It's not France, I have to tell you. Change is occurring and at the moment more is going on in the East, than in the West.

BLDD: Don't you think you were part of the wave that helped bring American design to the forefront?

GB: Indeed I do. I say it very immodestly. The fact is that I went to Milan where no American designer had been. It was a great breakthrough. It was in 1976 and I enjoyed it.

BLDD: What gave you the idea to go there?

GB: I went when I started making soft clothes. The stores had been used to my more constricted clothes. Kennedy Fraser, in *The New Yorker* commented: "How beautiful, but can they be worn?" I was practically reduced to tears. Then I thought about it, and I realized, "God, she's right." And I changed my whole approach to clothing. I didn't change it; I simply went back to the original way I'd started, which was chemises,

Geoffrey Beene, spring, 1984

loose, comfortable clothes. When I changed, the stores didn't like it. I had been wedged into stiff constructed clothes. I had a tough time. And I thought, "Well, if they don't like it on this continent, they'll like it on another." So I borrowed $140,000 for the show in Milan, and they loved it, and I bounced right back to America. Very often one has to go out of one's own country to do something innovative.

BLDD: Sounds like an opera singer.

GB: Not quite that lyrical—I hope the same thing will happen with my men's clothing in Japan.

BLDD: You're now working with a new wrinkled fabric in which the wrinkles are actually woven into the material. Are those intentional wrinkles an aesthetic innovation, as well as a technological one?

GB: Yes, because they give a new texture and a new meaning to usefulness. The idea of synthetic fabrics has always fascinated me. They perform so much better, and one day they will be perfected. I think the care and concern about the maintenance of clothing is too expensive, and too demanding of time.

BLDD: Do you think we Americans are overly clean, and press our clothes too often?

GB: Yes.

BLDD: For what lifestyle are you designing?

GB: Working women who have arrived, women concerned with our society. I do not think my clothes are bought by the bon-bon, Pekingese crowd.

BLDD: Do you ever find yourself mentally dressing, or re-dressing, people that you see in the street, or in a public place?

GB: Oh, yes. That's fun.

BLDD: Are you generally simplifying them?

GB: Yes, or glorifying their better features.

BLDD: Do you find that you're most productive working alone or with a team?

GB: I'm most productive in the morning at five-thirty, in my apartment, with my two dachshunds. I'm at my office at eight o'clock. Those are my best hours. Everything that I do in the day is conceptualized at that time. I adore executing my thoughts with my design team. Creative work with creative people is a rare joy.

BLDD: Your family in Louisiana—did they ever expect your work to evolve the way it has?

GB: No. They probably still think I'll go back to medicine!

BLDD: Did *you* ever expect your life to evolve the way it has?

GB: No. I never thought about it. I just wanted to be a good designer, if not a great designer, and perhaps make a contribution in that respect. But I never set goals or times, or anything. It's just working day-to-day and doing what one enjoys doing, one hopes with a sense of making a contribution.

BLDD: What do you think your most significant contribution has been? For what would you like best to be remembered?

GB: Perhaps shaking Europe up with American design in Milano in 1976. A concept of clothes that are very expensive and still modern, couture clothes that work. A shift in direction in expensive clothes, again, precious not by price but by performance and endurance, contributing to the modernity of luscious and costly fabrics.

BLDD: Is there any dream project that you haven't done that you'd care to?

GB: I'm a fairly content person.

BLDD: If you had your life to do over again, what would you do otherwise?

GB: Just more of it. The way I began my concept of clothing is precisely what I'm doing at the moment—fluid, comfortable, effortless clothes that make people feel good. I never thought design was more or less than that!

Geoffrey Beene, spring, 1984

BB

Bill Blass

Bill Blass is a one-man fashion conglomerate. He designs almost everything, including furs, shoes, perfume, chocolates, and even an automobile. His designs, the essence of American fashion sophistication, and his forty-year career on New York's Seventh Avenue have had a profound impact on the American apparel industry.

BLDD: Your background sounds typical of a small town American boy, but, somehow, unusual for a fashion designer. How does a high school football player from Fort Wayne, Indiana, grow up to become a celebrated New York fashion designer?

BB: It isn't that unusual. (Norman) Norell was from Indiana; so is Halston. The legendary Mainbocher, who was Main Bocker in those days, was also from Indiana. The one thing I think we all had in common is that we knew we had to get the hell out of Indiana!

BLDD: At what age did you decide to do that, and to become a fashion designer?

BB: Happily, I'm one of those people who knew from an early age what I wanted to do. Don't forget, I grew up in the Depression, when you could go to the movies on a Saturday afternoon for 15 cents and see Carole Lombard, Marlene Dietrich and Greta Garbo. I knew that making clothes for people of that sort could be the most exciting thing in the world. So from that time on—I was very, very young—I started sketching, and selling the sketches to New York manufacturers. When I was eighteen I came to New York to go to school and eventually to work.

BLDD: As a young man, straight out of high school, how did you make the decision to embark for New York City? Why didn't you go to Hollywood considering the impression those lavish movie costumes had on you?

BB: I knew that Hollywood was not the answer, that the only place to design was New York. Great clothes were being made here. Hollywood was already beginning to wane a bit. My family suggested that it would be more logical for me to go to the Art Institute of Chicago, but I knew then you had to be in New York. This is where it was happening.

BLDD: How did you manage to get a job once you arrived?

BB: First I went to school, but I always sketched, and I still do. It was no trouble at all getting a job on Seventh Avenue. In those days, the Seventh Avenue houses, such as the one I have now, employed a whole bevy of designers. There would be two or three head designers and numerous assistants. There was always a need, and always room for additional design staff.

BLDD: Unlike many other designers you never worked for a Paris couture house.

BB: It's my one regret, too, damn it. After I finally did get to Paris, during the war, I realized that it would have been a sensational idea, to work for a period in a Paris design house. In those days the French designers loved the idea of having American kids work there.

BLDD: If you had been apprenticed to one of the great Paris designers, do you suppose your work would be different today?

BB: The technique might be different, but I don't think that my basic approach to fashion would have changed very much. As I go over the sketches that I did as a youngster, they're reminiscent of the designs I'm doing now. The only thing that would have been invaluable is the technique you only learn in Paris.

BLDD: For whom would you have wanted to work?

BB: Jacques Fath, I think. It would have been more difficult to work for Christian Dior.

BLDD: Where *did* you receive your training in color, form, and fabric?

BB: I had no formal training. I know that it's wrong to say that. It's something that's very difficult to teach. I think it really is something instinctive. Fashion is easily acquired by almost anyone, but style is much more difficult.

BLDD: How has your concept of fashion varied from those teenage dreams in Indiana?

BB: It's not wildly different. The one thing I wanted to do was to make women as glamorous as I possibly could. I knew nothing about the life style of the people that I visualized in my sketches of that period. But that was what I aspired to.

BLDD: How was the fashion industry perceived when you first began, and what changes have you noted over the years that you've been involved?

BB: When I first started out, all the major houses were owned by manufacturers. Nettie Rosenstein or Hattie Carnegie were not designers. Hattie Carnegie employed a whole stable of designers, Norell among them. The major change, of course, has been the emergence of designer-ownership. This has only happened in the last decade. Previously, the manufacturer owned the firm and designers were highly salaried. They had marvelous jobs because they had two or three months vacation at one time, but manufacturers were then able to totally change their designs while they were away.

BLDD: Did they encourage you to take a vacation after you handed in your sketches?

BB: As soon as the collection was open! Then, gradually, we designers became involved in the business, too. I don't think any designer is instinctively a businessman. In my own case, certainly, I had to work to learn about the business of fashion. Now I find that almost as exciting as the creative part.

BLDD: Before the success of Norman Norell, was designer-ownership non-existent on Seventh Avenue?

BB: Claire McArdell was a partner. That was unique, and it wasn't until Norell himself bought out Traina that it became just Norell. That was the first.

BLDD: You are the president of a multi-hundred million dollar conglomerate, with ventures from chocolates to cars. Even backgammon sets!

BB: I dropped those. They were not profitable. I'd rather say chocolates to cars because cars still give me a great deal of pleasure, and I'm still designing them up to 1985.

BLDD: Do you play backgammon?

BB: Not any more. Not since that account.

BLDD: How do you still find the time to come up with a new clothing line at least twice a year?

BB: That is the least difficult, and at the same time the most complicated and competitive thing I do. And it's the most stimulating. There is loads of time for that. You make time for the things you really enjoy doing, and designing the couture line, as well as Blassport, is really the most stimulating part of my business.

BLDD: If you didn't design the clothes, would you have the licensees?

BB: I doubt it. The couture is the smallest part of the business financially, but it's the umbrella for everything else and it is what attracts the other thirty-one licensees. What excites me most now is the interest I notice in Japan. We've had our clothes there for three years. I'll soon have thirty-five to forty boutiques in Osaka, Tokyo, and the rest of the country. I go there at least once a year, usually twice. We're now seeing the emergence of the American designer on an international scale. That's why I don't want any more licensees here. I want to see the business continue to grow internationally.

BLDD: Have your plans for expansion been inspired by, or modeled after, any other fashion designer?

BB: Not really. I was the first American designer of women's apparel to go into men's wear, and I've designed linens along with every other designer in this country. I don't think I was specifically inspired by anyone else. My idea was that if the French designers were doing it, why the hell shouldn't we Americans?

BLDD: It was about 1967 that, as the first American designer of women's clothing, you branched out into men's fashions. Was there a particular individual, or circumstance, that prompted you to take this step?

BB: Yes. There was a woman then, the now legendary Mildred Custin, who was president of Bonwit Teller. When Pierre Cardin came to this country and tried to sell his men's wear, there wasn't a store on Fifth Avenue that was the least bit interested, but Mildred Custin had been willing to take a chance on Cardin. When she learned that I was also interested in designing a men's line she said she would buy the collection, sight unseen, based on what she knew of my own personal taste. She immediately opened a snazzy boutique and it was a fantastic overnight success. People didn't even try on the clothes—they'd just hold them up and say, "I'll take it." So it was Mildred who really put the stamp of approval on the men's line. My main concern even at that time was the fellow over thirty-five who wanted to look

"with it," but not ridiculous. Don't forget, this was the 1960's, when we were going through the most extraordinary revolution in men's wear that's ever taken place in this country. All sorts of fantasy was being exhibited and it was a terribly silly period. Grown men looked like their own sons, with long sideburns and bell-bottom pants and body jewelry. Oh, my God! I had in mind men, like myself, who wanted to be adventuresome but not too much so, who wanted clothes that were classic, and traditional.

BLDD: You once said that a man is happiest in what he wears from Friday to Sunday. How does that belief influence the way you design for men?

BB: There's no question that most fellows are happiest in what they put on Friday night. Now of course there are more occupations at which you can wear those same sport clothes. There's been a big change in the last five or six years in the way men dress for business.

BLDD: You said recently that the ultimate role of clothes is to please the individual, not to keep one hot or cool. Are there any practical concerns to which you make concessions in designing a garment?

BB: Of course. But I do think that essentially, the role of clothes is to give you some pleasure. We all know that there are certain things you put on in the morning that make you enjoy the day more. Sometimes people want to experiment with a new silhouette or color. And sometimes it's necessary to have clothes that are practical—that won't wrinkle, for example. Although I love linen to look wrinkled. I think in dressing you should please yourself. Mind you, there are occasions when women dress for men, and, certainly, when men dress for women. But essentially it's the way clothes make you feel that makes them right.

BLDD: Is there a typical American woman who buys your clothes? What is her profile?

BB: She's a composite of a lot of women. I make a lot of clothes for Mrs. Reagan, who is a certain height, and a lot of clothes for Mrs. Kissinger, who is another height, and yet the woman that I keep in mind is a composite of customers from San Francisco to Texas, to Detroit, to New York. It's a mistake to have the image of only one woman in mind. Frankly, it's always been my opinion that one of the problems of women designers is that they tend to design only in their own image. They rarely design anything that they themselves cannot wear. It's the reason for instance that a Madame Grès has never changed her style; nor did Chanel.

BLDD: You dress a lot of rich and famous women. How do their tastes differ from those of the not-so-rich or not-so-famous?

BB: The rich are exposed to more in the way of clothes, and life, and atmosphere in general than the average person is. Their needs *are* different; they go more places, they have more things to do. But today it's less true than it once was because most of these so-called very rich women work. They do something. In the last decade I think that probably the biggest influence has been that of the working woman—what clothes have to do for you during your business—even if they're charitable business—hours.

BLDD: How has the fact that more women are dressing for work influenced the way you design?

BB: They must command a certain classy quality. The clothes one wears in the daytime must last from one season to another. Actually, you can retire them and then bring them back again.

BLDD: You said that you design for women from San Francisco to Texas to New York—all over the country. Are there regional differences in taste? Is one part of the country more experimental, another part more knowing?

BB: Not in fashion. One difference is the fact that more affluent people live in the so-called sunbelt than anywhere else, and come November, people who have the dough travel, they get out of the northeast—so there is a difference in the weight of clothes I design. Texas is one of the biggest money areas in our country and one of the best for me from the business standpoint. Women there have very little use for heavy clothes. So there is a difference in the weight of clothes today.

BLDD: How many "seasons" are there?

BB: Two. Hot and cold.

BLDD: And what do we do in between?

BB: You make do! Those are the times you wear the more traditional things, such as a lightweight challis dress, blouses, skirts. The idea of

Bill Blass, fall, 1979

major seasonal changes today is ridiculous. The white suit has replaced the little black dress.

BLDD: What's the most fashion-conscious city in our country?

BB: New York. There's no question about it. Years ago it might have been San Francisco. After New York, I think of cities like Houston, Dallas, or Kansas City, that are full of very attractive, well-dressed women.

BLDD: And the most elegant city in terms of fashion?

BB: Probably San Francisco. I think that you take a good deal more interest in the way you look in San Francisco simply because of the look of the town itself.

BLDD: How do the clothes you design for the clientele that you mentioned, ranging from Nancy Reagan to Nancy Kissinger, differ from those of your less expensive line?

BB: Not much, really. We introduced a line called Bill Blass Collection a couple of years ago which was priced at $200 to $400 retail. All of those gals will pick dresses from that line as well. There shouldn't be any difference; the clothes are designed by me no matter what the price is. Couture clothes are expensive because I often pay $100 a yard for fabric, or trim it with fur, or use beads.

BLDD: It's well known that fashion reflects the values of society in any period: the encasement of tight corsets suited the Victorian age; the flapper look reflected the twenties; and the gray flannel suit expressed perfectly the conservatism of the fifties. How do you think that the clothes of today reflect the trends of current society?

BB: It has to do with the economy as well as with the conservatism of the political regime that's in power. Another era that was absolutely revolutionary in fashion was the sixties, when, for the first time in the history of fashion, inspiration came from the streets, from the young. And it was the madness of that period—when the drug culture, and a certain sexuality, influenced clothing—that caused a return in the '80's to more conservative clothes. Plus the fact that, because of the economy, clothes have to be an investment.

BLDD: Is extreme conservatism going to mark the shape of things to come?

BB: I would never venture to predict anything beyond next season.

BLDD: You have said this is not a time to be making fashion waves. What do you mean by that, and what do you predict for next season?

BB: I don't think it's a time to make major fashion waves as far as silhouette or similar things are concerned. I think the biggest change will be the return of the waistline, that even suits will be nipped at the waist again. And there will be a return of bright, vivid color. We've had season after season of dour, sad colors, and I think that next you'll see the brightest chrome yellow, red, purple, blue, and green.

BLDD: What's the current price range for your clothes?

BB: They start at about $1500 and go to $7000.

BLDD: *What* costs $7,000?

BB: Something with some sable on it.

BLDD: It must be a lot of sable.

BB: Not much . . .

BLDD: Do you sell a lot of those?

BB: Yup. Our $5,000 beaded and embroidered evening dresses are among the biggest sellers we have. You mean you don't have one?

BLDD: Why do they cost so much? Is it the fabric, the labor?

BB: They're hand-beaded, and I refuse to have the clothes made in Hong Kong or Taiwan, or another place like that. They're made here, from Eighth to Ninth Avenue. Even my knits are made by women in Ohio and Michigan. I'm an avid believer that we have to have clothes made in this country. Therefore we pay more money. The cost of labor is higher in this city than anyplace else. I'm a big supporter of the union, and I think the workers should be paid more. But the cost of labor and fabrication is what makes the clothing expensive.

BLDD: Why don't you give a few tips to those who have more taste than funds on how to assemble a wardrobe? If one had $500 to spend, how would you suggest it be spent?

BB: This year it would probably be wise to spend your money on accessories. As you know, there isn't anything wildly different about the jacket, skirt or trousers that you see in the stores this year. In my opinion, spend your

48

dough on the best bag, shoes, and accessories you can afford. That is what will make the overall look *look* expensive. Particularly shoes. I'm always very conscious of shoes.

BLDD: Do you design shoes?

BB: Off and on. The shoes have to be made in Europe. Sadly, no American shoes are being made anymore. I've done them periodically with an Italian manufacturer. At the moment I'm not.

BLDD: What are the five most important items for any wardrobe?

BB: It's very hard to designate five items because one of the things most important about clothing today is to dress appropriately. It's a funny word to be used in terms of fashion, but to wear the appropriate thing—not only in terms of the time of day, but in terms of whether it's a business or social occasion. A woman doesn't need a variety of suits, but she should have a variety of jackets, whether they're cardigan or notched lapels or tailored, that can be mixed with other elements. Even sweaters worn in school can be resurrected and worn with something that's new, and still look snappy. I don't think there are rules. If there's anything I hate it's those books about how to dress for success. That's a lot of bull. You should dress by instinct. That man who thought all you gals should go for an interview in a grey suit—how ridiculous! In a red suit you'd probably get a job more easily.

BLDD: What would you suggest to women who are looking for jobs or other interesting involvements?

BB: For the interesting involvement I suggest one of the beaded dresses! If you're looking for a job, you have to bear in mind the kind of job. If you are going to work for the art director in an ad agency, you're going to dress a little snappier than if you're going to work for a bank. Again, it depends on the job you're looking for, and the appropriate outfit to wear for that particular job interview. If the insurance company or bank you're going to work for tends to be conservative, you're going to look like a damned fool and probably won't get the job if you're too bizarre in your get-up.

BLDD: You made reference before to investment dressing. If you were to suggest one item of clothing that is really worth the investment, what would it be?

BB: I suspect, for a man or a woman, a Burberry raincoat. They're now $650.

BLDD: That *is* an investment! Do you collect clothes?

BB: All of us do. Certainly some of a man's favorite clothes are the sport jackets he's had—if he can still wear them—since he was in school. We all have favorite clothes that we wouldn't part with for anything in the world.

BLDD: One funny thing that I read about you, and you were the first to admit it, was that you can't keep a secret. How do you get people to continue to confide in you?

BB: I know several right now that I'm dying to tell you.

BLDD: Well, here's the question. What's the best kept secret that you know?

BB: The one that I obviously heard today that I can't tell you. I didn't realize I had that reputation—a blabbermouth!

BLDD: No, there's a big difference—you are just very generous in sharing a point of view.

BB: Particularly if it's forbidden!

BLDD: How do you manage, despite your constant travel and horrendous schedule, to always look so pulled together?

BB: I don't know about looking pulled together, but I do think that the traveling part of my career has been an important one. I realized early on that most American designers never went anywhere except Europe, or perhaps Palm Beach. But I decided that it would be very interesting to go to Detroit. I wanted to see who my customer was in Milwaukee. When I started out, years ago, long before anybody else did, I was really peddling clothes, but, I was also, more importantly, getting to know the people who wore them. Ultimately they became friends. I could anticipate what they needed because I knew how they lived in a particular town. Certain cities don't have restaurants, so all entertainment takes place either in a club or a person's house. Restaurant clothes aren't necessary in that case. The point of view in each city is somewhat different. I travel a lot. Last week I went to Paris, and from Paris to Lyons. I'm buying fabric now for next fall. The sad

thing is that we don't have any fabric in this country. Twice a year we designers are forced to go to Europe to buy our fabric. The great mills in this country are devoted more than ever almost entirely to making synthetics and volume fabric.

BLDD: With all of your experience both in fashion and in travel, do you have any suggestions on organizing a wardrobe, or on packing?

BB: I'm the biggest believer in taking everything you've got if you're going anyplace for any length of time. It's the only way. Nothing is worse for a gal than to go someplace and realize she didn't bring that favorite evening dress if she has an occasion to wear it. The same thing applies to a guy not taking a dinner jacket if there's a possibility that he may have a very exciting date. So, I'm the worst person in the world to advise about packing. I don't pack myself; and I think you take everything.

BLDD: How about some advice on how to take care of clothes? You said that sweater from your school days could still look snazzy—if it survived. With the cost of clothes nowadays, how do you give clothes that ought to be classic a longer life?

BB: One suggestion: no matter how fond you are of something, don't wear it every day. Clothes need to breathe and relax, too. And try not to send clothes to the cleaners if you can help it. If you can, spot-clean them after you've worn them. Cleaners devastate clothes. Anyway, I don't mind certain clothes looking quite beat-up. My sweaters are all unraveled—I have two dogs—and I don't mind that at all.

BLDD: So many women travel today both for business, and for pleasure. How has that affected your designs and the materials that you use?

BB: If you look at people in an airport, it's obvious that nobody thinks much about the clothes they wear when they're traveling. It's sad to see everybody in the airports looking so disreputable. But one doesn't take that into consideration at all.

BLDD: Everytime I pick up a newspaper or magazine, I see splendid fashions that are modeled either by very young girls or size 4 models. But the clothes are really intended for me and my pals. Do you think there might be a better way of reaching us?

BB: Certainly nobody wants to look at pictures of size 20 ladies! As far as the age thing is concerned, it does seem incongruous that since Miss Brooke Shields emerged on the scene—she was then 14, I guess—the most expensive sophisticated clothes are photographed on young girls. But you must bear in mind that the average size today is a size eight. I think ten years ago it was a size twelve, and then a size ten. Now it's a size eight, so one thing that's certain is that most people tend to be thinner.

BLDD: What do you think of that popular, familiar dictum that you can't be too rich or too thin?

BB: That was the Duchess of Windsor's theory, and I do think there's no question that as far as clothes are concerned you look a lot better in them if you're skinny. The toughest thing in the world is to make clothes for actresses. They tend to be bosomy. I can remember making clothes for Marilyn Monroe—while she was adorable, God knows she certainly wasn't easy to make clothes for!

BLDD: What did you create for her?

BB: Norell made her clothes for awhile but he went away at one point. She then lived in my apartment house and I made some clothes for her. All she cared about was that they were tight over the can. She was one of the few actresses who was more concerned with the appearance of her backside, than her front. But going back to this theory about clothes—you must remember that it is our ideal, in our time, for men and for women to look thin. Fashion magazines of the *Bon Ton* and *Lineator* magazines, in the 1920's and 30's, reflected the fashion figures of their time. In the twenties it was even more desirable than it is now to be flat-chested, with a flat tummy. So that is the image that the illustrator, the fashion photographer captures as the mood of his time.

BLDD: How important is the fashion press in determining, and shaping, the public's tastes and preferences?

BB: *Women's Wear Daily* is probably the most extraordinary influence on fashion reporting of its time. I think that it has a virtual monopoly. It's the only daily paper that is devoted entirely to fashion, and it continues to have an enormous influence. The fashion magazines such as *Vogue, Harper's*

Bazaar and *Town & Country* do, also. The fashion pages in newspapers, such as *The New York Times*, tend not to criticize fashion as they do theater or books. They tend to report on a collection almost entirely favorably. If they dismiss you with a paragraph that is far worse than a blast for half a page. But the importance of *Women's Wear Daily* continues today and perhaps always will. It takes only ten or fifteen minutes to read, so it's read by virtually all one's affluent customers.

BLDD: Creating a business as successful as the one you have requires practical ability as well as creative vision. Is the business end ever a headache? How do you manage to combine the two?

BB: A certain amount of the day has to be devoted to business, but I think that some of the instinct and insight that I have about clothes rubs off on the business end, too. You have to have gut instincts or reactions to something as far as the business deal is concerned. It turns out to be almost as exciting as the creative part of it. I don't have any designated time of the day that I spend on business, but I am concerned with it every day.

BLDD: Do you manage, with 32 or 33 licensees, to have a hand in every aspect of every design?

BB: Yes. The public can spot immediately when a sheet, or a scarf, or any other produce doesn't look like you. Though I have numerous assistants and a great deal of help, the overall thing has to be my decision and have my stamp of approval.

BLDD: How would you characterize the Bill Blass signature look?

BB: I think it's classic, timeless, and clean-cut. I even like to think that it looks "American" as opposed to European.

BLDD: How would you describe that American look?

BB: To an extent, it's lack of embellishment. European designers, probably because they're more influenced by their custom-made department, tend to have too many ideas on one dress or one coat or one suit. American clothes tend to be simpler, with more emphasis on fabric and line—and, this year, color.

BLDD: Do you design anything differently for American women than you do for anyone else?

BB: I don't know that I design at all for European women. The clothes that are done in Japan are manufactured in Japan, for the Japanese consumer only. It's obvious that the sizes have to be scaled down. Also, a Japanese woman does not have the same kind of social life at night, so there are less cocktail or evening clothes. The clothes vary according to what is appropriate to the woman's way of life in a particular country.

BLDD: What is the process, what steps do you follow from the original idea to get to a finished dress or ensemble?

BB: Last week was spent in Europe buying fabric. I look for fabrics that appeal to me within a thematic realm, either in color or patterns. Once the charts are made up of this fabric purchase then ideas come to me. I won't actually start the fall collection until January or December, but I make sketches on a table by my bed or in a plane or a car, little ideas that are then transferred to a larger pad when I get to the office. I then give them to my assistants with a swatch of the designated fabric. Often when we drape we find that when an actual garment is made up, it doesn't work out well. The process takes a long time because in a collection the shoes, the jewelry, the hats are as important as the clothes. Whether or not women really wear them, they are an essential part of a fashion show.

BLDD: If they're not worn, why are they an essential part of the fashion show—what is the difference between runway clothes and real-life clothes?

BB: What we try to do is convey an idea, a look, that is appealing to the audience. We have a very critical audience. This year hats are absolutely essential. Gloves, too, are having a big comeback.

BLDD: How much of the design is modified by external factors, such as cost to produce, availability of fabric and so on, rather than taste?

BB: Some clothes are modified because the buyer or store will like the idea but think the sleeve is too exaggerated, or not wearable. I have always tried to prevent that from happening. I tell them that either they send it out the way I designed it, or there's no purpose in making it.

BLDD: What's a typical day like—if there is such a thing—in the life of Bill Blass?

BB: I get up early in the morning and I'm in the office at 8:30. Most of the staff come in at 9 or 9:30. I like the first half-hour in the office even before my secretary gets there so that I can digest my agenda for the day. As a rule, there's an appointment every half hour, with one of the 32 licensees, or with fittings which take a lot of time. They're important and the thing I like the best. That's the time when you really think you're a genius, and that's rewarding. If the fittings have gone well the day turns out well. But there is no typical day, because I do travel so much that ordinarily, when I return, there's an awful lot of nitty-gritty, boring, business details to be taken care of.

BLDD: Is it all still fun?

BB: Yes, it is still stimulating, and I can't imagine being in any other business. It has always seemed that the opportunity to meet interesting and exciting people has come about through this business. I always wanted to go out and meet the customer, and I have done that, and that's gratifying, and fun, too. Most of them are my friends. My fashion shows at the Hotel Pierre are crowded with pals, as well as buyers.

BLDD: You've said that you feel partially responsible for bringing a new respectability to this business. What was it like before, what do you mean when you say a new respectability, and how have you helped to bring it about?

BB: Well, hell, lady, in the old days designers were never allowed out of the back room. I wasn't about to stay back there! Manufacturers didn't want it acknowledged that they had designers.

BLDD: How did people think they made the clothes appear?

BB: The manufacturers took care of all that. The clothes were all sent in from various design rooms or ateliers. The designers were anonymous, they weren't interviewed. They never talked to the press, and they rarely saw the buyers. I didn't like that. I remember when a great fashion editor at *Vogue* named Baron de Guinzburg came to one of the houses where I was working. He looked at the collection and said, "You know, there's somebody else making these clothes besides the regular designers." The things he was picking for that particular issue of *Vogue* looked different. He insisted on meeting me. And he eventually became a great fan and a great booster, God knows. That was when I really felt that I could no longer design clothes anonymously. I wanted to know not only the people who were going to wear them but also the people who were buying them for the stores.

BLDD: There seems to be a new respect for fashion apparel as a design art. To what do you attribute this, and what effect do you think it will have on the fashions of the future, or the kind of people who will become designers of fashion?

BB: I feel that fashion design is seldom an art. It attains that status under very rare circumstances. Balenciaga may be an artist, but not many others. To me, it's a craft. I think the recognition of fashion as an important element in our lives is a very healthy occurrence. I'm not convinced, however, that it is on the level of art most of the time.

BLDD: Are there some fashion designers historically, and perhaps even currently, to whose work you most respond? Is there anyone other than Balenciaga whose work informs your sensibility?

BB: There was an exhibition, at the Brooklyn Museum, of the work of Charlie James, an American designer who had enormous influence on world fashion though he made very few clothes and had a relatively short career. He was a genius. Madame Grès was a genius at cut and drape. It does happen. My favorite designer is Yves St. Laurent. He has a better knowledge of what the person of our time wants to wear, and needs, than almost any other designer. His clothes are also wearable. For years "wearable" was an obscene word in the fashion vocabulary, but St. Laurent changed that. I still contend, however, that rarely does fashion design become genius or an art.

BLDD: Are many designers your friends?

BB: Not many, but some of them are. Oscar de La Renta is an old pal, and so are some of the French designers.

BLDD: With whom do you spend most of your time?

BB: They're not really people in the fashion business. They're apt to be politicians—I like politics enormously. They're not theater people. I don't know why, but somehow I don't have that many theatrical friends. They're just people.

BLDD: Did you ever design for the movies, after that early influence?
BB: No! The funny thing is that the only time I ever did it was for a friend of mine, Gene Tierney, who was making a comeback and asked me to do her clothes. I've always stayed away from it. I don't even like doing clothes for the stage, because actresses are such a pain in the ass. Nevertheless it was fun doing the clothes for Tierney. I've done clothes for Streisand, which was an extraordinary experience because she's so knowledgeable. She knew more instinctively about fashion than almost anybody I've ever met. She certainly knew about her own body, her good points. She was an exciting woman to dress. Monroe was an exciting experience, for instance.
BLDD: Let's go back to politics for a moment. A *New York Times* article called you the Senator of Seventh Avenue, and a *New Yorker* cartoon once suggested nominating you to be Secretary of Clothing. In addition to being an ambassador of good taste, did you ever consider a political or diplomatic role?
BB: No. I don't guess I could afford to be a diplomat, and I never thought about politics, except I wouldn't mind being Mayor of New York City!
BLDD: What would intrigue you about that assignment? Do you think after Seventh Avenue anything is easy?
BB: I would clean up Seventh Avenue, start there, and let's go on. . . No, I think it's a little late for me to go into politics.
BLDD: The other career you might imagine for yourself is that of a diplomat. What intrigues you about that role?
BB: It's trying to show America's best face in other places. The most attractive Ambassadors are those who project the kind of American quality that can make our country so appealing to other nations. This is particularly true now that we are such a powerful country. Most people throughout the world dislike us, and so our Ambassador or attaché in those countries plays the very important role of making us more appealing.
BLDD: Do you ever consider yourself in a sense, an Ambassador from New York as you visit around the country?
BB: No, I'm a salesman. I'm just selling clothes.
BLDD: Have you ever considered designing clothes for what is often referred to as middle-America—your roots—a special collection, let's say, for Sears Roebuck, with your label?
BB: Well, Halston has announced that he will design for J. C. Penney's. But it has never appealed to me and I have no plans to do it. Somewhere along the line I would lose some of the excitement of going to Europe and buying these extraordinary fabrics, things of that sort. I do hope that the clothes trickle down to reach a good many more people than they do even at the Blassport or Blass III level.
BLDD: If you were to have a retrospective of your work currently, and examine what the most successful recurring, and timeless, elements have been, what do you think should be selected?
BB: As a matter of fact, I was going to have a retrospective, but I've postponed it until after 1985. My retrospective would be similar to the one that Givenchy had at the Fashion Institute of Technology. What I will try to project are timeless, classic, daytime clothes, and really glamorous, exciting evening clothes. The combination of the two.
BLDD: Would you include any of the fashions that you've designed for men?
BB: Oh, yes. Only the first early collections because those are my favorites. I still have those clothes and I know other fellows who kept them. I would also include the design for the first Lincoln Continental I did. Perhaps *not* the first chocolate!
BLDD: How have your thoughts about designing for men changed over the last fifteen years?
BB: Not much. It's the same philosophy about dressing that I had as a young man, and then as a not so young man, and still now. I dress in different ways for different reasons. I had a very square business lunch today; that's why I'm got up like this.
BLDD: It is something of a paradox that while men are giving up traditional business clothes, women are increasingly putting them on. We know how you feel about the dress for success philosophy, but is there any specific advice you would give to a woman who wants to look not only efficient, but glamorous at the same time?

Bill Blass, fall, 1982

BB: Much of it has to do with elements other than clothes: beautifully kept hair, clean, shiny, good skin. Not so much makeup. American women have a tendency to wear too much makeup during the day. Certainly not an over-abundance of jewelry. Pretty shoes. Good stockings. You notice I stay away from the clothes thing because I think these are the elements that make you look attractive to your employer, and, if not to your own husband, somebody else's.

BLDD: What is your most recent project? And in what direction would you like to go?

BB: I really don't want more licensees. I want to expand the European and Asiatic business. At this point in my life I'd like to put everything in its proper category and see that it works successfully. That is more interesting to me than anything else. I also want to write a book, my philosophy about clothes and what clothes do for us.

BLDD: A successful designer must be of his time and also be able to look toward the future. What do you envision men and women wearing ten years from now?

BB: To predict clothes is so curious, because in no prediction that I have read was the sixties ever anticipated. It was the first time in the history of fashion that fashion ever came from the streets, from the young, from the non-affluent. It depends entirely on the economy of the world in the next five years. And of course, war always changes fashion. The First World War changed fashion as we knew it in the '20's, and the Second World War brought about enormous change, represented by Mr. Dior's 'New Look.' God forbid there's a war, but it will always influence clothes.

BLDD: Is there anything that you haven't designed yet, that you'd care to?

BB: I'd like to get involved in some airplane design. I think that the interiors of most of them are so depressing. I wouldn't make them shocking pink, but I think that they could be more attractive.

BLDD: Have you ever designed uniforms for airline stewardesses?

BB: Yes, I did American Airlines for about ten years. Very disappointing experience. They used the most awful polyester fabric, and, while we had nifty blazers and skirts and ties for the gals and a variety of raincoats, by the time they were reinterpreted in what I consider third rate fabrics they lost a lot of their appeal.

BLDD: What's been the greatest satisfaction of your career?

BB: I'd be very dishonest if I didn't say recognition. There's something very appealing about being recognized and well-known for what you do. That's nice no matter where you are.

BLDD: In a world with an increasingly immediate need for gratification, you've said that you were glad that your success came later in life. What particular advantage would that have?

BB: Sour grapes, of course. I do think that one is more able to handle success after a certain age. Mr. St. Laurent is one of the few exceptions; he went to Dior when he was eighteen. Too often, success at an early age can ruin someone in so many different ways. Being a celebrity, being rich, can lead to all sorts of other personal problems. I've always found it better to have the background and experience and then eventually the success.

BLDD: Did you ever expect it to unfold the way it has?

BB: No, I reckon that I thought I'd make it, but I never thought I would do so many other things.

BLDD: If you had it to do over again what would you do otherwise?

BB: I would have taken a year or two apprenticeship in Europe, just to have had a taste of that. To have acquired some of the legendary technique that France has. After all, the French invented making clothes, the first couture houses, such as Worth, did develop there. I would have liked that when I was young. Later it was too late.

BLDD: Is there anything, by the way, in that three-and-a-half year Army experience, where you served as a sergeant, that you later applied to your professional life?

BB: Getting along with people. We were a camouflage engineer outfit to begin with, and then, as the war changed from defensive to offensive, we were changed into a combat engineer outfit. So the outfit, originally made up of artists, and architects, and painters, and people of that sort, added coalminers and taxi drivers, and a lot of other sorts. I think it was getting

along with people during that period that helped me more than almost anything else I ever did.

BLDD: You said that the French really invented it all. It seems to me that the Americans extended it all. What is the particularly American contribution to the world of fashion?

BB: Ready-made clothes. When I say the French invented it, I mean Marie Antoinette, in the 17th-century, too. In France there were dressmakers who made clothes, but they were made for the rich. In America we made the first ready-made clothes; we were the first to make mass-produced clothes; good-looking clothes for the masses. That had never happened before in any country. But we did it.

BLDD: Being a man, how much do you feel you have to understand the way women think in order to design for them?

BB: Well, I don't think anybody ever understood women. My role is to make them more appealing. I don't think you have to understand them to do that, you just have to want to make them look better.

BLDD: Is there any woman that you might cite who you find particularly appealing because of the combination of glamour and intelligence?

BB: In the media, I must say Barbara Walters. I've known her for 25 years and there's been a marvelous transformation of the woman as far as her hair, her skin, her clothes, her tastes. She discovered herself. Diana Vreeland says that most of us invented ourselves, and I think she's probably right. Nancy Reagan is another example. I knew her when she was the Governor's wife in California, but as she's emerged on the world scene I think she's improved, too. Nancy Kissinger, also.

BLDD: Would you like to see men's fashions change more frequently?

BB: I think it would be a vast mistake. It's funny—the husbands of those women who buy $5,000 dresses are reluctant to spend $750 for a suit. I think it's obvious that men's fashions shouldn't change very much. I don't think that the basic concept of men's fashion has changed in 100 years, anyway. A lot of it has to do with status. They are stuck with having to look a certain way to get ahead in business. Corporate dressing in this country still prevails.

Bill Blass, fall, 1985

Opposite:

Bill Blass, fall, 1982

OdlR

Oscar de la Renta

Colorful, fanciful, inspired—these are the clothes designed by Oscar de la Renta. Through his words and his work, we see what happens when a designer translates his love of vibrant colors, forms, and fabrics into art that can be worn. Dominican-born Oscar de la Renta was one of the first American fashion designers to mass market his products. Today his label is found on over eighty different items, everything from high fashion to household linens, sunglasses, umbrellas, and even the national Boy Scout uniform.

BLDD: So many of the things that you have created throughout your career have used such colors as reds, turquoises, yellows. Do you see a Latin flavor reflected in the designs and colors and even the ruffles?

OdlR: I think that my background certainly has to do with my color sense. I never wanted to be a fashion designer. I wanted to be a painter, and my sense of color really comes from my going through art school and trying to paint, and not from trying to design clothes. The Dominican Republic, where I come from, is a very warm Latin country and I'm sure it affected my color sense—my eye—as a painter.

BLDD: Many designers began sketching at an early age, but you actually studied abstract painting. Was this encouraged by your parents? Was there an artistic tradition in your family?

OdlR: Not at all. My mother has a very big family, from two different marriages. She had sixteen brothers and sisters. One of my uncles, who was in the diplomatic service for many years, is one of the best-known poets in the Dominican Republic. But there hasn't been anyone in my family before who was any kind of an artist. I have six sisters—I'm the youngest, the only boy, and so it was very tough for my father to accept the fact that I wanted to be a painter, and then a fashion designer. At the beginning, it was really quite difficult, and possible only with my mother's help. I was the only boy and the youngest, so she wanted to help me. That's how it happened.

BLDD: Why, and under what circumstances, did you leave the Dominican Republic?

OdlR: I went to art school there. At the same time I was going through high school. I graduated and had my first one-man show of paintings when I was seventeen years old. I convinced my mother, and my mother convinced my father, that I should go to Spain to study painting. One of my close friends who had gone to art school with me had gone there the previous year. At that time he was studying with a famous Spanish painter called Vasquez Diaz. So I went to the Academy of San Fernando in Madrid, and had private lessons with Vasquez Diaz. I lived there for quite a long time.

BLDD: How was your choice of a career influenced by growing up in an environment where there was, in fact, no fashion industry?

OdlR: Not really at all. My mother was a very strong influence in my early life—she died when I was nineteen—but she loved clothes and loved to dress well. Because there were no really good clothes in the Dominican Republic, when I was very young, my mother used to go quite often to Cuba, to Havana. She saw it as a wonderful, fabulous city, very gay, full of wonderful people. There was a famous store in Havana called El Encanto, the only store in Latin America that carried all kinds of European clothes, and my mother used to buy all of her clothes there—and, unfortunately, some of my clothes, too. At age fourteen I was still going to school in very short, wide pants while every other boy was dressing in long pants. I always felt very bad about it. But, though there was not a fashion industry in my country *per se*, Latin women care a lot about dressing, so I did see some fairly well-dressed people. At that point though I never thought of being a fashion designer. It never entered my mind.

BLDD: There you were in Madrid studying art, and suddenly you became a fashion illustrator. You had the good fortune to have a celebrated designer learn of your work. How did that come about, and who was he?

OdlR: My mother died when I was nineteen and my father remarried two years later. He then said, "Enough of that nonsense of wanting to be a painter," and asked me to come back to the Dominican Republic to go into his business. He was in the insurance business and he wanted me to sell insurance. I didn't see myself doing that, so I started doing fashion illustration. I tried to find some commercial aspects to my ability in art. Even though at that point I had already been a part of many gallery shows with other painters in Madrid, I hadn't sold any of my paintings. I wasn't making any money with my work, and I thought that one of the most commercial aspects of my being an artist was that I could draw very well. I started doing fashion illustrations for newspapers and magazines in Spain. I was making a little money, and going into the fashion houses and looking at the clothes and their designs. While I waited for a model to change, I'd think, "Well, if I was making that dress, I would make it different." I started doing sketches of my own. One day a friend of mine saw those sketches and asked, "Whose work is this?" I said, "Well, this is nothing in particular. It's sketches I have done from things that I have seen and thought that I could improve." He showed my sketches to Balenciaga, who was then already a very well-established designer in France. He had a fashion house in Madrid which was run by his sister. It was called Aisa.

BLDD: Why wasn't it called Balenciaga?

OdlR: Because when Balenciaga started in business in Spain, in San Sebastian, where he was born, the house went bankrupt. Then he went on to Paris and became a famous designer. But he never again could use the name Balenciaga in Spain, and that's why the house was called Aisa, which was his sister's name. He saw my sketches and thought that I was talented and asked if I would like to come to work in his place as an illustrator. At that time in Spain—and I think that some of the old couture houses in Paris may still do it—once the collections were made, they sent the sketches to clients in the provinces with color swatches of the fabrics, to see if they wanted to order any clothes. I did all the sketches for the clients. I worked there for almost a year, going into the sample rooms, to see how clothes were made, because I really never went to fashion school.

BLDD: How did you learn to make a pattern or even the proper kind of sketch?

OdlR: Well, I have never made a pattern. I learned from experience. Working at Balenciaga was a privileged break. If anyone came to my place today and asked for a job, it would be almost impossible, because you don't have the time to take on an apprentice and show him how things should be done. But then it was quite customary to bring in young people and train them. At the same time, they would do some sort of job, picking up pins and doing all sorts of other things. That is really what I was doing at Balenciaga.

BLDD: What caused you to move on from there?

OdlR: After one year, I just decided to do so. I never thought I would give up painting at that point. That came much later. I thought that fashion was probably something that was compatible with painting, and that the best place to be was Paris. I asked Balenciaga if I could work in his house in Paris. He said, "Well, I couldn't take you in that studio now because I would really like you to stay here for a while more, perhaps another year, and then you will come to Paris." But I was very, very impatient and, with the financial assistance of my sisters—who were all married—I was able to go to Paris for a couple of weeks. I started immediately at the top! The first house I went to was Dior. I went to Christian Dior with my sketches and told him I was looking for a job as an assistant designer. This was just the point, in 1959, I think, when Yves St. Laurent had some kind of nervous breakdown and left Dior. Dior was in the process of engaging new designers, but it hadn't been officially announced yet. When I showed my sketches to Madame Marguerite, the head of the studio, she liked them, saw I was talented, and offered me a job. She said, "I don't know what you will be doing because we are reorganizing our studio, but we will love you to work for us." She offered me very little money as salary, $150 a month. But, I was very, very happy, for the opportunity. That same afternoon I was walking down a street in Paris, and I met a Spanish friend and he asked me what I was doing. I explained. He said, "Well, a very good friend of mine, Antonio Castillo, is at the head of Lanvin, and he's looking for an assistant. Why don't you go and see him?" So, I went with my sketches to see Castillo and he loved them. He, too, offered me a job. But before offering me the job, he asked me if I knew how to drape.

BLDD: And we know by now, that you didn't!

OdlR: But I said, "Yes!" He looked at my sketches and said, "You know, I would love you to come and work as my assistant." And I said, "Well, I actually came at the insistence of this friend, because I have already

accepted a job at Dior." And he asked, "How much money are they paying you?" I replied, "They offered me $200." He said, "Well, what about if I pay you $250?" And I said, "Fine, but I need to go back to Spain and pick up my clothes. I really couldn't start before three or four weeks." He said that would be fine, and I asked for an engagement letter. That evening I went through the Yellow Pages. My French was very, very bad. I looked for a fashion school. I chose the biggest sign and I went to this private school the following morning. I asked for the head teacher and told the whole story. I said, "I accepted the job yesterday. These are my sketches. They asked me if I knew how to drape and I said yes, but I don't. So would you teach me how to drape in two weeks?" She agreed. The fact is that I don't know if I really could have done it because I was never put to the test, but, nevertheless, I went for two weeks, every day for four hours, to this lady, and she was wonderful.

BLDD: In addition to Balenciaga and Castillo, you've worked for Elizabeth Arden. How did being an apprentice to these great designers influence you in your work and your design aesthetic?

OdlR: My first job in the United States was with Elizabeth Arden. But she was different from the others, because she was not a designer per se. Working with Balenciaga and Castillo was a great influence on my career, though I never really worked that much with Balenciaga himself. He was creating the collections in Paris, and then the collection would be brought down to Madrid. But I was very much in contact with all his clothes and he was probably the designer I most admired and most identified with at that time.

BLDD: Did you learn the most from him, too?

OdlR: Yes. I learned a lot from him. There are very few people—except people who really know a lot about fashion—who know the name of Antonio Castillo. Young people, especially, probably know very little about him, but, for many years the label was Lanvin-Castillo, from 1952 to 1964. He made beautiful clothes. My sense for evening clothes really comes much more from Castillo than from Balenciaga. One of the best dressed ladies that I have known, who's now dead, was Mrs. Lowell Guinness, Gloria Guiness. She was a beautiful woman. She was a Mexican, married to an Englishman, and lived in Europe most of her adult life. She was wonderfully well-dressed, one of the best-dressed women I have ever seen. She used to dress from both the designers. They were both her very close friends. Half of her wardrobe was Balenciaga, the other half was Castillo. Several years before she died, I asked her, "What have you done with all of your old clothes?" She said, "Well, I gave all my Balenciagas away to the Metropolitan Museum in New York, when they had the Balenciaga show, and to the Victoria & Albert Museum in London, and a lot I gave to my family." Then I asked, "What happened to your Castillo clothes?" She said, "You know, those I never gave away, because all his evening clothes I still wear." He designed clothes that were not particularly important in that period, but clothes that are timeless. Whereas Balenciaga designed clothes that were so much of the period in which he designed, that I think it would be very difficult today for a woman to wear a Balenciaga dress and not look dated. There are lots of evening clothes designed by Castillo that are still valid and any woman can wear them and probably the outfit will look as contemporary now as it looked them.

BLDD: It seems to me that the very nature of fashion is "of the moment". But you are talking about timelessness and classic sense of clothes. Nowadays we hear a great deal about fashion "collectibles." I often think that's a gentle way to ease our consciences because of the soaring cost of clothes. How can you have "fashion" on the one hand, and "timelessness" on the other?

OdlR: There are certain garments that are timeless, that are classic, like a man's grey flannel suit. Probably you can wear the same suit for thirty years, even if the lapels go narrower or wider, if you don't wear the extreme version. The same thing goes for a lady's sweater. If you have a sweater that is a classic, it lasts far longer than something that makes a very strong statement. The eyes get tired of things that are very exaggerated, and that is why fashion changes.

BLDD: It's been nearly twenty years now that you have been in New York—how did you wend your way here from Paris?

Oscar de la Renta, fall, 1982

OdlR: It's going to sound as if I am a con man! I came to New York in 1963. I had already been working for about three years for Lanvin and Castillo. I had left the Dominican Republic in 1952 and had been living away from home for many years. I felt I could never go back home and exercise my new profession, because there was no tradition or fashion house in which I could work. I saw that New York would be a good compromise, and closer to home. Also quite a few of my friends in Paris had come to New York to work, and were doing very well. They were making a lot of money. I strongly felt at that point—and this was probably the most important part of my decision to come to New York—that ready-to-wear was the great future of fashion. Up to that time I had worked with high fashion houses where ready-to-wear was very unimportant. The year I worked for Lanvin, all the high fashion houses were already making ready-to-wear collections, but they were always treated as sort of second-rate. Castillo, who then had the house in Spain, used to come only for the big collections twice a year. The assistants, myself and another French boy, were doing the ready-to-wear collections, because they didn't consider them important. Sometimes we would do a dress with very pretty fabric that was reasonably priced and that was not too difficult to produce, so it could be a ready-to-wear dress. If the dress was too good, they'd say, "Oh, no. Let's keep that for the couture house." Ready-to-wear was not treated the way it is now. I felt that in New York they had a much better understanding of ready-to-wear and mass marketing than they had in France. I had two weeks vacation and I wanted to go home so I asked for two extra weeks, and I came to New York in November of 1962. I had written a few friends here saying I was considering the idea of coming to work in the States. I stayed on Madison Avenue and 55th Street at the Winslow Hotel. I think it's been demolished by now. The first day I arrived a friend of mine called me at five o'clock in the afternoon and asked me if I had a black tie. I said yes, and he said, "I hope you are not too tired. There's a charity ball tonight and I need an extra man. Would you like to come?" This friend worked in public relations. I went to the charity ball and sat next to Elizabeth Arden. Antonio Castillo had worked for Elizabeth Arden for five years and I knew a lot about her. One important factor with Arden, who was an extraordinary lady, then already in her eighties, is that she loved to fire people, but she hated anyone who ever left her. I knew that she would love to get even with Antonio Castillo. So, when we went to dinner, she asked me where I came from, and once she had learned that I was a designer working in Paris, she asked, "For whom do you work?" I said, "I work for Castillo." She said, "Oh, Castillo. He used to work for me." And I said, "Yeah, I seem to remember him mentioning your name one time." Obviously, I knew everything about his five years at Arden! She immediately said, "You really should come and work in the States." I said, "Oh, I love Paris. It's a wonderful city. In a few years I might decide to come work here." She said, "New York is so much more exciting. You can make so much more money." I said, "Yes, I know, because I have some friends that are working here. Perhaps I will consider it. I'm not saying no. I mean, if I were to find an extraordinary, irresistible offer, I might consider." Later that evening she came back to me and said, "Why don't you come see me tomorrow? I would love to see your sketches." I said, "Well, Miss Arden, I am very flattered that you would like to see my sketches but, first of all, I'm not looking for a job. Second, since I'm not looking for a job, I am not prepared, but I do have some sketches in New York. I am going down to the Dominican Republic and I have some sketches that I picked up as I was leaving Paris to give my sisters, but, you know, those are not really representative of my work. It's not a portfolio I have prepared to look for a job. They are not my best sketches"—which, of course, they were! She said, "Well, I'd love to see those sketches." And I said, "I'm going to give you my name and where I am staying. Why don't you ask your secretary to call me if you still want to see me tomorrow and I'll come. But, as I told you, I'm not looking for a job. But I will be very flattered to say that Elizabeth Arden asked me to work for her." She said, "Well, you say that if you had an irresistible offer you might consider it?" I replied, "Yes, I said that." The following day the secretary called and asked me to come, and I went to see her at noon. She went through my sketches very fast and then she said, "I would love you to come design a collection for me." She had had Sarmi work for her, and Castillo, as well as Charlie James. She said, "I would love you to do my custom collection." I said, "Miss Arden, I'm not looking for a job." At that point I was making $350 a month in Paris. I told her, "I will not work for less than $500 a week," thinking—this was 1963—that she would offer me $250 and I would jump! So, I said, $500 a week, and she said, "You got a job."

BLDD: How did you get the publicity that you needed when you first started out here in New York?

OdlR: In the same week that I got that job at Arden, I got another offer to design the ready-to-wear collection for Christian Dior in New York. I was quite tempted. I had never met Diana Vreeland, but a friend of mine in Paris who was working at *French Vogue*—and who years later became my wife—gave me a letter of introduction to Diana Vreeland. I called her and she invited me to have tea with her on Sunday. She asked, "What are you doing here? What do you want to do?" I told her, and I said, "Actually I have been offered two jobs. I have been offered a job to design the ready-to-wear collection for Christian Dior, and I have been asked to work for Elizabeth Arden." She told me, "Miss Arden's a very difficult person." I said, "Yes, I know, because Castillo worked for her for five years." And Diana asked me, "What is it that you want in the future?" I said, "I would love to be a well-known designer of ready-to-wear clothes." She said, "Well, then you should go to Elizabeth Arden, because at Elizabeth Arden you will make a name for yourself very fast." She said, "At Dior, you will be designing clothes for an established name, while Elizabeth Arden is not herself known as a designer, so she will use your name on the label right away, besides, because she is the strongest name in cosmetics, she has the power to really make your name known throughout the country." That's how it happened that I went to work with her.

BLDD: Does a man bring something special to designing for a woman, that a woman doesn't have?

OdlR: Yes and no. I think that there are very good women designers and there are very good men designers. Probably a man is more impersonal about fashion design. He can look at it in a more objective way. At the same time, probably the most influential designer of the twentieth century, the one who really changed dressing for women, was a woman: Chanel. She really created the Women's Lib Movement. She was the one who took women out of undergarments and created the modern woman of today. She is by far the most creative, and the most innovative, designer of the twentieth century. She could do it so well because she felt that way strongly herself. She wanted to be a liberated woman. She didn't want to be the Duchess of Westminster, because, she would say, "There have been many Duchesses of Westminster, but there's only one Coco Chanel." In that sense, she recreated her own personality in the clothes.

BLDD: It's been said that you, if not Freud, understand what women want. Just what is it that *you* think women want?

OdlR: It's sort of a guessing game. I think that women want to be dressed like women. What I try to do is to make pretty clothes. A decorator tries to make a pretty house; somebody who designs shoes wants to make a pretty shoe. If you bake a cake, you want to make it very good so somebody will eat it. You have to try to do the best you can. It all deals with illusion and temptation. You have to tempt people.

BLDD: Is it possible to get designer clothes at affordable prices?

OdlR: Yes. I design many, many different lines. Miss O is less expensive than the Oscar de la Renta couture line, which is my high-priced line. Miss O is relatively middle-priced.

BLDD: How much does a Miss O dress cost?

OdlR: I don't know exactly, probably around $200. Miss O retails from $150 to about $400. The very expensive line is mostly made of natural fibers and very expensive fabrics that all come from France, Italy, and Switzerland. That line retails from about $400 to about $12,000.

BLDD: What costs $12,000?

OdlR: There's only one article in my last fall line. It's an embroidered jacket. We sell them. I mean, we haven't sold a hundred but we have sold ten of them. The average price in the couture line is between $800 and $1,200. The very expensive ones are what we call showpieces. We sell really very, very few of them. Then, the Miss O line, which goes from about

$150 to about $400, is all silk. It's manufactured in Hong Kong. And we have the fabric printed in Hong Kong, Shanghai, and Korea. Then there's a line called Oscar de la Renta Sport—it's blouses and sweaters and skirts, and they sell from about $60 to about $125.

BLDD: Most dresses seem to be designed for very young girls or size 4 models. How about the rest of us?

OdlR: At that price range, the clothes are not really for a very young girl because a very young girl cannot afford to buy at those prices. My customer for the expensive clothes is really a woman over twenty-five or thirty years old. We see a professional woman who works and makes a lot of money or a woman who is married to a rich husband.

BLDD: In times past, fashionable women were expected to have fine shoulders, a large bust, and rounded hips. Nowadays, we think you can't be thin enough. What do you do to mask ample hips, and how much of a woman's body do you think should be left to the imagination?

OdlR: That's a very personal thing. It totally depends on the woman, what she wants to do. I specialize in a certain size range. The first sample I make is always about a size 8, and then we take that style and we grade it up to a 16 and down to a size 2. You cannot go any bigger. Why don't we design clothes for bigger sizes? It's just not what I like doing. The clothes I design are the clothes that I feel comfortable with and capable of designing. I sell to a small segment of the population because of the price range of my clothes. So I'm not really a mass market designer catering to a wide segment of the population.

BLDD: That is true in terms of clothes—but you also market so many other products, more than eighty. Can you tell us what some of the others are, besides sunglasses and umbrellas?

OdlR: I design shoes, costume jewelry, accessories, handbags, a full line of men's clothes, socks, shoes, clothing, shirts, sportswear, sweaters, knitted dresses for ladies, the Miss O line that I already mentioned, sheets and towels.

BLDD: Would you ever put your name on chocolates?

OdlR: Bill Blass is a designer I admire. He is also a good friend of mine. If he did it, I think it's right.

BLDD: Is there anything you haven't designed yet that you'd care to?

OdlR: Yes. I'd love to be doing more in home furnishings, but that requires a different kind of studio. To design is to have a feeling. When you design a dress, you don't design that dress in the abstract. You have a feeling for the woman for whom you are designing it. Or for that man, if it's a suit. You see that man or that woman in a certain environment. You see a certain lifestyle for those clothes. So it's absolutely natural that we should have a feeling for how that home or that office should look as well.

BLDD: Oscar de la Renta is an empire that designer licensing has helped to build. How much of a hand do you have in the design of all the eighty different lines that your company markets?

OdlR: I work with four assistants who design with me, plus three assistants that get involved in other aspects of the functioning of the studio. We design practically every product that is labeled with my name. Probably our biggest volume of business is the fragrance. Obviously, we don't design a different fragrance every day or every season, but I was very much involved in the creation of the fragrance. We are now going further with the fragrances into lotions and eventually into color—you know, cosmetics.

BLDD: I believe that your perfume is the number one perfume today. Is that correct?

OdlR: It's number one in the United States. We have limited distribution because obviously there are a lot of perfumes. We sell more than any other perfume in the stores we want to sell to. We're only selling in about 800 stores, while Chanel sells in 20,000. You can buy Chanel in a drugstore or a discount store. Oscar de la Renta you can only buy in an established store like Saks or Bergdorf's or Bloomingdale's.

BLDD: It used to be important that a scent was "French perfume." That no longer seems to be the case. Who, and what, was responsible for that shift?

OdlR: Actually, my fragrance happens to be made and packaged in France, but, again, that was out of choice. We worked with different perfumeries, American as well as French, and it happened that the fragrance I liked most was the one that was created by an innovative

French house. Also, I think that the French understand quality in packaging. At the same time it was a question of mechanics. We felt that for the markets around the world where the name of Oscar de la Renta is not as well known, as it is in the United States, it would be much more important to have a perfume made in France with the name Oscar de la Renta than one made in the United States, where there is not a tradition for making fragrances.

BLDD: How much of the success of the perfume do you attribute to the successful marketing of a successful name?

OdlR: I think that it's very important to the marketing of a product to sell that first bottle. But the success of a fragrance comes when a woman identifies with that fragrance and buys it a second and third time. At that point, the important thing is really the fragrance itself, because the woman or the man will not buy the fragrance again if they don't like it. They can try once because of successful marketing, but the second time they will buy it just because they feel they like it and they identify with it.

BLDD: How does it feel to be in a crowded room, an elevator, or an airport, and realize what an influence you've had, not only on body covering, but the personal habits and self-image of so many people?

OdlR: It feels wonderful. That's what I work for, and I have been very, very lucky. I don't feel that I am more talented than other people, who perhaps haven't had the same opportunities that I have had.

BLDD: How has the perfume market changed in the last decade, in terms of the shift to American perfumes, the use of television for marketing and so on?

OdlR: People keep saying designer's fragrance is a new thing, but Chanel was originally created by a designer. Chanel No. 5 is probably the best known fragrance. And they talk now about designer fragrances as if they were a new thing! But they are not. Every designer who has established a name dreams of having a fragrance. I always call a fragrance an invisible dress. My legacy is what the woman that wears my dress smells like. American women now have a much better understanding of fragrance than ten years ago. The big difference is that a European woman will wear a fragrance as a second skin. She will wear the fragrance and walk into a room and when she leaves the room they say, "Oh, So-and-so was here," because she leaves that scent. An American woman likes to play more—there are designers that make sports fragrances, and evening fragrances, and American women change and wear one scent one day and the next day something else. I suppose that is part of the freedom of doing anything one wants. But I like the idea of a woman wearing only one fragrance, because it becomes herself. If that fragrance can be Oscar de la Renta, then that's even better!

BLDD: Why don't we talk about that identity for a moment? You are a kind of oracle on the subject of glamour. Perhaps you might help us define what that difficult term means. What makes a woman glamorous? Is it her clothing, her grooming, her posture? Or is it really some other, more mysterious, quality?

OdlR: It starts with oneself, with the image that woman projects. Glamour has nothing to do with beauty. Even a badly-dressed woman can have some glamour. The glamorous woman has a certain glow, and that glow is something that she has to create herself. Glamour is an illusion. It's entering a room and dazzling somewhere, somehow, and sometimes for the wrong reasons.

BLDD: Is there any public figure that personifies that certain quality for you? For example, Lauren Bacall is admired for having a very personal style, and so is Jacqueline Onassis.

OdlR: Yes, but a personal style has nothing to do with glamour. Glamour is something else. A woman can be glamorous and not have style. When you talk about the Hollywood stars—let's talk about the dead ones so that the alives won't get hurt—I mean, Jean Harlow was glamorous, but I don't think that she was elegant or had any finesse. She had style, but it was not a style I tremendously care for. She had sex appeal and she was glamorous, but she didn't have all the other qualities that I admire much more in a woman.

BLDD: Is there any other woman, alive or dead, that personifies those qualities for you?

OdlR: A lot of women. What I admire in a woman, first of all, is her intelligence, her intent. For any human being, the most important beauty is the inner beauty. The most important beauty is not the beauty you were born with, but the beauty you create for yourself. Real beauty starts when the beauty that you were born with ends, because you can be born with certain gifts but after awhile they fade. Then there is that inner beauty that comes through. That, for me, is far more important. It's what one makes of oneself that is real beauty in human terms and in intelligent terms. Those are the important qualities. That's the kind of beauty that I admire, and that I care for, and that's the kind of woman that I am interested in.

BLDD: That's a very serious and philosophical reply. Being a name designer today is obviously a very serious business, too, and it requires a special business sense as well as aesthetic ingenuity. How much of your time do you spend on the bottom line rather than the hemline, and is it all still fun?

OdlR: Yes, it is all still fun. When I started my own business in 1965, I spent 90% of my time designing clothes. Today, I probably spend more like 30 or 40% of my time designing clothes. That is the time I enjoy most. Unfortunately, my business, like almost any other, has changed in the sense that the promotional aspects of it have become very, very important.

BLDD: You're very good about going to stores and talking to customers. How much do those conversations affect what you eventually design?

OdlR: A lot. New York today is by far the fashion capital of the world, not only because of the tremendous amount of designers working in the city, but because we are designing enough clothes for a very, very big market.

BLDD: America used to be the poor cousin of the European market and now, obviously, it sets the pace. How do you account for that success and that change?

OdlR: For years Seventh Avenue was controlled by manufacturers, and not by designers. That changed in my time, when I came to Seventh Avenue. Until then most of the names were either connected to a manufacturer or the name on the label was the name of a manufacturer and not the name of a designer. Early in the '60's the designers started to emerge as the stars on the label. American manufacturers had been buying from the European market, bringing the clothes to the States, and copying them. But in the very early '60's and even in the '50's, people like Claire McCardle and Norman Norell launched the idea of the importance of the American designer, and created what the market is today.

BLDD: It's been said that good taste is almost as rare as genius. Would you agree with that, and how would you define good taste?

OdlR: Good taste comes from appreciation of life and from learning. No one is born with good taste. You can be born in certain surroundings where it comes easier, but it is something finally that one learns.

BLDD: You're known to millions of Americans not only by your clothes but by your publicity. There are not many designers that appear on the cover of *The New York Times Magazine*, or are featured with such regularity in the national and international press. Did you ever expect the media to celebrate you, or your work, the way they have?

OdlR: I never expected, but I always hoped—and it happened.

BLDD: What next? Where are you headed and what are your plans?

OdlR: I'm quite happy doing what I am doing; I couldn't handle any more work right now. I make very good money, a very good living. I have a very happy life and I'm just working hard to keep what I have.

BLDD: Your involvement in the world of foreign affairs includes friendships with many diplomats, politicians and other officials. If you could dress the leader of your choice, who would it be, and what sort of ensemble would you create?

OdlR: I don't know. I don't know if there is a leader of my choice! It depends on the time of the day. I like a lot of people. But, for example, I would not get Mrs. Gandhi out of her sari.

BLDD: Would you take Mrs. Reagan out of that other designer?

OdlR: No. I think Mrs. Reagan dresses wonderfully well and she should keep doing what she's doing.

BLDD: If an actor can be an ambassador, why can't a fashion designer be an ambassador? Is that a career you might consider?

OdlR: Not really. I still have very strong ties to my country, to the Dominican Republic. I have been offered, more than one time, to be the Dominican Ambassador to Washington, which I cannot do because I am an American citizen, and I don't want to lose my citizenship.

BLDD: How about the reverse, the American Ambassador to the Dominican Republic?

OdlR: That hasn't been offered. I think that I am a much better ambassador just being myself. I serve my country of birth better by being Oscar de la Renta and by going there as myself, and I feel much happier as an American doing what I am doing, because that is what I do best.

BLDD: Have you been able to influence fashion in the Dominican Republic?

OdlR: If I had gone to my country, probably I would have been a very influential designer—but nobody else in the world would have known about it.

BLDD: Do you spend much time in the Dominican Republic?

OdlR: About six or seven weeks a year. I have a house there and I'm involved in different things. I am very much concerned with an orphanage and a day school. I have 300 kids that I take care of, and I love that.

BLDD: Do you ever get a chance to paint anymore?

OdlR: No, I don't, unfortunately. Because I was a professional painter, it would be very difficult to become a Sunday painter. There are so many different things that a person with talent can do. But to do something well, one should only do that one thing. I say that one day when I can afford to, I'll paint again, but I'm not doing it now.

BLDD: What do you consider the best training for a young designer today?

OdlR: School. I didn't go to a fashion school, because I went in through the back door. But I feel that the fashion schools, especially in this country, are absolutely wonderful—Parsons, F. I. T., Traphagen. I think that Parsons is by far the best school. Probably going to work directly with a designer the way I did, is the best school, but today that is non-existent. That was a wonderful opportunity then.

BLDD: In addition to your fashions, I think you are one of the few designers as well-known for your role as host, for the various homes that you live in, as for the fine cuisine that you offer your guests. Are *you* mainly responsible for this, or is this your wife?

OdlR: My wife.* Not only is she responsible for everything you mentioned, but I think that it's a big advantage for a designer to be married, especially to a woman like my wife, who has been involved in fashion for so many years, and who sacrificed her career in fashion to be married to me. My wife is French, born in Paris, and up to the time we got married, in 1967, was Editor-in-Chief of French *Vogue*. She had lived all her life in Paris, and not only did she have to give up her job, she had to give up her city. Which she doesn't regret. She is my strongest critic. We have tremendous disagreements about fashion, because she understands it in a completely different way.

BLDD: What's the difference?

OdlR: I do a lot of things that she doesn't identify with. She doesn't wear ruffles!

BLDD: Then how does she manage to wear your clothes?

OdlR: Well, there are a lot of things I do that have no ruffles! I have very talented assistants that I work with, and it's nice to know that if I designed something that my assistants hated, I would expect them to say something about it, and they do. But regardless of how close a friendship we have, and they are all my friends, I'm still the boss. With my wife, I'm not the boss. So she can really come forth and say it. She can come to the collections and be all smiles in front of the public, but afterwards, she'll say, "That was terrible."

BLDD: Who is right more often?

OdlR: We are both right in a sense.

BLDD: Wouldn't you make the perfect diplomat . . .

OdlR: I have a good story about my wife. In the late '60's, the company that makes Ultrasuede was a company in Japan called Torai and they were my first licensee in Japan. When they were going to introduce Ultrasuede in the United States, they sent me ten yards of the fabric and said, "This is a

*Sadly, Francoise de la Renta died since the interview was conducted.

Below:
Oscar de la Renta, fall, 1982

new fiber that I think is going to revolutionize the market, and we would like you to launch it in the States. We are going to give you a year's exclusivity on it if you make an important group of clothes with this fabric." I took my ten yards, saw that the fabric felt fabulous, that it could be washed, didn't need to be pressed, that it had all these great qualities that an American woman loves. I made a dress, size 10. I gave it to my wife and said, "You know, this is going to revolutionize the market. I want you to tell me what you think about it. Would you wear it?" She put on the dress and the following day, I said, "Don't you think it's fabulous," because it was well tailored to her. She said, "American women will never wear it." I asked why. She said, "It feels terrible on your skin, and women will never wear it." So, *I* didn't use Ultrasuede. Somebody else did, and made a tremendous business out of it! For a while Ultrasuede was a huge thing and it was very, very successful in this country. But, actually, it never sold in Europe. My wife reacted like a European woman. The American man is much more refined about what he wears than a woman is. You will find a lot of men who will not wear a polyester shirt. A man will want to wear a 100% cotton shirt, because polyester doesn't feel good to his skin and doesn't breathe well. On the other hand, a lot of women will put on a polyester dress with the greatest of ease. This is the paradox.

BLDD: Have you ever designed for the theatre, or for films, and would you like to?

OdlR: I have done some clothes for films. Right now I'm doing some clothes for the new ballet of Twyla Tharp. And I love it. I would love to do some ballet costumes and some for opera, because I like opera. But again, the problem is lack of time. I don't physically have the time to do it. Jerome Robbins from the New York City Ballet, is a very good friend of mine, and I would love to design a new production of "Scheherezade," because it's something that I understand. But the fact is, that I don't really have the time to do it.

BLDD: If you had it to do over again, what would you do otherwise?

OdlR: Probably, I would do it the same way. There are a few mistakes, but they are not that important.

Opposite:
Oscar de la Renta, spring, 1982

Oscar de la Renta, fall, 1982

Opposite:
Oscar de la Renta, fall, 1982

PE

Perry Ellis

The clothes designed by Perry Ellis are well known for their bold combinations, for their comfort, and for their originality. In a short time he has made his adventurous designs a major force in American fashion.

BLDD: You grew up in a small Southern town, one that I know well, in Tidewater, Virginia. What effect do you suppose the area has had on your decisions about work?

PE: I suppose one's environment is always terribly important to one's work but I don't know how important it is, or its direct implications. But certainly growing up in the South is different from growing up in the Midwest or in New England, or in the West, though the differences have never been particularly important to me.

BLDD: So, you don't find yourself or your orientation particularly Southern?

PE: Perhaps I'm a Southern person. I feel the values that I have, perhaps some of what I appreciate in life is Southern, but then I meet people from all parts of the world that enjoy and like the same things I do.

BLDD: Your education is different from that of most other fashion designers, too: a B.A. in business, and an M.A. in retailing from New York University. Did you always intend to pursue fashion as a career?

PE: I really didn't know I would become a fashion designer. I chose business at the College of William and Mary because I knew I did not want to be a doctor or lawyer. Business seemed to be a wonderful catch-all. The only thing I really liked was stores, particularly clothing stores, and especially those that sold beautiful men's and women's clothing. They tended to be rather small specialty shops. The trip to the big city was to Richmond, Virginia, and to go into stores like Miller & Rhoads or Thalheimer's, which are regional department stores. They had glamour, excitement, fragrances, and women who were very beautiful. For someone from a small town, it was terribly exciting and stimulating, but I didn't know how I could make a living at it. So I went through undergraduate school learning about business—actually not learning very much about business, but having a pretty good time. After undergraduate school, I decided to concentrate on retailing, and I went to NYU which had a wonderful department of retailing in the Business School. I finally found an area in which I was fascinated and totally comfortable. When I left there, I went to work for Miller & Rhoads.

BLDD: How, and why, did you get a job with that Richmond department store?

PE: There was a time when stores from all over the country used to send representatives to New York to hire students who went to the School of Retailing. Miller & Rhoads was one, and since I was from Virginia, I talked to their representative and he invited me to come down and spend a vacation. I always loved the store, and it seemed like a perfect place to work.

BLDD: What did that experience teach you about design, or about the needs or desires of consumers?

PE: I certainly don't remember learning anything about design or about consumers. Most of what I know today has to do with instincts, what I learn from my travels, observations of what stores are actually like, and what they need. Personal observations inspire most of what I do.

BLDD: Just how small was your small hometown?

PE: Portsmouth, Virginia, now has a population of about 100,000. But actually, I lived in a suburb called Churchland, which was even smaller. It's lovely—a lot of flat land, surrounded by beautiful rivers. Suffolk, which is close by, is the peanut capital of the world, and Richmond is the tobacco capital. There's a lot of Chesapeake Bay influence on that tidewater part of Virginia. It's a wonderful part of a great state.

BLDD: When and how did you make the transition to become a fashion designer?

PE: I don't know the exact moment that I became a designer. When I was buying women's clothing for Miller & Rhoads, I was very strong and very aggressive, about almost everything I wanted to buy. I wanted to change everything I saw. I couldn't understand why certain things weren't done; I was constantly redesigning other people's clothing.

BLDD: How large a chain is Miller & Rhoads?

PE: Today, I have no idea. In those days, it had thirteen stores and I was buying for all of them. Therefore when I walked into a showroom in New

York City, people would pay attention to what I had to say, and how much I had to buy. Much of what I redesigned became terribly successful for them, so they started asking my opinion. Manufacturers came to Virginia and wanted me to look over a line before opening in New York. Then a couple of them asked me to do something for them. Finally one manufacturer asked me to come work for him—John Meyer, from the company John Meyer of Norwich. I accepted. That was about 1967.

BLDD: What was important about that time for you?

PE: I was full of ambition and fire, and had a passion for retailing.

BLDD: What is it that you like so much about it?

PE: Number one, I love clothing, and I was buying clothing. It was almost like being a merchant—to buy and to sell, and to make a profit on it. It's a very interesting feeling. What you decide affects the sales of a store. You have a lot of power as a buyer; you see results immediately. Clothing is unpacked in a warehouse, brought to the store and put on the floor, and you know instantly if it's going to be successful or not. You can almost tell the first day when something is put on the floor. If it sells quickly, you can turn a $100,000-budget into a million-dollar budget. There's a whole method to how quickly you buy and sell—it's called turnover.

BLDD: Does that aspect most engage you?

PE: Then it did. For example one took a department which was making $100,000, and within a year's time it was making a million dollars. It's very exciting. It may not interest a lot of people, but merchandising and buying and selling is something that is in the blood. When it is in the blood, you can't stop; you can do it night and day. That's why I think most of the successful merchants in this country are workaholics. The pleasures that they derive from their work are extraordinary. Ultimately it's only those who have it in their blood that become successes in the retail business.

BLDD: Was your family fashion conscious?

PE: Not really. I have some aunts and relatives who always cared about clothing. But it's not just clothing—it's style. They look at life aesthetically and want it to be very pleasing and beautiful. They wanted beautiful rooms, beautiful houses, in a certain sense to simply have a beautiful life. In my first years in fashion, the vigor of business appealed to me. It wasn't so much the aesthetics. I have always loved picking among fabrics and suggesting certain styles, but the early pleasures had to do with the volatile business of fashion.

BLDD: Then it truly is the fashion business that engages you, not so much the business of business?

PE: Yes. It was the fashion business. I suspect that the pleasure was heightened because it was fashion, but I may have derived the same amount of pleasure had I been buying housewares. There is a business side of me, of any merchant, that simply derives pleasure from business.

BLDD: How would you describe yourself?

PE: I can't describe myself. The more I know about myself, the less I can say that doesn't seem contradictory.

BLDD: You said you knew what really was important to you. Can you share some of those things?

PE: There are three areas which I truly care about. The first is my health. The second is my work. I have always been aware of my health and very attuned to my body. But health has to do with one's mental as well as physical well-being. And that of course has to do with my work, which I love dearly. The last part of the triangle is my love—physical passion and the person I share it with. When those three areas of the triangle are in balance, my life is extraordinary. I have true peace and happiness and joy, and I feel wonderfully fortunate. I feel blessed that all three of the areas which are important to me are occupied and fulfilled.

BLDD: Let's go back to some of the specifics of how your career has unfolded. You spent a period with John Meyer of Norwich. What made you decide to leave that company?

PE: I had been there seven years, and I did what I did very well but I had been doing the same thing for a very long time without any movement. It was a challenge in the beginning, and maybe it was really good for me the first four or five years, but then I found that I had free time, with hours to think about other things. When a phone call came from another company, I

was ready. I think there are moments when one is ready to move on to another challenge. The challenge presented itself.

BLDD: What was that company?

PE: That was the Vera Company, a part of Manhattan Industries.

BLDD: And that was one of the fortuitous circumstances in your life?

PE: Yes, because the first time I spoke with them I was not very interested—the company made polyester clothing. The president, Matt Shaw, insisted that I meet the founder Vera Neuman. I'd learned not to say no too quickly. I took a trip up to Ossining, New York, to see her and I liked her instantly. She explained what her needs were, and I was moved by them and felt that I might be able to help her, help myself, and have a challenge. So I accepted.

BLDD: What did you do when you first went to Vera?

PE: Vera was an artist, and her paintings were first on scarves, and then on sheets and blouses. Her prints were on many products. She had been very successful in her sportswear, but then the company started having trouble. She needed someone to work directly with her, to help her make decisions about what to paint for her prints, and someone who could literally design sportswear.

BLDD: Are you a painter as well?

PE: No, but I enjoy painting. I just don't have enough time to do it.

BLDD: Paintings and ballets and art exhibitions, film and travel are all some of the raw materials of a great designer. From which of the arts do you draw inspiration?

PE: I'm never quite sure. I am inspired by anything that is beautiful—an extraordinary film, a stage production, a television production, a book. A painting can be terribly moving and inspiring but that doesn't mean that I run back to my studio and create something. It's never that way. They're quite separate experiences, complete in themselves. When I enjoy a movie, or an art exhibit, it makes me feel wonderfully fulfilled. That's enough. I don't have to take it directly to the office.

BLDD: Can you tell us briefly how you made the transition from designing for Vera to having the Perry Ellis label?

PE: The clothing that I was designing for the Vera Sportswear line started to get special recognition. Editors from *Vogue*, and editors from *Women's Wear Daily* came in and liked it, and they were very encouraging.

BLDD: How did you get them to come to your shows?

PE: In the seven years I had worked on Seventh Avenue with John Meyer, I had established a few friendships. Out of respect for what I had done at John Meyer, these people came to see buyers at Vera. Their job is to cover markets. Their encouragement led me to have the confidence to ask Vera if I could, in addition to doing her line, start another line for myself.

BLDD: Within the Vera umbrella?

PE: Yes. And we agreed on the Portfolio, the first label that I designed under my name. It became an instant success. When I say "success," it was. For a couple of years, starting in 1976, the media covered it broadly and faithfully, long before retailers knew how to support a line of that kind.

BLDD: From the very beginning, your clothes were unlike anything else done on Seventh Avenue. What made you believe that the innovative features that you were trying to introduce, like big shoulders and long skirt lengths, and what I would call the "boxy jackets" would be attractive to consumers or to retailers?

PE: I never know what is going to be attractive to consumers. I must design what I feel I have to design. For many years I wanted to express myself fully. It never occurred to me that one person, ten people, or a thousand people would be interested in what I was going to say. It just had to be said. One doesn't write a book for an audience or paint paintings for the people who are going to buy them. One paints because one has to paint. And one writes because one is driven to write. People can write books, people can design collections for a specific audience. But it never occurred to me to do that, and still doesn't today.

BLDD: How do you explain the rapid acceptance of your early designs?

PE: It wasn't so rapid. At first it was very much touch and go. Fortunately the press supported me so strongly in the beginning that stores were almost forced to buy and support my line. Retailers love to come in and discover something the press is talking about. Without the press, I wouldn't be

PERRY ELLIS

sitting here talking to you today. It plays a major role in the success of many companies and designers.

BLDD: Did you ever expect the media to celebrate your work the way it has?

PE: I can't say I expected it but I was very pleased, obviously. I felt my work was strong and good and valid and deserving of what it received. There were enough key people who supported me—Karen Gottfried of *Women's Wear Daily*, who no longer works there, instantly recognized my line as being something exciting and different and new. She put it on the front page, and Mr. John Fairchild, publisher of *Women's Wear Daily*, saw it and liked it. We had so few orders we couldn't have kept the business going.

BLDD: How did you keep it going?

PE: We were under an umbrella, and our overhead was not terribly high. We worked out of the Vera showroom. Three of us did the whole thing. That allowed us to keep our expenses down to the bare minimum. Also there was a wonderful man named Frank Brockman who was then president of the Vera Companies. He was very astute in running the business, so we could sustain it, and the few orders were just enough.

BLDD: You've described some of your early designs as satires, in which you poked fun at the fashion establishment. Give us an example of one of those designs, and explain, too, if you would, how and why satire translates into clothing.

PE: In those early days when I first started, I felt so much of fashion was terribly pretentious. As I looked at clothes, mannequins and models, they were all so serious and almost untouchable. I didn't know who would be interested in so serious a vein of clothing. I wanted to bring some lightness, an amusing quality that would make people smile about clothes and feel that they were, as I used to say, friendly, rather than something to contend with. There are pretentious stores, and there is pretentious clothing, and I wanted to push all that aside and let fresh air into Seventh Avenue in a way that perhaps hadn't existed. I wanted hair to be free and loose, and makeup natural. I tried to remove and reduce fashion to its bare elements and make them wonderfully carefree and amusing. That was my original intention.

BLDD: How has that philosophy evolved?

PE: It has changed and broadened dramatically. That's one of the great things about fashion and a career in fashion—it changes virtually every day. The backbone of the works remains, but the body of it evolves over a lifetime. After it's all done one might be able to say, "It went from there to there." But in the middle, right now, I don't know.

BLDD: I believe it was the innovative sweater design that first established your reputation in the fashion industry. What was it, and what is it, about your knitwear that the public finds so appealing?

PE: The thing I most love about sweaters is the fact that they can be knitted by hand. Generally the most beautiful garments in the world aren't made on machines. So the average person never gets to see the beautiful yarns available, unless he goes into yarn shops and selects them for himself. What I wanted to accomplish with knitwear was, first to have it knitted by hand, and then to use these extraordinary yarns that I knew existed, but which one never saw in stores.

BLDD: What kind of yarn?

PE: There are beautiful raw yarns from Scotland and Ireland, for tweeds and beautiful plaids. My first sweaters were like big, giant heavy yarns. The idea was just sitting there. Handknit sweaters had been done before, obviously, but a designer had never focused on them. So, I started to, and they have become a mainstay of my designs.

BLDD: What is your design process like? How does it evolve? Where do you begin? With sketches? With mannequins? With fabric? With an idea? With a season? With a store?

PE: It's pretty simple. There is a calendar year. The first thing is the selection of fabrics in Europe. There are several fabric fairs where the most creative mills in the world bring all of their selections. You can spend a week just looking at fabrics. It is one of my inspirations. I see extraordinary things. In Europe, there's still an industry of artisans and craftsmen who care very much about quality and they're willing to do limited editions for designers who want special colors or special finishes on fabrics. I make selections and in three months' time I have them in my studio. Then I have to decide what fabrics to order. I look around the room, and all of these fabrics literally tell me what they want to become. They want to become jackets, or shirts and skirts. I select them and see how they work together. After that, there is another deadline, a show of a collection.

BLDD: How often do you do that?

PE: Twice a year. That's probably about average. Some people do it more frequently and some people do it less.

BLDD: How do you decide what color to feature in any year? Is there some agreement in the industry that it will be black and white one year, and wine and gray another?

PE: There are companies that advise people on color, but mine are totally instinctive. I can only do the colors that interest me at the particular time that I am designing a collection. I don't turn to anyone and say, "What color are you doing?"

BLDD: Are there any colors that recur in your collections?

PE: I always love neutral colors, like khaki and all the shades of gray and tan, and offwhite. They are the backbone of my work.

BLDD: Are there any colors that you never use? I hope you detest orange, as I do.

PE: No, as a matter of fact, orange is probably my favorite color, outside of the neutral range of tans and the beiges. "Orange" covers a lot of different colors. The oranges that I mean are the ones that you see in woven Persian carpets.

BLDD: You mentioned that the support and encouragement and publicity of the fashion press was important to your own career. One writer said that the customer to whom your clothes appeal the most is the one who wants to experiment safely. What do you think of that description?

PE: It's very difficult for me to comment on that kind of observation, because it may only be true for that particular person.

BLDD: It seems to me that more American designers than ever are concerned with creating what I would call grown-up clothes for a working, active and health-obsessed population. Does that affect what you do?

PE: I never, ever think about that sort of thing. Instinctively I think about health, and physical condition, but I don't start a collection and say, "This year I'm going to do a collection for health-conscious Americans, or for all of those women that go to the office."

BLDD: How much of a design is modified by external factors such as the cost of production or the availability of the fabric?

PE: Very little. I'm always aware of what fabrics cost but I have never stayed away from a beautiful fabric. I find that the starting point of a good design is the fabric. Some women respond to extraordinary fabrics in the simplest of cuts. I try to balance a collection so everything is not expensive. There are less expensive fabrics in the couture collection. But I try not to be deterred by any factor if the design is something I want to express.

BLDD: Are you so disciplined that you know how to edit in advance?

PE: Some fabrics can't be produced, obviously. But we have attempted to work with very fragile fabrics. To satisfy my own need we will do a limited production. There are enough fine stores that buy our collection. Some stores, like Bendel's, love having specials. We do many things that are exclusive that I know we couldn't do for all stores, because we couldn't get enough fabric.

BLDD: How much control do you have over the final product that comes from your studio?

PE: I have almost total control over every product that has my name on it—even all of the licensees. I can't get involved with the production of most of the licensees—there's just not enough time, but we do try to "police" them, and we try to be very careful in selecting the licensees. Within my own men's and women's sportswear company I have total control.

BLDD: How many other licensees do you have now, and how broad is the range?

PE: There are sixteen licensees, ranging from socks and shoes and men's clothing, shirts, and neckties, to fur coats.

BLDD: Is there anything you wouldn't put your name on?

PE: There are a lot of things. Many people that come to us want my name

and not my talent, but I'm not interested in designing anything, or being a part of anything, that I don't supervise myself.

BLDD: In lots of consumer products, from shampoo to champagne, a lot of test marketing takes place. Does that same procedure take place in the fashion industry?

PE: We should do a lot more of that, but there doesn't seem to be time. We do our own testing in minor ways.

BLDD: How do you do that?

PE: Within almost every collection there are sort of "background" pieces, like basic pants and basic jackets, and then there are experimental pieces which are terribly new and different. Sometimes the experimental pieces become the backbone of lines in future seasons. Each season there are new ideas that are introduced into the line, and if consumers respond to them and if I continue to love those designs, we follow through with them the next season.

BLDD: In a sense, a design trickles down or up. What is once experimental may have a more paramount role in the collection several seasons in the future—and that is one of the ways in which you do your own test marketing. Are there any sophisticated marketing techniques that you use?

PE: Seventh Avenue is not educated—that's been one of my major complaints about it, but it is also one of the things I love. We are an emotional lot. Although the number of those with college degrees is increasing on Seventh Avenue, generally it's been an instinctive market, filled with a lot of heart and soul and sweat. The younger generation seems to have degrees so perhaps one day everybody on Seventh Avenue will have M.B.A.'s.

BLDD: And then you won't have to have designers. Computers can do it all.

PE: I don't think that day will ever come, because there's one thing that computers will never be, and that's creative.

BLDD: You are known for your willingness to experiment. Which innovations of yours do you consider to be the most successful?

PE: It depends on how one measures success. Success can be an extraordinary picture of a design, something that may be in *Vogue* magazine. In one way that's a successful design.

BLDD: But by your standards?

PE: I like to have it all. I like the extraordinary photograph, and the beautiful product, and I like it to be successful in stores.

BLDD: Among the things that you have brought to your profession, which do you think have been the most successful? What Perry Ellis idea is the core of your designs, and has influenced others as well?

PE: I've been very successful not because of any one, two, or five design ideas. The body of work is what is important.

BLDD: How do you gauge the success of a design?

PE: In many ways—but most frequently by how many designs one sells, how many the stores sell, and how well it reorders. That's the obvious way. But very experimental designs that I think are very beautiful only go into a few stores. The fact that those stores support an experimental design makes it successful to me.

BLDD: What considerations do you take into account when you design clothes for men and women? There must be some requirements that are shared, but also some that are very different.

PE: The only consideration and difference is the obvious one—I can wear men's clothing so it is first-hand. For women's clothing I need a lot more imagination and fantasy. This makes designing for women a very different experience.

BLDD: What do you think is the most neglected area of fashion design?

PE: Selling in a store. If stores had stronger salespeople fashion might be more easily transmitted.

BLDD: Do you see those circumstances improving?

PE: No. I think they are getting worse. For example, with Bloomingdale's we now share the expense of the salesperson. We select them, and we pay part of their salary, so that this person is almost educated by us and then put on the floor.

BLDD: That's a great idea, and one way of getting your product out there. Do lots of designers do that?

PE: I have no idea.

BLDD: Are those people paid by commission as well? What incentive do they have to really get out there and sell?

PE: They do receive a percentage from the store, but the main thing is that they are an employee of ours.

BLDD: Was that your idea?

PE: Not mine directly, but one that the company evolved.

BLDD: You are part of a conglomerate. What is your relationship to that company?

PE: We are a subsidiary of Manhattan Industries, with all of the corporate structure that goes along with that sort of thing. For the most part it's been a very good relationship.

BLDD: I can see it being a help to one's career to be part of a larger organization but can it ever be a hindrance?

PE: I'm certain that it can be. But ours basically had been very good. Corporate structure generally means bureaucrats, and fortunately we haven't had very many of them.

BLDD: What is your favorite garment to design?

PE: I haven't a favorite—it would be like asking a mother who was her favorite child!

BLDD: I don't think I've ever seen you, in person or in print, wearing anything other than a blue shirt. A blue shirt of your own design, I might add. Is that your fashion signature?

PE: I wear it a lot. I'm not certain about fashion signatures. It could be called a uniform because I tend to wear it almost every day. I'm very comfortable in it.

BLDD: Why do you wear the same thing every day—a "uniform"—when you want to encourage the rest of us to do the opposite?

PE: I don't encourage people to wear something different. I think people should express what they actually feel. This particular shirt and these pants are terribly comfortable, and I love them. It's simply a personal part of me, and I don't try to make it right or wrong, nor do I suggest it for other people.

BLDD: Is there any design you wish you had never introduced?

PE: I can't think of one. Not all are brilliant or successful, but of course, I'm pleased with the body of my work.

BLDD: What would you most like to design that you haven't yet?

PE: I'm really very satisfied at the moment. I recently did a play, Noel Coward's *Blithe Spirit*, for the Santa Fe Arts Festival.

BLDD: Would you like to do more of that?

PE: I would love to do more for the theater but I would like to have it closer at hand. Santa Fe is far away, and the clothes had to be sent over and back. I'd like a closer personal experience with the theater, and more control over all the visuals—the sets as well as the costumes.

BLDD: Have you ever designed a theatrical set? Is it known among the theatrical persons, that you'd be interested in doing that?

PE: No.

BLDD: You talked about aesthetics as a way of life, not only important for body coverings, but for special rooms, and environments. Looking at your offices, it's quite clear that you have a very strong sense of interior design, as well. Are you deeply involved in the interior design of your workspace?

PE: The architect, Jim Terrell, is an old friend of twenty years. We've spent so much time together that it's very easy for us to work together. My ideas and his ideas combine to make an extraordinary space, but I know nothing about building or structures. All I can do is talk, and then it is up to him to define my ideas. And he's brilliant.

BLDD: Has he designed your home as well?

PE: Yes.

BLDD: Is it similar in feeling and spirit to this?

PE: It's much more personal than this. He was able to put modern detailing in an old brownstone and blend it beautifully.

BLDD: Do you collect anything?

PE: I collect Chinese export porcelain which was made from 1700 through 1840.

BLDD: How did you first become interested in it? Was it your Virginia upbringing and influence?

PE: It was always around, and I've looked at it all my life.

BLDD: Is there an aspect of it that particularly engages you?

PE: I really love the whole body of work; I love the multicolored pieces and those with the patterns. I probably have a hundred pieces. It's all boxed up in basements and shelves and bookcases.

BLDD: Don't you want to exhibit it?

PE: I've never had the opportunity. I'm always rearranging my living room. Occasionally, I will have a dinner party with fifty or one hundred pieces of unmatched porcelain. I find when I get too much of it around, I don't see any of it. I keep my house quite bare, and that's why most of the porcelain is in the basement. I bring up one or two pieces that draw my attention. When I stop noticing them, I get two others and replace them.

BLDD: It's been said that taste is as rare as genius. Do you agree?

PE: I would say that about extraordinary taste, yes.

BLDD: How would you define good taste?

PE: There are all kinds of taste. There is good taste and bad taste and taste that is in between. It's all very personal. Ultimately I find that there's only personal taste. Some people judge whether it is good or bad. When I see something that is extraordinary or beautiful, that's how I see it. Ten other people could totally pass it by and not even be interested.

BLDD: Where do you see the center of design today?

PE: I don't know if there is a center. There are a lot of hubs that are important. There was an era and a time when Paris was the center. Today, New York is as important as Paris. Milan is important. Tokyo is becoming important. It's all relative.

BLDD: Even though you poked fun at the fashion establishment, you are now a very major part of it. How has that affected you or your designs? How does it feel?

PE: I'm not sure whether I became a part of the fashion establishment or if the fashion establishment became a part of me. I didn't make any overtures, and haven't sought the fashion establishment. I'm part of it, and I don't know how it happened. Perhaps my work has changed enough, or perhaps the fashion vocabulary just expanded enough to include me. I'd like to think that the latter is more true.

BLDD: How has it affected your business?

PE: For the good.

BLDD: What could be nicer than having something to say and having the opportunity to say it? Seven years ago almost no one heard of Perry Ellis. Since that time, you have become one of the most celebrated American designers, not only here, but abroad as well. How do you think it all came about so quickly?

PE: "Quickly" is a relative word. Seven years is a long time. First of all I always believed in talent—talent that is recognized—and a lot of hard work.

BLDD: What aspect of your career has brought you the greatest sense of satisfaction?

PE: The greatest satisfaction comes from my design—the creative moment is what I love most. The highlights are a design coming from the workroom or the show being completed.

BLDD: And the greatest disappointment?

PE: I have not had any great disappointments.

BLDD: There must be some sacrifices that you've had to make for your career.

PE: I wish I knew of some. My success came late enough. I'm now 43, and seven years ago, when this started, I was 36. That's a long way on the road to maturity. I have always been a pretty quiet person; I've always had relatively few friends. That has not changed. I have not been drawn into anything that has really changed my life. It has remained stable throughout.

BLDD: There must be some external differences.

PE: There's obviously more time, more to do, but also it's good and exciting in terms of work. I don't feel I have had to sacrifice. I don't feel any disappointments.

BLDD: What do you see as the greatest challenge lying ahead of you?

PE: I don't plan; I have always taken life every day. I don't go beyond what the book says that I must do today.

BLDD: What impels you to operate that way?

PE: Every day I try to leave my office feeling very complete, that things are in order. Peace is very important to my life. I love to be relaxed, and I sleep very well.

BLDD: Did you ever expect your life to unfold the way it has?

PE: I never really thought about it. My only ambition was to be very happy at what I was doing. And that's what has happened.

BLDD: If you had it to do over again, what would you have done otherwise?

PE: I don't know one thing that I could improve on or change.

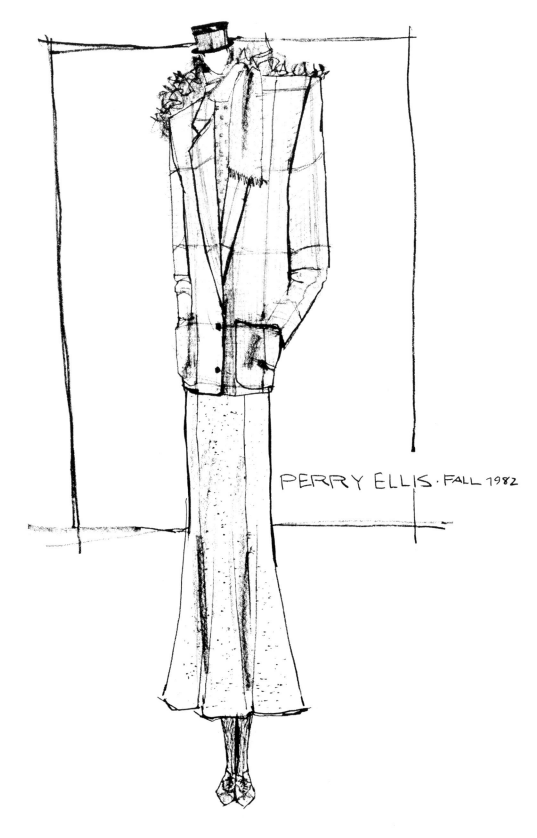

PERRY ELLIS · FALL 1982

Perry Ellis, fall, 1982

Perry Ellis, spring, 1983

JG

James Galanos

The meticulously tailored dresses, suits and spectacular evening clothes of California-based James Galanos are considered by many observers to be the closest thing this country has to the custom-made fashions of the great French designers.

BLDD: Was there a history of design in your family?

JG: Not that I know of. My father was artistic. He was probably a frustrated artist, who was never able to pursue that desire, because of his background, coming from the old country. It was one of those stories of the immigrant coming over and having to work so hard just to make a living. He had to subjugate his personal desires to take care of other necessities—family over there, and here.

BLDD: Where was he from?

JG: From Macedonia, a small town quite well known in Greece, near Salonika. A very beautiful place.

BLDD: Have you been there often?

JG: Only once. However, I go to Greece often, but not always to the area where the family is from. He was a restaurateur. How he became one I don't know, because there was no background of that in my family either. It was just a question of survival in the new country.

BLDD: And how did you know at such an early age, around 14, that you wanted to become a designer?

JG: Earlier than that. It was just there. I didn't want to be a painter. I didn't want to be an artist in any other area. I must have been about eight or nine years old, when for some reason I just made sketches of clothes.

BLDD: And what did you sketch, and on what?

JG: On scrap paper or whatever was around. I used to sit behind the cash register in my dad's restaurant—we all used to chip in and help—and while I was sitting there I'd always draw. Whenever I was able to muster enough money to buy a fashion magazine—at that point I was about 13 or 14—I would spend my money on a *Vogue* or *Harper's Bazaar*.

BLDD: Was there a particular person or circumstance that influenced you?

JG: No, not at all. No one.

BLDD: What about movies? Did they influence you in any way?

JG: I had secret desires and ambition to be a film designer. I grew up in a succession of small towns. I was born in Philadelphia, but my parents moved when I was about eight or nine months old. The two small towns where I grew up and went to high school were typical, nice little towns with no museums or anything of that sort from which I could draw inspiration. I had to search on my own, which I did. In school I took an art class which was compulsory, but that was insignificant and had no design studies.

BLDD: And at that early age, did you try to influence the fashions of your mother and your sister?

JG: Yes, always. I would always shop with them and make their decisions for them, and they actually listened. I would say, "No, I don't like this." Or, "I like that," or "you can't have that," or "you shouldn't."

BLDD: What were the rules then?

JG: No particular rules. It was just a question of whether they could afford it or not! My eye always went to the best, so there were times when they would say, "Well, we can't afford that." I would say, "Well, let's wait until we can."

BLDD: Do they still listen to you?

JG: Not particularly, no.

BLDD: Did you ever receive any formal schooling in fashion design?

JG: Yes. When I graduated from high school, my father sent me to New York and I enrolled in the Traphagen School of Design. I just chose it by looking in the magazines. I had no one to guide me. At the time there was a school headed by Karinska, a very famous stage designer. She was Russian, and she did the clothes for the great ballet companies, so that sounded very interesting to me. When I came to New York, I tried to contact that school but I think it had gone out of business. I didn't know about Parsons, and Traphagen seemed to be advertised more and more people were talking about it. I believe it is the oldest, and the first of that sort of school.

BLDD: Did you learn anything there?

JG: I enrolled for three years and my dad paid the tuition but after I was there a couple of months, I became disenchanted, because what they were teaching me, I'd already developed on my own. I found it a little frustrating and a waste of time. I was very impatient. I did continue to go to school, but if I felt like doing something else, I would. I only took the courses which I thought would be beneficial to me. I decided to take classes in draping, and life classes but was not really interested in painting. I developed my own style for sketches, which is adequate, but I didn't have the patience to become an artist, or make detailed renderings. But I did take the draping class and I had an excellent teacher who inspired me. Her name was Smalley. I don't know if she is still alive, but she was interesting and she inspired me because she would talk about the great dressmakers, like Vionnet, for example. She had style, and there was something about her that appealed to me. So I would listen and I'd learn more just by being around her than I did by taking all the other things that the school had to offer. After the first year I decided not to continue school. I went out on my own and made sketches and knocked on doors along Seventh Avenue. That was my means of making a little money to exist, since I didn't want to burden my dad with my problems.

BLDD: He was very encouraging, wasn't he?

JG: Yes, he was. I always came home when I was desperate because New York and New Jersey are not too far apart. In those days, back in the '40's, I lived on $25 a week, and that was a lot of money. He was very supportive in his own way. He would have preferred I'd stayed at home with him, but nevertheless, since I was so determined, he let me do what I wanted to do. When he saw me look very despondent at times, he said, "Why don't you come home and we'll do something together?" That was impossible. I said, "You'd have a miserable young boy on your hands."

BLDD: Why were you so discouraged?

JG: For anyone in any field—particularly in the arts—it's difficult when you're young and trying to get ahead.

BLDD: It's difficult when you're old, too!

JG: I had not had much training. I'd look for jobs but they were not available. At that time, there was not the youth explosion that there has been in the past ten years, and to get a job in a responsible firm without any experience was very, very difficult. Also we did not have the system of apprenticeship here in the United States, as they have in Paris, in which young people are given the opportunity to work in the great couture houses.

BLDD: You had that opportunity. How did you manage to save the money to take, at that time, the almost obligatory trip to Paris.

JG: One of my teachers at the school liked me very much. She taught style and fashion, and we became friendly just because she thought I had talent. Miss Rorabach sort of kept an eye on me. When I left school, she would call me every now and then and we'd converse, and whenever I felt blue I'd call her and she stimulated me. Eventually, she came across an interesting situation. Someone opening a business had called the school looking for a young designer. She called me immediately and said, "Jimmy, why don't you call these people and see what it's all about? I will recommend you." I called up this person and brought some sketches. His name was Mr. Lawrence Lesavoy—a big businessman, or entrepreneur—and he had a whole floor of the Empire State Building. It was very impressive.

BLDD: What was his work?

JG: He had cotton mills in the South and bought and sold commodities, that sort of thing. He was a highly educated Russian immigrant, who came to America and made a fortune overnight. He made many fortunes, and lost them and remade them again. He was married to a beautiful woman who was much younger than he was. She had everything in the world, because he gave her everything: a beautiful penthouse, a chauffeur, clothes. I guess she was ambitious or bored—I don't know. She wanted to get involved in the fashion business and so they were looking for a young designer who they could groom. I was introduced to her, and I had some sketches with me, and in that meeting they told me the setup. They had contacted a friend, the chief tailor at MGM in Hollywood, and somewhere along the line they started talking. "Why don't we start a business? You have the expertise in the tailoring. We'll find a designer for you, and we'll put the components together and open a business." Well, of course, that was very exciting to me, since I always wanted to be involved in the movies, and because back in the '30's and '40's Hollywood was glamorous and there

were some great fashions. At the time I was eighteen years old, and, for some reason, they took a liking to me. I kept going back to their office, and had several meetings with the wife. I don't think they really knew very much about sketches, but neither did I! I said I didn't want to sign my name to a contract, thinking "Tomorrow I'm going to become a big star and I will be tied up." What did I know? At first I said no, I didn't want to do it. They said, "If we take a chance on you, you've got to give us the same opportunity." So I gave in. They signed me up for three years and gave me a starting salary of $75 a week. That was a fortune to me.

The next step was to send me to California. They were first going to get a building and start something out there. A year elapsed and nothing much materialized and, of course, I was sitting in New York not doing anything, waiting, waiting, and going back home. I was a very sensitive young man, and was despondent all the time. But these people took a very special interest in me and they said, "Be patient. Be patient. Everything will be all right. If you need anything, we'll take care of it." Anyway, finally I did get out to Hollywood. In the interim they were divorced, and it was a bit of a shock after spending a year there to realize that there were too many problems for this situation to work out.

So, there I was in California, not doing anything, just biding my time. Mr. Lesavoy, who acted like my second father, said, "What can I do for you?" I couldn't hold him to a contract. I managed to live on what little I had. When I was really desperate, they would advance me money against the contract. He asked whether I would like to go to college. I thought about it. I said, "Well, I've always wanted to, but I made a decision to go to art school instead of college and having tried that, I decided that wasn't right for me either." Then I thought about it and called him back a few days later. I said, "If you really want to do something for me, would you send me to Europe? If you send me to Europe, I promise I'll pay you back whatever it costs. I'd like to study or work in Paris." I was as green as they come; in my mind there was Hollywood and Paris. He said, "I'll arrange a scholarship for you and we'll send you there and I'll see that you're set up with a family to live with," which he did. He sent me to Paris a year later. I was supposed to enroll in the L'Ecole des Beaux-Arts. But it was the same situation. I didn't know it but the Beaux-Arts is primarily a place to study painting and has nothing really to do with fashion. When the time came for me to enroll, I had a talk with the administrators and they said, "You're pursuing the wrong direction. You should become involved with the Chambre Syndicale de la Couture." So I spent the time just learning what Paris was all about, going to museums and absorbing the atmosphere. In the meantime, I was doing sketches and sending them to America and making a little bit of money.

BLDD: To whom did you send them?

JG: I had found a resource, a man who sold sketches by the young designers to the New York designers on Seventh Avenue and to custom dressmakers. And I would just go on my own to some manufacturing house that did great volume, and they would buy some of my designs. They were doing nice things with them, and they kept buying. It was a little source of income for me.

BLDD: What was the $5 design that you made, that turned into a half-million dollar fashion idea for someone else?

JG: I don't exactly remember. It was a blouse design, but the volume on it was tremendous. The manufacturer told me himself. He was so pleased. I made ten or fifteen dollars out of the whole deal. I was happy if I could get $2 for a sketch, that was the working price for sketches in those days. We used to go up and down the elevator and stop in every house. Some designers would see you, some wouldn't, but it was a way of making a little money. When I say "a little money," I mean if I made $25 or $35 a week, I thought I was in heaven.

BLDD: How long did you stay in Paris?

JG: I spent a year there. When I decided not to go to school, I called Mr. Lesavoy and said, "My understanding of the school was all wrong and I'd prefer not to enroll. Do you mind if I stay over here?" He said, "You can stay as long as you want. You can stay three or four years, all expenses paid. You can travel. Learn everything you can. See everything you can. Don't worry about anything." When he said that, I decided to try to get a

James Galanos, fall, 1982

job in one of the couture houses. I didn't speak any French and I was very shy in those days. I was living with this very lovely French family, an elderly couple who fortunately spoke English. I said, "Would you call up some of the houses that I'm interested in and see if you can arrange an appointment for me?" I didn't know how to do it on my own. I was frightened. The lady of the house agreed and she called them. In those days, back in 1946–47, my favorite was Balenciaga, whom I had met once very briefly in California in '45. I thought I might be able to see him. There was Robert Piguet, whose work I only knew by photographs, and I liked it. The only house I was able to get into was Piguet. So I went, taking my little portfolio. He didn't speak any English, but he had a secretary who did, so she interpreted for us. He saw my sketches and said they were very nice but there wasn't anything he could do. But the next day they asked me to come back and see the director rather than Mr. Piguet. He said, "Mr. Piguet liked your work very much. But we're not prepared to pay you very much money. What is your status?" I explained that I was there on a student visa. He said, "You know, we wouldn't be able to pay you money without working papers." I answered, "I don't care. I'll work for nothing if you'll just let me work in the house. I want training and I'll do whatever I can to get that."

BLDD: Did they let you do that?

JG: Oh, yes. They agreed. I could have earned a little money, but it wasn't important. I had enough to live on. I spent a year there. Marc Bohan, who is now the head of Dior, was the modelist there. They gave me a little cubbyhole outside the door of Mr. Piguet, and I made sketches.

BLDD: Did you learn?

JG: Oh yes, mostly by observation.

BLDD: Then why did you decide to leave?

JG: I was terribly ambitious and a little lonely. During the influx of the American buyers and manufacturers at collection time, several manufacturers recognized me and asked, "What are you doing in Paris?" I said, "Studying." I got a couple of job and training offers in the States, so I decided to come back. I got a job on Seventh Avenue for a big, big house which doesn't exist today. They were the original copiers of Chanel clothes in America, Davidow, Inc., coats and suits. Very, very famous and they did a terrific job with a certain casual type of clothes, basically based on Chanel. I worked there for two years, but it was depressing, and not encouraging.

BLDD: Where was Mr. Lesavoy during that period?

JG: He was in New York and I would always see him.

BLDD: Did he live to see what he helped to create?

JG: Oh, yes. I kept in contact until he passed away a few years ago. I fulfilled my obligations. He was a lovely man. He always kept an interest in me, and vice-versa. Anyway, I didn't like my job there. Frankly, I didn't do a good job, because I was not encouraged to be innovative. Secondly, it was the wrong style house for me. It offered no challenge and no one really took enough interest, so I left and came back to California.

BLDD: That was, I guess, almost thirty-five years ago, in 1951.

JG: Yes. I've been in business nearly thirty-five years now.

BLDD: You were about twenty-six years old when you founded Galanos Originals in California. It was a rather original and bold idea for a young man. Why California?

JG: Because I couldn't get a good job in New York, I decided to come back to California. I'd been here before, liked it, though I didn't know too much about it, and decided to try the movie studios again.

BLDD: What did you do once you arrived here with a lot of courage, and a little capital?

JG: Before I went to Europe I had worked for a period of time with Jean Louis at Columbia Pictures, so I tried to get a job there again as a sketcher, but there wasn't one available. It was Mr. Louis, a friend of mine, who was actually responsible for my going into business. He encouraged me and introduced me to a friend of his, a fine French dressmaker. "Why don't you make a few models?" he said, "and Marguerite will make the clothes for you. I'll finance the first few models and you go to the big stores here and see what you can do." And that's how it all started. He advanced enough money to make a few models, and I made the clothes with Madame

80

Marguerite, who shared a little tiny shop on Beverly Drive. There was no plan whatsoever, just an idea.

BLDD: What were those first models like?

JG: I made seven or eight dresses. I made them on the niece of Mr. Louis, a charming little French girl with a beautiful figure. We then called the local buyer at Saks Fifth Avenue and she came to look at them. The next day she gave me an order. So that was the seed.

I didn't know the first thing about production, or about making production patterns, nor did Madame Marguerite. She was a custom dressmaker.

BLDD: How did you manage to fill the order?

JG: She made some of the clothes free hand, because there was no system whatsoever, and I saw it as a challenge. I found a small contractor who was willing to take over some of the work and we started that way. Within a few months, I started building up a little business. By the following year we had a half-dozen people working for us. And from there it just went on.

BLDD: How has living in Los Angeles affected your vision of the clothes that you design?

JG: Well, strangely enough, it has not affected me in the least. Everyone assumes that California means a different style of living. My clothes are totally sophisticated and international. From the very beginning it has always been that way. I was never influenced by the sun and the ocean. In fact, I never see them. My idea of elegance and quality is what it's always been and I've just pursued that. I was always closed in my own little world and I never really looked around. I have never been involved socially in this town. I always pursued my ideal of sophistication, or what elegant women should look like, and made my own look, and my own clientele. They do not come to me, I go to them.

BLDD: An enviable circumstance. Why don't you describe that ideal? What does that look of an elegant or sophisticated woman mean to you?

JG: First of all, it has to do with a certain refinement, *quality*, a paring down, elimination of the superfluous in the clothes that I make. The cut, the line *is* of the utmost importance and so is the fit of the dress, and the ultimate components of fabric, color and proportions. When you see it all together on the right person, it's a thing of beauty. Aesthetically, it's very exciting to me to see someone that knows and understands what you're trying to do. We make so many things that are never understood except by a very few people. Generally, taste level is not very high in fashion as in many other fields. It's a mediocre world we live in today.

BLDD: More mediocre than ever?

JG: In technology it's fantastic but aesthetically, I don't think we've progressed very much. We're losing so much of the beauty and fineness that was. Craftsmanship is slowly fading away. Young people are not into it very much because, unfortunately it's not the most promising area in economic terms in relation to the amount of work involved. It's amazing to see some of the people I have here, and they're mostly Europeans—my whole factory is really all European—sit there and do such unusual things. What we do here, they just don't do on Seventh Avenue, because they no longer take the time or have the know-how. We develop people who want to work with me, who are interested in their craft, and take some pleasure and pride in it.

BLDD: Are there regional differences in taste? For example, is the West Coast more experimental, the East Coast more knowing?

JG: I think it equals out. There is always a commotion about the differences between California and New York. California obviously has certain things that New York doesn't, and vice-versa, simply because there is a difference in climatic conditions, the style of living, and so forth. You have some very talented people out here, and there are a lot of things that start here and filter into New York, and vice-versa.

BLDD: What in fashion currently starts in California, New York, and vice-versa?

JG: The casual type of clothes that one wears here, the beach clothes. Young people are very athletic here and live mostly outdoors, so the clothing has to be different. But that's far away from what I do, because my clothes are not outdoor clothes. They're occasional clothes. They're really city clothes. We don't have a city life out here, really. Just look at the way people dress on the streets! But, then, I don't think they dress any better in

New York. In certain areas they do. In New York, where do you see the well-dressed people? A few in the Park Avenue sector, a few in the fine restaurants, and the rest of the city is a conglomeration of every look that there could possibly be. I don't find it all that attractive.

BLDD: Do differences in what women are wearing in Los Angeles or New York or Houston or Chicago or Washington, D. C., affect what you design?

JG: I never worry about areas and people. I make what I like, and then I have to find my audience for it. So it either appeals or it doesn't appeal.

BLDD: What city do you currently see as the center of fashion design?

JG: There's no doubt that New York is the most important city, because it's still the melting pot. It remains the focal point of everyone who comes to America. And then you have people who migrate out here, but international people usually make their first stop in New York, and that stays their second home. You can't get away from that. Today, there are lots of Europeans coming to California, creating a whole new look on Rodeo Drive. All the fine shops are exploding on the scene, but I don't know how much that affects the look out here.

BLDD: Paintings, and ballet, and art exhibitions, and films, and travel are generally the raw materials of the great designers. How do *you* get an idea for a design?

JG: That is true subconsciously but not consciously. I love books, so as a hobby every week I go to a bookstore, and I have every book that's available. I look through them and in certain ways they feed my imagination, but when it comes to actually designing, their effect is very minor. It's very hard for me to take an eighteenth century painting and say, "Oh, I'm going to make a design from that." I know a lot of designers do take from those periods. We were taught things like that in art school. But that is not the way I design. It's a matter of very hard work and working directly with the fabric. It's a project. The most inspirational moment comes when I work on a live body, rather than sketching. I make a lot of sketches, but out of a hundred I eventually may use only one. That just keeps the juices going. You may get an idea and jot it down, and that forms a little blueprint, a line, for your assistants to work from. But the actual gown materializes once you start fitting. You may have a shell of an idea on paper. You say, "Well, I'll work up a muslin like this." But I'm actually tearing, pulling, rearranging and sometimes then, by accident, I come across a design because through things that happen while you work, you see things that you can't when you sketch. You have an idea, but sometimes that idea is static. In fabric, things happen. When you drape on a body, the fabric may slip off the shoulder and you go to catch it and something happens with that material. If you're sharp enough to catch it, you'll say, "O.K. That's it. There's a good line there." And that's what excites me. When I design I change constantly. I start off with a model and an idea and sometimes it's okay, it's logical, it's not bad, but it's never good enough. What I try to do is make it even better. Or take a given design—there are, after all, a lot of things in the public domain—like a chemise. A chemise is a chemise is a chemise, but within that given shape you can do something that will make yours a little different and a little better than the next one, or you can refine it to a point where it says something else. That's the challenge of designing.

BLDD: How do you know when it's right? How do you know when to stop?

JG: Instinct. It's a question of personal taste. It's simply my taste against someone else's.

BLDD: By what period of history and by which designers have you been most influenced or inspired?

JG: I'm 58 years old, so when I left school and started my career in 1942, I grew up with the most famous, the most elegant designers, who were Balenciaga and Christian Dior. Schiaperelli had just gone off the scene. They were at their peaks in the '30's when I was a teenager, so I didn't know them. But I knew their work because I collected magazines. The one who was most inspiring, because to me he was the absolute perfection of quality and elegance, was Mr. Balenciaga. There was a mystique and a mystery about the clothes he made, they were pure elegance. It's a totally different kind of look today. Today everything has to be young, sexy and vulgar. In those days everything had to be the ultimate. That's still what I'm trying to do, but in a more contemporary way. Look at Gloria Guiness. Why, for me she was the goddess of all time. We don't have very many people like that.

BLDD: Do we have any?

JG: I have to say there are very, very few. I'm sometimes infuriated with *Women's Wear Daily* and publications like *Vogue* and *Harper's Bazaar* who play up certain ladies again and again. To my mind some of the people they play up are neither very elegant, nor well-dressed. When I see them in real-life I wonder, "Is my taste so off, or who are they trying to kid?" I know lesser, "important people" insofar as name value and even financial standing that have far better taste, but they're people that . . .

BLDD: . . . don't make a story?

JG: But that do have taste and quality.

BLDD: How important, how significant, as figures in fashion were people such as Condé Nast and Carmel Snow and Diane Vreeland?

JG: They were very important. I grew up on *Vogue* and *Harper's Bazaar*, and there was a taste level back in those days, when those magazines were really the arbiters of fashion.

BLDD: Are they no longer?

JG: To my mind they still are. I think they're reflective of what's going on today. Unfortunately, I'm not very keen on what's going on today. However they are reflecting what is happening today. But I think they have a tendency to vulgarize, rather than to make clothes more aesthetic and appealing. Maybe clothes just aren't thought of in that way anymore. In the late '50's, '60's and '70's, Norell and I were highly visible in the fashion magazines. The editors would have pages for Mr. Norell and me, and usually feature a special section just in our collections, emphasizing our point of view. That was great and made sense! We were used as a counterpoint to the French Couture, and inasmuch as we showed so late or after Paris, a special interest was generated. I have always shown when I felt it was right for me, and I'm not always concerned with the commercial aspect of manufacturing a collection.

BLDD: Why do you choose to show so late?

JG: It just happened that way years ago, and it works for me, but, unfortunately, I can't make the magazines, because the issues today are made at a certain time and the pages are closed much earlier.

BLDD: How interrelated do you think the pages of magazine text are with advertising?

JG: Tremendously. Let's face it. Today you pick up a *Vogue* or a *Harper's Bazaar* and practically every page in the editorial area is Calvin Klein, Oscar de la Renta, Halson and Bill Blass. And if you look at the advertising, who has the most pages all the time? Many important designers are ignored! The same goes for *Women's Wear*. When Calvin Klein takes ten pages of advertising, they must be reciprocal. It's sad, but that's the way it is. I understand that.

BLDD: It's surprising to hear you say that you feel you had your high moment in the '50's and the '60's.

JG: The '50's and '60's were my first big splash. I was young, new and exciting, and within three years of starting my business I received all the important fashion awards in rapid succession. The Neiman-Marcus Award in those days was as prestigious as the Coty. I won that twice and shortly thereafter was voted into the Hall of Fame. It was a "high" for a young unknown talent. And, of course, I had constant press coverage because of all this and my youth. Now there is a new group of young designers who are making news and it is their time, rightly so, and we must admit to it, and accept it. Remember, I had thirty years of success and acclaim!

BLDD: But don't you think you're more celebrated than you have ever been?

JG: Oh yes, I am, and it would be nice if the magazines made some kind of effort to celebrate my thirty years in the business, to understand the dedication, expertise and the continuity of that time span, the progression through the fashion changes of the last decades and still be on top! Now I just do my job and get on with it. I don't concern myself with the publicity. I take it as it comes.

BLDD: You say that sometimes what you read or look at doesn't directly affect your design. Is it distilled and filtered through all of your experience?

JG: Yes. For example, I have a painting on the wall near my desk that is red and black that I see every day. Somewhere along the line I'm going to use red, black and gold or what-have-you. Or I will see something on the

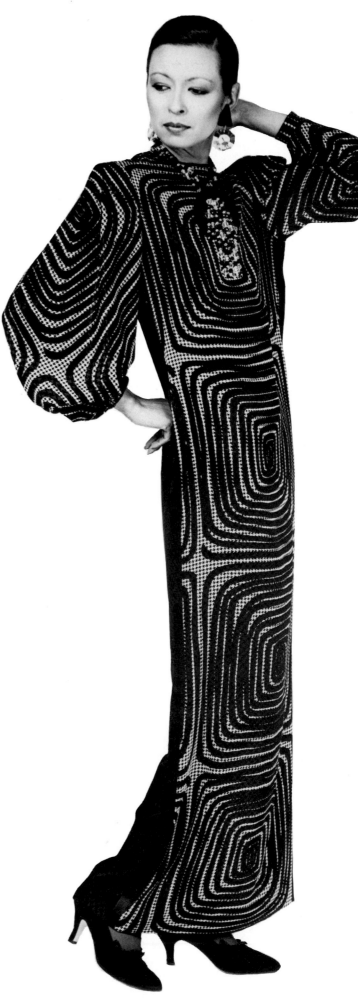

street. I was watching joggers one day and I saw a jogger wearing little shorts over the jogging pants. I was walking through Central Park and it was wintertime and it was pleasant. There was something special about the little shorts over the jogging pants. It immediately struck me—I thought, "I'm going to do something with that," and went home and made a little sketch so I wouldn't forget it. Last spring when I made a collection I said, "I'm going to use that and make it high couture."

BLDD: How did you do it?

JG: I did a silk print jacquard pair of shorts, stitched it together with a pair of men's bright English wool and I made a blouse out of the same fabric as the shorts. It was a terrific look—different, special. It had a lot of style. So I saw something which I translated into my medium. Whatever you see, you absorb.

BLDD: Does the eighteenth century particularly interest you? Somewhere I read that you are surrounded by eighteenth century French furniture. . .

JG: I do have some. I have a little of everything. I have no special interest in the eighteenth century, but lots of very beautiful things were developed in that period. There was a certain refinement, but, there was also a lot of fussiness. The good things are quite beautiful, quite elegant and they've never been surpassed. But that's just one period. I never hold to just one thing. There are many other things that I like as well.

BLDD: The respected *New York Times* fashion critic, Bernardine Morris, has characterized your designs as the closest thing to French custom-made that this country has to offer. Is this description accurate and pleasing to you?

JG: Yes, it is, and it is accurate. My cut and detailing is Parisian. I put a great emphasis on detail, what I call "hidden detail," so as not to be fussy and overdesign, which I find the Italian designers do. There's just too much going on in one particular design.

BLDD: Are you talking about the current wave? The ones who are influenced by architecture?

JG: That's a lot of nonsense, the architectural design. It's a nice statement, but it doesn't hold water. It always rubs me the wrong way when they say architectural design. You don't wear architecture. You wear clothes that work with the body. Forget the architecture. If anyone knew anything about architecture, it was Mr. Balenciaga. He understood line, proportion, refinement, and knew how to apply it to the human form. The others just make all these cuts and go nowhere. They're basically all taken from Mr. Balenciaga anyway. But what's better are details which are subtle and blend into a particular design and don't hit you in the eye. They're all very time-consuming in the making of a particular dress. That's why we are not copyable in many respects—at least so the manufacturers have told me—because they just can't put those details into a mass-produced dress. Even our ready-to-wear clothes are made as they would be made in the couture. Every dress here is singly made, moulded. Every piece of fabric is shaped and worked directly on a form before ever seeing a machine. It is custom-made inside and out.

BLDD: How do you shape fabric?

JG: You stretch, you pull, you steam until you get the line—without damaging the fabric, naturally. The inner linings retain the outside shape. This is a system that just doesn't exist in ready-to-wear on Seventh Avenue.

BLDD: The clothes that you design are ready-to-wear, but they look and fit as if they were made to order. How do you manage that?

JG: That is the expertise in the working of the dress. They are individually made on a mannequin, not just cut and sewn by a pattern. All of the nuances that we put into the original model are put into the ready-to-wear product. It is made exactly as I made my original sample, because it's the same process and takes the same time. It takes a minimum of one week just to make a dress for production. Some dresses take longer, according to the specific model and its intricacy.

BLDD: What sort of women do you envision wearing your clothes? Must they all be thin and rich?

JG: No, because all women are not thin and rich. But of course it's helpful if a woman is nicely proportioned. It's not a question of being skin-and-bones, or like a model. In fact, I have many customers who look better in my clothes than the mannequins who wear my clothes, because they have good figures and their proportions are right. But, one has to have the feeling, the instinct, and also the attitude of the clothes to make them come alive. It's the difference between two women in the same dress. One makes it click and the other does not.

BLDD: What's the price range of your clothes?

JG: They retail from about $2,000 up.

BLDD: At those prices, how should one take care of clothes so that they last more than just a season or two?

JG: To begin with they're going to last longer than that because they are of superior fabrics. I've been told a thousand times that my customers have dresses that go back twenty years and they still wear them, including Mrs. Reagan, who keeps bringing back her clothes that date from the '50's, and they are in A-1 mint condition.

BLDD: Why does she bring them back?

JG: Perhaps to alter something. In fact, just last month she came in to visit, and she brought a dress that was about fifteen years old, and it was immaculate. It was a gorgeous print from Staron, one of the great print houses. She said, "Jimmy, what can we do with it?" There wasn't too much we could do. I took in the skirt a little bit. It had an A-shape, so, to make it a little more contemporary, I straightened the skirt, changed the hemline a little bit, added a belt and a piece of black fabric around the armhole, and it was a perfectly new dress.

BLDD: How do you hang, or clean, the clothes so they retain their shape?

JG: A woman who buys good clothes takes good care of them. She doesn't have to clean them. The less they're cleaned, the better. But I know many of my clients, and I see the way some of them put their clothes away—they stuff the dresses. Their maids will take out the few wrinkles that may exist, and if the clothes are selected carefully and the fabrics selected carefully, they don't need very much care. There's also the question of lining. We usually line our dresses, but not as we did in the old days, when everything was layered underneath with hard shells. Today, clothes are soft, and should feel like nothing on. Couture clothes still have the luxury of careful work underneath, and that's one of the hidden things that we do which a lot of people don't.

BLDD: How do you manage to achieve such outstanding quality—those intricate hand-faggoted seams, for example? How close an eye do you keep on all the work that goes out?

JG: I'm constantly in the work room, and the people who are in charge there have also been brainwashed by me so it just comes automatically for them. Even when I'm away from my plant they are carrying on the tradition that we started. They don't cheat, because there's no point in it. They would not gain anything by cutting corners.

BLDD: How much time do you spend away from them?

JG: Twice a year I make my personal appearances at the stores. Today, designers in our category have to help sell their merchandise. Because of the tremendous price of the clothes, women like to see a full collection rather than only what the store is offering. No store can buy everything you make. So this gives a customer the opportunity to see everything to build her wardrobe.

BLDD: To how many stores do you go?

JG: I visit five key areas in the country—New York, Dallas, Houston, San Francisco and Chicago—because that's where the affluent clientele is. At my price range, we don't do very much in the Midwest. In all the cities in America, there are just a handful of ladies who have money. Let's say Mrs. Jones likes a Galanos. She won't buy it in Milwaukee. She'll go to New York to buy her clothes. Years ago I used to sell in Minneapolis. I don't today because the stores won't invest in my clothes. They don't have enough business to warrant it. It always bothered me that a lot of the buyers would not buy the right clothes to satisfy these women with tremendous buying power, who are world travelers. Buyers would always end up with the most nondescript kinds of things. Maybe the buyers don't have the guts. There are very few really great buyers. It's understandable but it is also frustrating. Women from all over the United States, as well as Europe, will come to Bergdorf's or Bonwit's or Saks or Martha in New York because they can't find the merchandise where they live. And they have the money.

So it's not just a question of money.

BLDD: Where do you obtain all the lavish fabrics for which your work is so well-known? Do you select them all personally?

JG: Oh yes, absolutely. Twice or three times a year I go to Europe. I just came back two months ago. I picked out my spring fabrics. I go to Milan, Como, and Zurich, because they have one of the great houses there, and Paris. Sometimes I go to Lyons, where the silk center is. But most of them are in Paris.

BLDD: For how many seasons do you design?

JG: We have the spring and summer line and the winter and fall line.

BLDD: Do you think that approach more accurately reflects the way women dress now? To have a broad range of all-weather clothes, and then a few things for very warm weather and a few things for very cold weather?

JG: You have to face it, there are seasons. Once upon a time, Cardin in Paris said that he was going to make one tremendous collection with everything—winter, summer, the whole lot in it, and you would have it all there in front of you. Well, that really doesn't succeed. Like it or not, you must work with the seasons. You cannot wear a summer print in the wintertime. You can, but it's not proper or it doesn't look right. Because of the high price of our clothes, we try to make clothes that can translate over a larger period of time, and clothes that can travel with our clients, who are always traveling—they go to Europe or Palm Beach or some resort in South America. We make clothes that can be worn in California as well as in New York or Paris or wherever they're going. My clothes hold up. That's why a lot of European women come and buy my clothes in New York. I met a lady there who owns a very famous gallery in Paris. She comes over every season. She wears my clothes in Paris because there everyone's wearing Yves St. Laurent or what-have-you. She says, "I feel different in your clothes." She was very stylish and she picked the most avant-garde clothes that I had. Whereas most of my ladies wouldn't be caught dead in them. They just don't understand those kinds of things. It was very pleasing to see someone understand my clothes.

BLDD: You mentioned Cardin. He seems in some ways to be the very model for some American designers as the king of licensees. Many designers aspire to design everything from cars to chocolates. Is licensing among your aspirations?

JG: At the moment I have my perfume which is now two-and-a-half years old. And I just signed a contract with a wonderful fur company owned by Mr. Dion in New York, a gentleman who is enthusiastic and wonderful to work with. We are sympatico, and all the ingredients are right! So this is the second license I have. Early in my career I had every kind of offer thrown at me. At that time I was a fair-haired boy. I had offers from TWA, American Airlines, and Fieldcrest. All these people asked me and I said no. I just didn't want to get involved. I didn't feel that I could handle it. I didn't realize then that all you had to do was put your name on those things and they did all the work, unless you were truly concerned with their products!

BLDD: You wouldn't be willing to do that anyway, would you?

JG: I couldn't. Unfortunately, too many do it, and that's why they come in one season and they're out the next. There are a few that do get a little more involved. Wherever I would have done it, I would have been involved. I thought I just couldn't handle that much. I've had many, many offers and I keep saying no. In fact, an airline came to me just a month ago, and I still said no.

BLDD: Well, what can an airline hostess do in a Galanos? How can you carry an airline tray wearing your luxurious fabrics?

JG: You make a design that's very practical. Valentino did a very nice one for Alitalia.

BLDD: Wouldn't it upset you to see it in synthetics?

JG: If it's well done, no. You'd pick something that is suitable for the particular moment and for the particular function. That's easy.

BLDD: Is there anything that you haven't designed yet that you'd care to?

JG: No. I'm not that ambitious to do a lot of things. I should have built an empire, but I didn't. I didn't have a person behind me to do the business end. I'm an instinctive man and whatever I do, I do on my own. I'm not a trained businessman, but I am good enough to keep my business under

control. However I'm getting younger instead of older, so I still may do it. Who knows?

BLDD: And to what do you attribute that desirable state?

JG: You mean staying young? I have a young outlook and I don't surround myself only with people of my own age. I have a diverse group of friends. And I'm active. I have a lot of energy. I don't know why, but I do. I have more energy today than I did when I was in my 20's. I'm still ambitious, I hope, in the right direction.

BLDD: Let's say a favorite niece came to you with more taste than funds. What would you suggest if she had $1,000 to spend? How should she equip herself to be a well-dressed young woman? She's obviously not going to be able to wear your clothes with that budget!

JG: She wouldn't have to worry about it. She could have them.

BLDD: Well, what advice would you give your niece's best friend?

JG: I would say buy less and buy better. Buy one or two things that are good quality, that have good lines. Of course, there's a question of how much taste you have. Buy things that are not trendy, that are not in one season and out the next. The penchant for trendy clothes is the fault of the magazines. The critics all promote some sensational thing that hits the fancy of the public, and two months later it's obsolete. That's why there's been a big switchover, why we are on top again, and why young people are thinking in different terms. Talk about quality is back, because prices have escalated so much. The quality things last, look good, and hold up.

BLDD: Did you ever consider designing a more affordable line?

JG: I never really cared about doing things en masse. I always wanted to do the most expensive, the most elegant, clothes, for a very special public. I never really think in terms of the big areas out there. It doesn't appeal to me. I'm not interested. You have to have a different mentality to do what Calvin Klein has designed. He was born in a different era than I was. And, let's face it, his training was Seventh Avenue production stuff. He had an idea, and what he does, he does fantastically well. It holds up. It's good, but it's mass appeal. It has nothing to do with couture. Now that he wants to be a couturier he may have to think in two directions.

BLDD: So many fashions seem to be designed for an ideal world, one with temperate weather, disappearing stains, door-to-door limousines, endless amounts of spendable money. What are the rest of us to do?

JG: You just have to pick and choose, sort it out and find what works for you, that's all. You cannot listen to or take advice from anyone.

BLDD: For those who might be able to afford only one of your own designs, what style would you recommend?

JG: It's all according to the person's figure. It's not a question of style. It's a question of what you can carry, what your figure says.

BLDD: What's your own favorite ensemble to design?

JG: I really don't have any favorite. I'm known for evening clothes but actually we do as much, if not more, with daytime suits and coats. I enjoy doing suits. I like doing everything. It's a challenge. I have a reputation of doing very glamorous evening clothes but sometimes I like to do the unexpected. I like to make them very tailored, with a certain anti-romantic flavor, which takes a lot of style and know-how, a lot of instinct, to wear. But, it's a challenge to do any category. Some designers are very good in one area and not as good in others. I think most designers like to design evening clothes because naturally you have a little more leeway to fantasize. But the challenge, the most difficult thing, is to make the absolutely simple, "nothing" dress look exciting. That is a project that never ends—making the most beautiful little black dress, one that is absolutely pure in line but has impact. Whenever I come up with a beautiful little black dress—it doesn't have to be black, but black seems a good medium to work in—that excites me. I'm always advocating black. I always say, "Look, you can't go wrong with black." Most women fight it and say, "Oh, it's not good for my skin." And I say, "Oh, that's a lot of nonsense. Everyone looks good in black as far as I'm concerned. It will suit you whether you have olive skin or white skin." In fact, I have quite a few little black dresses hidden under jackets this season. They're so nothing that it's a throwback to another time we've almost forgotten about. It looks great.

BLDD: It's hard to reconcile the artistic and the practical aspects of fashion. Most of us don't want to wear uniforms, nor can we wear only

James Galanos, fall, 1982

costumes. What are your suggestions on combining clothes to create outfits that can make the transition between night and day, city and country, office and dinner?

JG: Sometimes I think it would be a good idea if we did have uniforms, because at least if we had uniforms, everyone would look all right. Now there are too many people that don't know how to put themselves together. The uniform hides everything.

BLDD: Has the need for adaptability been a consideration in your own design?

JG: There are some women who like the idea of wearing the same thing all day long and switching just some little accessory for the evening. I tend to feel it's more interesting to change several times a day. I'm old-fashioned in the sense that I like women to be women, to be gorgeous and glamorous, and I don't want them coming from the office and wearing the same thing to dinner. I think it's boring. As long as we have fashion, and we have clothes, why not utilize them and present yourself as a new person in the evening? There are times when perhaps you can adapt the same outfit, but I think it takes something out of life when one believes there is so much to do that there is no time to indulge. I like to spoil women. I think women should have the most beautiful of everything, and I like the idea of them taking time to glamorize themselves in the evening or to entice men in the evening. That's a thrill. What more do you need when you go out than to see a woman who's sensational or elegant looking? I don't want to see her in some uniform that's just something to wear to cover the body. I hate that.

BLDD: You deal with some of the most beautiful and glamorous women. What's the quality that makes them glamorous or alluring to you?

JG: The clothes can only help you to a certain extent. It all really has to do with what you are. It's not a question of physical beauty. If you have some special personality, that comes out, and everything else becomes interesting on the body. There are lots of objects that are totally magnificent to look at, but you lose interest in them after a while. So they have a beautiful dress on—that's it.

BLDD: The empty suit syndrome?

JG: Yes. In a sense that's it.

BLDD: Is the burden of being a dream merchant for the too ample, or too tired, or too jaded, or too ambitious, sometimes too great?

JG: Yes, a lot of that can get in the way, but I think you've got to equalize everything and make it all come out right.

BLDD: Is it still fun for you?

JG: At times. At times it's very hard, and sometimes maybe I make it too hard for myself. I get depressed by business because I'm constantly here. I'm a worrywart and I like things to be right. I probably spend too much time with my business and too much time on the details, and don't give myself enough air and let other people take over. It's a problem in my personality, but one has to accept what one is, I guess, and go on from there.

BLDD: Not only do you design the clothes, you pick the fabrics, drape the clothes, stage the fashion shows, and visit the stores to talk with your customers. You obviously have a lot of energy, but how do you find the time to get it all done? Aren't you ever tempted to relax and let somebody else do some of the work?

JG: Oh, yes. I have a wonderful crew. There are technicians here, and they carry on, but when you have a business like this, a very personalized business, it stands for you, and your assistants can only do so much. The reputation relies on *you*. If I slacken in my work, then the people who surround me are bound to, and that's going to affect what I do. That is what happens to the big conglomerates and certain big designers who have everything going for them. They have tremendous help, and they do less and less themselves. It finally shows in what they're doing. You can see it on page after page after page. It's only because of your care and attention to detail that whatever you're doing comes out right. You cannot give it to anyone else to do. It's very, very important, and I don't want to get so far away from what I'm doing that I lose interest. If I do that, then I might just as well close up. As long as I'm here and somebody wants me, I can give my utmost—until the day that I dry out, which could happen. There's always a question within yourself as to how good you are. Every season is like starting all over again, with the feeling that I just don't know anything. It's like pulling teeth. I get hysterical because I feel I'm not designing enough, or it's awful, I don't like it, I hate it. And then that one big surge comes where you know you've got to get the job finished and then you make the big effort. But sometimes while you're working, you'll procrastinate. You're not happy and things are not going the way you want them to. And it's not a question of how many years experience you have. I've had enough. I know what's right and wrong. I know what's professional, but professionalism is not enough. There's got to be that one little extra thing that snaps and says, "O.K. I'm proud of it and I'm not ashamed to show it." If I just had to make nice clothes to show, and they were good professional clothes that had viability as far as sales go, that would bore me to death. If it doesn't excite me, then I feel I haven't done very much. It has to excite *me* first, before anyone else. If I don't like it, then I know it's no good.

BLDD: You have evolved from the fair-haired boy of fashion to . . .

JG: An old man!

BLDD: To what is often thought of as the dean of American fashion! How have your ideas about fashion changed? How have they evolved?

JG: I am not a philosopher. I just do my job, that's all. I really never analyze anything. My only aim is to make beautiful clothes and I hope that somewhere out there someone likes them.

BLDD: Where is fashion going nowadays, and do you want to go with it?

JG: We keep bitching about where fashion is going, but at the same time it's exciting in a certain way. I think that's what really keeps me going. I get furious, but there's a challenge in seeing what the young kids are doing, and the kooky ways they they're dressing. I hate it and yet I love it, because it's so totally what I don't do. I think it's fascinating to see the way some of these young people find trash clothes out of ash cans. There is something very, very interesting about it. It's not a question of taste. It's something else, because, as I said, there are rules, but you can break the rules. Sometimes what you do works and at other times it doesn't. For Balenciaga and other designers in those days, everything was measured, everything was proportioned, and yet he sometimes did things that would seem out of the norm. It's a question of breaking the traditional rules. Some people can get away with it, and some people can't. That's the excitement.

BLDD: What's been the greatest satisfaction of your career?

JG: Just being able to do what I'm doing. It's a lovely opportunity to be able to do something in this country. Although I was born here, I have the traditional mind of the European, like my parents, or immigrants. When you see how difficult it is in Europe in many, many respects for young people to get ahead, it's amazing what young people can do in this country. Designers today are movie stars. It's ridiculous, the acclaim they get.

BLDD: How do you explain it?

JG: I really don't know, but I think clothes are probably the most important thing, in a sense, after food, which one needs to exist. There is expression in clothes. There is vanity. It could be because it's the last glamorous thing that's available. Everything seems to be a downer. I don't know why, but there's such a vulgarization of things today.

BLDD: We know the effect of films on clothing designs. How about television? Do you think that has influenced the way people look and the way people design?

JG: No, because television just reflects what's going on. Television is a horror and a drug. There are good things on it, naturally, but most of it is junk. It's the same with films. I think films are exciting and I love them but I don't go very often because I no longer have the patience nor the time to stand in line to see a film. And I don't like what I've seen in films, the idea that we have to look at the lowest aspect of life. That seems to be the only thing that is portrayed on film.

BLDD: But there is another aspect of the impact of television: do you think there is some effect on a wide number of people who have seen Mrs. Reagan at an Inauguration Ball, or some other event, wearing one of your designs?

JG: It would be nice to think so. If it does, great. When Mrs. Reagan went to England to the royal wedding, she was on all the TV shows, and was fortunately wearing a costume of mine. She photographs like a dream. She was a movie star once, so she's a pretty lady. I know her from back in the

'50's, when she used to come into the local shop, and she was always properly but simply dressed. She has developed now into a more sophisticated woman. Mrs. Amelia Grey, whose shop she went to, really guided Mrs. Reagan, to whom she was very attached. Unfortunately, Amelia's not around anymore. She's been bedridden for years. But Amelia helped develop Mrs. Reagan's taste for my fashions and style. Mrs. Reagan used to buy the samples, and this woman developed a style and became more in the public eye with her husband. She's impeccable in a sense. She's appropriately dressed and she seems to know her look, exactly what suits her. Sometimes I may get carried away when she comes here, and I'll try different things on her. She's very petite, she's very tiny. I've tried to lift her out of a certain mold that she gets into, and I'll say, "Nancy, let's get away from this little suit look that you have." Yet it's charming on her.

BLDD: It's a uniform in a way; a convenient and easy way of dressing.

JG: It *is* a uniform for her life. And I will say, she looks very nice in it. If something is wrong, she won't say anything, but you know and then you look twice. Sometimes I'll say, "Well, did I get carried away with my designer's imagination." Because she's got the figure and she can wear it, she looks good. And many times I realize that she was right. But there are times when I want to change her look. At night she does look very glamorous.

I was invited to The White House for the dinner for Prince Charles. It was my first time, so I was excited about it. She wore a Galanos. It was very sophisticated and she looked beautiful. Everything was done well—the hair, the makeup. And she looked like a queen in her element, and it made me feel good, because she should be a showcase. I resent all this nonsense that went on about the clothes. I think she should be dressed well and have the best. I don't care whether it's mine or somebody else's. It could be Adolfo. He makes lovely clothes. It could be Bill Blass. But she should have the best of the American designers and no one should criticize her for it. She is the First Lady of the country. Do Americans want to see the President's wife wearing some dowdy little dress? Is that going to please them? Or are they going to be proud of her if she looks great and people talk about her? It's a sad position she's in, because no matter what she does she's criticized. When she went to England, we got a tremendous number of calls. Very elegant people would say that she stole the show from everyone. So she did have influence. People did look. And I think it makes young people, who do not wear clothes of that kind, think a little bit. It's a good example, if this woman, at her age—and I don't exactly know what age she is—put it together and did have influence for a while. People cleaned up, tried to look nice again, wore little white gloves and that sort of thing. It does help, and I think that's important. When a public figure makes an effort to look great, it rubs off somewhere; because we are constantly looking and we all have our idols, whether it's Mrs. Reagan or Mick Jagger.

BLDD: If you had it to do over again, what would you do otherwise?

JG: Probably do the same thing all over again. Who knows?

BLDD: And what next?

JG: Nothing. The satisfaction is being able to do it. I'm not that interested in building tremendous wealth. I have a little simple house that's very nice. It serves my purpose. It's pleasant. I have a car. The only thing that my business affords me is a certain independence. I can go anywhere. I don't care whether I have millions of dollars. I'm satisfied with ten dollars if it'll do the job. Money is only good if it lets you do something, and not worry about cost. That's what's important in the long run.

BLDD: Are you saying that money can give you more diverse choices?

JG: Sure. If you work hard, the rewards should pay off in a certain way. It's not disagreeable staying at the Ritz in Paris instead of the Hilton. That's all it means; it's nothing more than that.

BLDD: Is there any secret project that you haven't yet done that you'd care to? If you had enough time and assistance, is there something that you'd like to do?

JG: I'm an amateur photographer, not in a very serious way, but I do enjoy taking pictures, and I have a pretty good eye for composition. So every now and then I play at that. One day I would like to spend time, and travel a bit, and really develop my photography, because here and there I have done some fairly nice things, not terribly experimental, but tasteful.

James Galanos, fall, 1982

Opposite:
James Galanos, fall, 1983

CH

Carolina Herrera

Venezuelan socialite Carolina Herrera turned her finely-honed fashion sense into a career as a clothes designer in 1981. Her first collection, priced for a wealthy clientele, was praised for its workmanship and artistry; its clothes featured hand-sewn details, and were distinguished by original—and often dramatic—embellishments. Since that première, Ms. Herrera has become an internationally-respected designer. Her fashions are acclaimed for their elegant sophistication and glamour.

BLDD: You were born in Venezuela and still reside in Caracas for part of the year. What impact did your early experiences in Venezuela have on your decision to become a fashion designer?

CH: I have had an interest in fashion all my life. My mother and grandmother were always very smartly dressed. I come from a family that was very interested in fashion. I suppose that influenced me; I took fashion for granted.

BLDD: How did your mother and grandmother dress? Did their style influence your own fashion aesthetic?

CH: My grandmother wore Balenciaga designs, and my mother always liked simple, elegant clothes. When I was growing up we did not buy ready made clothes—we always had them custom-made. Everyone had their clothes made by a dressmaker. That had a great deal of influence on me. It is why I insist that everything be made well.

BLDD: Do you have any sisters? What about their interest in fashion?

CH: I have three sisters. My youngest sister, Maria Eugenia, who lives in Caracas, has just started designing clothes for young girls. My two other sisters, Cristina and Maria Alexandra also live in Caracas. They have children and lead quiet, married lives.

BLDD: Is your designer sister manufacturing clothes professionally?

CH: She is. She started 5 months ago and is very successful. It's difficult to design for young girls—from 12 to 16—but she has great ideas.

BLDD: Did your late-blooming career surprise your family and friends?

CH: I suppose it did, because they were not expecting me to do this.

BLDD: Did you ever expect to make a business out of fashion?

CH: I didn't start as a hobby. I started as a business.

BLDD: You said that your opportunity to enter the fashion business occurred by chance. What chance was that?

CH: I have designed clothes—some evening dresses—for myself for many years. And when I would go to New York or Europe for the season my friends liked my designs—they had something that women noticed. My friends would ask me who the designer was and I'd say it was me. Many people encouraged me to start designing professionally. Rudi Crespi always encouraged me. He'd say, "Why don't you do it in a professional way?" So finally I said, "Alright! Let's see what I can do." I went back to Caracas and started a small collection of 20 dresses, all made by a seamstress that I had. That was in 1980. Then I came to New York with my collection. Lauren Wyse, who had been with me from the beginning, called the buyers from Bergdorf Goodman, Martha, Saks, and Neiman-Marcus, just to review the collection and to see their reactions—to see if it was saleable, if it was a good idea. They all wanted to order it immediately. But I didn't have any production system, so I started looking for a backer to open this company. I found a very good one, Armando DeAramas, a Venezuelan who owns one of the biggest publishing houses in Latin America. By pure chance we met and it's been working very well from the beginning.

BLDD: What led you to begin designing?

CH: Sometimes you design because you want to have something that nobody else has. I like my designs. Other designers have suited me, but I wanted something more personal.

BLDD: In which other designers' clothes were you most interested?

CH: It all depended. I had my Italian years, my French years, and my American years. Sometimes I used to wear Valentino or St. Laurent. I remember my first evening dress, when I was seventeen. I got it at Lanvin. I went with my mother and she, of course, wanted to give me a white dress because when you come out in South America you dress in white. But I wanted to be a vamp and to have a black one! Needless to say, I got the white one. It was very beautiful, very fresh and very young. But I wanted something more interesting.

BLDD: What did you first design?

CH: I did many things—evening dresses and daytime wear—a little bit of everything.

BLDD: Your first collection was presented in April, 1981 at the Metropolitan Club in New York City. What was the response of the press?

CH: It was good. I got very good reviews.

BLDD: The first Herrera Collection became one of Saks Fifth Avenue's best sellers. To what do you attribute your immediate popularity?

CH: I suppose to the fact that they are feminine and wearable, and also because of their quality and the detail.

BLDD: How does your family feel about this great success of yours?

CH: My husband loves it, and I think my children love it, too. It's very nice because when you have somebody who is supporting you in what you are doing, it's wonderful, no? Then it's not a problem and you have strength to do more.

BLDD: Is your husband at all involved in the business?

CH: No, he's not. He's a landowner in Venezuela and is involved in real estate. He also works in publishing with the DeAramas Group.

BLDD: What does the DeAramas Group publish?

CH: They publish and distribute most of the Latin American magazines—*Vanidades, Harper's Bazaar* and *Cosmopolitan* in Spanish, and 15 other magazines and newspapers. They also publish textbooks.

BLDD: By what fashions, or what time, or what designers have you been most inspired?

CH: Fashion is inspired by everyday life. For instance, my big sleeves that are mentioned all the time are Elizabethan. They're old-fashioned. I liked the way they looked and I interpreted them in a contemporary way.

BLDD: You are perhaps best known for your opulent evening designs. Which garment is your favorite to design and why?

CH: I love the glamour and sophistication of evening especially. For evening I think a woman should make more of an effort and look her best. So I like glamorous, feminine and sophisticated clothes.

BLDD: What makes an ensemble glamorous to you? Is it the fabric?

CH: Glamour is a combination of everything—the way you wear the dress, the way you move, the way you act, the colors you're wearing. It's everything. There are certain people that are very glamorous, even if they're not wearing a glamorous dress. And others are never glamorous, no matter what they wear. "Glamour" is an American word, you know? It came from Hollywood, all those "glamorous" stars.

BLDD: Is there a counterpart in Spanish?

CH: "Glamoroso" is the word in Spanish.

BLDD: And as an idea, is it any different than in America?

CH: It's the same idea everywhere, but I think it's an American invention.

BLDD: You epitomize the well-dressed, glamorous woman. Do you have any advice for those who would like to transform themselves or their wardrobes?

CH: First of all, I think a woman has to be very sure of herself and know exactly what looks well on her. If something does not look right for her figure, or type, she should not wear it because it is fashionable. You have to know yourself. It's very important for a woman to have a looking glass in front of her. There are certain things that don't go well with certain types. A woman may think that to be in fashion she has to wear something even if it doesn't look right. That's a big mistake. You have to know exactly what looks well on you. For instance, I would not wear a miniskirt now, even if it was in fashion and everyone else was wearing it, because I know it doesn't look right on me.

Women should dress according to their age. Women who want to look younger think that if they wear young clothes they're going to look younger. They don't! They look older.

Also, the less makeup, the better, because you look fresher. Some women who are not very young put on lots of makeup because they think it hides lines. It's not true. It makes their faces look like masks.

BLDD: If a young person came to you who wanted the look that you epitomize but couldn't afford your clothes, what would you tell her to buy?

CH: I suppose skirts, blouses and trousers and convertible things. Two short evening dresses. It all depends on the way this young girl lives.

BLDD: Are there any basics? I remember asking Bill Blass that question, and he said, "Get a raincoat, a good raincoat," because it covers everything.

CH: Yes, but sometimes you have to leave the raincoat at the entrance and no one sees it. You're not always in the street.

BLDD: So, *that's* the difference between a female designer and a male designer!

CH: Exactly.

BLDD: What special insight do you think a female designer has?

CH: A woman designs for other women. As a woman she has tried the dresses on and knows what feels best. Men are very good designers, of course, but they don't really know a woman's point-of-view. They're testing to see whether it *looks* well or not. Sometimes they design things they would love to wear, but cannot!

BLDD: Is there a typical Herrera customer? How would you profile that person?

CH: A Herrera customer is sophisticated and secure, she knows what she wants: she wants to be very feminine. It flatters me when a woman wearing one of my dresses comes up to me and says, "You know, my husband loves it!" I receive so many compliments from men. To me, that is the greatest compliment. Women give compliments, but it's not the same. When a man notices what a woman is wearing, it's good.

BLDD: You've said that an important consideration of yours is creating clothes that are molded to show a woman's figure. But surely not all who would like to wear your designs are interested in revealing all their figure's details! Is there anything that you do to mask figure flaws?

CH: Sometimes, yes. For example, the very long-waisted dress with a little skirt, not tight, is a very good seller to women who are very small-waisted with big hips. That style covers everything.

BLDD: For someone so new on the fashion scene, your clientele is already rapidly growing. What do you offer that other designers in the fashion market do not?

CH: I suppose they like my designs and my materials. I offer the best fabrics, hand-finishing, and details. Every one of my dresses has to be very well-finished inside and out, because if you are buying one of these dresses, I suppose it's a little investment, so you want to have the best. Our prices are not expensive, when you recognize the materials and that they are hand made. I always get my fabrics from Europe—France, Switzerland or Italy.

BLDD: What's the process of the design? Do you select the fabric first, or create the design?

CH: I gather all the materials in front of me and then I start designing. After I finish each show I start selecting the materials for the next season immediately. I don't wait even one week. It's one after the other.

BLDD: How much of a hand do you have in each step of the design process?

CH: I'm involved in everything, from the beginning. I sketch, not very well, but I do my little sketches with every single detail and notes on the side, and then I have my assistant put them into a more complete form.

BLDD: How many assistants do you have?

CH: One.

BLDD: And how large is your staff?

CH: Forty-six.

BLDD: Your designs are very often described as feminine, and sometimes exotic. Would you agree with those descriptions?

CH: More glamorous, more chic than exotic.

BLDD: You would prefer to characterize your work as glamorous? What does "exotic" mean to you?

CH: Eccentric and with too many details. "Exotic" is too active. I like simple lines with one extravagant detail. You cannot add two or three details, or you destroy the lines. If you want a big bow, it should be only one. If you're going to add a ruffle, it should be only one. If I have big sleeves, I don't do anything at the skirt.

BLDD: Closely tailored outfits seem to have been popular over the last few years. Now it appears that looser fitting clothes and the chemise are back once again. What determines the popularity of a certain shape or silhouette? Why do so many designers decide at the same time that it's a good idea to reintroduce the chemise or to reintroduce the mini?

CH: That's something that I've never understood because you can get an idea although you haven't seen anything else like it around. It's like

Carolina Herrera, spring/summer, 1984

scientists on different continents making the same discoveries at the same time. One reason might be the type of materials that are offered because the same collections of materials are offered to all designers. When you see a new season's fashions and everything is in black and white and brown, you ask yourself, "Why is everything in black and white and brown?" It's because all the materials that were offered to designers that year were black and white with a brown background.

BLDD: How do you decide which colors you'll feature in any season? You often use bright primary colors.

CH: I love colors! I *love* color! I don't use many prints. I prefer to mix materials and colors, but not with prints.

BLDD: Your work, along with that of several other contemporary designers, has been described as "architectural." What does that term mean to you? Is it appropriate in describing your designs?

CH: "Architectural" clothes are constructed clothes that have square lines, like Shamask's designs. "Architectural" is not a fair description of my work. My clothes are softer. They are constructed, but not "architectural." I see "architectural" as very square, all lines like a Leger drawing. My clothes are designed to mold the figure and create an illusion of thinness and height. They have to be simple and yet striking.

BLDD: For years your presence has been an important feature of international society events. Do you wish that you had had more formal training in design in addition to that informal education in what your typical customer wants to wear.

CH: I don't think so. I feel good about my designs. Formal training sometimes limits you to what you think you can do.

BLDD: But in your own career, did you ever wish that you had some of the skills that are gained through formal training?

CH: No. It doesn't matter. The most important thing for a designer is to have a good eye for proportions and colors and taste. I don't think you can learn any of these things. Some people who are studying design don't have the eye, and don't know how to combine colors. I insist the most important thing for a designer is to have an observing eye.

BLDD: Have you been influenced by any particular painter?

CH: By many. By colors from Matisse, Picasso, Braque and, of course, the German Expressionists and Ingres, that marvelous quality he gives to the materials; and Holbein, Whistler, Sargent; and the primitives. There are so many. I see exhibitions of the new painters because it's very important for a designer to see what's going on. Sometimes you see one detail that you can add to your clothes. I just went to the Morgan Library to see the Queen's collection of Holbeins. The color is extraordinary.

BLDD: Did you find a detail in the Holbein show that you plan to adapt?

CH: It was something I already use—a sleeve.

BLDD: How do you do your research, generally? Do you have a theme, for example? Do you study certain periods?

CH: Yes, sometimes I do, but it all depends on my first idea. I work on that and I follow it through. If I see that it works, that's the collection. I'm not like Mary McFadden, who will do an entire collection that is inspired by Napoleon.

BLDD: Your firm, like many other designers, is now negotiating licensee contracts for shoes and furs and, I assume, some other things. Is this for distribution abroad as well as in the United States?

CH: I do have a licensing arrangement with Japan that has already been signed. Some of my clothes are going to be manufactured and sold only in Japan. It's my collection, with minor changes. We'll use the same materials. Japanese ladies are very classical in their looks and they have great taste. For them I may change the skirt or the sleeves a little. It's the basic idea, modified.

BLDD: Why do you think the Japanese market was particularly interested in your designs?

CH: That's a good question. I don't know. They're interested in many designers, Valentino and St. Laurent. Maybe it is because the Japanese are very classical, and my clothes are also classical: they last. My last season's designs can be worn this season and not look dated.

BLDD: Do you have any other licenses planned for the future?

CH: I have many proposed licensing arrangements. I'm working in fur now.

BLDD: Did you ever consider designing a less costly collection?

CH: The one that's going to Japan is less expensive. I think it's too soon in the United States. You see, I have only had two years in this business. I'm quite new. So I think I need to wait a little.

BLDD: Are your clothes offered in Caracas?

CH: No. My customers from Caracas travel a lot and they buy them here. That is not the only reason. It's also that this house is growing very fast and I have to supply America first. I have to be ready for the U.S. market. When I will have a production big enough to be able to deliver wherever my designs are in demand I will start with South America. I think it's very important to do it right.

BLDD: How did you, from beginning with just twenty dresses and a seamstress, hire a whole production staff and establish a very professional operation within a year?

CH: My backer helped to put all this together.

BLDD: How did you find the people?

CH: Lauren Wyse, who I mentioned earlier, helped put together this operation. Between the two of us, we found all the people, and all are still with me. I have been lucky. Every day gets better. At first, you make many mistakes—but you have to—then everything gets better.

BLDD: Have you ever designed jewelry?

CH: I design the jewelry for the shows and I work with an Argentinian jewelry designer, Eduardo Costa. He did my last show. The earrings are real leaves, laminated, and with rhinestones. We worked together. I gave him the idea and he understood exactly what I had in mind. I think that is important. These beautiful leaves with rhinestones came out precisely the way I wanted them. We are going to do it again for the next collection of spring-and summer wear in November.

BLDD: And what colors do you think you'll be interested in then?

CH: I don't know yet. I have to put all of them together to see what I have. I have chosen fabrics in many, many colors. In all my collections you'll always find yellow because I love it.

BLDD: Is it a color that you wear a lot?

CH: I do, and it looks well on me although I'm blonde. I also love to wear white. It's one of my favorite colors. Black, as well, even in the summer. And I have lots of bright colors. But I never wear any red.

BLDD: I imagine there must be great changes in your personal life now that you have a professional life. Has it changed dramatically?

CH: Now I also work, in addition to being a wife and mother. Before, I took care of charities, my house, my children and husband. All this is a great change. But I am well organized. I have time for everybody.

BLDD: Have you always been well organized?

CH: Yes, and I try to be.

BLDD: Did you learn that from your mother, too?

CH: Yes! She was a very well-organized woman. I feel this office is like my house and I try to run it like my house—it is a big family.

BLDD: How does that work, this extended family?

CH: It has been working very well. You have to like what you are doing and you have to love your workplace. I love mine! I don't mind having to stay here for hours and hours and hours, because it's mine. I am building this, you see.

BLDD: And you think this is just an external expression of what you've been working on for twenty-some-odd years? Were all the years that you designed for yourself part of your education and training?

CH: Yes, and I was brought up in a very strict way and I think that it shows.

BLDD: Did you ever expect the press or the public to receive your work the way it has? It's one thing to hope it. Were you surprised?

CH: At the beginning I was. I was surprised because you never expect something like this. How can you know?

BLDD: How important has the press been to your success?

CH: It's been very important. It's one of the most powerful things on earth. In presenting the first collection, I was a little blind; I was offering *my* idea, the way I saw it. And I didn't know whether it would be accepted. So I was like somebody learning how to walk. I was very lucky that it was accepted. My greatest success is that women buy my clothes.

BLDD: And they're your best advertisements. Who were your first customers? Were they friends of yours?

CH: Many people were not friends, of course. But I never mention names because I think it's not right to make publicity with people's names. If they want to say that they wear my clothes, I'm very flattered—but I'm not going to say who they are.

BLDD: When you wore other designer's clothes, wasn't your name mentioned?

CH: Many times.

BLDD: How did you feel about that?

CH: Sometimes I didn't feel it was right. That's why I don't do it. Making publicity for yourself by saying that so-and-so bought that dress isn't right. The dresses have to sell themselves.

BLDD: But don't you think that publicity and promotion are an important part of fashion?

CH: Yes. The best publicity is to describe the dress, to say how it looks, and how well finished it is, and how wonderful the design is, not to give the name of the person who's wearing it.

BLDD: What's the most surprising thing that you've encountered in your brief career?

CH: The quick acceptance of my designs . . . seeing all these women wearing my dresses. It's the most flattering thing in the world to see. It's like seeing all your babies around.

BLDD: How do you feel if a woman isn't wearing it properly, or hasn't accessorized it correctly?

CH: Sometimes you feel like saying something.

BLDD: Do you ever do that?

CH: Not very often!

BLDD: What's the most disappointing thing that you've encountered since you've been a designer?

CH: I have experienced so many good things that it is difficult to think of the most disappointing moment. When you've designed something that you feel is great, and it's not accepted the way you thought it was going to be, that's very disappointing. And it has happened, of course.

BLDD: Do you ever try to reintroduce such designs again?

CH: Yes, because you have to stick to your ideas. Nobody can make me change. When I have an idea, I want to follow it through.

BLDD: What's been the biggest satisfaction, so far, of your career?

CH: My biggest satisfaction is having created all that you see around me.

BLDD: If you've done this in two years, what are your future plans?

CH: There are so many future plans. I suppose everybody wants to get bigger and bigger and bigger and to sit on top of the world in your own discipline.

BLDD: How can you get bigger and maintain the standard of quality that you have in mind?

CH: That's a real problem. That's why I don't want to grow so fast. One of my main concerns is controlling the quality of the clothes. My clothes are compared with couture, which is wrong.

BLDD: Why?

CH: This is not couture—it's the *look* of couture. It's ready-to-wear. When you have a dress hanging on a rack, not fitted, it is not couture. I have never understood why they call my clothes a "couture line." It's really prêt-à-porter. My clothes are extraordinary prêt-à-porter.

BLDD: Do you ever try to clarify this misnomer?

CH: I have been trying to, but everyone insists on calling it couture, which for me, is made-to-order with fittings. If you come to me and say, "I want you to make me a dress," and I have fittings for you, that is couture. But I do that very seldom, only for certain private clients.

BLDD: Is there any particular reason that you chose to be situated uptown on 57th Street, rather than in the traditional, conventional Seventh Avenue garment center location?

CH: It was easier for me here. This is a wonderful location and very near everywhere. I didn't think of going to Seventh Avenue. I thought I was going to stay uptown. There are many designers uptown—Adolfo, Halston, Scaasi, Kamali, Giorgio Armani. But I also have offices on West 39th Street.

BLDD: How many hours a day do you spend here?

CH: You couldn't believe it. During collections I sometimes arrive at nine or ten o'clock in the morning and leave at twelve or one at night.

BLDD: And the rest of the time? Are you here every day?

CH: Yes, I come here every day. Every single day. It's important that I be here.

BLDD: Aren't there some things that you wish you had more time for?

CH: Now, I realize how wonderful the weekends are. Before, I didn't realize. I didn't understand when I heard people say, "Ah! I'm so glad that today is Friday." So what? Now I'm counting the days, "Eee! Tomorrow's Friday!" Now I realize it. I love to stay in my house on week-ends, quietly.

BLDD: Do you go to the country?

CH: It's not my favorite thing. I prefer to stay in town and have a very relaxed day, to just stay in the house and not move around. To go out for a whole week-end is a whole production.

BLDD: How do you manage to work long days and to go out at night to some of the many events that you went to when you were not so actively involved?

CH: I always go to bed early. I go to bed at eleven-thirty or twelve—a must. When I go out to all these parties, I try to go to bed early. I love sleep. *I love it.* I could sleep for fourteen hours if they would let me. One of my passions is sleep.

BLDD: What are your other passions?

CH: I love to read. It relaxes me. I read everything. Novels, history, autobiographies, everything.

BLDD: What are you reading now?

CH: I am reading a book on Misia Sert. I am amazed by her. She was fascinating, yet she never did anything. She was the friend of such people as Chanel and Renoir. She didn't produce anything, but she inspired them all. Her art was to fascinate. Isn't that marvelous?

BLDD: Do you think it's important that your children produce anything with their lives?

CH: It all depends on what they decide because I cannot decide for them. I would like them to do something, to produce something, if they can. I'm not going to push them and tell them what to do because I think that's not fair. They have to do what they can.

BLDD: Do you wish that *you* had started earlier?

CH: There's a time for everything in your life. Now was the best time for me to start because of the ages of my children. I am Roman Catholic. I am also very superstitious.

BLDD: How does that manifest itself?

CH: There are some things I'm superstitious about. When I start a collection and I come back to the showroom before the buyers arrive, the clothes have to be hanging in the same way. And the shoes have to be in line in pairs. That's good luck for me.

BLDD: What else?

CH: I'm superstitious with people, and with dates, numbers and things. I think everyone is a little superstitious. I have so many lucky numbers that I don't even remember the bad ones.

BLDD: Did you ever expect your life to unfold the way it has?

CH: No, I wasn't planning this. It came out like this, and I'm delighted and I would do it again. Absolutely. I love what I'm doing and I think the best thing about it is that I love it. I have lots of energy. If you stay with me the whole day, I'm sure that at the end you're going to be lying on the floor exhausted. And I don't take vitamins.

BLDD: Do you think it's psychic energy?

CH: You have more and more energy when you are doing something you really love. If you do something you don't like but you have to do then your energy is lowered. You say, "Ah, should I do it? Why do I have to do it?"

BLDD: If you had it to do over again, what, if anything would you do differently?

CH: Nothing. I would do *exactly* the same thing.

NK

Norma Kamali

Norma Kamali, a designer and businesswoman, is the recipient of two Coty Awards, and in 1982 was voted the outstanding American fashion talent. Owner of the Manhattan boutique appropriately named OMO for "On My Own," she is best known for her flamboyant, sensuous use of fabric, such as sweatshirt cloth, snakeskin and feathers coupled with soft velvets. Kamali is presently expanding her designs to appeal to a more diverse audience, including the design of children's clothes.

BLDD: You were born in New York City. I wonder how much you attribute to growing up in New York during the 1950s and 1960s as an influence on the development of your fashion style?

NK: I think everybody exposed to the city is influenced by it. If you're born and raised in Manhattan, the influences are even stronger because that becomes your point of reference for the rest of your life. If you live in New York, in a sense you live on the street. You don't stay in your apartment, you go out on the street. That's what we did as children. If you live in Manhattan and it rains, you tend not to go home, but you go somewhere together in a group to get out of the rain. We would go to museums. In spite of myself, I was bombarded by what the City has to offer, which is a lot of pretty terrific stuff. I became as familiar with the inside of the museums on either side of Central Park as with playgrounds. We spent a lot of time in both the Metropolitan Museum and the Museum of Natural History.

BLDD: Did you live close by?

NK: I lived on West 77th Street. If it was raining or snowing outside, we would walk through a museum and play hide-and-go-seek there. While you'd walk through, you'd see things and become familiar with them. I knew every wall, every crack, every nook and cranny in them. It was very comfortable and familiar to me. I think all of that had a lot to do with what I'm doing now.

BLDD: In speaking of your teenage years, you've said that you were always doing strange things—and that wasn't going to museums—such as literally stitching yourself into pants and creating rather sexy blouses from doilies. Did out-of-the-ordinary clothes characterize your wardrobe during those years?

NK: Yes, and there are a couple of reasons for it. My mother was the kind of person that was always making something out of something else, usually a household object. She'd make a bag out of a piece of an old carpet; she's like the household tips lady. But, beyond that, because she painted as we were growing up, we always had easels and paints in the house. I thought everybody's mother was doing the same kind of thing. So that's what I did, too. I wanted lots of clothes to dress up in, and since we weren't the wealthiest people in the world, I became creative out of necessity. I went to Washington Irving High School, right around the corner from Klein's on 14th Street. I would go there, spend $2 for a dress, take off all the ugly trimmings and buttons, make it shorter or cut off the sleeves, add stuff to it, get my own lace and decorate the dress. Then that dress was mine, my own creation. That's how all of it started. It was just that I wanted more, and I wanted to decorate it.

BLDD: What was the reaction of your peers to your ingenuity?

NK: A lot of people liked it. When you're sixteen, seventeen, eighteen, you're still living at home. You don't have the responsibilities of a job or an identity and you have an opportunity to experiment and be creative. I decided I didn't want to have eyebrows, so I shaved my eyebrows off. I decided I wanted to have lots of color and makeup on my face and wear clothes that I liked. I didn't see them in any fashion magazines, or anywhere else, but I didn't care. When I took the subway to go to school, you can be sure that I was looked at as if I had landed from some strange planet. But it was my opportunity to be strange because I didn't have to earn a living. I didn't have a job to be responsible to. It's during those years that you can really do it and do it to the hilt. You drive your parents crazy, of course.

BLDD: What was their reaction to this experimentation?

NK: My mother was dismayed, but because she was not exactly an on-course person herself, she was not unhappy about it. I wasn't doing anything wrong. It was just that she didn't think it looked that great.

BLDD: How about your father? Was he a traditional businessman?

NK: My father wasn't alive then, so I didn't have the pressure of that male

Overleaf:
Norma Kamali, fall, 1983

figure. I think what I did then is now seen in the clubs, it's the newer version of punk.

BLDD: What *is* the newer version of punk?

NK: I don't think it has a name yet, but it's evolved from the whole English and Japanese thing. If you look at those people, they're sixteen, seventeen, eighteen years olds who live at home, and they're also doing it to the hilt. That's such an important time because that's when you can be foolish, silly, ugly, pretty, everything at once. You can do it and it doesn't matter to anybody so long as your parents can live through those years and not get exhausted by it. That was my time of playing.

BLDD: Did you ever expect that this creativity, this almost natural genius for improvisation and regard for the other-than-usual, would evolve into the multimillion-dollar business you've become?

NK: I never, ever wanted it to, and it wasn't my goal. I wanted to paint. I thought that's what it was really going to be about. It wasn't. I didn't ever think of it for the dollar. I don't think I do now either. I've learned to appreciate what money can bring as far as freedom. But still, I'm not going to do a collection because it's going to bring me money. It wasn't a multimillion-dollar business that was the goal. It wasn't even fashion really that turned out to be my goal. It just didn't work that way.

BLDD: In describing your mother and her own resourcefulness, you've told me that she made not only clothes, but toys for you during your childhood. Obviously that same resourcefulness is evident in your work, and obviously, too, she has had a very marked influence on you. Do you ever consider that perhaps she was born twenty years too early to fully realize *her* talents?

NK: Absolutely, I'm certain of that. I didn't have the kind of mother who would say, "now you have to get married, and I want you to meet the right kind of man to take care of you." That was *never* the kind of conversation I had with my mother. My mother said, "You should learn how to be an independent person, how to earn your own living, have your own security. And when you choose to get married, make sure that your marriage is based on other things and not on your need for someone to take care of you. First be who you are." Nobody else's mother was telling them that.

BLDD: Let alone any mother of Basque and Lebanese descent. Independence, personal, professional success are traits that don't appear to be encouraged for women in those cultures.

NK: No, not at all. Not at all. But she is an independent soul. That's the way she is. She's very much ahead of her time. She still works—in fact, now she does all the crocheted children's clothes we carry. She does the crocheted bags. We're working on some hats together. Her talent is there and it's incredible. She's sixty-seven. I think she missed something, but she's so productive, that I don't think a day has gone by where she hasn't lived it completely. Her energy is unbelievable. I think it's part of what this company is about: everybody is like a family to each other.

BLDD: Does it compensate for the other-than-usual family that you did not grow up in? Or were you part of a very large and extended family yourself?

NK: My mother's family is very large, but we were basically a small family, which is fine with me, because I don't feel a need to communicate with family all around the world. In this type of business you become so much a part of the lives of the people you work with. I think our family spirit has been a very positive, helpful thing for this business. I like the comfortable feeling about it, and I think everybody else does, too. If somebody doesn't fit in with it, it's apparent. It doesn't work without this blend.

BLDD: You were graduated from the Fashion Institute of Technology in New York just about twenty years ago. What were FIT students wearing during your years at school?

NK: I was in the Illustration Department at FIT and all of a sudden I decided that because I really wanted to paint, clothing was not going to be important to me. And here I came into a fashion school and I noticed that in the design classes everybody was very, very aware of what they were wearing, how expensive it was, and who the designer was. Twenty years ago there were very few designers' names that anybody knew, but there was such an attitude toward status in the school even at that time.

BLDD: Who had high status then?

NK: I think St. Laurent, certainly. It was very strange and it made me very uncomfortable to even think about what people were wearing. It was more important to me how good it looked. People were very dressed up with pocketbooks and shoes to match, and stockings. It was that time. It had to do with a very polished, put-together fashion school look. I think that could be expected twenty years ago.

BLDD: Do you ever sketch your own things?

NK: I never sketch anything before I do it. I sketch it afterwards.

BLDD: How do you do it? Do you sew it yourself?

NK: I did sewing for many years. Up until three years ago I made all the patterns, and I still do some of them. I think a new design comes from something that doesn't exist. If you can draw it, you're limiting what it can be. It can only be the drawing. I start with a concept before I start with a fabric. I might write words because that's not my medium and therefore it's not going to interfere with what I'm creating. I'll write down what I think about a shape for a collar and then I'll do it. I don't sketch it because I don't want it to be trapped by my sketch. When it's complete I can sketch it.

BLDD: What was the first job you had after you were graduated?

NK: I worked at a buying house. They had artists to do creaky, stiff little sketches. These sketches were put together in a book and would become next season's line. It was my first taste of what the garment industry was about. It was so restricting, so uncreative, and it told me so much about the fashion business that I said, "I think I'm in the wrong business. This is not for me." It was too limiting. I think it was a good experience to see what that was about, and it made me realize I didn't want to stay on Seventh Avenue. So I left. I did a couple of freelance illustration jobs that were very nice because I was finally drawing a human body and making something happen. Then I realized how very few jobs were or ever are available for fashion illustrators. I didn't want to be limited so I decided to travel, and I went out and got a job at an airline. I said, "That's it. I'm going to go do something else." I worked in an office for Northwest Orient. I didn't know how to type or do anything, but I said, "I have to try something else right now. I know that this is the time." I worked there for four years and learned so much about computers and office procedures. I traveled every single weekend. For $29 I could travel roundtrip to Europe. That was pretty good to do in a weekend. I experienced London as if I were living there. And I would go to Paris. It was the sixties and I was part of what was happening. It was a wonderful, wonderful thing for me.

BLDD: So the job really became a vehicle for your travels?

NK: Yes, and I was good at the job, too. I think I was excellent. I became the head of the Tour Department. If you are good at whatever you're doing, it's rewarding. I decided I was going to make the best of that time. I thought to bring back some of the clothes from Europe would be a way to try something new. Everybody wanted what I brought back from London. Then I saw an ad in the paper for a basement shop on 53rd Street at $285 a month, and thought, "I've got to be able to pay that rent. I have to be able to do this. It's ridiculous not to." So I got the shop in 1967. I worked at the airline, and I ran the shop with my now ex-husband who also was going to school. When he wasn't working, he was in the shop. And when I wasn't working, I was in the shop.

BLDD: Where did you find time to get married during the course of all these activities?

NK: I guess when you're that young, you find time to do a lot of things. I was twenty-one years old. He was a student of economics and I was working at the airlines.

BLDD: Did he share your interests in fashion?

NK: I don't think he was really that interested until it became so popular. The store became so important, much more important than either one of us expected. We really had to look at it as a business that we had to contend with. Because so many people had expectations for it we had to keep restocking the shop and making it more than what it was before. Then we decided that we really were involved in this business, and that we had to learn about it and make it better. For the sixties and the seventies you could experiment, you could take a chance. The risk of $285 surely wasn't that great. So we did it. Around 1970 or 1971 I left the airline because it got to the point where I didn't see as many wonderful things in London. I finally decided that I was going to make the clothes to sell in the store. That's when I started sewing and learning how to make

patterns, with my mother helping and working and getting the stock into the shop.

BLDD: What were the first things that you designed?

NK: I remember that the very, very first thing that I ever made and put in the store was leather and suede and snakeskin—nothing like starting with the most complicated. But that's what it was. It was an appliqued design of snake and leather on a suede jacket and suede pants.

BLDD: Who were your first clients?

NK: It was a time when people were decorated and dressed experimentally. I don't think it was a certain type of person, but because my clothes were a bit more extravagant, my customers were probably involved in rock-and-roll and music because music was very important at the time. It was important to everybody. It was that time. People in the music industry spent a lot of money on looks and a lot of time on the visual presentation. So I got involved in that a lot, and I liked that. It was a lot of fun, because I could continue my sixteen, seventeen and eighteen year-old fantasy of how to dress up.

BLDD: But here you were, making things yourself. What was the transition from loving hands at home to a professional manufacturing capacity?

NK: It went on for quite a long time because I was still growing. I didn't even think of myself as a designer. I continued selling for three or four more years as one of the key sellers with somebody else also helping. Then we hired someone else and I did most of the cutting. Eventually, I did less sewing, and more cutting and patternmaking, then more cutting and patternmaking, and up until three years ago only patternmaking. So I stayed with it and I still do. I'll sit down at the machine if I want to try something new. I can't expect someone else to do something unless I know how to do it myself. It's important for me to have my hands on it.

BLDD: Your headquarters, your shop, your offices have always been uptown, away from Seventh Avenue. Why have you chosen to remain apart from Fashion Avenue? Has the physical separation been important to you, and has it made your acceptance by the rest of the so-called fashion establishment complicated?

NK: At the beginning I was very anti-garment industry. Then after the initial thing of "I know that's not for me," I just felt it was something that wasn't happening. I was a retailer first, and I still consider myself a retailer first, so my store was the most important thing.

BLDD: Obviously you've made a very careful statement in your shop at 11 West 56th Street (in New York City). You've taken over an entire building, gutted and redesigned the interior.

NK: Yes, the store is the key. My business is first about retailing. This store represents to the public what I'm doing. I have sportswear, swimwear, evening clothes, day couture that we make, children's wear, shoes, hats, socks, gloves. It's all part of what I present to the public.

BLDD: When did you find out you had outgrown 53rd Street?

NK: We grew at 53rd Street until we were in the basement and on two upper floors. It was very successful. But as a result of what also happened in the seventies, that particular street was doomed by a methadone center. The area was plagued by drugs and their effects. We had to move for survival. Madison Avenue, on the second floor—it was no man's land on Madison Avenue at that time—was the next opportunity, something we could afford.

BLDD: What ever gave you the idea then to go to a second floor shop in a street level shopping area, where everyone stumbles from one lure to another on the ground level?

NK: Purely economics. We didn't even know if we'd still be in business. The move to Madison was very scary because it was really the only other street to go to. The second floor was all we could afford. The question was, how are we going to get people to come up to the second floor.

BLDD: And how did you do that?

NK: As I'd always been in a basement or in an off-street-level store anyway, I knew how to get people to look down or sideways by doing windows that would be interesting and creative.

BLDD: Did you design the windows?

NK: Yes, I've always been very involved in that. The big change was that on Madison Avenue feathers and velvet and all of that stuff just wasn't

going to make it. It was time for me to grow up and mature, and I wanted the clothes to be different.

I also decided that this was my chance to make a break from what I was doing and grow up and mature in another way. So I hired European tailors and learned about tailoring. I made beautiful suits for women at a time when the man-tailored look was really not the fashion. But they were so beautiful, the styling was so nice and clean, that it helped me find a direction. I had beautiful lace dresses and suits, and that meant not only a move to Madison, but all new customers. Very few of my old customers could handle this change that I wanted. So it was six months of "do you think anybody will ever come up here? What can we do to carry them up the stairs and get them up here?" When we thought it was all over, people started to come up. And I got more and more creative with the window.

BLDD: What did you do with the windows that enticed people? What was the most unusual or eccentric windows that you did?

NK: At that time most of the window displays on Madison Avenue were flat displays. Mannequins were not used. An English company, Adele Rubenstein, who had just come to New York, started to bring in their mannequins, and I found them in Soho and decided to use them. The department stores didn't even have them then. Mine was the first store that had many mannequins in clothes that didn't look like anybody else's. I used whatever kind of prop that would suit the nature of those clothes, and I'm talking about big props. One time I had a whole bunch of work clothes, and we did a Con Edison display with a big tube and Con Edison stands with flashing lights.

We did grafitti windows with big sheets of paper and grafitti all over it with spray cans and all that. This was the seventies, and very shocking because everybody was becoming disturbed about grafitti in the subways. It was just beginning to make people crazy, and here I was putting it in the window. I think that was probably the first time it had been done. So the window was a key to get people up.

BLDD: How long did you stay there?

NK: I stayed till '77. The store remained two years after I left. The company matured having the store on Madison Avenue. It became a different kind of company with a new look and it got more recognition. Also I was growing up, and so was Eddie Kamali. The business was definitely an important part of our lives. We both were very involved in what was going on. But when you work together and live together and you have an emotional connection, it's a big disturbance when it doesn't work. It was not easy to make the decision to leave. It was probably the most difficult decision of my life; I never thought I really would be able to do it.

BLDD: What gave you the courage to leave?

NK: I thought that if I stayed there I couldn't grow. I felt that there would be too many things—they're personal things that I don't want to talk about—but that would stop my growth.

BLDD: So then there were two Kamalis.

NK: Yes, two Kamalis then existed. And I left, and I was scared to death because I said "nobody knows me. I'm the one that's hidden in the back. Does anybody know that Norma Kamali exists?" Nobody ever heard about me. I thought all I can do is just try to be good at what I do.

BLDD: Where did you get the funds to do anything like that?

NK: From everybody in the world that I knew. It was the most difficult thing in my life to ask anybody but the bank certainly was not going to go for it. Until that time I allowed myself to be a woman without a credit card, a woman without a bank account, because I thought—who needed it? I was so happy doing what I was doing—that I became the person that had no identity and no nothing. A salary wasn't important to me. Nothing was important. Then I realized, "This is not acting grown-up. You have responsibilities and you want to do this and you don't have the money to make anything new happen." I got money from my mother, every relative in the area, every friend I'd known that had ever saved a penny. People not only loaned me money, but they extended credit beyond the time that anybody with a brain in their head would allow credit to be extended. Those are the people that you never forget.

BLDD: Do you wholly own this business yourself?

NK: Yes.

BLDD: And whatever happened to Eddie Kamali and the Madison Avenue shop?

NK: He decided not to stay in business. After two years he closed everything. I think he's back in Iran.

BLDD: From there, you started to become Norma Kamali, businesswoman, and opened what you refer to as OMO, "On My Own." From what were you declaring your independence?

NK: OMO was just a symbol. Every lawyer I knew said, "You must find another name to connect with your name so that there's a clear difference between Norma Kamali and Kamali." I kept thinking about a name, and I thought initials that didn't really stand for anything would be good, and initials that looked nice, that really said something would be even better. OMO looked very nice, and they said "On My Own."

BLDD: Did you make it up yourself?

NK: Yes. I wanted people to know that Norma Kamali was on her own; she wasn't part of Kamali anymore. It wasn't any big political statement. It was simply survival in a business where two names were the same. But in the end, it really did have all of the other meanings. I learned how to be a grown-up. I learned how to be a woman who could take care of herself, which was very important to me as a person, and I learned how to run a business. Everybody assumes that if you're creative you don't do those things, that you don't know how to do it, but I love it. I think it's so exciting, and so much fun. It's only helped me as a designer to know about business.

BLDD: What is your own personal fashion style?

NK: There are no words ever for that. That's something that happens within a person. It's just the way you do things. It's the way you sign your name. The minute you describe it, it's no longer your style. It's something else. It's something you don't describe, and it's always changing.

BLDD: How do your fashions reflect your own lifestyle?

NK: I'm somebody who lives in the eighties, an active and energetic person involved in business, who has certain needs to express herself. I need to be comfortable, to look pretty, whatever the word "pretty" is for that minute. I need to say something about myself, and not be trapped by my clothes, either. I want to be able to rise above them no matter what. I do that for myself, and I do it with the clothes. If there are any other women that think the same way, they can also find their way by doing what they want with my clothes.

BLDD: You've described yourself as a "designer for street people." How does this concept affect what you design and its pricing?

NK: Because I haven't been rich and have always had to be smart about the way I spent my money, I think about price. Today everybody is aware of price and what they're getting and how they're spending their money. I am aware of the same things and want my clothes to be priced well. I want them to be fun and exciting and give pleasure, because that's the business I'm in—to give pleasure, not to make machine guns. I want that for my customer because I want it for myself. It's very simple.

BLDD: You've called fashion design an art form, and have regard for the kind of respect Europeans accord to design. But as you've pointed out, you also recognize the business side of fashion and have acknowledged that you'd like to be successful in terms of making money. Is the making of beautiful clothes, and the making of money, incompatible in any way in your life, or in your work?

NK: The creative time must be separated from the business time. I do that. When I'm designing, I'm doing what I want to do. I experiment. When I finish with the design, I sit back and look at it and say to myself, "Do I want to experiment with lots of people with this particular design, or do I want to put two of them, or three of them, in the store and see how it works there first, and see what happens with it?" That's when my business brain gets involved. But the day that I say, "I'm not going to do that design because it may not sell, or it's not a good business idea," and I don't take the chance, then the business will be interfering with the creative part. I don't think that'll happen. It's not what I want. You have to separate one from the other, and then you have to pull them together.

BLDD: What features would you describe as the most Norma Kamali-like? For example, wide shoulders?

NK: I think you would say that. But five years ago you wouldn't have said that, or ten years ago you wouldn't have said it, and three years ago you might have said, "but her swimsuits are really more important." You can't do that with fashion. There's an essence in everything, whether they have shoulder pads or a bathing suit, that people recognize as me. It's like a signature, you don't know what it is, but it's there.

BLDD: Are there any women that you know of, or have observed, that you would characterize as women of style? Women who you think have a wonderful way of putting themselves together?

NK: The most creative people are those that don't have a lot of money to spend. Style definitely has to come not from what you can afford, but what you can do with what you can afford.

BLDD: Now that you are pretty far removed from that sixteen-year-old both in terms of your life, your work and the rewards that have accrued to you, do you still feel in touch with that look and that feeling?

NK: I don't need to be that way anymore. I did that. Nobody wants to be the same all the time. That's the great part of it—that you become a better picture of yourself. As the years go by it becomes finer and better and perfected. That's how you can see the person emerge in their thirties and really become who they are in their forties. It's very exciting to see all of that experience come together to create a new person. The evolution is fascinating and I'm a product of my evolution.

BLDD: Are there any contemporary designers to whom you respond? Whose works do you most admire?

NK: The personality that Calvin Klein offers to the American woman is very important, because the American woman is clearly different from the European woman. She has needs, and characteristics that are special. He understands that. When he's doing Calvin Klein, he's doing something very special for the American woman. Ralph Lauren is another one who is very clear about who his woman is, and when he's true to himself in what he presents to the public, it's terrific. It's really fantastic. They also understand American business, and they do it incredibly well. It's really an amazing business. It's not me, and it's not what Norma Kamali is about, but I appreciate that part of it.

Then there are European designers that are very talented in different ways. There's something wonderful about most European designers. Their creativity is so spontaneous and exciting. The ones I like best are those who are the most true to themselves. I also think there's something interesting that will come from the Japanese designers that will evolve and become part of what we're all thinking about, and we won't even know it.

BLDD: You talk about the business sense of Calvin and Ralph. Let's talk for a moment about the business sense of Norma. Your line has expanded to include children's clothes, shoes, bathing suits, hats, coats, socks, tights, hosiery design, all sorts of things. In how many different areas do you design?

NK: You named them all and it can't be much more than that because I do design each collection. I don't have a staff of designers. They're also things that I've always wanted to do and finally had the opportunity to do. I've been wanting to do shoes for years. High-heal sneakers—that was twelve years ago. All of the accessories are really part of finishing off the look or the character.

BLDD: It's now possible for a woman to wear Kamali from head to foot. When you design an item—a dress, a suit—is a total Kamali look in your head?

NK: Not at all. It's almost like talking about an abstract picture. I think it's probably not attractive to see the total look, even though I do most of the time. I want to put the personalities of my customers first, and then the clothes. So if anybody sees my clothes first, before they notice the person, then I think something is wrong with the picture.

BLDD: Speaking of pictures, why are you so reluctant to share yours? Why is there never, by choice, a Norma Kamali photograph published?

NK: It has to do with what my business is about, and how I see myself in this business. There are a lot of designers who are superstars. But I am my customer, and I don't want to be separated from her; I don't have that star quality that the other designers have. I think my fortune is that I am like my customer, and I don't want to be different. I like being the same, and I want to be in touch with her all the time, and also be me. I don't want to be

Norma Kamali, fall, 1985

recognized, and I have to protect myself from that. That's why I don't have my picture taken.

BLDD: Does a woman designer bring something extra, something different or special to the design of clothes for women?

NK: I can only speak for myself. It's a personal need and desire to look a certain way and have certain things. I think because I have a particular taste, I reach a lot of women.

BLDD: You really do try to reach a lot of women. In fact, in your boutiques from time to time you even wait on the customers. Why do you do that, and what do you learn from the experience?

NK: First of all, if it's a busy time in the shop and somebody needs help, I am hardly going to turn away somebody's question or ignore a customer. That's usually how it comes about. If I'm in the store and something has to be done, I'll do it. By doing that and by getting notes from everyone in the company, I get the information I need about what people want.

BLDD: What do you mean by getting notes?

NK: Each person in my company who is connected with the public in any way must write me a note once a week. They tell me exactly how things are fitting, what colors are doing well, if they think the store needs to be rearranged, or anything, including, if they want, something about their boyfriends. This way I can stay in touch with what they're about and what the store is about.

BLDD: Seventh Avenue designers always work months ahead of the current selling season, because of merchandising and manufacturing schedules. In contrast, the work you do from your boutique allegedly allows for greater design immediacy. Is that accurate, and what are the advantages of such immediacy?

NK: I find it very exciting and satisfying to see my work in the store right away and see it on customers. And the opportunity to experiment is endless. I can do whatever I want, whenever I want to. What more can you ask?

BLDD: You said that the time of experiment in the 1960s is responsible for the kind of work that you do today. What did you mean when you said that?

NK: The sixties gave everybody the opportunity to do things today that they would never have done before. They were very special, and I think in modern times have had the most revolutionary effect on everybody's life. How fortunate it was to be a part of that. I learned a lot. I had no limitations. I was never told, "Yes, you can do this, but you can't do that." I learned that experimenting and trying new things is very important. To stay the same is just not stimulating. It's not exciting, and in this business it's death.

BLDD: Since you're always so conscious of your own evolution, what can we expect next? In what direction do you want your life and work to go?

NK: It is very important for me as a woman in this business to begin to include my personal life more into what my business day is about. As far as my future goes, I want to do this until the day I die, but not of course the same thing every second. It's who I am. It's what I am about, and I'd like it to go on forever.

BLDD: How do you feel about imitators, and how do you feel about their infringements?

NK: It's what the business is about. When I was young and less mature and less secure, it drove me crazy. I thought, "That's stealing. They're taking my styles." But what I learned is it forced me to do the next thing right away!

BLDD: How has the rapid expansion of your design activity in the past five years affected your life and your perception of the way the company's direction should go?

NK: The concept of being small was very important for me until I realized the possibility of doing a collection that would be affordable if I did it with a large company. I had no idea that it would be successful and that it would make me big, but it did. Many people appreciate what I do, and it gives them pleasure. As a result of that, my business is big now. I've learned that to limit myself is a negative approach to life. And I realize that you can be big and do something that's kind of terrific at the same time.

BLDD: You talk about always doing something fresh and new. Are there any Kamali designs that you think of as classics, or that you'd like to have become classic?

NK: I think the sleeping bag coat is not going to go to sleep on us. It just keeps wanting to come back. It came from my sleeping bag, and it worked, that's what gives it a long life. The concept of a coat made like a sleeping bag, that you could roll up into the bag you got it in originally, that stores well, is light and comfortable and warm in the winter is what it's about. There is only one sleeping bag coat. It works. I'm not going to change it because nothing that anybody else did or that I did was better. Sometimes it's better to leave well enough alone. I've changed color every once in a while, but that's it.

BLDD: Whatever gave you the idea to design children's wear? Your mother's talent? Your friends' children?

NK: It came about when I did sportswear. We did a window with big dolls in it. We made miniature versions of all the sportswear and put them on the dolls. I opened a can of worms. People said, "Hey, look at this. What kid wouldn't want that?" Then I thought, "Yeah. I guess you're right. It is kind of cute." The best thing I ever did was actually doing that, because I've learned so much from children.

BLDD: Your clothes look exciting, trendy, from time to time—wild. Is that a great contrast to the kind of life you lead personally?

NK: I am conservative. I come from a time where drugs were very important and I never took any drugs. I look like something else, and I'm not. I'm the complete opposite I think. What I express in my work is all that stuff inside. I have a conservative nature and I want to live a very simple way. Nothing is complicated. Nothing is wild and crazy. It's very basic and simple. But it's not boring. It's a lot of fun.

BLDD: In spite of your self-described "Calvinist" lifestyle, people within the trade call you "Hot Kamali." How does that make you feel?

NK: It's my bathing suit. I think it started with my bathing suits because they were the tiniest little things. A lot of very straight women shop in here, lawyers that are very, very well-respected in their fields that look like they would never wear any of my clothes. But they wear my wildest bathing suits. So I guess there's a side of everybody that would wear something like that. It doesn't make *me* a "Hot Kamali" though.

BLDD: As Norma Kamali grows older, will her fashions mature with her? What happens to that sense of humor, that sense of whimsy, irony, and often impracticality?

NK: That will be there. It has to be. I think I'm going to be wilder when I'm in my sixties and seventies than I ever was. I'm looking forward to it! Then there will be total freedom to say, "Hey, why not."

BLDD: You're very involved in physical fitness. Do you think the growth of the physical fitness movement has influenced your fashions?

NK: Since I've been involved in swimwear for nine years, I can't help but be aware of physical fitness, the body, and fabrics that deal with exercise and dance. When the whole exercise thing became important, a lot of the clothes I was doing worked for it. And I've done more.

It's a dream to exercise in the privacy in your home with a cassette and let your fat fly, and look terrible and silly and obnoxious while you're doing it. It is such a great opportunity to take care of yourself, if you want to, privately. If you're an active woman being physically fit is very important. That doesn't mean that we're that way all the time. I stopped smoking two years ago and gained twenty pounds. I thought, "I can't believe that this is happening. But I don't want to smoke anymore." I'd decided that was it. So I dealt with this weight and the trauma of it.

It was devastating, especially every time I had to do another collection and think about looking good in clothes. Here I had this body that I never saw before in my life. It was as though I had to be that weight so I could understand being that weight and wearing clothes. That helped me understand the trauma of putting something on and feeling horrible, especially with my clothing and sportswear collection. I thought about clothes that looked great that don't show everything—it was key to being helpful. I learned, "I don't want to be this way. I know how to do clothes to make me look better, but now I just want to lose this weight."

It took concentration, changing my diet, and changing the food I ate.

When I saw weight coming off I decided to get my body back in shape, and I got a Jane Fonda tape.

BLDD: Did you ever anticipate the popularity of your sweats? Do you think their popularity has distorted your image by focusing a disproportionate amount of attention on what is actually a very small part of your work?

NK: The sweats in that sportswear collection represent affordable sportswear for a lot of people, including me. It makes sense and it's practical, and I have a lot of freedom in sportswear to be creative. Then when I want to do things that are not so practical and maybe more expensive, I have the other part of my business that gives me that freedom. I reach a lot of people with the sportswear. It's not stopping my creativity by any stretch of the imagination. It's giving me more opportunity to do other things.

BLDD: Is there any dream project that you have yet to do?

NK: Cosmetics. That's going to be a lot of fun. I've been talking to people, and we're in the negotiation state. I have ideas that I don't think are out there right now. It's the challenge that's exciting.

BLDD: You seem to respond eagerly to a new challenge. Is that how you are generally perceived?

NK: I still don't think I'm totally aware of how people see me, but I'm surprised when people know about who Norma Kamali is. It's almost like Norma Kamali is another person and I'm who I am. I *am* who I am, and Norma Kamali is who everybody thinks she is. They're two different people. I know that because people act differently toward me when they know I'm Norma Kamali than when they don't. For that alone, I know I want to keep her over there and keep me over here.

BLDD: What do you want to become important for you?

NK: The only thing that is very important to me right now is video and communicating fashion through video.

BLDD: You've used multi-level video cameras as window display. It may be the ultimate contemporary communicator. Why do you use that to represent you, and how is video connected to your life as you see it now?

NK: The whole form of communication through video is at its earliest stages, and it works for music and fashion because music and fashion are of the moment. Video captures a moment spontaneously in a simple way. As we use it more, it'll be simpler still and more and more people will be able to touch it and be a part of it. This is a kind of communication that I have to know. We're producing a video every season that we do a collection. This is exciting in itself because it's a new form of creativity for us. I just know that that video is going to become like a catalogue, something else that's a part of what our world is about. Women who work want to sit at home and look through a catalogue. It makes life easy, especially buying stockings and shirts and things. Taking that one step further, when you can sit and put a video on your screen and say, "Oh, that's great," or "that moves very well." Then you're communicating again in another way. And that's just the beginning of it. How exciting it is to see where it's going to go. I want to know everything about it because I want to use it for my business and personally, too.

BLDD: If you had a young friend, a cousin, a niece, who had more taste than funds and wanted to put a new wardrobe together, what advice would you give to her?

NK: Everybody's needs are different. Once people realize, first of all, what they look like, not what the girl in the photograph looks like in that dress, but what they look like and they say it out loud, then they can go anywhere and try on clothes and build up the terrific and diminish the negative. That's the basics. Everybody can look at any fashion magazine and see what's the latest fashion, but it's how you do it for yourself. That's the most important thing.

Norma Kamali, fall, 1985

HK

Herbert Kasper

Kasper's designs redefine our idea of comfort and luxury. His clothes are in tune with those who have a keen eye for enduring design—design that pays attention to details and to one's budget: classic clothes at affordable prices.

BLDD: There's something that I've always wanted to ask you. Is Kasper your first or your last name?

HK: Kasper's my last name. It's *Herbert* Kasper. But soon after I began working, Lord & Taylor decided they would like to promote me as one of their young American designers, and they came up with the idea of Kasper. So it's been Kasper since then.

BLDD: You've always known the value of words, and you've known, too, what your clients want. Advertising, which you studied as an undergraduate, depends on a very finely tuned sense of both. Was your study of advertising good preparation for your career as a fashion designer?

HK: I would say that it's removed, yet in a sense related. What helps a designer more than anything is just life itself. I think advertising's interesting. I think studying English would be interesting. I think studying the theatre would be interesting. A designer should be aware of what life's all about, and what's going on, and then to tune into that part of life he or she would like to serve. Whether you're a junior designer—a misses or contemporary designer—I think the point is to use your knowledge of what's happening in the world and then to zero in on what suits your talent, your taste and your potential market. So, I'm sure advertising has in some way affected me, but, what is more important, is the sum total of many influences.

BLDD: Right after college, you served with the Occupation Forces in Germany. What kind of assignment does a business major from New York University get with the Army in Germany?

HK: I wasn't really a business major. I was marking time, trying, with a very decided goal, to have a general education. From the time I was about ten years old I wanted to be a designer. Not that I was that aggressive about pursuing it, but in my mind that's what I always thought I would be. Whatever I did was to get to that. In the Army I started out as a company clerk in the medical corps. After that I was transferred to Special Services and I became a glorified chorus boy. But I was then sent, after a period of time with the company, to battalion headquarters, in Wiesbaden, Germany. There is a large opera house in Wiesbaden, and the USO, and Special Services, and all forces that had to do with that kind of work, used the opera house. While I was there the band in one of the shows had jackets—I guess you could call it a single-breasted men's jacket—made of some white fabric. They washed them and they shrunk. In my naive way I said, "Well, why don't you just cut them down and make little mess jackets out of them?" That was my first experience as a designer, and I think I was labeled "designer" after that.

BLDD: Did you continue to design for your company?

HK: I was really bored being in some of the shows as a glorified hoofer. As a child I had been to dancing school. But then, the quality of talent in the Army is not always the highest. I started designing costumes for soldier shows. I did one show and it was a tremendous experience; it was really more guts on my part than talent. Certainly I was not professional. It was funny and sad at the same time. On the day of the dress rehearsal, when all the people on the stage were in the costumes that I'd designed, they did not look that bad. But as I looked at the positioning of the clothes and the players, I realized that it's quite another thing to place one color and design against another. That revelation has really been most helpful to me in designing. Because I spent a lot of time with a photographer, especially early in my career, one of the things I've always done is to look at clothes as if it were through the eye of a camera. Designing a dress, whether it's putting the buttons on, or seeing how it fits a woman or how it moves—which is also terribly important—I think of it through the eyes of a camera or like looking at the stage. Since you deal a lot in architecture, you know what I mean when I say I think about a design in terms of levels.

BLDD: What happened when you were ten years old that gave you the idea to become a designer?

HK: Somebody asked me, "And, little boy, what would you like to be when you grow up?" And I said, "A fashion designer." Actually, I never said "fashion designer." I'm sure it wasn't in my vocabulary. I might have said "dress designer," at that age.

BLDD: After your experience in the Army you returned to New York and entered the Parsons School of Design. Soon after that you had the good fortune to become the protegé of a milliner. How did that relationship come about?

HK: It's a funny story. I met John Fredericks, who had been a partner of Mr. Fred during the Depression since the early '30's. The company was called John Fredericks—"John" for Mr. John and "Fredericks" for Fred Fredericks. When I met him, I was in my second year at Parsons School of Design. During the course of a year you have two projects, and at the end of the year a jury selects certain designs for the fashion show of that year. Both of my designs were selected. One of them had a fabulous cape, all cut on the bias—it almost looked like a cocoon. It was quite wonderful. Today it really doesn't mean as much, but it was done in beige wool and lined in beige and black polka-dot. At that time, as I remember, nobody used print linings in coats. Anyway, it was the one that Fred Fredericks bought. I didn't know it was he who bought it; he sent his designer to buy it because he was afraid that I might want too much money. He didn't know how excited I'd be to have him buy it, as most kids would be. About a week later, he called saying that he had bought the coat and asked if I would like to come and see him. Of course, I went. He said he thought I had a lot of talent and he would hire me to work for him. I had decided to spend my third year in Paris so I said no. He gave me letters of introduction, said "Send me sketches," and was really very nice. Through him I met one of my very, very dear friends, who was one of his oldest friends. His name was Maurice van Moppes. He was a famous Dutch illustrator living in Paris, a quite wonderful man, who died in an accident about ten years ago. The fact was I could not draw a hat on a head. I couldn't draw four legs on a horse and make it look like the horse was standing. And I was too embarrassed to say I couldn't sketch. I tried, but I guess I didn't try hard enough, because I couldn't do it. About six months later, Fred came to Paris, and we went around the shops, buying fabrics and ribbons and so forth. He asked if I would send him sketches, and I promised and then he went home again and I didn't send any. About two months later I got the most horrible letter I have ever received from anyone. It frightened me so, because he said, "You're an idiot. You're selfish. You're lazy," everything negative that could be said. And he added, "On top of that, you're blowing it, because you're losing the contact of somebody who can be very helpful to you." I thought about it again, and decided I'd better do something.

BLDD: What did you do?

HK: I bought *Chapeaux*, a magazine that was devoted solely to hats, and I started tracing faces, heads, and hats, and started to get the hang of it. I suppose I was just frightened into it. I started to sketch and then I just didn't stop. I had already done a great deal of research. I would go to the museums in Paris and look at wonderful paintings, and to the library, and see shapes of hats, and it was very inspiring. I had lots of ideas. I just couldn't put it on paper. But when I started sketching it was like a well running over. I used to send him sixty to a hundred sketches a week. He was very, very excited about it and loved what I sent him. I did crazy things, like jeweled buckles for evening pumps, and all kinds of novelty boutique ideas.

BLDD: What did he do with all your sketches?

HK: He used some of them. One thing I did became quite a fad in hats. When I was at Parsons, "the New Look" came in, and we used to sew horsehair in the bottom of those big full skirts to make them stand out. This was 1949. I guess I had horsehair on the brain, but I thought to myself, "There must be something better to do with horsehair than have it in the hem of a skirt." I started playing with it and draping it around, making crowns. And I came up with the idea of taking a sailor hat and turning it inside-out so the crown goes one way and the brim another. I did a hat with a crown made out of mesh, out of net, and then used the horsehair for the brim, creating the wonderful shimmering shadow that horsehair has. It was quite beautiful and very sexy. I then continued playing with it and draping it, and putting jewels in the middle of it. It was really the beginning of all the nose veils that women wore in the early '50's.

BLDD: Were you involved with millinery when you returned to this country?

HK: I went to work with Fred Fredericks and stayed there about three months and hated it. During that time I did the clothes for a play, as well as the accessories and hats, everything, but I just didn't like it. A friend of mine told me about a job on Broadway, which is really the wrong side of the tracks. I got a job in this tiny little company through the only friend that I had in the business. He told me that they hire you in the morning and fire you in the evening. I kept that job for about three months and the buyer at Lord & Taylor's bought some of my clothes. One of them turned out to be the best dress he ever had. I still joke about it—I don't think he knew if I had talent or was just lucky. But he kept coming back, and he bought more clothes, and that was my introduction to Lord & Taylor. That's when they decided to promote me.

BLDD: Going back to when you were in Paris, I assume you went because you wanted to work for a couture house. In those days and perhaps, still, an apprenticeship in Paris was practically a prerequisite for any aspiring designer.

HK: I did it more on a freelance basis. First I went to school and then I started to freelance. I worked for Christian Dior, and Jacques Fath, and a few other houses, but I wasn't apprenticed to one house.

BLDD: What did you do?

HK: I would go see them and they'd show me things. And I sold a lot of sketches to magazines. It was a rounded training. I think it would have been interesting to work in a couture house, but this gave me something that I wanted, and I liked the maneuverability and the opportunity to travel a lot.

BLDD: Do you think your designs would be different now if you had never lived and worked in Paris?

HK: It's hard to say. I was weaned on the couture and yet when I went back to New York, because my clothes were "young," yet sophisticated, and I was young, my designs were set at a much more moderate price range. That was completely different from my training and thinking, because at that time even at Parsons everything was done in the manner of the couture. We did all our own sewing and every detail was done by hand. That was the whole idea. You would never have a button without a buttonhole, and the buttonhole would always be handmade. Today you might have a dress with rows of buttons without one buttonhole.

BLDD: Is there any hand tailoring or hand detailing in the clothes that you make now?

HK: Oh sure—not to that degree, but a lot of clothes are made in the Orient, and therefore they do have more handwork, because there it's more feasible.

BLDD: In your experience, who would you say are the most legendary figures in fashion? Which ones have been the most influential, in general, and for your own work?

HK: Chanel, absolutely. Chanel is like Carole Lombard. Every time you look at it, it's just right. There's a picture of Chanel, wearing a sweater, I think, and a sailor hat to one side, with all the pearls and the jewels that she wore. It was probably done about 1936. I think she's sitting down, wearing a pair of what looks like wide-legged trousers. The classic sense of quality about Chanel was certainly inspirational for me and always will be. Norman Norell was influential because I grew up when his career was ending and mine was just beginning. He was certainly a classicist with great taste. Mainbocher was wonderful. He had a sense of detail that was fabulous, a true dressmaker. Balenciaga was also a dressmaker; his sense of purity was like Norman Norell's. Before that, I would say Vionnet because she draped her clothes. They were all done on the bias and the intricacy of the work was incredible. Poiret had great imagination and fantasy.

BLDD: And to the work of which of these designers do you think your work most responds?

HK: I would like to think it's closest to Chanel. Another incredible designer was Claire McCardell. She used fabrics with such originality. And she had a sense of simplicity.

BLDD: Did she introduce American "sportswear?"

Herbert Kasper, fall, 1981

HK: She's recognized as one of the first American designers of sportswear, also one of the first American designers of renown.

BLDD: You mentioned earlier that you were promoted by Lord & Taylor. I wonder if the policies of that store, or any other, were particularly important in vaunting American fashion? American fashion, as I understand, was in pretty much the same boat as American art until post–World War II, not highly considered.

HK: That's absolutely true. I would say that Lord & Taylor made a reputation of fostering the American designer. Dorothy Shaver, then president of Lord & Taylor, was responsible for that. Obviously she was brilliant. In the '30's, stores that were in competition went to Europe to buy collections, brought clothes back and had them copied. The "American designer" may have existed, but never received recognition. Not even in the '50's, as I remember. Until the '60's, a store like Saks Fifth Avenue rarely promoted a designer unless he was confined to them. To them merchandising meant promoting Saks Fifth Avenue's name on their clothes, not the designer's.

BLDD: That must have been the pre–designer label era, when the store's name was thought to be more important than the designer's.

HK: I don't think the designer label really became important until the '60's.

BLDD: What caused that change?

HK: I think it was a natural evolution. In post-war art and design, one designer after another had a successful career, and it became a growing trend.

BLDD: I guess before that most American fashion houses were known by the names of their manufacturers rather than their designers.

HK: That was true, too. Today, some designers own their own companies, and have their own label and some have their name plus that of the company, but it's always the designer that's promoted.

BLDD: If we were to pursue that analogy of art and fashion, would it be accurate, or merely chauvinistic, to say that American fashion, too, is now pre-eminent in the world?

HK: I think that in France, the French designer is still much, much more important. They are very guarded and jealous of that position. There's great talent over there and the designer's position is well-deserved. American fashion is not as accepted there as it is in this country, though many French people love and buy American clothes.

BLDD: Is American design imitated by French designers at all?

HK: In some ways. I wouldn't say imitated, but influenced. When designers come here they take something of the American atmosphere and spirit back with them. Look what's happened to jeans. It's a universal fashion.

BLDD: Have we made any other contribution to fashion through native American dress, other than jeans?

HK: One big contribution is sportswear. The Europeans never thought of fashion in terms of sportswear until it became a big thing with the Americans and then throughout the world. Sportswear—the concept of dressing in pieces and parts—started here in America.

BLDD: Was it because of our less formal lifestyle?

HK: That has a great deal to do with it. You have to remember that until the late '60's a great deal of the designing was only done by the couture, and copied and filtered down in Europe, in France and in Italy. Prêt à porter didn't really begin until the '60's.

BLDD: What does prêt-à-porter actually mean?

HK: Prêt means "ready," porter, "to take". . . It's off the rack, versus custom-made, and therefore less expensive. It's opposed to couture, high fashion, which was always made to order.

BLDD: You talked earlier about designers being the sum total of their experience, that they really have to know about life before they design something. Paintings, ballet, art exhibitions, films, and travel are all part of the raw materials of a great designer. From which of these arts do you especially draw inspiration?

HK: All of them, but the visual arts make the major contribution. I've seen dozens of Matisse shows. When I was in Paris in 1970 I saw this incredible Matisse show, with all the bright colors that I had seen dozens or maybe

Herbert Kasper, spring, 1981

hundreds of times before. For some reason it just clicked in my brain and I responded to it. The colors were really right. Within legal means, I swiped paintings or parts of cutouts of Matisse, and I had some textile designers work on these ideas that I wanted using postcards and books, and I did a collection of prints centered around Matisse. It was fabulous. I did organza, crêpe de chine, and cotton, and the color derived from that collection. I think most designers are always attracted and influenced by the arts.

BLDD: You are very much interested in the visual arts, and a collector yourself. In addition to Matisse, is there any other artist to whom you especially respond?

HK: At the moment, Léger.

BLDD: And what has Léger done for you lately?

HK: It's what he may do. I am now being influenced by many things in the Art Deco period. Something will probably evolve out of that. I've already seen it in some print designs from various collections all over the world. Whether that influence will exhibit itself in the colors or the sharpness of the design or in the actual design, I'm not yet sure. But Art Deco will certainly be an influence.

BLDD: Do foreign countries or history inspire you?

HK: I remember being in a museum in Leningrad and looking at some clothes. The excitement of the color and the embroidery was so interesting. That was a tremendous influence on my collection, and in many others at one time. The Hapsburg era has been another inspiration.

BLDD: And what can we expect in the future?

HK: I'm not sure. The obvious thing is to bring back the bustle. I don't really believe in it as a way of life, but I do think dresses with back interest will be part of the collection for next fall.

BLDD: Can you picture women in the mid-1980's wearing a bustle?

HK: No, but I could see some kind of fabric being draped up in the back, and maybe a big train or a cascade or a hemline that is short in the front and long in the back. I think it is sad that designers are always very guarded about their talent or their ideas. They don't have seminars or talk sessions, nor do they ever have anyone except very close friends visit their collections. Doctors on the other hand may have other doctors read their journals or their reports, or have sessions which may be meetings of the mind. Ideas obviously influence designers, and one idea leads to another, but I always feel that what's important isn't whether you take an idea from somebody or what it is—it's how you use the idea. In other words, if you just lift something and say, "O.K. I'm going to take this neckline and put it over here and make it my neckline," that's copying. But if you look at something, let's say a beautiful open neckline, and you respond to its openness and begin to play with it and create something that's your own, that is taking an idea and going on to something of your own. I think that's growth.

BLDD: How much of that exists among fashion designers?

HK: It happens more than people admit. I could list five designers who go to a collection and I can see what they take from it. The point isn't that they've been influenced but how they use that idea.

BLDD: Are there any designers whom you consider among your close friends or associates with whom you discuss professional matters?

HK: No. One doesn't really talk about them. Though I know many designers, I'm not that close to most of them. It's difficult for people within the same field to be very close. In some way you hold back. I've had young people show me their portfolios, but they don't want me to look them over on my own. Print designers respond like that. I'll say, "Well, look, if I were to take this, that would be one of your ideas, but hopefully you're going to have a lot more ideas than this, or you'll never go on." That's the essence of it. People are very guarded about their work and their ideas.

BLDD: You began your design career in the early 1950's based on what you called, I think, a "collection premise." What did you have in mind?

HK: That goes back to my training in Paris. One of the great trials and tribulations of my career is the fact that I never had any apprenticeship. When I had the job that I told you about, I was given one sample hand, which is someone who sews, and she had one machine, and she cut and sewed the clothes after my sketches. I followed the process step-by-step

and learned it on my own. I did this for a few months and the world didn't fall apart, but then I did a spring collection—my first collection—and made about fifty designs. I didn't know anything about merchandising—if you have so many slim skirts you should also make some full skirts, if you have no waistlines, make some waistlines, if you have mostly short sleeves, make sure you also have a full sleeve. I just made what I liked, and it was a phenomenal overnight success. It was brilliant as far as the audience could see. My problem was how to go on to the next collection. Now that I was a full-fledged successful designer, I didn't know what to do. I didn't know how to begin the next collection. I became frightened by my own success.

BLDD: And what did you do?

HK: I stumbled through it, and, luckily—knock on wood—I stumbled through it well. It was a learning process for me. I've gone to schools and talked to students and told them that one of the most important things is to have a learning period from which to grow. I had to have my own learning period. So, for me it was rather difficult at first. The fact is that you have to begin somewhere. When I began designing my first collection, I just did clothes I liked. For the second collection, I had to think differently—they still had to be clothes I liked, but I had to know why I was doing it. I zeroed in on an audience. I didn't really know who my audience was at the beginning, but I learned. For example, I did a lot of clothes with back interest. As a matter of fact, one of my very first dresses and one of my biggest successes was a dress that could be worn backwards as well.

BLDD: What did it look like?

HK: It was a wrap dress, with a high bateau neck in the front, short sleeves, and a wrap back, but you could take the back and wrap it around the front and have a V-neck with a high back. At that time it was rather novel and interesting. I really didn't have a premise at the beginning because I really didn't know what to do, except to make clothes that I liked. One thing that I did learn, and it has always stayed with me, is the fact that when women bought clothes at the couture—and I used to go to all the shows and watch and listen—they went planning to spend thousands of dollars. In the same way a housekeeper or wife might go and shop in the A&P, the typical customer had a marketing list. She would say, "Well, I'm spending three months in Paris and I'm going to St. Moritz for Christmas and I'm going to South America in February . . ."

BLDD: The way everybody lives.

HK: Obviously more so today. Then it was really the chosen few, and they would buy clothes to fit the schedule for the year, a certain amount of clothes—not a lot necessarily—that would suit that lifestyle. What I learned as a young man and have used in my professional life, is to design a coat, and with it a skirt and a blouse, and then perhaps a dress to go with it as well. Then sometimes I would do a short evening dress that would go with that same coat, either in the sense of its colors, texture or fabric. What I tried to do was to present a capsule wardrobe within the collection. In a sense, that is the premise of sportswear, to buy pieces that work together. Now, for example, if you're wearing a jacket, that same jacket might be worn over a slim black silk dress; it could be worn with the print of the skirt of its own; you could wear it with a long dinner skirt or a pair of evening pants or even a pair of wool pants.

BLDD: Shortly after Joan Leslie was founded about twenty years ago, along about 1964, your label was included in its collection. How did you come to work with Joan Leslie, and just who is Joan Leslie?

HK: Joan Leslie is a fictitious name; it's a trade name. There was an actress named Joan Leslie in the '40's or '50's. She played the girl-next-door. In the beginning a lawsuit was brought against the company because she sued them, but the judge came up with the fact that her name was as fictitious as that of the company, so they both had a right to the name. I had been with another company, and before I left I met the principals of the company I'm now with, and we liked each other and decided that I would work for them. That's how it began.*

*It ended after twenty years in March, 1985 when Kasper started an entirely independent company.

Herbert Kasper, fall, 1982

BLDD: You've said you believe that clothes should not wear the woman, she should wear the clothes. What do you mean by that?

HK: It's about using a wardrobe. I think that clothes really have to become part of the woman, her wardrobe, her life and her style. Once you're aware of what you're wearing, you are no longer yourself. Clothes have to have ease, flexibility. Originally this was more an American concept: you have to make your own wardrobe. Let's say that you bought this off-the-rack, ready-to-wear dress. A lot of other women will buy the same thing. Rather than look like one of a bunch of cookies from the same mold, you might wear your hair differently. You might wear different makeup. You might take the jacket and wear it with something else. You might wear the dress at the same time, but it's the way you wear it, the way make it feel, so that it becomes part of your life and part of your style.

BLDD: If I could buy just one thing for my wardrobe this year, what should it be?

HK: It changes. Sometimes skirts are in, or pants are in, or the shape of a certain pant is in one year. A few years ago it was a shawl, stole, or scarf. If you're buying one thing—I hope you will buy more than one thing—it should be either a slim skirt with some sort of side opening or a front opening to show leg, or an easy sweater, with dropped shoulders, something that is a sweater-blouse. But the skirt should be the focal point.

BLDD: Any particular color?

HK: I would say black, because black is something you might wear in the day and also in the evening, and I would buy a longer length. That's what I would buy for fall.

BLDD: What do you mean, a longer length?

HK: We're now showing skirts just touching the knee, about a 30-inch length. And I think that if one has the right proportions for it, a longer length with a slit on the side or a front opening would be very elegant, because it would be pretty in the winter, and you could wear it with boots, and it would be a wonderful skirt to wear in the evening. It's something that could fit into your daily life.

BLDD: Let's talk about those who have more taste than funds. If someone had five or six hundred dollars, was about to start a new job or received money as a gift, and wanted to start a new wardrobe, what would you tell them to buy, particularly emphasizing clothes that could be used for multiple purposes? What's the basic wardrobe for a limited amount of money?

HK: Obviously I would say you should buy sportswear. What's very important about fashion today is that there is no "one" look. I think versatility is fashionable. Different lengths, silhouettes, colors, and fabrics make fashion what it is. It isn't one thing only that makes fashion.

BLDD: How about a coat? How can you buy a coat in that price range and still have money for everything else?

HK: I'd better become a comparison shopper, not a designer, because I'm not sure of prices. I know they exist, but to ask me how to buy a decent coat is an unfair question, because I really don't know prices. I know what *my* prices are, and I know there are lower prices, but I'm not sure what you could get in the stores for a particular price. Probably the largest investment would be for a coat. I'm sure you could buy a nice coat for $200. I would buy a slim skirt, and I'm sure you can get a good-looking skirt for about $100. So that's $300. You could certainly buy a pretty blouse for about $60. You could buy a blouse that you might wear for day and a blouse that you might wear for evening. So that's $120. We'd better make it $600! Let's say you wanted to buy a sweater. What might look very new is a turtleneck sweater.

BLDD: All over again?

HK: Yes. So, you could buy a turtleneck sweater for about $50. So that's close to $500. I'd say the other thing is to buy a pair of shoes. Could you buy a decent pair of shoes for $50 or $60? Probably if you really looked around, I'm sure that you could get some things for a little less. Then you might be able to buy a pair of pants or trousers. And I think that would be fabulous. But I would like to add something about price. If one really has a limited amount of money—and it's the way I've lived my own life when I didn't have a lot of money to spend—I would rather buy one or two things that have some kind of quality and pizzazz about them, not necessarily faddish, of the moment, but classic. Whether it be a coat that's a trenchcoat or another style, it should be something that will have longevity. I'd rather buy two things, or maybe even one, and have it be fabulous, because it makes everything else more interesting. Unless buying that wardrobe is what you want to do or what you have to do, I would say buy only a few things, because less, is really more.

BLDD: I've heard that before. Is it more important to have fabulous shoes or a fabulous bag or a fabulous sweater? If you're going to indulge yourself in one item of clothing, what should it be?

HK: I've always believed what's important is a good-looking bag or a good-looking pair of shoes. And they are expensive. I shopped for a bag for Christmas, and I know what they cost. But there are lots of wonderful-looking clothes that are very much with it, elegant, stylish, and can be had for prices that fit into that budget. I do feel that putting money into clothes is a worthwhile investment, because one beautiful item will always add tone to what you're wearing. People do see it and respond to it. That is very important in dressing as well.

BLDD: Provided those items of clothing last. What is the best way to take care of clothes?

HK: For a bag or shoes, some kind of cream or polish is necessary to keep the leather well-lubricated. If you're really being careful—regardless of what you have—if you really care, it's best to take a bag and put it in a sack or in a drawer at night, not just fling it some place and have it get scratched and worn out. It's like taking care of your body or taking care of your home; it's all part of the same thing. One has to have a respect for clothes and to take care of them the same way.

BLDD: When a woman enters a department store and is confronted with racks and racks of clothes, and hundreds of choices, what do you think determines what she's going to select?

HK: I think she should look for a Kasper and buy it and go home immediately.

BLDD: And that's enough! What do you think it is that women look for? Is it style or fabric or fit?

HK: I think that women respond first to color. If you see racks of clothes, you're going to respond to something that comes out at you. If everything on the rack is black or grey or blue and there's some color that intrigues you, you'll reach out for it. The next thing is, when you reach for it and hold it up, you're touching it. I think if the touch is pleasant you respond to it. Then you actually look at it, and if you like the style, you'll put it on. I would put price last. If you really love it, unless it's totally out of your range, you should buy it. I have always said that one has to have a love affair with a dress or a coat or a blouse, whatever it is.

BLDD: That's asking a lot from an article of clothing.

HK: In a way you have to, because what clothes do for a woman or a man, is to give an emotional release. When you put something on and feel good, you feel different about everything, about yourself, and where you are. Clothes do that for you. You do respond to clothes emotionally, so that although the price is important, it may be the last thing you consider. Obviously once you put something on, it has to fit and look well. If it does, that's the clincher.

BLDD: And how much of it depends upon advertising and promotion?

HK: A lot. People often ask for particular items that have been advertised. Why do stores run full-page fashion ads? Because it brings people into the store. Advertising is tremendously important.

BLDD: I know you're very much interested in classic design. You made reference before to fads. What is the difference between fads and fashion?

HK: A fad is something that's short-lived, that might last for just a few months or a season. A fashion is like a good idea, the evolution of many things. It's a growth process. As it evolves, a fashion may go through a beginning, a rise and even a decline. But a fashion usually stays with us over a period of time.

BLDD: What are you working on now?

HK: I'm in the middle of doing what I hope will be a big success in active sportswear for fall. It's what I'm calling "weekend wear," clothes you may not even wear for sports.

BLDD: So it's not a jogging suit.

HK: Well, I'm also doing jogging suits. If you look in the streets today, in New York City on a Saturday, you'll see people wearing jogging suits not only for jogging but for shopping and as a way of dressing, a uniform. It's like wearing jeans; it's that kind of dressing. I'm beginning a large collection this fall. The major items are dresses and sportswear. I also do scarves and sweaters.

BLDD: Does the design of furniture interest you?

HK: Yes, but I'm more interested in visual things in the sense of lifestyles, for instance, place settings, tableware.

BLDD: Have you done that?

HK: No, but I would love to, and I think I would do it very well. I would love to design furniture, but I don't think that I would be able to design a series of furniture collections. There are those people who do it far better than I can and who are knowledgeable. Not that I wouldn't have a sense of style about it. But I might do only one chair. It would be a whole other way of life for me, and I'd really have to get involved in it.

BLDD: It's obvious by looking at you that you have a keen sense of personal style. Have you ever been intrigued by the idea of designing for men?

HK: Yes. I also do men's clothes, and I'm now going into weekend wear for men.

BLDD: How has your own style of dressing changed over the years? Have you always put yourself together so carefully, and so colorfully?

HK: It's what we call "calculated casualness."

BLDD: Well, it works.

HK: I would say so.

BLDD: Are you less formal today than you were in the past?

HK: Much less. I think the world we live in is much less formal. Sometimes I go to work in a turtleneck sweater and jeans or a sport jacket and trousers. But when I first started I always wore a suit and a shirt and a tie.

BLDD: How would you define "style"?

HK: "Style" is taste. "Style" is originality. "Style" is being yourself, being personal.

BLDD: How do you define "glamour"?

HK: "Glamour" is an illusion. Going back to the idea of a love affair with clothes, glamour is really an emotion. It's a feeling and that's what fashion is all about.

BLDD: Is "glamour" allure—that sense of mystery, or drama, in small or large measure, most women, and I suspect many men, would most like to achieve?

HK: Yes. When you just said "glamour," I thought of mystery. That is certainly a part of it. But today, the free style of life can also be glamorous. "Glamorous" is in essence appeal.

BLDD: Who best exemplifies those qualities for you?

HK: My wife. But there are lots of other people. It's not just one thing alone. A woman may be mysterious, exotic. Another woman may be fresh and alive and clean-cut.

BLDD: Whatever happened to sensuous dressing? Is that a part of all this freshness and openness, too?

HK: It's another way of dressing. Fashion is multi-faceted. Fashion isn't one look. One can be sensuous at night or one can be a sensuous human being in one's particular style. One might be casual, clean-cut and simple and yet glamorous. Would you say that Katherine Hepburn was a glamorous woman in her youth? I think she was. I certainly think someone like Carole Lombard was glamorous. You go back to the sirens such as Jean Harlow or Marilyn Monroe—they were glamorous people.

BLDD: Who are their contemporary counterparts?

HK: Meryl Streep comes to mind, but I don't know if I would call her glamorous because the parts that she plays create an illusion that's not necessarily one of glamour. Karen Black is a more sensuous being, as far as actresses go. Maybe it takes time. One may react to stars because of their success, but it takes time for a legend to become a legend. When Marilyn Monroe was alive, obviously everybody thought she was glamorous, but I don't see anybody now who has the style to create that. Racquel Welch is certainly glamorous and sexy. Lauren Bacall is glamorous in her own way.

BLDD: You said you can't feed your ego by designing clothes that no one will wear. What special means do you use to find out what interests the

Herbert Kasper, fall, 1981

Herbert Kasper, fall, 1981

women for whom you design? Who do you see as your audience, and what do you think they want to wear?

HK: I like to think of my audience as being educated, not only in terms of schooling, but also educated by traveling and doing things, people who are multi-faceted. It's the woman at home with the children, the woman who has gone to college, who may have worked, may still be working and who's interested in lots of things. I'm interested in that kind of person because clothes become part of her life. She makes clothes part of her style. I find that kind of a woman more interesting and more demanding to design for. Rather than saying, "O.K. This is what you wear. This is the way you'll look," there has to be a give-and-take. I am educated by going out and talking to people. I like to meet all kinds of people—it's a way of life. It all helps me in my work.

BLDD: By the way, how do you feed *your* ego in this design process?

HK: By being successful!

BLDD: How important is the fashion press to the popularity of a design? Do you liken the work of a fashion writer to that of a theatre critic?

HK: Oh sure, of course. It's all part of the same thing. A designer shows a collection about five times a year. There's what we call Fall One and Fall Two, the total of which is a fall collection. Then you do a holiday cruise collection. Then you do a spring collection, and a summer collection. Each time you do one, like in show business, you put your head on the block. It's very difficult. Obviously applause, a pat on the back, is what feeds one's ego.

HK: And sales?

HK: Absolutely. Like show business, it's very difficult. Each time you begin a collection, even though you have a reputation and you are successful, it's like starting all over again. Last season's or last year's success is really short-lived, and the new success or failure is going to be based on what you do now.

BLDD: If each season is like beginning all over again, how do you sustain yourself?

HK: By that very thing. It's the excitement that's created each time. That's why I always consider myself lucky—not only because I am talented and I have made it work, but to be in a business as interesting as it is. Though at times I absolutely hate it. It is demanding and it is difficult. But there are very few businesses or careers where you can turn yourself on so many times a year just by looking at new colors and new fabrics and new ideas. There's a sense of keeping yourself bubbling and thinking and going all the time.

BLDD: If you had it to do over again, what would you do differently?

HK: The only other thing I really would have liked to have been would be a psychiatrist. And that's not so far-fetched. Being a designer I'm involved and interested in people. You're giving something to them. I am very much interested in psychiatry, psychology, the mind, and human behavior.

BLDD: Did you ever expect your life to unfold the way it has?

HK: Well, I said from the time I was ten years old I wanted to be a fashion designer!

Donna Karan and Louis Dell'Olio for Anne Klein

Donna Karan and Louis Dell'Olio are the recent names behind the celebrated Anne Klein Label.* Classically tailored and crisply elegant, the clothes they make are intended to suit the lifestyle of the sophisticated, multi-roled contemporary woman.

BLDD: Under what circumstances did your collaboration with Louis Dell'Olio begin?

DK: I became an assistant of Anne Klein's in 1968, when the company was first formed. I was still a student at the Parsons School of Design and stayed for quite some time. But, unfortunately, after working with Anne for a good many years, I was fired. Then I came back to work. We had a marvelous relationship. Later when I was pregnant and just about to give birth, Anne was taken ill. Louis and I had always discussed working together so I said, "Louis, why don't you come work with me, because I don't know where my head's going to be. And I know Anne's going to need some help because I'm going to have a baby. I want to stay home and take care of her and I don't want to have the responsibility." He agreed. There were interviews back and forth, and Anne said she was against having the three of us—her, me, and Louis because she felt there would be trouble with three people working together. Unfortunately Louis never did work with Anne for she died before he came to the company. I took over the company eight days later. I was working on an early fall collection, and Anne was in the hospital. We did a preview capsule version of the collection. We had just come back from Europe together, and I had finished fabricating the fall collection in Europe by myself. We did the Versailles show in Paris in 1973, an absolutely incredible show. A group of five American designers were invited to participate with the French to show what American design was all about. I was eight months pregnant at the time.

BLDD: It was one of the first times American design was treated on such an international scale. What precipitated the Versailles show?

DK: It took a lot of work with Eleanor Lambert, Marie Helene Rothschild, Oscar de la Renta, and a number of other people who convinced the French public they should be interested. At that point American design was definitely a stepchild. The fashion world was Paris. Even Italy didn't exist, it was only Paris.

BLDD: Who were the American designers whose work was shown?

DK: Among them were Oscar de la Renta, Bill Blass, Halston, and Anne Klein. As soon as we came back from Versailles Anne became ill. It was January and I had to finish up the early fall collection. I had the baby in March and the collection was due to open in days. The owners of the company and Anne Klein's husband, Chip Rubenstein, asked, "When are you coming back to work? You have to open the collection." I said, "That's ridiculous." Anne was not available at all. After I had the baby they said again, "When are you coming back to work?" When I said I couldn't they said they would have to bring the work to me. And with that the entire company came out to my new house in Lawrence, Long Island. It was quite exciting; I had just brought home my new baby girl. I said "How fantastic, everyone's coming out to see the baby." They actually came out with the clothes. And that very day Anne Klein died. Isn't that amazing? I was going to see her the next day. All this occurred within seven days. I hadn't been to see her at the hospital during my pregnancy. And then she died. I came back to work literally the day after she died. We opened the spring collection and then went to work on the fall collection. I could not stay home and take care of my baby as I had wished. Everyone was happy that "Anne Klein" was going to continue to exist. We had owned a lot of real estate in the stores and people didn't know if the company would continue without her. I don't believe there's an American company that exists today with the name of a deceased designer other than ours. There are of course two French companies that do: Dior and Chanel. But otherwise no other company has existed after the designer died. Anne Klein, God bless her, and her company live on. Louis and I have actually designed the collection for nine years, longer than Anne did. She was fifty when she died and had been designing since she was a young girl, but the Anne Klein company

*Donna Karan and Louis Dell'Olio in the spring of 1985, decided to end their collaboration. Donna Karan now designs under her own label, and Louis Dell'Olio designs for the Anne Klein label.

only started in 1968, and she died in 1973. Before that she designed for Junior Sophisticates. Anne Klein basically established the first American sportswear company. People say that Claire McCardell really organized American sportswear and I believe she did do it, but Anne was responsible for designer collection sportswear of the modern age. She said suburban women were going to wear blazers and trousers and coordinated separates, rather than couture ensembles.

BLDD: Was she the first person to do this?

DK: Yes. Claire McCardell did it years ago, in the '40's. Then there weren't designer's collections of better priced, luxury sportswear.

BLDD: You know a great deal about the recent history of fashion. One of the reasons, I assume, is it could be said you were born into fashion.

DK: I was brought up on Seventh Avenue, there's no doubt about it. Fashion is what we talked about at home. My father who died when I was three, was a mens clothier, and made custom-made suits. The suits he made for my mom were absolutely extraordinary—the shoulder cut, the balance, the proportions were just incredible. My mother started out as a showroom model on Seventh Avenue and later became a major sales representative who sold on the Avenue. Through my mother I made my connections on Seventh Avenue. She worked for Chester Weinberg, Bill Smith, all the main designers. My mother is deceased now. For some reason, openings and death in my family have been quite close. My mother died six years ago on the day my spring collection opened. I did grow up in fashion—I knew the names, the games, and I knew the business. I felt it, I felt clothes, I felt the operation. I felt the hustle and bustle of the showroom. But I was never involved, truly involved in what we consider the main game of the business.

BLDD: What is the main game?

DK: I keep a very low profile on a social level in "the fashion business." I don't luncheon.

BLDD: Why do you choose to do that?

DK: My private life is terribly important to me. I would not be able to dine and lunch and get everything else done and be a mother and a wife. Those two facets of my life conflict with fashion.

BLDD: For how long have you been married?

DK: Happily, for a month and a half. Actually we've been living together for six years, and I've been involved with my husband practically my whole life. We met a long time ago, but the age difference was just too great then—there's ten years between us. I met him when I was 18, and I fell madly in love. He is so wonderful, an artist, so off the beaten track. He has two children. So I have stepchildren now who are twenty and eighteen. My family life is quite active. I miss living in Lawrence, but it wouldn't work to have a home there. Being a working mother is not easy. But I think I'm coming to grips with that, perhaps because my daughter's a little older now. She's nine, and we have fantastic communication. But it wouldn't work with them being in Lawrence and me in Manhattan. Now when she needs me I'm home on a dime, and if I have to run up to school, I run up to school. My daughter is terribly sophisticated, very much into the fashion business. She loves it, loves the models, the clothes, the work concept. Her idea of an ideal vacation would be to stay in my office. She loves to watch the fittings, loves to answer the telephone.

BLDD: Would you like her to follow in your footsteps?

DK: She's asked if she could, and already says she wants to take over the business. I said she could have it!

BLDD: Was there ever any question in your mind that you would not pursue fashion as a career?

DK: Yes, a lot of questions. I loved dance, and I wanted to be a dancer. I loved to illustrate, so I wanted to be a sketcher. Then I figured out by being in fashion I could be involved with the body. I love women and I love movement. And I like to watch clothes move. It all just evolved into fashion. It wasn't something that I thought I was going to do. I started as a salesgirl and I was a very good one at a retail store in Lawrence, Long Island.

BLDD: What did you sell?

DK: Clothes, sportswear. It still exists. It's a very inexpensive young kids store. The kids used to love to come in and I would put them together. I have a knack of being able to tell people what they should wear, how to

wear it, how to make their wardrobe lives easier. The best thing I do is help ease women's lives.

BLDD: How have you done that?

DK: By explaining how you can put yourself together simply and not get crazy. When women shop, they see so many clothes and accessories. I suggest they step back for a minute and take a look at their wardrobes, and try to figure out the fundamentals they need.

BLDD: Can you give some advice? How can one simplify a wardrobe? Can you suggest eight easy steps?

DK: I would start with black; I always prefer black as the base. Women look extraordinarily elegant in black, and they can wear it from day through evening. It can really function as a background for their personality. Every woman should own a fabulous black skirt. Then she must own a great fitted pair of black pants, with those I would suggest a cashmere sweater.

BLDD: Black also?

DK: Black. You can then wear jewelry, which I think is terribly important as your signature. I don't think clothes ring out as your personality per sé. The body should become a linear form and let your personality emerge. Then everything starts working together.

BLDD: Do you see the clothing as "scaffolding," in a sense, as background for personality?

DK: Perhaps. I think my husband has had an effect on my ideas of form and silhouette. One of my own physical problems had led me to understand the body more. I have relatively large hips, which most women do, and I have large shoulders. I explain to women that they have to maintain a strong shoulder line if they want to make their hips look narrow—that one's "hanger" for clothes should come from one's shoulders. What you're trying to achieve is a man's shape, which is a triangle. There's nothing worse than a woman who looks like a pear. Basically fashion is dealing with form. Afterwards you need a marvelous scarf; scarves are fabulous because they are part of your personality, they're warm and they're cuddly. They're sophisticated and they have flair. You also need a marvelous accent jacket, perhaps in another coloration that you can throw on with anything—such as a white shirt. From there I would go to grey flannel pants. Avoid prints. Then have additional items—a beautiful sweater that you think is fantastic. I don't believe you have to own a dress, but if you do, for me the ideal is a cashmere dress.

BLDD: Not everybody can wear a knit dress.

DK: They can. I believe that women should buy their clothes oversized. For example, I would buy a men's extra large sweater. I don't get hung-up on size. Clothes are more an attitude than a size.

BLDD: Do you often buy men's clothing?

DK: No, I wear my own clothes. But I do buy my husband's, and I buy him extra large things so I get a double wardrobe!

BLDD: What would you design for men if you had the opportunity?

DK: Actually, I'm too busy designing for women. I don't know how some of these designers find the time. I've been designing Anne Klein II which is our second collection, and it is an enormous new responsibility.

BLDD: What does Anne Klein I, Anne Klein II mean? What do these various generations signify?

DK: Anne Klein II was set up to accommodate the customer. Anne Klein clothes are very fairly priced, but by the time you put a whole outfit together, you're talking about a thousand dollars at retail. That's a lot of money. It's much less expensive to wear a dress than a silk shirt, that costs about $300 with a jacket that costs $500 and pants that cost $250.

BLDD: Before you know it it adds up to more than $1000 without accessories. Is there now a less expensive version?

DK: There is a customer who wants to wear designer clothes and just can't afford it, a working class woman who needs clothes. Nobody is catering to her. Many of these women look at the clothes and say, "What is Anne Klein doing? What is Calvin Klein doing? What is Ralph Lauren doing? Why don't they design clothes for me? Or should we try and knock them off?" Nobody can knock us off better than we can.

BLDD: So you chose to do so?

DK: Right. Anne Klein II has the same spirit as the regular line, and it is less expensive.

BLDD: What are the differences?

DK: The fabrication. Anne Klein would have the more advanced point of view. Anne Klein II is a more classical company. For example, one of my frustrations as a designer is letting go of what I consider a good thing, like certain sweaters I did about three years ago. I sold about 100–150 of them, because at designer prices, the sweater cost about $600–700 in cashmere. You don't sell that many.

BLDD: Why would a cashmere sweater cost $600–700?

DK: It's the design. The sweater is cut and sewn, not made by machine. My cashmere costs $80 a yard. So by the time I manufacture it the cost is very high. The question is, why can't I do it in the inexpensive jersey?

BLDD: Why can't you?

DK: I do, for Anne Klein II. I don't do it for Anne Klein, because my customer is cashmere-hungry, and once you wear cashmere you're not going to switch. But the woman who doesn't know cashmere can go to wool jersey, or cotton knit, or sweatshirt fabric, or something else. That's why I've applied the designs in less expensive fabrications. I have the greatest fitting blazer, but it is $500 in red cashmere. Now I do it for Anne Klein II in a red shetland for $250.

BLDD: Is there an Anne Klein III on the Horizon?

DK: Please, no. I couldn't handle it.

BLDD: How would you describe the characteristics of the Anne Klein Label?

DK: A sophisticated sportswear, rather bold and aggressive, in which women feel absolutely wonderful. The clothes make you feel good. They're not clothes that dictate to you, but clothes you yourself have to be involved with. They're clothes that move, separate pieces that can be worn independently or together. Right now our customer is buying ensembles. She's buying a different look, she takes away the pieces and then she wears the clothes.

BLDD: What is the design process like here?

DK: Fabrication first, then the design. We design all our own fabric. Eight weeks before a collection is due I'm still not ready to design. Sixty percent of my time is spent developing fabrics. When you walk into a store the first thing that hits you is color. So I go through yarns and create colors that didn't exist. Our collection has been called a little tough.

BLDD: What do you mean "a little tough"?

DK: It's an unfortunate cliché. *Women's Wear* or someone referred to us as "tough chic," because our clothes are more aggressive. Our clothes have a bit more snap than namby-pamby clothes.

BLDD: How would you like to have the clothes described?

DK: As sophisticated: they are for a woman with presence. Although you don't notice the clothes, they make a statement. They enhance the woman.

BLDD: Approximately how large is the volume you manufacture annually?

DK: In volume, the company does $30 million annually. We dress less than one percent of the population, that is approximately one million items.

BLDD: How does that make you feel?

DK: I never think about it, it's not something I'm hung up on. My high is my work room. It is also people telling me how much they love the clothes, really getting off on them and understanding them, and realizing that they aren't necessarily how they saw them in *Vogue*, but that they can become "love" items.

BLDD: What does that mean?

DK: It means that they really become your friends.

BLDD: That means that you want to keep them for a long time. How do you then sell additional clothes?

DK: You constantly update them, you change proportions. I never throw out clothes that I love. At these prices, I don't expect my customer to either.

BLDD: How do you decide what color to feature in a season?

DK: I can't answer that. Why am I suddenly looking at your scarf? Why does that green all of a sudden look new to me, what causes me to notice that green. Maybe next year I would think that green was terrible.

BLDD: Does the Color Council have anything to do with your color selections? I have often wondered how come one year everyone is interested in peach?

Donna Karan and Louis Dell'Olio for Anne Klein Co., spring, 1981

DK: To this day I can not figure out how Calvin Klein, St. Laurent and I did Glen Plaids the same fall, because we each designed them from scratch. These patterns never existed. I never saw them at a fabric show, nobody had them in their collection. Our plaid was based on an old scarf that we gave to someone to make into a fabric for us. Then to see someone else had made a zebra pattern with a plaid was so crushing. I thought my design was unique.

BLDD: How did it happen that all three designers did Glen Plaid?

DK: I don't know. You go into the market and see some natural themes. Afterwards you evolve your own ideas. Because of timing the first thing we design is our shoe collection. The shoes must come first. So I go to Europe and I work on the shoes before I design the fabric. Then we start to build.

BLDD: If you start with shoes then haven't you dictated the length and color of your clothes?

DK: No. I could be wrong on that. But we do enough shoes to cover every base. It's a shoe collection that sells incredibly well. I start with bunches of swatches and fabric boards. Suddenly a form starts to take place, and then designing starts. It starts to build, and build, and build, and then we play the proportion game.

BLDD: What does that mean?

DK: We play short over long, long over short, big over narrow, narrow over big. You know, "I've got this jacket—what shape skirt do I want with it? Do I want to fill it out? Do I want to keep it narrow?" And we play. Really, we play with the model. We accessorize her. We get her head big, we get her head small. We give her hanging earrings. We give her button earrings.

BLDD: What do you do, and what does Louis dell 'Olio do? How does the collaboration work? Who decides?

DK: We work as a team, pure team.

BLDD: Well who decides?

DK: It doesn't matter. It's an equal decision. I like it, he likes it, we get it. Both of us must like it.

BLDD: Do you know each other that well and that long?

DK: Oh, yes, ten years, a long time.

BLDD: Who starts the design process? Do you sit down together? Do you work in the same room?

DK: We work on one desk, face to face. We don't sit and draw all day. Maybe I'm fitting, or with my assistants. There is a lot of space. We have four floors, a shipping department downstairs, and on the upper floor the studio which does all the accessories—belts, jewelry, handbags, gloves.

BLDD: How many licensees do you have?

DK: About seventeen domestic and ten international licensees.

BLDD: Is there anything you haven't designed yet that you'd care to?

DK: Oh, god yes. Lots of things. I want to design men's clothes and children's clothes. I'm dying to do a swimwear collection. I want to take a vacation. I want to design myself a gorgeous vacation.

BLDD: You can do that, can't you?

DK: No, I can't, I don't have time.

BLDD: Did Anne Klein consciously groom you to take over the company?

DK: No, she was a young woman when she died. We worked as associates. I was her assistant at first, really rock-bottom, assistant. My big job was getting her coffee and sharpening pencils. Then I graduated to shopping for fabrics. That's where I learned a lot, and of course watching her. Every once in awhile she would take a vacation and it was my turn to play.

BLDD: It sounds like a union of two very independent and strong-minded temperaments.

DK: No matter how strong and independent I am or was, she was far stronger and far more independent.

BLDD: Louis, what gave you the idea to go to Anne Klein?

LDO: I think I saw an ad in *The New York Times*.

DK: You were working on the Avenue before you went to Parsons.

LDO: I worked with Norman Norell for a summer, after high school. But I had already been accepted to Parsons.

BLDD: How did you get a job with Norman Norell who was probably the then leading designer?

LDO: My uncle worked in the union part of the Ladies Garment Union. He knew all the designers, and was very friendly with Norman Norell. He got me the job.

BLDD: Did you learn anything?

LDO: You always learn, even when you are not aware of it. It was a fantasy—I thought the fashion business was working for Norman Norell. But I did learn some very basic things there. I remember going to Norell's apartment to bring some clothes for a photography shooting. I volunteered: I was dying to see his apartment and anything that belonged to him personally. The man for whom I worked directly told me to do something. Soon afterward someone else asked me if I had anything to do. I said I didn't because I wanted to bring the clothes over to Norell's apartment. My boss heard me and said, "Let me teach you a lesson. You can do anything when you work here, but always do what your boss tells you to do first." That was a lesson well learned: "You can bring the clothes but you have to do what I told you first." He brought my head right out of the clouds.

BLDD: What else did you learn?

LDO: I guess the most significant thing I observed was extravagance. The whole place was so extravagant. The first thing I saw when I walked into his showroom was a rack of eight dresses. Each dress was the same style but each in a different color. They were chemise camisole dresses, straight, with ruffled bottoms and a big flower, totally covered in sequins. It was like a carnival. They were gorgeous. They might have been flashy, but everything he did was gorgeous because it was so well made.

BLDD: Did you sketch and design as a child?

LDO: Oh yes, I have books of sketches that are so funny. My parents moved recently and I saw the sketch books I made when I was thirteen years old. I saved them all because they are so funny. They're little stick figures with little sayings next to them. I guess in those days the magazines used to write little captions, so I wrote little balloon-encased captions.

BLDD: How did you both come to know each other?

LDO: Through Lesley Mesh, a mutual friend, with whom I went to high school and Donna went to summer camp.

BLDD: Where is she now?

LDO: I have no idea where she is. The last I heard she was on a commune. She was a little weird. I guess we were all a little weird then, but it was the '60's.

BLDD: Does she know what she helped wrought?

LDO: Sure. I've been in touch with her since I've worked here. She called out of the blue one day.

DK: When we went to Parsons we were the only two kids who lived on Long Island; so we needed companionship. Louis and I really grew together out of necessity.

BLDD: How old were you when you met.

DK: Seventeen. When we first met I was sitting on a stoop in short shorts and Roman Gladiator sandals way up to here.

BLDD: And what did you look like Louis?

LDO: Very preppie.

DK: Horn-rimmed glasses and a button down collared shirt and short pants.

LDO: I was preppie. I still am pretty preppie actually, I don't think I ever left that look.

DK: One year I decided to turn Louis mod.

LDO: One day Donna re-did me all in white. When we were in school we went to Florida on vacation and almost sun-burned ourselves to death. She dressed me in white bell-bottomed, hip-hugger pants. I don't remember what the shirt was, all I remember is that I had this nautical silk scarf around my neck, and a big white hat and sunglasses. We even took pictures of ourselves in this photobooth.

BLDD: How would you best like your work to be described?

LDO: So many clothes have such a stamp on them that no matter what the woman wears, they're wearing that stamp. I think our designs are a little looser than that. Our clothes only look well on women who understand clothes. Our proportions are special, they're not the norm.

BLDD: In what way are they different?

LDO: They're a little longer: they're a little sleeker. They're cut with more savvy.

BLDD: Do you make many personal appearances?

LDO: No, very limited because . . .

DK: They don't really work.

LDO: They don't. You get women who come in to complain that you don't make clothes for them. You get women who come in and are devoted fans but don't really know the first thing about what you're doing. And you get a very small percentage of women who come in because they want to learn. Most of them don't want to learn. They want to come in and make your clothes conform to what they want. And if it's not for them, they shouldn't be buying the clothes. If a woman comes in looking for a little tiny Ralph Lauren blazer, she's not going to find it with us. That's not what we do; that's not what we're about.

DK: Some designers do personal appearances. When we have, we have sold incredible amounts of clothes. But we open five collections a year. We have two operations. You just have to say no to some things in your life, and unfortunately, in ours, it became personal appearances. Unless it's a very special event we do video tapes.

LDO: We have road people who go out to do our shows.

DK: To educate the customers. So we do a lot of trunk shows. Our customer knows designer clothes. She is very sophisticated, and knows the international design theme. She knows about proportion, she knows about sizes that are cut with the size. The customer whom Anne Klein Two is catering to has never really experienced designer clothes at all. She has to be educated to understand that its okay if your jacket is a little big. She's frightened. They don't understand our blouse cuts at all. But with our old customer there's true communication.

BLDD: Do you think that you've helped bring them along?

LDO: Absolutely. From the first line we ever did here to today.

BLDD: What's the difference in the woman for whom you design?

LDO: First of all, we were terribly frightened. We kept saying "Is this Anne Klein?" We doubted everything we touched. We kept saying "Is this Anne Klein?" And then finally we said, "This season we're going to break away." It was time. We did a crude line that didn't have a blazer in it. It had big easy loose shapes because before everything was so tailored and fitted.

DK: The new world blazer. I think we were a forerunner in promoting a look that had never existed.

LDO: A totally relaxed look.

DK: Relaxed sportswear.

LDO: It was relaxed. Anne Klein had been noted for tailored, constructed suit separates. Ours were different; there wasn't a fitted thing on the line except for one very fitted blazer.

DK: And the pants were very baggy.

LDO: Everything was easy and people were scared.

DK: They thought we had lost our marbles. We did a collection in fuchsia, orange, turquoise.

LDO: Rust, purple.

DK: Rust and purple. No white or black. It was jewel-toned silk-linens. We asked our customer to wear skirts on top of skirts, double colored skirts. We had a shirt on top of shirts. We asked them to wear two colors together that they would never have worn in their wildest dreams.

BLDD: Did they wear them?

DK: Absolutely. They did, but the stores freaked.

BLDD: How important is the fashion press to the popularity of your designs?

LDO: The press can kill a designer. But there are times when we've been creamed and we've sold incredibly well, anyway.

DK: They hated this past fall's collection and we honestly thought it was our best fall collection. They didn't get it at all.

LDO: The stores didn't even understand it.

DK: The stores hated it. "How could you do a collection on two colors?" We just did white and black and that's it.

LDO: And it sold out incredibly.

BLDD: What do you think the press is looking for that they don't find in your clothes now?

DK: Continuity. They're complaining that we don't do what we profess to do. What we do is show options. The press wants to see one direction. They felt very uncomfortable with the fact that we have alternatives.

LDO: It's a political thing. It depends who's doing it. We're not the darlings of the press: we never have been. But in the fashion field the apex is presentation—the shell, the clothing. Fashion is creating clothing, a look. It's very difficult to put into words, but it pleases me when I see clothes that work, that look wonderful: they don't even have to be my clothes. When I see a woman walk into a room and she looks fabulous . . .

DK: That's the high.

LDO: Yes, the business part of the business is the low. Then it is who you know, and how you behave, who you cater to and who you don't cater to, and who is "darling" and who isn't "darling." In this business—and in the entertainment business — it's at its showiest, it's all up front, it's all personalities. Unlike more conservative businesses, it isn't covered up.

BLDD: What changes have taken place in fashion since it became a personality designer business versus a business-business?

LDO: It hasn't really changed. Before it was the designer, it was the company.

BLDD: Is the clothing label really the scaffolding that you hang licensees on?

LDO: Absolutely.

BLDD: Is there anything you wouldn't design, if asked?

DK: No, as long as its in good taste and has merit. But I often have problems with the design, how it's designed.

BLDD: Because of the lack of control that most people have over their licensees?

DK: I will tell you that right now I would not put my name on the back of jeans. I'd put Anne Klein's name, but I would never put my own. I don't want to walk down the street and see my name there. My name is private.

BLDD: How do you feel when you see someone wearing your clothes and it doesn't look so good? Do you have the urge to go over and say "please take that off" or "please don't . . . " So what do you tell them?

LDO: If I know them very well, I'll say, "Can I help you? I mean, you're wearing this a little cock-eyed."

BLDD: Do they like that?

LDO: Oh sure, they love it. But when someone comes in and is wearing an unflattering suit and colors, who has put it together that way and thinks they look good, you can't start ripping them to shreds and say, "Your hat's wrong. This is wrong." Then they walk out like you've beaten them to death. One of my greatest problems today is that I don't like seeing the clothes worn. Sometimes I think I would prefer to see them kept like jewels! I don't like to have the obvious thrown in front of my face. I sit here playing with my model and having a great time doing, say, a plaid jacket, and going through all the emotions I have about it. Then all of a sudden I see the jacket coming down the street on a heavier woman, or a skinnier woman than the one it was designed for, and I want to die.

BLDD: You wouldn't prefer no one wearing them! Do you feel they're unique works of art rather than body covering?

DK: I have to live with the fact that this is a business, and probably one of the more successful businesses. I produced it that way.

BLDD: What do you think is the most important accessory?

LDO: Shoes. Shoes create the leg. Basically if you wear the right shoe you're finished.

DK: If the whole thing is in proportion, it's absolutely perfect. It's non-jarring.

BLDD: In the twenty-two years that you two have known each other there's obviously been an enormous shift in the whole concept of fashion, a very basic one in terms of the importance of shape and fit and a very relaxed and less formal style of dress that bases itself on a well-tuned body. Your designs are a part of that whole transition. In fact, you have stated that they are in the forefront of that transition. In light of that, what do you see as the future direction of fashion, in general, and the direction in which you are going specifically?

DK: I could give you the answer today and when the time comes along it may not be the answer, because fashion moves so quickly. It turns on a dime. I can't believe how fast it moves sometimes.

LDO: I have always said that there will always be easy comfortable clothes, we will always have the light style.

Donna Karan and Louis Dell'Olio for Anne Klein Co., fall, 1982

DK: Who would ever think that people wanted fitted clothes again, and yet last spring they tried to do it.

LDO: It didn't last long, but I think if it had been done properly it would have. Donna will say it quicker than anyone else: when you're pregnant and you have that baby you can't wait to get into tight clothes in which you can feel your body.

BLDD: I would think many people would want fitted clothing. With the great interest in health and fitness, and such wonderful bodies, you'd think they'd want to show them off.

DK: I do.

LDO: They do.

DK: When I'm feeling fit, I've got to tell you I want to show it all. I don't want it constricting but I want it soft and molding. And when I'm fat I want it big.

LDO: We would never do an Oscar de la Renta dress here. That's Oscar and we don't relate to it. But I think they're fabulous. Donna always said she'd love to design a Bill Blass gown, but she never has the opportunity and we never do that kind of thing. But we do an extensive evening collection. Because we're sportswear designers, once the stores buy the collection, they don't have the money to invest in the evening collection. So they'll buy dribs and drabs. But now evening is selling. People are going out again because they're getting a little more relaxed about spending money, and there are places to go. We went to the St. Laurent show at the Met, and there was everybody in those corselette tops, and those little constricting things. Women found them appealing, sexy. They are damned uncomfortable. But they give you a certain tension, a certain feeling about yourself—and obviously women liked them, and thought they looked good in them, otherwise they wouldn't have bought them.

BLDD: Are you suggesting that to be really glamorous you can't be too comfortable?

LDO: Yes, because you don't always want to feel the same all the time. There's always a time when you want to feel a little different, not quite yourself. Even a man goes through that and expresses it, by wearing a tuxedo. Men don't wear tuxedos very often, so when they do, they walk differently.

BLDD: In our mass-oriented technological society, almost everything is mass produced. How personal can one's dress be in light of the mass production that is necessary?

DK: Today? Phenomenal, because the options are endless. Just look at the big world of design. Everybody says everybody's doing the same thing, but I don't think everybody's doing the same thing at all. One of the healthiest things that's happening today in fashion is that each individual designer is coming into his own and developing a stronger image of who and what they are.

BLDD: Do you particularly respond to the work of any current designer or one of the past?

DK: Individually, I like things of many designers. I love the tailoring of Armani. But, though he has great ideas, there are some things he makes that I think are unfortunately contrived. I was amazed at the St. Laurent exhibition. His range blew my mind completely. I thought it was a fantasy; and it is true that some of his clothes have longevity that I have not seen with any other designer. He can cut a garment and make it look like it was just a piece of fabric. That is genius; he has always been one of my favorites. I appreciate what Calvin and Ralph and Perry have done to the American market.

BLDD: What have they done?

DK: Their personalities, and the health of all of our businesses have really promoted the American fashion industry into what it is today. I'm not negating Oscar, Bill and Geoffrey, who are also geniuses and talents, but I think the whole movement towards the American modern woman was captured by the sportswear divisions. So I appreciate what they're doing, and I like the idea of all of us separating right now. There was a time when it was getting confusing for me. We were a little too symbiotic in what we did. I think Perry's become his own person. Ralph, most definitely has carved a niche for himself, and a magnificent one. I respect him a lot.

BLDD: Because his look is such a consistent one?

DK: Absolutely. He's an independent, it's not so much based on creativity, but on good taste. He has the best of the licensee operations.
BLDD: Why?
DK: Quality. He paved his mark on a T-shirt. Anyone who can out-Lacoste, Lacoste, God bless him.
LDO: In Europe they'd rather wear Ralph Lauren than Lacoste. He offers a broader range of colors.
DK: Lacoste just stayed there, it didn't change; Ralph picked up and became the modern Lacoste.
LDO: Many of the designers in this country are in the world marketplace. Norma Kamali put pads in a sweatshirt, gave it a little sex appeal, and created an empire overnight. You can't beat that. She's a smart business lady, and she is very, very creative. I don't always love what she does, but I have a lot of respect for her. I don't always love what anybody does.
BLDD: How about your own work?
LDO: I don't always love what I do. I like it at first but often I look back and think, "God, that was a mistake."
BLDD: Are there any designers whose work has been an influence on your career?
DK: Claire McArdell. I think she was modern; she was sportswear, and she understood clothes had to be easy and simple. Some of the clothes from the '20's, '30's, and the '40's are still good to me. To me the classicism of those periods is the basis of fashion.
LDO: Without fail, I get tons of inspiration, every season, without even realizing it from such Hollywood designers of the '30's and '40's as Adrian and Plunkett. They were brilliant. All the French designers today are still using clothes from the movies. Movie designers created shoulder pads for Joan Crawford that the world is still using—those suits! What they did for Marlene Dietrich in a white gabardine trenchcoat! That didn't come out of Europe; it came right out of Hollywood.
BLDD: Do you think that there are regional differences in taste? Is the West Coast flashier? The East Coast more conservative?
LDO: Absolutely. The lifestyle in California conditions what people there wear. I hate to put women in a category—everything has its exceptions—but you walk down Rodeo Drive, and they're in jewelry, jeans and high heels. It's all showy, bright colors. They never wear toned-down colors.
BLDD: And how would you characterize the East?
LDO: Much more subtle, much, much, more subtle. Darker colors.
BLDD: And the Midwest?
LDO: The Midwest is a mixed bag, because they're in the middle. They're very fashion conscious. We've been to the Midwest and gone to their affairs, and the women are very attuned to what is going on. They read everything.
BLDD: How about the South and the Southwest?
LDO: They still like pretty clothes.
BLDD: Would you contrast the South and the Southwest, for example Virginia versus Texas? Two different looks?
LDO: Definitely. Texas is big money. In Texas they want the whole collection!
BLDD: By the way, for which women do you design? Is there any one group you can focus on?
DK: Perhaps one more urban, more East Coast, more New York—although we are very, very successful on the West Coast, probably one of the most successful designers there.
BLDD: Because there are so many East Coasters on the West Coast!
LDO: Not only that. I think when they come into the store, they're looking for a certain kind of sophistication that they know they can get from us. Sometimes we're called the "tough chic" kids. Sometimes we like it and sometimes we don't. But there is a certain zestiness, a certain sophistication about our clothes that lets the woman show through. They know that.
BLDD: What American woman, or women, would you say have had the most impact on the course of American fashion during the last two decades?
DK: Jacqueline Kennedy, bar none.
LDO: What she did to America!
BLDD: What in your view did she do?

124

DK: She said, "Ladies, get up, let's dress, it's not so bad to be cerebral and fashionable."

LDO: She woke up the masses. She definitely woke up America. There's a tug-of-war with American women. In some circles you don't want to be too concerned with clothing because your achievements are in other areas.

BLDD: Do we have a Princess Diana in this country? A woman with the same fashion impact?

LDO: No, I don't think we have a personality like that. Jacqueline Kennedy was the last personality who was a focal point.

BLDD: Do you think women in the "columns" have real impact, and serve as role models for other women?

DK: I think they dress to please themselves more than anybody else.

LDO: It's very funny, the jet-set women are still the same women that you read about twenty years ago. Where are the young new jet-set women, if there is such a thing, which I don't think there is?

BLDD: What about Diane Keaton's impact on fashion?

DK: I think Diane Keaton has a wonderful statement.

LDO: She has a personal style. What she looks like on the street makes it clear that she's not just created for the screen like some actresses are.

DK: The other one is Lauren Hutton—she's fabulous, she's got taste, she's got style.

BLDD: Is there such a thing, and if so, are there many women who personify American beauty today? How would you describe that American look?

DK: Alive, wide eyed, active. Jane Fonda personifies it. There isn't another woman around who has more of the American dream body. What she has done for exercise is unbelievable.

LDO: I think it definitely comes from within. So many of the fashionable women that you hear about have a dead quality to them.

DK: Candice Bergen is another American beauty. So is Cheryl Tiegs.

LDO: And they don't necessarily have the best style nor are they the best dressed.

BLDD: What's the most neglected area of fashion design?

DK: Licensing should be cleaned up. There should be less prostitution of the label.

LDO: The most important thing for us is educating the customers. We try hard, but we haven't been able to. If we had, people would not be wearing polyester.

BLDD: How much quality control do you have over your licensees?

DK: Not enough, but we try. It is a constant battle. You're very lucky if you have a good licensee who respects you and wants to please you. Unfortunately no matter how hard that licensee tries, the store wants to take that name and splash it in the weirdest places.

LDO: It all starts with the consumer. If they buy a product there's nothing we can do to stop the store from selling it. The buyers will say, "Hey, our business is booming on this little thing." It's tough to fight success.

DK: The public is buying these little bags with lions on them and thinking we do them. And we don't do them but it's an incredible multi-million dollar business and you don't throw that away. You think, say, "God bless poor Sadie Schultz, whoever she is—(I hope the name doesn't exist.)—she's buying that lion bag right now and she loves it. Why take it away from her. But in fact we had nothing to do with creating that lion.

BLDD: How did the lion become a symbol of Anne Klein?

LDO: She was a Leo.

BLDD: How does it feel for you two low-keyed people, to have your lives so quickly evolve this way? Is it a tough thing to deal with?

DK: I don't think it's been so quick. I feel old! I have been selling clothes since I was sixteen and seventeen, and my life has been here since 1968.

LDO: I was sketching dresses when I was twelve years old.

BLDD: Do you think you will ever stop working in fashion?

DK: Yes, absolutely.

BLDD: Do you picture that as a possibility for you?

LDO: Someday it may not have the importance it has for me now.

DK: You'd be a craftsman.

LDO: Yes, I'd like to work in crafts. Anything which is hand-made. I love making things: ornaments, Christmas ornaments, anything. Out of dough,

paper. I like busy stuff. That's more fun for me than going to a store and buying something.

DK: I'm so jealous. My daughter likes his Christmas tree, his Santa Claus, his model, his girl. And says, "Mommy, you don't know how to draw."

BLDD: Do you?

DK: No. I'm not as good as Louis is in terms of artistic ability. I have a different type of artistic ability. It's incredible what Louis can do with his hands. I can't make those Santa Clauses. And he can also make earrings.

LDO: I like detail work.

DK: I hate detail work.

BLDD: How about the environments in which you live? How closely do they reflect the work that you design?

LDO: I have a beige apartment. It's all tile and raw silk.

DK: Our apartments are similar.

LDO: They're totally different.

DK: Mine is eclectic and very antique. Yet it is contemporary because it has a modern-base. I don't want to say modern—because it's not modern.

LDO: It's not modern.

DK: It's contemporary, but it's eclectic. There's more in it because I came from a house into an apartment. Little love objects and things like that. Louis started later than I did, so his place is fresher, and less cluttered. I would love to hang out in his apartment, and there are times that I think Louis would like to come over to mine.

BLDD: Do you socialize together?

DK: Once in a while.

LDO: I don't go out often. I go out to dinner and to the movies.

BLDD: What changes have you seen on Seventh Avenue since you began observing it?

DK: I've become snobby about it. I'm embarrassed to admit it but I will. I used to walk from Penn Station to my office at 39th Street liking everyone I saw. Now I'm afraid of the people.

LDO: It's definitely changed.

DK: I'm scared.

LDO: When we started, you never heard that after a certain hour you couldn't go out on the street at night and get a cab. The whole city has changed in that respect. It's seedier; it's dirtier.

DK: It's more druggy, I smell grass all over the place.

BLDD: What do you do to try and upgrade the quality of the neighborhood in which you spend most of your life?

LDO: Committees have tried to do things. They put up planters along Seventh Avenue, but it's all hopeless unless people care.

BLDD: What do you see as the major difference between European and American clothes today? Is there a difference?

DK: Absolutely. We're not as gimmicky; they're much more contrived.

LDO: They're still into the show, into the flash, into the presentation. They make a collection to show, and then a collection to sell. And we always used to do the same thing. Now they've learned from us. The American market has become so strong for them, that they're starting to show what they sell.

BLDD: How strong has the European market been for Anne Klein?

DK: Fabulously strong.

LDO: We don't sell our merchandise in Europe right now because the duty makes it too expensive for us.

BLDD: If you had your life to live over, what would you do differently?

DK: I would hope to do the same thing, with less effort. I would have liked to have known at the beginning what I know now, I love my life—I think it's outrageous, but I wish I could get past a lot of stuff that holds me back. The greatest thing in life is to create, to re-create, to change. My life is very safe, very comfortable. I love the excitement of opening a collection ten times a year. The track record is good. I can't imagine we would ever produce a bad collection.

BLDD: Do you have the same confidence?

LDO: Absolutely. We've grown. We've reached a certain taste level. Sometimes we're such perfectionists that we defeat ourselves. But we'd never create something that wouldn't be successful on a certain level.

BLDD: Did you ever expect your life would unfold the way it has?

Donna Karan and Louis Dell'Olio for Anne Klein Co., spring, 1983

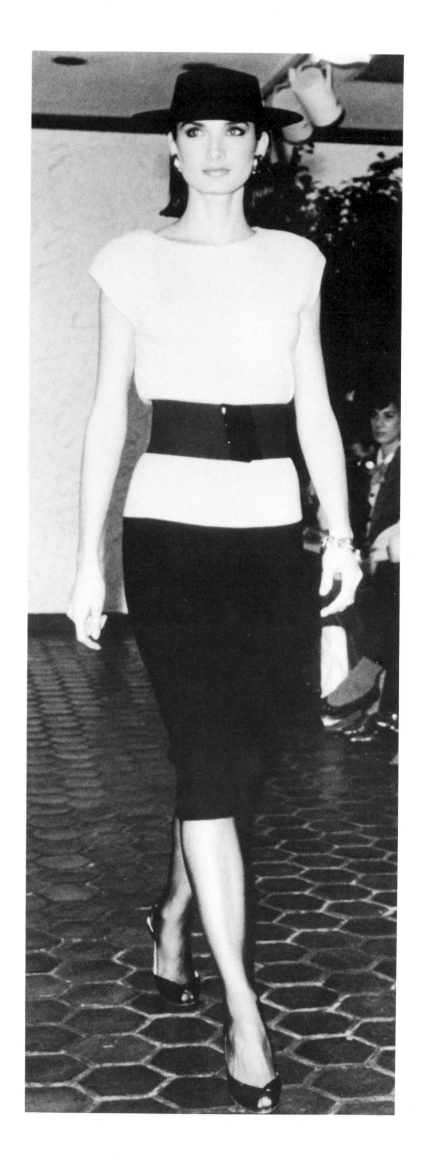

DK: Yes. And I have more dreams and goals to fulfill.

BLDD: What are they now?

DK: I want to be international. I want it all, and I know I'll probably get it because we're very diligent. We're hard workers and we respect ourselves and others.

LDO: It's very funny about being successful designers, sometimes it's timing and sometimes it's luck. But if you ask a designer when they decided they wanted to be a designer, most of them will tell you they made up their minds when they were very young. They never seem to have had a problem achieving their goal. I don't know of one designer who ever had a struggle making their own talent known. I always believed that I would take my time achieving what I wanted and that the success would be very secure.

BLDD: There are obvious advantages to working as a collaborative team, as the two of you do. I can understand that there might be some limitations too. Can you tell what some of each have been.

LDO: One advantage is that it takes off some of the pressure.

BLDD: Is there any other firm that works as a team?

DK: We're the only ones. Because there are two of us, we can go into different aspects of the business.

LDO: Most designers don't design by themselves anyway.

DK: They need other people to assist them. But Louis and I literally are "the" designers, we give each other the power.

BLDD: How involved are you in the business aspects of the business?

DK: Quite a bit. Not the banking aspects, but the totality. This company rotates around the design room.

LDO: There isn't anything we don't do—from production to buying fabric. Every department has its head but we are always involved.

BLDD: Do you think you would have accomplished as much if each of you were on your own?

DK: No. Maybe. We have a tremendous organization behind us. I knock on wood that we're special; we're lucky. Anne Klein is a brilliant company and a talented organization. Because our product is finer in style, a lot of very talented people are involved in creating it.

BLDD: How much of an influence has technology been on your career?

DK: Not enough yet.

LDO: However Purolator is God's gift to us. A delivery takes two days from Europe instead of a week. Saving time is very important.

DK: If we change a sketch or color, we are at the mercy of the Europeans and their schedules.

LDO: That's their big advantage.

BLDD: Why haven't we developed an American counterpart to all those fabric mills?

DK: It'll never happen.

LDO: It's years and years and years of craftsmanship, handed down through families. It would be interesting to see what happened if American designers had the same fabrics available as the European designers do.

BLDD: Do you think that is such an advantage for them?

LDO: They think we have the advantage here.

DK: They think we have exposure. The French live in the French way; the Italians live in the Italian way. They are jealous of what we have here in New York City—the pulse. The world is happening right on our block and it blows their minds. They come here and they drool.

LDO: They all get crazy.

DK: And we go over there and we just want to see culture.

Donna Karan and Louis Dell'Olio for Anne Klein Co., spring, 1983

Donna Karan, fall, 1985

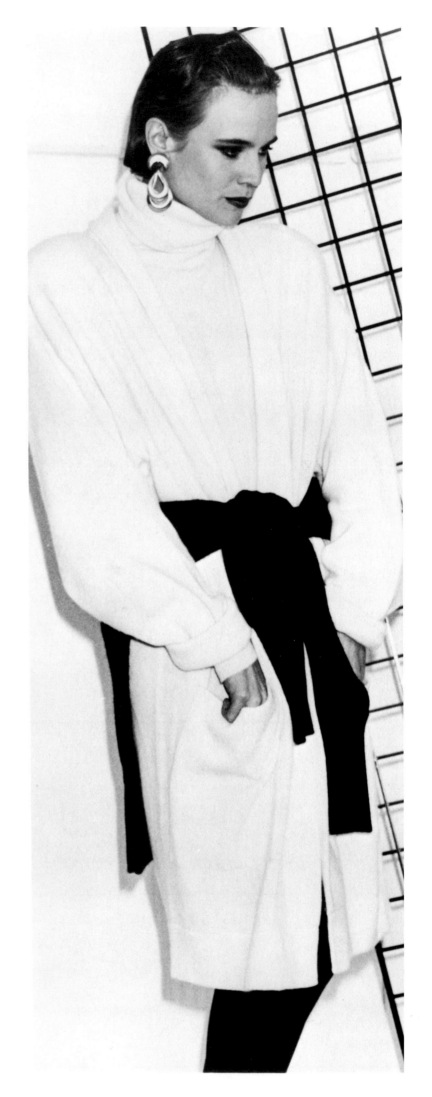

RL

Ralph Lauren

Ralph Lauren manages to mix youthful exuberance with a respect for the traditional in his designs for the American public. Starting as a designer of men's neckties in the 1960s, he is now a designer of a lifestyle: clothes, cosmetics and home furnishings bear his ubiquitous label.

BLDD: How does someone who grew up in the Bronx get to be so interested in—in fact to get to look like—an authentic cowboy?

RL: I don't think it matters where you grow up. All kids grow up with dreams that motivate them to make a life they would like. But along the path of life most people change their mind because somehow their dreams don't materialize. When I grew up in the Bronx, it was just a nice area of America. It did not have the connotation that it has today. It was happy, middle-class. I played basketball and baseball in schoolyards, and I was very happy. I wouldn't trade it for anything. As I see my kids growing up today, I realize I wouldn't trade with them either.

BLDD: What's the difference in your upbringing? What do you think they are missing?

RL: I think it's the camaraderie. They're missing the freedom of being able to look out their front window and see their friends in the schoolyard, or on the parkway, and putting on roller skates and skating, joining them on the street. I never had to think in terms of what New York City is today, of some areas being unsafe, or of kidnappings, or other crimes. The Bronx was beautiful to me. It was happy. At that time my goals were to be Joe DiMaggio, or Mickey Mantle, or Wilt Chamberlain, or Bob Cousy, the great basketball star. My goals at that time were not really to be Hop-A-Long Cassidy, I wanted to be an athlete; and I was a good athlete at the time. Loving the atmosphere of the West did not come at that period of my life. It came later on. It happened when I became more sophisticated and more traveled. Fortunately, my background and my parents' training made my values clear as to what I considered important in life.

BLDD: Let's talk about your background for a moment. What were those values? Was there anyone in your family, for example, who was interested in fashion or working in the fashion industry?

RL: No. I have two brothers and a sister, and my father's an artist. So I grew up in the art world to a degree. But it was not a sophisticated art world in that it was not about the fine arts as we traditionally describe them. My father was a mural painter. He worked in buildings and showrooms downtown, in the fur district at 30 West 30th Street. He painted a whole New York scene on the ceilings.

BLDD: I don't imagine that many of your pals in the Bronx had fathers who were artists.

RL: No, it was very rare. He came from Europe, from Russia. He learned the craft, and somehow had the talent. He did housepainting when he couldn't get a job doing the other things. There were good times and bad. Occasionally I used to help him painting and carrying his paints. He'd make walls look like wood. He'd do *faux bois* and marble. He could make a wall look like marble. He's done some things for Suzy Parker over the years. She'd import marble or wood from different places and he would match them up, by painting them. That was his life; he is a very artistic person.

BLDD: And you worked with him?

RL: I was never taught. I just helped him. I was just a kid, and helped him out carrying things.

BLDD: Did you ever paint or sketch?

RL: I tried. I sketch, but not well. My whole family is very artistic. My sister went to Music and Art High School and she was an artist. Eventually, she became a dental hygienist. Of all those in my family, I'm the least artistic in terms of drawing talent. They're all very good.

BLDD: Your mother as well?

RL: No, she's just a normal housewife.

BLDD: She was the nurturing spirit?

RL: Yes, very—I had a very nice lifestyle, very happy, very good home, very nice values in terms of not being frivolous. My father and mother are still alive. Now my father plays the violin. He taught himself to play the mandolin and the violin, and he paints. For relaxation he played the mandolin and violin. We'd close the door. So that's the kind of background I came from.

130

BLDD: What about your brothers' artistic ability?
RL: One of my brothers works with me as head of the men's design division, and another brother is in the plastics business. My parents are very proud of me because they saw me build my business by myself. They know they didn't hand it to me, and they're very thrilled.
BLDD: How important do you think formal education or training is in a career such as fashion design?
RL: I never had any formal training. So I think any kind of extra help you can get is great, but you have to have the instinct for fashion. You can't say, "I'm going to be an artist" or a painter or a designer and not have that touch inside. I think fashion particularly is an instinct. It's inside, a feeling about life. It can't be learned, you've got to have it. School, formal training can guide you, and might develop your other areas. Any kind of formal training can help if you have the instinct, but if you don't have it I don't think training is going to make a great deal of difference.
BLDD: How did your own education affect your design aesthetics? Is there any relationship, or is the way you lead your life and your own aspirations of more significance?
RL: I think it has a lot to do with my own aspirations, my own goals.
BLDD: What was your training? Where did you go to school?
RL: I went to the most unusual training school—Yeshiva University. My family was religious, my mother, particularly. So I probably had a very different morality than most people. I had a good education in Hebrew and the Torah. The course of study was really for people who were studying to be rabbis.
BLDD: Did you ever consider that possibility?
RL: No, I never considered it, but as I look back I think it was a good education. I went all the way through Yeshiva University, as well as the Yeshiva University High School.
BLDD: Is that morality and value structure very significant in your own training?
RL: Yes. I had some of that, but I also went to public high school—DeWitt Clinton in New York City, and to City College for a while. My education was as solid as it should have been. I went to summer school, to day school. I went through a lot of different periods. I wish I had gone to Harvard or Princeton or Yale, but I didn't.
BLDD: But your kids will.
RL: Maybe. Hopefully. But what it did do is give me an enormous drive. You have to sort of make your own, if you're not born into it. I didn't think I had the talent that my father had, so I had to create my own way, I was out there saying, "All right. What am I going to do?"
BLDD: So what *did* you do? What was your first job?
RL: Counselor in a camp. I wanted to be a history teacher. I liked the gum-soled shoes and the tweed jackets and the pipes. I was always very atmosphere-conscious. I never thought I liked the business world because I wanted a life that was free of not being honest or straightforward. I was that way as a kid. I thought the business world was always a little devious. My friends were teachers, and they were much freer in their thinking and their attitudes toward people. I had a lot of that exposure. My first job was a counselor in a camp that was typical of camps in the mountains. I went to a place called Camp Roosevelt. And I became the captain of one of the color war teams, an event when the entire camp split into two sides and competes in all sorts of activities. It is a major event in most camps.
BLDD: So you thought of yourself as a leader from your earliest days?
RL: That's right. There was something there that was a little special. In terms of my professional career in fashion and clothes, my first job was to hang up returns at Alexander's Department Store! If you returned something to Alexander's, you'd have to go up to the sixth floor to bring it back to the return department. While I was going to high school, I wore a stock boy uniform and would hang up all the returns. It was a part-time job. I guess I always had a flair for something in that world, whether it be movies, or clothes, or images and lifestyles. I didn't know what the words were at the time, but I know I had a "romanticness" about what I believed in. And that's the way it went. I worked for Alexander's when I was about sixteen and seventeen years old. Then I worked for Allied Stores, a buying

corporation. I was called an assistant buyer, but I really wasn't an assistant. I was in the buying office.
BLDD: How did you move from there to fashion?
RL: These places were fashion areas, even though at the time I didn't know exactly what I was going to be. I just went where I felt I had some flair. Also, as the youngest member in my family, I was the beneficiary of exposure handed down to me.
BLDD: Did that include the clothes of your older brothers?
RL: I was always wearing hand-me-down clothes. I was the third boy. Having all older brothers and seeing what they wore always made me more advanced than other kids my age. Kids would ask me where I got things. "Where did you get that?" they would always ask. Somehow I got them. No one had the money. I had to go out and earn the money myself and buy myself clothes.
BLDD: What was your early look?
RL: I was always preppie. I was the preppiest kid you ever saw! When I was eighteen, I was preppie, even before preppie came the first time! I wore tweed Bermudas that I had made for myself. That was my style. When I was nineteen I went to work for Allied Stores and then went into the Army on what was then the six-month plan. When I came out of the Army I worked for Brooks Brothers for a while selling, before I got another job. I wasn't quite sure what I wanted to do but I went toward areas that I liked. While I worked at Brooks Brothers, someone recommended me for a selling job. The job was with the Rivetz company which made neckties for Brooks Brothers. They were in Boston, Massachusetts and they sold real Ivy League kind of ties. I watched them, I then knew nothing about designing but watched how things were done—and listened to the people coming from Europe. I was then a salesman for the tie company, and used to sit in on meetings where they'd discuss the fabric. I would say, "Well, why don't you do this, and do that," and the main boss, Abe Rivetz, after I had been there about six months, said, "You've got it, and when I retire, or whatever, I want you to be the guy that's going to do the work here."

I was going to discos and wearing custom-made suits when I was twenty-two years old. I thought I was very sophisticated at a very young age. And I went to L'Interdit when that was considered a great club. Most people who went there were European. The clothes were flamboyant and had great style. I was always the leader, in terms of what I wore, in America and certainly in my industry. Wherever I was people would say, "Where did you get that?" I sort of felt like I had something that was different and special.
BLDD: Were you designing what you were wearing?
RL: Yes. I would say, "I want this made . . ." I was always interested in the look of Cary Grant and Fred Astaire. I never even thought about being a designer. I didn't know what a designer was. But I went to work for the Rivetz Company. The guy who said that I should take his place in the company died the very day I got married. He was very good to me. But, of course, his son-in-law took over. He knew I had some flair, and I started to design some things on the side. I'd started to see that I had some talent, and so did the people whom I worked with. They also knew I wasn't getting anywhere. Finally I said, "Look, is there such a thing as a designer? I'd like to come out with this idea." Pierre Cardin was just coming along. The son-in-law had a different reaction. "Ralph, there's no such thing as a designer in this business. The world is not ready for Ralph Lauren." I felt frustrated. So I persuaded a tie company called Beau Brummel to let me start a division for them. The division was called Polo, and we operated out of the Empire State Building.
BLDD: Where did you ever get the idea of a Polo symbol? Where did you ever get the idea for wide trousers?
RL: Again, it was images—what I related to, the taste, the style that I somehow developed at a very early age. It was Ivy League, and then influenced by England. I became very sophisticated very early, and admired European style and horses and the whole atmosphere of the good life. I wasn't merely interested in fashion. I'm not a fashion lover, but I knew what I admired.
BLDD: How *would* you describe yourself?
RL: I don't know if I can describe myself, except in terms of what I admire:

style, and not flamboyance, but sophistication, class, and an aristocratic demeanor that you can see in people like Cary Grant and Fred Astaire. They were my inspiration. As a result the things that I designed had more of an antique quality than a contemporary, with-it feeling. I felt that if I wanted to wear something, or if I was in love with something, there must be other people out there who would agree. People were always asking me what I was wearing, and I thought there must be some reason for it. So I followed my own instincts and designed an entire line. It was very successful, and that was where it started.

BLDD: And where did you get the notion of Polo as an appropriate name?

RL: When I was thinking about a name, I talked to many different people. I've always liked sports and athletics, and names were not important to me. I was not a guy that would wear a designer name. I wouldn't wear Christian Dior, Bronzini, or any of the names of that period. So I came up with my own style, which was a sport that had an aristocratic image, and that was Polo.

BLDD: How did your career move from Beau Brummel and wide Polo ties? How did you make the leap to designing other things?

RL: At that time there were no designers, except in the women's business. I knew that I couldn't exist on my ties and wanted to do other things. I liked clothes, and I was interested in a whole look. America, at that time, was very Ivy League. When the tie came out, they were saying, "Well, what shirt do I wear with this wide tie? It doesn't go with my lapels." I knew the look because I was going to custom tailors for my own clothes and telling them, "I want this." So I knew what styles could go together. A guy by the name of Norman Hilton became my partner. He is still a clothing manufacturer, and a very fine gentleman, and he financed me. Norman Hilton is about sixty-five now. He put up practically all the money and became my partner, and he got me started with $50,000 cash. That was about sixteen years ago, in about 1967. I made the clothes and shirts. I did the shirts for Bloomingdale's, other stores in New York, and Neiman-Marcus. The shirt became a hit. Everyone bought it, and they came out with wide lapels, natural shoulders. In other words, I designed for America—Pierre Cardin was European, very spiffy; mine was more Ivy League, more elegant and traditional.

BLDD: I guess you are more than partially responsible for the preppie rage . . .

RL: Brooks Brothers was the foundation, and I revived it. I worked for them, and wore all their clothes; I also left them as a consumer when they started making dacron and polyester. They no longer had a style, and I was a traditional guy. So I saw the opening in the whole market and said, "Well, I want to look like this, and I don't want to shop here anymore. They're not moving"—they did change, but they became more ordinary, more mundane. I was not going to be high fashion, but I did believe in individual sophistication, a more customized look—what Brooks Brothers used to be when they were great. That was what I went after, what I love, which is a lifestyle. Men who had a lot of money would go into Brooks Brothers to buy shirts, and say, "Give me three white, three blue and three pink," and they'd walk out. They'd do it every year, year in and out. They weren't interested in what was the latest this, or the latest that. I recognized a certain mentality and security about them. Working there was like going to an Ivy League school, there was an in-ness, a quiet in-ness about that kind of place. Anyway, I understood the philosophy, and the motivation of people, and also what motivated me. It was a fantasticness, not just a consumer going to buy a pretty shirt.

BLDD: Isn't it ironical that you never wear a necktie these days?

RL: I do.

BLDD: But when?

RL: You know what happened? I do so many things that I don't want to get up in the morning and have to think about what I want to wear. At one time I was so into clothes, that now I actually don't care about them.

BLDD: Do you wear what you're wearing now—jeans, denim shirt and worn boots, on a daily basis?

RL: Unfortunately, yes. I love beautiful clothes, but I don't have the time to get them! If you saw the shirts that I've worn, and if I showed you how ripped the elbows sometimes are, you'd flip out. Somehow I've gotten more seedy as time's gone on.

BLDD: Maybe it's the shabby elegant look that you're after now. I suspect you know just what you're doing . . . and what better sign of having arrived, than to have frayed cuffs or collar?

RL: That's true. But you know what happens? I used to see people who would do that, and I never understood it. I work here all day, with so many things going on that I don't have the time to think about what I am wearing. Sometimes I'll see a friend of mine wearing something, and I'll think, "Gee, why don't I get that?"

BLDD: From your own line?

RL: Yes! They'll look great, and I'll call up and say, "Can I get that?" And they'll say no, that the item is gone, or all sold out.

BLDD: By the way, are you still that rugged sportsman? When do you have the time?

RL: I make the time to do whatever I have to do—I ride horseback, play tennis, drive sports cars . . . That's what I like, that's relaxing to me.

BLDD: What are your favorite designs, and do they project that kind of look?

RL: I've always admired things—it's a cliché because it's been on my advertisements—things that get better with age. I like it when my tweed jackets get worn. Americans never understood that. Europeans did.

BLDD: Do you think we understand it yet? And is it the economy that's making us understand; the fact that clothes really are so dear that we had better hold on to them? If we can recycle buildings, we might as well start recycling our clothes.

RL: A better education is available now. Americans have become much more sophisticated; they're ten times more knowledgeable than they were ten years ago. They'll be better in the ten years to come. Taste is getting better, travel is getting better. America has become an exciting place. Now whether that's going to change in a year or two I don't know. Over the last five years, wherever you go in Europe, there is an excitement about Americans.

BLDD: What about the Japanese influence on fashion? Do you think that's for real, or is it media hype?

RL: I don't think it's media hype. I think it's real. You know, fashion is—that's why I don't like fashion—always looking for something new, something new to sell, something new to promote. Stores need business. They need to stimulate business. I'm for anything that's exciting, that's interesting, that has individuality.

BLDD: You say you're not a fashion lover and that's why you're not for fashion. You also say that you are interested in timelessness and classics. How would you describe what you are interested in?

RL: I love things, and I don't love to throw them out. It's not that I'm a hoarder, but when I buy something—I want to live with it. I want it to be mine.

BLDD: You must be a careful shopper . . .

RL: I am. We all have things that we love. You have your jackets or you just become attached to certain things that you love. And sometimes you buy something, wear it once and say, "I made a mistake. I should never have bought this." I try to design the things that you'd love. That's my goal. I could have done a lot of different things that I don't do, because they would have become trendy and too fashionable.

BLDD: For example?

RL: My philosophy of design is the very opposite of the Europeans'. They operate on what's in this year and what's out next. The shoulders are big this year, the hemlines are short next year.

BLDD: Why should your potential audience keep on coming back for more if your things are so classic and so timeless, why do we need more Ralph Laurens?

RL: It's a matter of adding to your wardrobe to stimulate it. One of the reasons you like clothes is that they make you feel good and another reason is that they make you look good. In other words, I believe in building a wardrobe. My designs of last year can be worn with new blouses this year, to make the whole look different. So things are never to be thrown out or discarded, but added to, to create an eclectic look, that doesn't look like it came out of a magazine. That's what I prefer.

BLDD: What's the most important purpose of body covering today?

RL: I haven't read all the history of clothing, from what an Indian would wear, and what it represented to him in the social sense, or what they wore in the caves—I'm sure there was always status to what people wore at different times in history. But today clothing sets your taste, it's your outward expression, it's the first shot, it's what you say about yourself to the world. After that, it's supposed to be the backdrop. To me, it is the backdrop, but it is your presentation of yourself.

BLDD: If clothing is a backdrop, then our environment is an even more significant "backdrop." Looking around your eclectic office, with its pleasing and surprising juxtapositions: mirrors, cast-iron ornaments, an Adam-style mantle, a Persian carpet, an Indian rug, a glass and steel table, a classic architect's chair. Every element makes a statement.

RL: I'm for an education in taste. Europeans have had a much broader education than Americans in many ways. What I've tried to do is give the American consumer the elements that I love, whether it be in clothes or home furnishings. The things I do are very simple, and uncomplicated. I was once complaining to a fashion writer that I never got the kind of press that I thought I should get.

BLDD: You?

RL: Well, I got press, but when you're intimate with your own business and your own reviews, you begin to see how your reviews are read and how they're written. I know when reviewers, or the fashion press, will come to my collection, walk out and write a review. And I used to think, "What did they write about?" I remember speaking to one editor who said, "Ralph, I don't know what to write about, because there's no new arm, there's no new shoulder. It looks familiar. It's something we know, and yet it isn't; but we want it." However it hits the consumer. It hits the consumer much more than the press. I think the press is not very sophisticated, they are in a different world. Their life is different, their work is their life. They want to be at the right seat, the right place. They do a lot of things that are misleading.

BLDD: Or misguided?

RL: They misguide the public. When consumers come in they say, "I've got money in my hand, and I'm going to spend it, but I'm not going to spend it easily, so let me see what you've got." They walk into the store and say, "Okay. Show me. Teach me." They're putting out their hard-earned money to buy something. *They* are the real critics.

BLDD: Has the press been important to the success of your work?

RL: Not at all, because I never got press.

BLDD: Do you think they've understood your unified lifestyle approach?

RL: I think they're getting it now. Now they're saying, "If this guy is so successful, let's watch." Quite frankly, I never got great reviews, nor negative ones, not the kind of reviews that I've seen others get. It's follow-the-leader in the press, and there are very few leaders. Obviously there are good press people—a handful of very wonderful writers that look and make critiques. They're not politically oriented. They don't want to be wined and dined. They look at the clothes, and they say, "This is what I see and this is what I think is important"—

BLDD: Is there a need to hold hands with the press?

RL: Very definitely.

BLDD: More so in the fashion press than in other professions?

RL: I don't know if it's more, or less, so. There are individuals in every area that you have to cater to. It is natural to become familiar and friendly with people that you work with.

BLDD: An age-old problem, particularly in specialized areas—how do you get involved with your colleagues, and still maintain a professional distance?

RL: I think it's difficult on any level, but there are personal likes, and personal friendships which are sometimes natural.

BLDD: What are your work habits like? You have so many divisions—how do you divide your day, and your time?

RL: I go through my day like a football player.

BLDD: Does that mean well-disciplined and regimented?

RL: It's regimented in that I'm handed a sheet of paper by my secretary who says, "This is what you've got to do at 9-10-11-12-1-2-3." Most of the time I don't have lunches; I go straight through each day. But I try to run every morning. I've seen the marathon on TV, and I would love to try it and train for it. I don't know if I really want to run in it, but I would love to be able to do it on my own, quietly. I seem to get on it, and then get off it, because I have to go somewhere. I guess it's not a strong enough desire on my part. Anyway, going through my day is interesting in that although it looks like I'm doing many different things they are all connected, and I'm very much connected to what I'm doing.

BLDD: I've been told there are two thousand products in your Home Furnishings Division. How much of a hand do you have in each?

RL: I'm involved in everything.

BLDD: How do you manage that?

RL: I don't know. If I have to think about it, I get real scared.

BLDD: Who decides what to keep in a line and what to throw out? To whom does Ralph Lauren talk?

RL: Well, I talk to myself. I talk to my assistants, people that I've grown with in this company, that are talented and very much a part of my life, and I talk to the individual manufacturer, or the people that I respect who have knowledge of the industry. To many of my designs, people say, "Ralph, this is not going to come off." Or sometimes they'll say, "It'll never happen." And I'll say, "No. It's got to happen." Some things do go off the line because they can't be made or the factory won't have enough time to produce them.

BLDD: Do they ever come back on the line?

RL: Usually if I believe in something. The interesting thing is that I've gone by my own instincts, my gut feelings, because I have not been trained in any of the businesses. But I have an instinct as a consumer. That's what I've worked with. I have never known what was right or what was wrong; I just did what I believed in.

BLDD: What part of the business do you like best?

RL: At this point, I like starting new things. I love the challenge of new things. I like launching them. I enjoy the advertising and the promotion. It's almost like doing a movie. I think that would be my ultimate goal—to try and do something like that.

BLDD: A movie?

RL: Yes. Making it say something important.

BLDD: Which part of your work do you like least?

RL: I don't know. It's such a unit now. It's very hard to say, but I guess doing the women's clothes—not that I like it the least, but it's the hardest to do. I have a very major business and I want to keep it going, but the hardest thing in this business is to re-design. Doing a first line is not hard—but staying there . . . It's very hard to have to draw—for me, particularly. The question is how can I be interesting on a very simple note, say something with simplicity, and also newness. How do you do a show—a thousand people come to the show—and have them walk out and say it's wonderful? How do you say something quietly, simply, elegantly three or four times a year?

BLDD: Who do you regard as your competitors?

RL: I don't know. I mean, I don't know about competitors, because each designer—and this is not trying to get out of something—who does his own thing is a designer, and he's not a competitor because he does *his* thing. So I don't think it's a matter of competitiveness, but there is stimulation . . . If someone is out there doing something and gets a lot of notice, I say "What is he doing that I'm not doing?" Or "What am I missing?" It gives you a little shot in the arm. So I don't know if I have a main competitor. I think all designers are competitors. I think anyone in the business is a competitor.

BLDD: Who's your role model, or who do you admire?

RL: It used to be John Kennedy. Now I don't know anymore.

BLDD: You started out with Fred Astaire and Cary Grant . . .

RL: It was a very superficial image. I have gotten to know a lot of people I admired and it has been very interesting.

BLDD: Did they turn out to be what they looked like?

RL: Cary Grant is a very nice, very clothes-conscious man. He has great style. But I don't think I have a role model anymore. I think it's myself.

BLDD: How do you compete with yourself?

RL: It's easy. I think there's always somewhere to go.

BLDD: What would you like to achieve now?

RL: I'm not sure yet. If you'd asked me five years ago I would have thought I had done everything I wanted to do. I don't know. I love challenges but I'm not quite sure of what they are now. I'm looking for perfection in life, how to live a proper way. We haven't really learned how to enjoy what we have, and to relax about life the way the Europeans, the English, have.

BLDD: It may take several generations to do that but since you've accelerated every other stage of your life, you might manage this one, too.

RL: I have lived at a highly accelerated pace, but I'm not that kind of person. There's a contradiction.

BLDD: You have all these beautiful residences and vacation houses. How do you find the time to visit and enjoy them?

RL: Well, I make the time. I have a family and I'm married, and we use the houses whenever my kids are off.

BLDD: Your family seems very central and important to your life.

RL: I am a father and a husband, and through my parents learned the value of those roles. That's important to me, and a very private feeling. The other things come and go. So I try to make as much time for them as possible.

BLDD: Do you emphasize more of that part of your life?

RL: I do now. I never changed. I'm home at seven o'clock every night with my kids. I yell at my kids just like everyone else does.

BLDD: But once you're there, what do you do? How often do you go out?

RL: Not much. I go to a movie, go for a hamburger or—

BLDD: Your days appear to be so rich and full that by the time you leave your office, there's not much left for the end of the day.

RL: I don't go to parties. I don't really have the patience for them.

BLDD: And what about your wife?

RL: She's probably more private than I am. She is trying to do things she loves. She's trying to find her own career and to express herself.

BLDD: Is she a designer as well?

RL: No, not at all. She doesn't have a particular career, but she's interested in art and interested in photography. She recently went to China and took some great photographs.

BLDD: Who do you have in mind when you design?

RL: Probably her, because she's beautiful. She lives a very natural sort of life. She takes care of a family and is a wife and a mother. She's not a frivolous girl that goes shopping in every store and wearing today's look every day. But she's an active, young, bright girl—and that's who I design for. She's been my role model.

BLDD: Both of you are very tightly-wrapped packages; you may have wanted to be Wilt Chamberlain, but you are indeed not his size. So with whose stature in mind do you design?

RL: I have models. But when I first started the clothes were very small, I really designed for very thin girls because I'm interested in people keeping their bodies together and being slim and trim and feeling good about themselves. I think that's a goal for a lot of people.

BLDD: What's your favorite look?

RL: I don't know if I have a favorite look. I love elegance. I love casualness. I don't have a favorite look. But whatever it is, it's got to be pleasing.

BLDD: How would you define "glamour"? How do you think a woman should look?

RL: Glamour is very personal. I think a girl on a horse with a string of pearls and a denim jacket would be glamorous—that's what I admire. Glamour for a man is a different thing. It's not a matter of what I see personally. I don't admire a man or woman that's very conscious of clothes. If you sense self-consciousness and concern about clothes, it's very unglamorous. Glamour comes from the inner self, it's a sense of style, an attitude, an intelligence. I mean, I could see a glamorous girl in a low-cut dress, who was beautiful—there is a mystique. From one point of view that's very beautiful. But to me naturalness and earthiness is most appealing. Glamour in a man is probably the sense of power he gives off.

BLDD: So you agree that power really is the ultimate aphrodisiac?

RL: I do think power is the most glamorous thing in a man, from what I've observed and what I think people relate to. A woman doesn't have the same drive for power that a man has; a woman wants to express herself but her need for power is not equal to his, nor would she flaunt it as a man would.

Ralph Lauren, fall, 1983

Ralph Lauren, fall, 1983

I've worked with a lot of women, and I like them. They are very good executives and leaders.

In terms of what makes people attractive, I don't think clothing is important. In terms of what expresses power and what expresses sex appeal and style, I think you can be wearing anything. It doesn't really matter. What becomes appealing is the personality and that is what makes the power. A guy could walk in here wearing an ordinary suit. If you found out that he does a lot of important things, and that he's a great guy, you'd say wow, he looks great. The fact that he is sloppy and doesn't care becomes appealing. If a guy comes in here with nothing but a spiffy, up-to-date suit, he becomes a very unimportant guy. I mean, models look great, but they have nothing to say. Now I can understand why Marilyn Monroe would be attracted to Arthur Miller versus Clint Eastwood. And you learn that as you become more mature.

BLDD: How do you explain your own professional expansion into home fashion? Was it your career unfolding, or your own personal needs? You have such a definite point of view, that I suspect if a product doesn't exist, you will design one to fulfill a personal need.

RL: That's exactly what it is. First clothing was my personal need and now it's home furnishings. It's all very personal. I don't use everything I make, but the designs are aimed at particular tastes and lifestyles.

BLDD: If that's the case, is furniture next?

RL: I've done some furniture . . .

BLDD: Where do you go from here; where does this all end?

RL: I only get involved where I can make a contribution. I like antique furniture. I like wonderful contemporary Italian furniture. I don't think I'm all things to all people. I don't think I can do everything. I'd like to think I can, but I can't. I think my talent is knowing what I can do and what I have to say, and not thinking I can say more than I can. I know my limits. I know who I am, and I know what I want to say, and I think there's an audience like me. I don't think I'm the world's greatest designer. I don't know what that is. I don't know what clothing design is. It's art, but it's not a painting, because when clothing doesn't sell it gets thrown into the dustbin and it becomes a rag.

BLDD: You've often said that fashion is a function of lifestyle, and in a way you design for the leisure hours, not for forty or more hours a week that most people spend working. Or is it that you would like to see American businessmen and women wearing Polo in the boardroom and the office?

RL: No. I've done all kinds of clothes for all kinds of living. I've designed pinstripe suits, and I design things for weekends, too.

BLDD: The costumes that you designed for "Annie Hall" were tremendously popular, and still affect the way many people look.

RL: Let me clarify that. In "Annie Hall," I didn't design the costumes. There were a lot of clothes that were mine that were personally selected by Diane Keaton or Woody.

BLDD: It is the Diane Keaton look that I am talking about.

RL: I don't want to take the credit for Diane Keaton.

BLDD: Was it her own interpretation of your look?

RL: Diane Keaton is a very stylish girl with great flair, and with her own style that made that movie. It was her own taste level. It was her own way of wearing things. The only thing I can say is that Diane wears a lot of my clothes, or has worn a lot of my clothes. She used to come to my shows when no one would even flash a bulb at her. One year she came to a show and no one knew who she was, and the next year the cameras were all over her. It was the same girl, very quiet, nice, and with great style. Her taste is very similar to mine, in what she thinks is exciting. She admired my clothes and I admired hers. So I don't want to take the credit.

BLDD: There was a period when even Ralph Lauren wasn't Ralph Lauren either. I'm sure it wasn't fun living through that. To what do you attribute, after that momentary lull, the really sharp turnabout in your business, when it all just escalated and exploded?

RL: Shaky, yes. Well, I can tell you a little about it. It was a tough time in that I had been in business about seven years, and was doing everything under one roof. Everything was done here. It was probably the darkest moment, one of the darkest moments of my life. That year I'd won a Coty Award. It was a very tough time because I began to realize that a few people

in the company with whom I had placed some financial controls weren't watching them and that there were a lot of loose ends. I always thought you go out of business if you don't do business. I was doing too much business, and didn't have any cash flow. So I had to fire some of the people that ran the financial end of it. Do you know what happens when rumors surround your business and people start to call? I started to deal with the sharks that appeared and said, "Well, we want this and this." Anyway, what happened fortunately, is that I decided to license my business, my women's business on Seventh Avenue. I hadn't licensed anything until then. That was the beginning of licensing for me, and I always thought if you license you've got to lose control, but I found that I had to license or else I would have lost my business. So, in order to get some guaranteed capital into my business, I decided to license the women's business which was then a very young one. It was causing me problems because I didn't have the right controls, and I wasn't handling it like a real business. I was handling it like a fun thing. But once I started handling it correctly, everything changed.

BLDD: Everything from perfume to home furnishings. Give us an idea of the range and diversity of your licensees. How many do you have?

RL: I don't even know the numbers. I have cosmetics, fragrance, home furnishings of all types. The home furnishings are everything that has to do with the home. And, of course, men's wear. I own all the men's companies. Polo is my company. I have licenses in Japan and Canada, too.

BLDD: The only things that I can think of that you haven't done yet are chocolates and automobiles.

RL: I've turned down chocolates, and automobiles I would love to do. I've turned down automobiles, actually. I'm talking about really designing automobiles, which I don't think I'm capable of. I'm a big car fan, but would never put my name on anything I don't know how to do myself.

BLDD: What haven't you designed yet that you'd care to?

RL: I think I'm doing everything. If I'm not designing something, it is because I'm not capable of it. I've been offered phones, toilet seats, chocolates but I think I'm doing enough and in areas where I have a statement to make. I think my designs have made a contribution.

BLDD: What's been your most successful design?

RL: I don't know. There are things that have gotten more play than others, such as the Prairie look in Santa Fe, which got a lot of exposure.

BLDD: By the way, you said it wasn't your early life but your later evolution that caused you to be so interested in the West.

RL: I think growing up in New York and living in this world of chic and sophistication, made me begin to look for a freedom, an outlet that was a little different. And whether the Old West existed or not, I was looking for something that was not sophisticated but that was natural, that was spacious, and that was very honest. There's too much around here, too much movement, too much that's too fast. Everything is style, fashion, pace, movement. So I was looking for an escape in my own life, and I think the West gave me that. It's inside of me, too. I have the most beautiful ranch in Telluride, Colorado. I spend the month of July there, and weekends when I can.

BLDD: For a fellow who grew up on the subways, what's it like to have your own airplane?

RL: It's great! It's heaven! It's a dream! You can go anywhere you want. It's like getting in a car, but you're up at my house in Colorado instead of Pound Ridge. I've been on that Long Island Expressway and it's taken me four hours to get out to Montauk. In four hours I could have been in Colorado.

BLDD: How often do you get to go to those houses?

RL: I use Jamaica when it's cold—it's a nice contrast.

BLDD: I assume, to use an inelegant phrase, everything is grist for your mill, that no matter where you go there must be some idea that touches or reaches you; for example, that Jamaica white look. Are there particular sources for your inspirations?

RL: People. Everything. When something comes into me, it's a blend of what I feel and what I see. I love every place. I'm a very happy person and I'm very happy and thankful about my life. I've got as good a life as you can have.

BLDD: How do you manage your overwhelming professional commitments and your private life?

RL: Well, if you ask my wife, she'll say I don't balance them. I just do my best to make everyone happy.

BLDD: There are a lot of people that you have to make happy. How do you stay so calm and appear to be so centered?

RL: I look calm, but I'm probably not. I am easy, but I have my stresses.

BLDD: Did you ever expect your life to unfold the way it has? In your best fantasy, did it ever approximate how it has turned out so far?

RL: No. I don't think I could have ever wished for this. It's too much to take. It's hard, but it's wonderful, but sometimes a little hard to cope with. It's hard to understand; I do as best I can.

BLDD: How do you manage to make sense out of it all?

RL: I just do it. It didn't happen overnight although it may look overnight to somebody else. So you grow and build with it. You live with the pains. I work my ass off just like anyone else does. I have things that go wrong every minute, right and wrong, up and down. And so I am busy and I work. The fact that I've been rewarded financially is wonderful, because it gives me a chance to escape, to have the flexibility to do anything I want to do. Having a family, I have one set of rules. If I were single, my life would be different than it is now.

BLDD: From what one knows about you and what you so consistently have described you are a very private, philosophical person with a hierarchical set of values. In many ways they're not unrelated to that very early classical training of yours, however orthodox. How do you communicate those values to children who are growing up in a whole other way that is even beyond what you could have imagined?

RL: Actually, it's not very different. I'm with them. I talk to my kids. I work with them, and so they see me, they see how I act. They see me with people. They watch my wife. There's a unity and a love, and I hope they will see what I do and what my wife does, and they will improve on it. But there is a lot of care and a lot of love and a lot of attention, no different than any other home. Maybe better in a lot of ways. We don't have some of the struggles that other people have financially. But I have probably equal pressure, maybe more pressure, than other people have.

BLDD: Do you think they miss something not having to struggle?

RL: I have two boys and a little girl. Fourteen, twelve, and nine. They struggle because they want to make their own mark.

BLDD: Do you see them interested in your field? Do you see a budding Ralph Lauren?

RL: I don't know yet. My son likes music. I see a lot of sensitivity in my family and thoughtfulness. They're nice kids.

BLDD: What do you see as the future evolution of fashion design, in the nineties, the year 2000? Will we have disposable fashion? Will we have overly complicated fashion? How will your own fashion goals be affected, if at all?

RL: I don't know. I don't want to think about it. Some people have asked what designs we'll be seeing worn in the year 2000 or 3000, or whatever. Your clothes have to do with your life. You know, people don't wear the same clothes they wore twenty or thirty or forty years ago. They wear a lot of the same clothes, but if for instance your life gets to be faster then you need clothes that are sturdier. There are new technologies every day. As the new technology evolves, the clothes change but people are still wearing warm tweeds, they wear cashmeres, they wear flannels, they wear scarves around the neck, they wear Chanel kind of shoes, and they get on planes. It would be a little weird to fly on the Concorde for three and a half hours wearing the same kind of clothes you wore fifty years ago. Somehow there's something that's not connected.

I'd like a little cottage in the country. I don't feel like living in a space-age house, although I admire some of the new technologies. One needs a balance of things. People still need comfort, they need warmth, they need coziness, they need a sense of realness. So I can't really say what the new technology is going to do, what people are going to be like, what the clothes will be like and I don't know how important clothes or status will be.

BLDD: Are they important now?

BLDD: I think they're less important now. There's so much out there.

BLDD: What is the new status?

RL: Be yourself. Have your own mind, and a sense of yourself. That's what people are moving to.

BLDD: What are the implications for you?

RL: Great. I love it, because I think that I cater to an educated consumer.

BLDD: Some things endure; I see a picture of the Duke of Windsor hiding behind a potted palm on your office wall. What does he represent for you?

RL: A wonderful style. I don't know if I like him as a person, whatever I've read I haven't liked. But I like his personal style, elegance, and charm. It's interesting to read that a guy who was a king and had all that prestige still cared about his own status. I could never quite understand that.

BLDD: Do you ever picture "abdicating" as he did? Just enjoying yourself and going to all those houses and having a wonderful time?

RL: Yes.

BLDD: Not only on a tired, rainy Monday morning, but in reality?

RL: More often than that.

BLDD: What would you do?

RL: I have a working ranch. I'd work with my ranch and cattle. A one hundred-year-old cabin and two newer cabins, a cookhouse, some breeding horses, and 1,600 head of cattle. It's fabulous.

BLDD: Could you picture living there?

RL: Not all the time. I think that I love too many things and love seeing different things.

BLDD: If you had it to do all over again, what would you do otherwise?

RL: Nothing. But actually, I don't know anyone who's done everything he wanted to do. There are very few people that can do anything they want to do. I can almost do that on my own, within my own world, on my own terms. I can't do everything, but I have control over what I do. I make things happen. I think you've got to believe in yourself, and if you believe in yourself, then you'll make it. If you're not sure, you'll make it halfway. If you're not sure at all, you won't make it at all. If you're totally sure and can stick with it, you'll make it.

BLDD: What advice would you give to young designers?

RL: Believe in what you're doing. You can't be somebody else. If you believe in yourself, then you've got to keep going and don't let people tell you it's not right.

BLDD: Are you saying practice makes perfect, or nothing without much labor, or both?

RL: I think you've got to work and I think you've got to have luck. I wouldn't want to start again.

BLDD: Is it possible for a young designer to become a Ralph Lauren nowadays? Is there any way in, now?

RL: I think it would be real hard. There's so much competition today; there was not a hell of a lot when I started, now it's a whole new world.

BLDD: You mentioned earlier that you can picture those ads talking, that you can see it all moving towards making a film.

RL: Well, I love quality things. I think there's a lot to be done in film that hasn't been done in terms of taste and quality.

BLDD: What kind of film would you make?

RL: I don't know yet. I have to be inspired by something, but if I did it, I would do it right.

BLDD: Do you want to write it, or produce it, or act in it, or all of the above?

RL: All of the above!

BLDD: Why not? Who plays Ralph Lauren in the story?

RL: Woody Allen.

Ralph Lauren, fall, 1983

Opposite and overleaf:
Ralph Lauren, fall, 1983

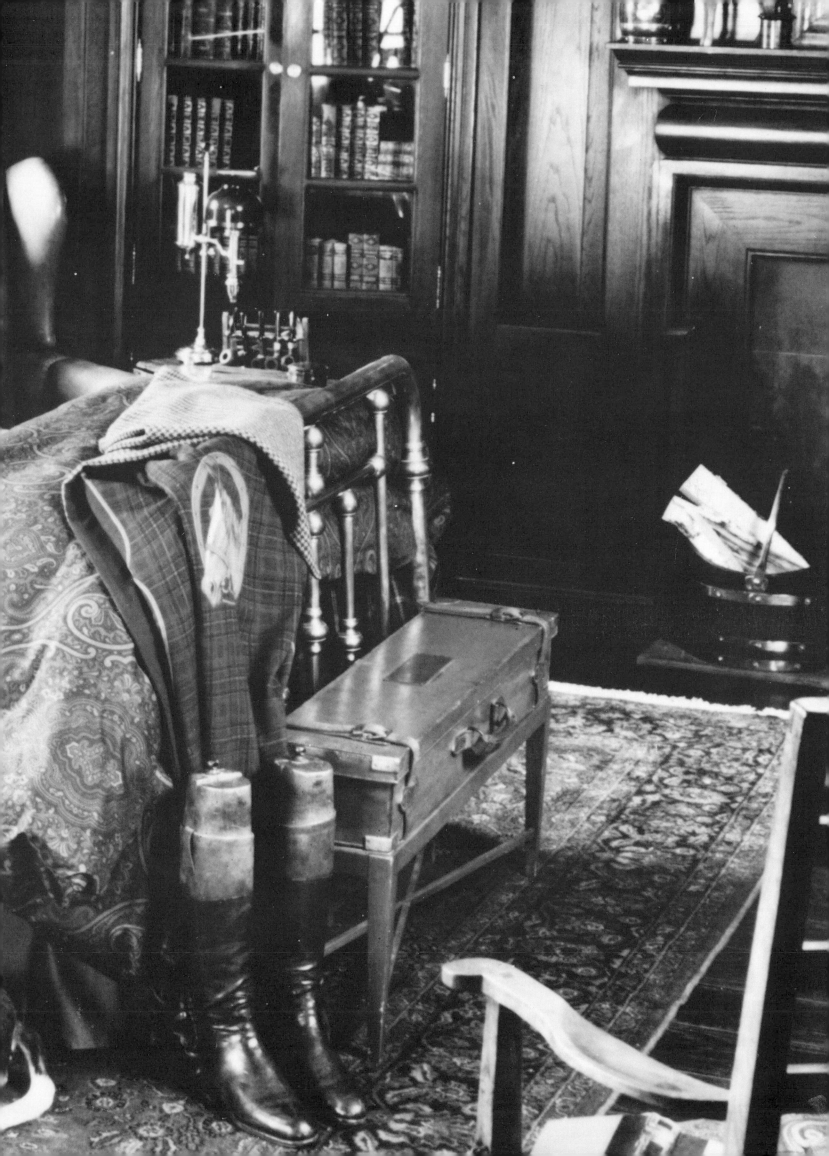

MM

Mary McFadden

The clothes, jewelry, and furnishings designed by Mary McFadden are often described in terms that are used to talk about art. Her work is derived from many sources, including cultures far and near, familiar and ancient. The result is designs that are contemporary and timeless.

BLDD: Others think of your work as synonymous with exotic, hand-painted and shimmering fabrics. How do you see your work, Mary?

MM: I see it as something that's evolved over a long period of time. Ten years ago we started working with China silk. At that time, it was very inexpensive, about $2.25 a yard, and everyone else was working with jersey. Then I decided to do everything possible with China silk: paint it, quilt it, and pleat it. I realized then that a natural fiber cannot be permanently pleated. After a year I found a polyester satin back in Australia, which we still use today. We had it refined in Japan. Then we developed marii pleating, which is created by a heat process that produces this very rich effect in the fabric. We have about twenty different patented varieties of pleating.

BLDD: I've often thought of you as your own very best spokesperson, the very model of style and grooming. Would you give those of us with more taste than funds some tips on developing a personal style?

MM: It requires a lot of looking into the mirror and getting to know yourself. I don't think it happens overnight. American women take a long time to find their sense of style, as opposed to the European woman, who seems to have an innate flair for it. Maybe she spends more time in front of the mirror. I haven't figured that out yet, but I do think it's very important to understand what you are inside, and then learn to project what you think you are. I think it's a very important and a very charming thing for a woman, or a man, to do in their contacts with people.

BLDD: What is that mysterious quality that we know as "good taste"? How would you define that?

MM: I really have never figured out what it is, but I do know what bad taste is. It is not harmonious, and good taste seems to be in perfect balance and harmony. There are so many types of tastes today and there have been so many different styles over the centuries. It took maybe a hundred years to refine the shape of a Ming dynasty piece of jade or an astrological disc until it reached perfect balance. I consider that a form of perfect taste.

BLDD: Perhaps more than any other fashion designer, yours is the total aesthetic, encompassing most everything, from your own one-of-a-kind clothes and jewelry—did you design the earrings that you're wearing?

MM: I've been making jewelry for ten years. It's one of my most favorite things to do. We have our own factory, in fact. These earrings come from the current collection which was based on Islamic art from the period between the sixth century and the thirteenth century. Those reflect a later period of Islamic design.

BLDD: Your respect for the work of craftspersons is evident in your own collections. How do all of these interests of yours nurture each other, and how do they reflect themselves in your work?

MM: I think that an artist or designer or a writer, for that matter, is a product of his total education, and that the better the education, the stronger the stamp, and the depth of the work. It will have a much stronger sincerity and clarity and intellect. Let's take the example of Picasso, who encompassed all cultures in his work.

BLDD: How important is research to your work?

MM: It's a starting point, but essentially my work is all a fantasy of my creation. I think that most people need a starting point, an inspiration. And that inspiration is sometimes much stronger one year than the next, which is why one collection is better than another. The inspiration, or the person to whom you may have dedicated the collection, have not been strong enough. Sometimes I dedicate collections.

BLDD: Who has received this honor in the past?

MM: I dedicated the recent collection to my business partner, J. Patrick Lannan. I've dedicated one to my daughter, and another to a friend.

BLDD: The clothes that you design are quite different from the kind of practical and durable garments that you must have been accustomed to seeing as a child growing up on a Tennessee cotton farm. What influence did those experiences have on your current interest and work?

MM: I can hardly remember the Tennessee farm. My only visual memory of

142

the Tennessee farm is that it was all made of glass, very much in the style of Philip Johnson. Can you believe it? That was so far back.

BLDD: A farmhouse in glass?

MM: No. It wasn't a farmhouse. It was an incredibly beautifully glass house that stood on a hundred acres, some of which were cotton. My father was in the cotton business and he also loved cattle, dogs, cats, pigs and everything else that goes with a farm. We had a couple of donkeys, as children, and they used to knock me off as soon as they got to the salt lick. I remember we used to stroll through the irrigation ditches before the floods, where I can remember encountering four-legged eels. My father died when I was very young, so I left the farm when I was eight, and have no visual images beyond those I described.

BLDD: Was your first interest in fabric a result of that early involvement with cotton?

MM: Well, we only saw cotton growing. I never knew what it was to see it spun or woven on jacquard machines, or looms, or any of the things that I've seen since I've been in the business.

BLDD: After that early age you came to New York and then eventually, as you've recalled, were a student of sociology at Columbia University.

MM: I came down to the New School for Social Research for supplementary classes in sociology, and then I studied philosophy with the so-called "faculty in exile" that had come from Europe. There were some wonderful thinkers that were so powerful that you went to class just to listen to them think, or speak in a beautiful manner. Actually, I never really understood very much of what they were saying; their ideas were so lofty.

BLDD: For you, the transition from the world of academia to the world of fashion was a swift one. It's not everyone who goes directly from being a student of sociology to becoming the international director of publicity for a celebrated fashion company. How did that come about?

MM: That was another lucky chance. I had been a very serious scholar, and consequently I used to get up at six and work until midnight every night. I did it for three years without really taking a break, all through the summer, too. One night I was invited by the head of Christian Dior to a cocktail party, and heard that they were looking for a girl to run the public relations for Christian Dior–New York. I went up to the Executive Vice President and said, "Listen, I'd like to interview for the job." And he said, "Come down tomorrow at ten o'clock." So I went to 498 Seventh Avenue. I guess I was 20 or 22 years old then. I said to Henry Sherman, who was later to become President of Christian Dior, "I don't know anything about public relations, but if you hire me I'll be a fast study. I'll learn the business within two months, and you don't have to pay me for that time. And if I do well, then I want to be paid. He said it was a deal. At the end of two months, he said, "You've done a fantastic job and now you can be paid."

BLDD: How long did you stay there?

MM: I stayed there three years. It was very interesting to be on the inside of a company like that. Christian Dior always said that his name would be remembered for his licensing empire, and Henry Sherman was really responsible for building up the licensing empire internationally. And so I learned about the building of a licensing empire. It isn't like licensing today. At that time they just licensed the name Christian Dior to the best manufacturer, say, for women's stockings, women's shoes, whatever. It was not the huge design input that designers give now to licensing.

BLDD: You are involved in every aspect, I assume, of your own licensing designs. I know how involved you were with the design of the bottle for your perfume, which resembles the pleats used in your clothing.

MM: It was a very interesting experience. We took a piece of fabric and just twisted it, then asked a sculptor to work on it. It took about a year to make the perfect clay models—it's an asymmetrical bottle—and discover how fabric actually flows, in glass. Originally it was all too perfect, and we were slowly able to work into it natural imperfections, which enhance the beauty of the bottle.

BLDD: From 1964 to 1970, you lived in Africa. What circumstances brought you there?

MM: The first time I went there was at the invitation of Jane Engelhard, whose husband controlled most of the uranium and platinum and other fine metals in the world. They had huge holdings in southern Africa, and

invited me to their house. I thought that it would be great fun to see what Africa was like. That was in 1964. I'd just come back from spending two months on the Nile, which was great fun, except traveling on the Nile was rather exhausting in those days.

BLDD: Were those holidays from your work, or were you between engagements?

MM: In fact, in South Africa I was doing licensing for Dior, but the Egyptian trip was a holiday. We set up a licensing system for Dior, for men's shirts and ties—the usual, dull but practical merchandise that Dior has all over the world. Dior's licensing empire is about the third largest in the world. There I met my first husband. He was a director of De Beers Diamonds, and that meant that he traveled around most of Africa operating the diamond mines. If you're living in a diamond mine, it's like living in a prison. It is so isolating that most people find it very hard and crack up. So the actual management of people on the mine is a difficult problem.

BLDD: Did you find it difficult to live there?

MM: I loved my years in Africa. I became editor of *Vogue South Africa*. That gave me a chance to see everything that happened in South Africa. I learned how to write. I no longer had to rely on journalists. As a public relations woman, you're always inventing stories for journalists to write about, and that was one thing I really resented doing. I felt that it was like being the leech, in effect. When I started as office editor at *Vogue South Africa*, thanks to Mrs. Vreeland, who got me the job, I learned to write and to edit the magazine. I learned about merchandising and everything there was to know about South Africa, from the political point of view, from the African's point of view.

BLDD: Did you write about political things as well?

MM: I did. *Vogue South Africa* closed a year after that. We had increased the circulation to about 25,000. It was a glossy quarterly, published in England. The printing presses were in England, because they didn't want to put the investment into South Africa for political reasons, naturally. Mr. Patcévitch was then running Condé Nast. I went to visit him in England and asked him not to close down *Vogue South Africa* because there was a real possibility that it would make a lot of money, because it had a strong position within the market, but he didn't believe me. He thought the political situation was going to collapse any moment. Needless to say, it's going to go into the 22nd century, probably. The magazine was closed down, and I became a freelance writer and a columnist on the Rand Daily Mail, and worked for probably the most brilliant group of writers and editors anywhere, any time. They won all the prizes for writing and several of them, of course, were given one-way passports to leave the country because of the prison scandal. I also left South Africa and went to Zimbabwe—it was then called Rhodesia—where I married my second husband, who was the director of the National Gallery there. Together we developed the Vokuto workshop schools for the Africans.

BLDD: What does Vokuto mean?

MM: Vokuto is a word used by the Mashona, which is the largest tribe in Zimbabwe today. The Vokuto bird is a small pigeon that lives in a huge valley there.

BLDD: And what did you do at this workshop?

MM: Well, the Mashona were an extraordinary tribe with a unique culture. They had the keeper of the peoples' memory, and they had a huge fantasy world of animals that were half-human, half-bird. There were rock edifices from the 11th or the 13th century that are without mortar, in huge conical shapes. No one knows if the Arabs built them for gold, or what the reasons were. It's still shrouded in great mystery. But there have been carvers of stone since the 13th century and it's like an inborn skill. All their sculptures were made in serpentine, which exists in very few places in the world. Serpentine is, in fact, powder or talc. It's a very soft stone, and easy to carve. It exists in Russia and in Rhodesia, and the pre-Colombians used it in Mexico. At any rate, you could tell that they had an incredible genius for carving in serpentine, and their fantasies ranged from tree growth symbols to all the early symbols of design one can think of, that also occur in other prehistoric cultures.

BLDD: What happened to the sculptures that emerged from this workshop?

MM: We sold them to twenty-three different countries. They had a show at the Musée Rodin in Paris.

BLDD: And what did that experience teach you?

MM: That was, in fact, the beginning of my inspiration, to become a designer. I had always believed that I would be a writer for the rest of my life, living in front of my typewriter, translating from my head to my hands, which is an interesting and a very creative form of exercise. But I had never ever thought that I'd make a dress, for instance. In Africa, however, I did have to make a couple of dresses, because I couldn't find anything that I liked. Then I was sent to Madagascar for about six months to do stories. I was the first journalist into Madagascar, which is a fascinating country. And there I bought some of the most beautiful Madagasch silks. I didn't know anything about sewing, so when I came back I created something very simple that an African could sew. I made a square, and I cut out the head on one side and I put a little hole in the middle of the square, letting the fabric fall on the bias. It became a beautiful tunic, and I used pants underneath it. But it was a very simple thing that anyone could do. The fabric was, of course, extraordinary.

BLDD: Were those your first designs?

MM: Those were the first designs and, when I came back to New York, they were photographed for the cover of *Vogue*.

BLDD: How did that come about?

MM: I wore them to work one day, and people thought they were beautiful. I had been going back and forth to Madagascar even after I'd written the stories on the Madagasch people and their history. I went back to collect sculptures from the tombs of the dead. A Chinese gentleman helped me to negotiate the deals. It is desirable to have a lot of cattle on Madagascar. There are more cattle than people—I think ninety million cattle to six million people. So I traded cattle for tombs. The theory is that you're more important when you're dead than when you're alive, that the spirits of the dead are in the corner somewhere watching. You can't just rob a grave, you must placate the ancestral spirits, and you can do that by paying with cattle. There are all kinds of strange rituals on Madagascar. When you die, they prop you up in the middle of the desert and people come to visit you for about two months. When the stench gets too terrible, they bury you in a huge hole in the mountain. If a father dies, the eldest son jumps in after him to take the spirit from him, and then they throw rocks over the corpse. There are about thirty-seven different tribes in Madagascar and twenty-seven different dialects, and each tribe has its own very bizarre way of taking care of its dead.

BLDD: Why don't we move on to the living for a moment? Would you be good enough to tell us how you moved on from Madagascar to New York?

MM: In 1969–1970 the political situation closed in again in Zimbabwe. There were only 250,000 whites and something like thirteen million black people, and it was pretty obvious that the white people would have to leave very shortly, and that South Africa would not come to their aid. Since we'd supported black enterprises, we were not exactly *persona grata*. My husband said, "I think it's about time we leave." He then decided to spend the rest of his life at sea and I decided to seek my fortune in New York. I came to New York and immediately went to meet Alexander Lieberman. He still is, and will probably always be, one of my friends. I admire him tremendously. He is the editorial director of all the Condé-Nast publications. Diana Vreeland also came to my aid, and said to Alex, "Mary's in town. Why don't you give her a job in the art department?" I worked in the art department tediously for about three months. This was 1970. I wasn't sure they were going to give me a permanent job, but after a month Alex said, "I think we'd better hire you." He realized that I was better in the journalistic area than doing layouts, and made me Special Projects Editor, which meant taking care of all the home furnishings, doing the house photographs for which you earn lots of awards, thank God. We were then a bi-monthly and there were more pages not devoted to fashion. I did all those pages—there were about twenty each issue. I did the beauty pages and all the photo-reportages of personalities and their lifestyles. That lasted for three years. And then one day my dress got on the cover of *Vogue*.

BLDD: Simply because you wore it to work?

MM: Yes.

BLDD: That was about ten years ago, and in that period you have been transformed from an interesting globetrotter to an incipient tycoon. How did your experience as a fashion tastemaker and commentator influence your own development as a designer, or your own design and marketing technique?

MM: At the beginning we made tunics. They said, "Once the dress is on the cover, go and get a merchandising credit." I'd just done a story on Geraldine Stutz (the president of Bendel's in New York) on her houses in town and in the country. I thought well, maybe she'll see me. I knew that every Friday the designers came with their work, so, I went over. Jean Rosenberg, the Vice President, sees new work on Fridays and you can line up, as I did. I presented her with these three tunics and she said, "Why don't you come back next week and let Geraldine see them?" Geraldine loved them, and she bought about thirty of each.

BLDD: Where did you get thirty of each tunic?

MM: I didn't have any! I had three!

BLDD: So, what did you do?

MM: I had three different styles. I had one made out of the most beautiful pongee made in Hong Kong, and two of these toga types and pants that went with them. That's what I was wearing as my evening uniform. So I said, "Listen. I don't know how to sew. Can you please help me out? I don't know anything about pattern making or draping or anything like that." She suggested that I see a man called Mitsu, a very highly qualified Japanese technician, trained in Japan. And he said, "I'll leave my business"—he was in some pattern company—"and we'll start making these clothes together." He took a little basement in the East 80's. It was so hot, no air conditioning, and we had a mirror over a sink and one seamstress. I used to have to climb up onto the sink to see the proportion in this tiny mirror! That was August. In September we delivered the clothes, on time. Mitsu cut the patterns. We had, I think, at that point, a million dollars in business!

BLDD: All in this one-room basement?

MM: Yes. Geraldine gave me a press show and invited the national press, as well as some socialites, and through that show I was able to book a million dollars worth of business.

BLDD: How influential has the fashion press been in terms of your own continuing success?

MM: What we always say about the fashion press is that if you get a great deal of good publicity you should expect to fail.

BLDD: Do you think that's limited to the fashion press?

MM: No. I think that's probably true about life. Any new star gets incredible press, and I was terribly lucky to have four-star collections for three or four years in a row.

BLDD: And then what happened?

MM: Then I went down to one star and I'm still struggling around at one star. Maybe next year I'll do better. But, at any rate, for about six years I was at the top and it was incredible because I didn't really know anything about designing.

BLDD: Have you since learned about pattern-making and other design skills that you didn't know originally? Or, is that not important because you inform yourself by other means and you have managed to find the Mitsus of this world to support the areas that you don't know?

MM: It took me ten years to get the most highly sophisticated machine in terms of the best production manager, the best pattern-makers, the best duplicate makers. It's all produced in-house now. Nothing is contracted out, because we now own everything. The best administrators, the best salespeople, the best accountants, the best lawyers.

BLDD: You sound as if your life is in perfect shape. Enviable!

MM: Now I can become a playgirl!

BLDD: Is that your next agenda?

MM: Well, I think I'm doing a pretty good job right now!

BLDD: Your involvement with American culture, especially crafts, is extensive. How does that involvement affect your work, or the place where you work?

MM: I met Patrick Lannan in 1973—he's my business partner. He also owns a large foundation that is dedicated to young artists in Palm Beach, for which we are going to build three auxiliary museums. I'm the curator.

144

From 1975 to about 1977, we bought heavily in all the glass artists internationally, all the ceramic artists, the artists working in fiber, and those working in textiles and jewelry.

BLDD: What are your goals as the curator of the collection?

MM: Patrick has really outlined the goals. The artists we support are usually without galleries or not highly established. For instance, in the case of Julian Schnabel, we bought him before he was hardly known. Today, how can you afford to buy a Julian Schnabel? We've been very lucky. I think our track record has been incredible in the discovery of new talent across the country, in the areas of painting, sculpture, kinetics.

BLDD: Does your curatorial work inform your work as a designer?

MM: The only thing I can see that's related to what we do is that we have used glass for jewelry and at the foundation we've worked with glass artists. We've worked with all kinds of unique young artists in fabric development, because we're very involved in that area, because of knitwear and throws in our own collection.

BLDD: Have you ever commissioned any fiber artists to design anything for the Mary McFadden couture collection?

MM: I do that pretty much by myself. I give them a design. But some of my technicians might articulate it better than I, given the conceptual idea of the design.

BLDD: Nowhere is your interest in the arts more evident than in the places in which you live and work. Would you describe those two places? Why don't we talk about your showroom which is filled with pieces from your own collection?

MM: From the East 85th Street basement we were able to move to 264 West 35th Street, which Mitsu found for me. We had a little cubby corner there, too. That's how it started. Now I have four floors. I think we practically own the building! Mitsu suddenly realized that he couldn't handle all my production. How do you produce a million dollars' worth of goods? It was out of the question. So, we both went our own ways. He has his own floor, now, too, and it's been highly successful, which greatly pleases me. We see each other in the elevator and still remember the old days. First, we took a half floor, then a full floor. Then, about two years later, we had three and after ten years, we had four floors. The showroom you see today was created about five years ago. We painted it dark blue to conceal its miserable architecture, because it's just an old loft, and we filled it with the most extraordinary pieces of art. There's an Alan Shields there. We have work by a new man called McFarland who is an incredible talent working in graphite. We also have jewelry on display there. There's even a table by Mark DiSuvero, and work by the late Dennis Valensky.

BLDD: In fact, there are even two framed Mary McFaddens that appear to be ready to go to the Metropolitan Museum's Costume Institute.

MM: One of them was a wedding dress with the most beautiful macramé work in it. I wanted just to save it as something that will hardly ever be seen again. And the other is a hand-painted chiffon in an incredibly beautiful pastel configuration of abstract flowers.

BLDD: Your apartment is as spare and serene as a Buddhist temple. Do you have any advice for those who find it hard to cut down on clutter?

MM: Every three years I send a whole bunch of goods to auction. Then I notice I've got quite a lot of money in the bank again. Then I go out and redecorate. That's what I did this afternoon.

BLDD: Was this afternoon pruning or buying?

MM: This afternoon was looking. I went over to Sotheby's. I had received two catalogues from them because one of my pieces was being auctioned in an Islamic collection. And I saw another piece of Islamic art, from the 10th century. It was beautiful but in terrible condition. I know how to get it restored so it'll look like a hundred million bucks when it's finished and framed. Anyway, I noticed that it was not valued very highly, so I told my assistant to bid on it tomorrow. Then, of course, you get trapped in these places. They happened to have an exhibit of European furniture and there were three things from the Italian Baroque period in there that I have my eye on.

BLDD: One of the things that you're not trapped in is any one location or any one style. You moved from a very large apartment that was rather formal to a glass-enclosed box and now you're going to the Italian Baroque period. Will that influence the design of your clothes as well?

MM: I haven't thought about that yet. It's a secret what the next collection is, but we're researching it.

BLDD: Can you give us a little preview of what the spirit or nature of that collection will be like?

MM: We decided we're going to do a collection based on the Napoleonic period. There were three empires. But, in fact, the second empire was so short that it really didn't exist because Napoleon's son died when he was twenty. We're dealing in basically a highly neoclassical period. We have chosen all the fabrics for the collection already. In the last collection we had some beautiful fabrics. These are even more beautiful because there were more beautiful fabrics available. We're working with several fabric houses in Europe, to whom we give fullscale pattern designs that they can print on beautiful face fabrics that we have chosen.

BLDD: Since your clothes are unique, is there a way that you can test-market your ideas before manufacturing them? How do you know that an ensemble will convey the kind of magic that you have in mind to the potential buyer for the store and to their ultimate customer?

MM: I have always believed that the closer I have stayed to classical designs and shapes, the greater our sales have been.

BLDD: So do you learn to be true to your own instincts?

MM: Well, no. Most of the collection is actually the opposite, it is rather flamboyant, and everything I do that's flamboyant never reaches the production stage. The dress you're wearing, in fact, was the best seller we ever created and it was a dress that I never thought was going to make the production line. It was created after the collection.

BLDD: Is it the color or is it the style?

MM: The color was a large part of it. It's been made in every color, of course, but it was shown to the buyers in the purple color you are wearing. I thought that the dress I have on would be a top seller and that we'd cut 500 units of it, but we didn't.

BLDD: Do you ever make that many of any particular style?

MM: Oh yes. We made three or four hundred units of the one you have on.

BLDD: Your work has always relied heavily on an excellent color sense. How do you make decisions about color? How do you decide that one year it's black, and one year it's purple, and another pastel?

MM: About two collections back, my inspiration was the Olmec Collection. It was the mother civilization of the pre-Colombian period. I went to Mexico and became fascinated by that period. I think of Mexico as a land of rusts and earth colors with bright hot pinks and a lot of brilliant green. That's how we came upon those colors.

BLDD: How does that relate to your work at the Color Council, of which you are one of the fashion members?

MM: We are all asked to submit the spectrum of colors that we think will be the color range for the following year. What usually happens is that colors seem to roll in a rather interesting cycle. The seven or eight people often all choose the same colors.

BLDD: What's in store for us? Will you give us a fearless forecast of new colors?

MM: Right now what is very important is black and white. I can't tell you why people are buying it—maybe it's because of the recession. That'll change. It's been strong for two seasons now.

BLDD: If that's the case, do we go to red next?

MM: What I mean to say is that very graphic colors like red and black or black and white have all been strong. You can see them in practically every collection. What's going to happen next? For the next collection we have a peach and rose group, black and white, of course, and we have a beige group, which you almost always have. This time the groupings were chosen according to what was available to us in that incredible fabric show that appeared for the first time at Parsons School of Design and from a few other sources.

BLDD: What's the current price range of your clothes?

MM: $500 to $3,000 at retail, and the average falls at a thousand bucks.

BLDD: Why do they cost so much? Is it the labor, the fabric?

MM: It's everything. The fabric, the marii pleating which comes in at $14 pleated and landed, and the labor that goes into the making of these dresses. It looks very simple, but whenever anything looks very simple, it's actually very complicated. The simplicity shows the perfection. I think we've become experts in dealing with fabric. Even though it's imitated every day, no one has learned the actual perfection of how we do it.

BLDD: One of your favorite combinations is a long, loose tunic worn over floating loose pants or a long skirt. Is that a classic type of ensemble?

MM: That was the first garment I made. It started the trend of tunic dressing in the evening. And I almost do it as a good luck sign in every collection.

BLDD: But is it, in addition to being one of your trademarks, because you think it's a permanent style, a classic?

MM: I do. Every woman can wear it. It disguises the mountains and valleys of a woman's figure. If you're fat, it doesn't show your fat. If you're thin, it makes you look like a goddess. And I don't do it only in marii pleating. I do it in silks and in every kind of fabric—in lace, for instance, combined with other materials. I feel that it elongates a woman. Maybe because I am small, I want to have a very columnar feeling. I don't think the designer can ever, ever separate her own body from her designs.

BLDD: You've mentioned a columnar feeling. In fact, your designs are sometimes described as architectural. What does that really mean?

MM: I have been very, very upset by the feeling of wearing a Chanel suit that is boxy and that didn't fall on me properly, perhaps because I am too small. So when I did go into design, I wanted to correct all the things that I had hated about other designers. And one of them was just that. Balenciaga is certainly considered an architectural designer. I wanted the clothes to be fluid and to move with the body, *not* have their own architecture. I think we've achieved that from the very beginning with the so-called "soft" dressing.

BLDD: Who do you see as the most influential designers, and who are those that most influence your work?

MM: I'd say the people who forced me to go my own way were the designers that I hated the most—the two designers that I've just mentioned.

BLDD: Is there a particular age group to which your clothes are geared, or do you think anyone can wear them?

MM: Brooke Shields is our youngest client, and she's been buying since she was fifteen. And we've got a couple of clients that are getting close to a hundred years old! Maybe they'll last to 120. Who knows today!

BLDD: How do you recommend using jewelry and accessories to keep an outfit looking fresh and new, particularly since the clothes are so distinctive. I would think if I went any place wearing this wonderful purple fantasy, and were to return, my tunic would be very well remembered, and that isn't what most women want. Are your clothes so distinctive that there is sometimes a problem with wearing the same outfit twice?

MM: I think we've had that problem in the past with the hand-painted tunics that were so extraordinary. The reason they never really sold is because they were so obviously a strong design statement. We never had trouble with the pleats, oddly enough, nor with the quilted coats. They keep on selling each year as if we had just created them. But a woman will feel uncomfortable wearing something that is extraordinary, like a very bold fabric design, two or three times a season for fear that someone will say, "Gee, you must be so poor you only have one dress." It's really true.

BLDD: You've created a line called Couture for the Working Woman. What is your own personal dress for success philosophy?

MM: This year I've been much more of a peacock than in other years. There were years in which my grandfather always wore the same grey suit. I think he had about fifty of them at one time. He was a physicist and an extraordinary man. He was an honorary doctorate five times in his life, which to me is high achievement. I admired him enormously, even though I couldn't work even a slide rule. He said the reason he had all the same clothes was that he didn't want to have to make a decision every morning. The suit was there, and it was very elegant, and there were no decisions to be made. I adopted that philosophy for a long time, until recently. I met a couple of movie stars, and I realized that they were making a terrific effort to be very attractive at all times. So I threw away my uniform, which had been black in the winter and white in the summer, and decided to make some fantastic daywear clothes. This is my year of the peacock. I have fantastic daywear clothes now.

BLDD: It would seem that your approach would lend itself especially to costume design for the stage or for film. Is that an involvement that you've had or that you would like to have?

MM: I'm reading the script of "Gorky Park" right now, which will star Gregory Peck. And I'm going to be reading a script for Jack Nicholson. He's going to play Napoleon and Jack Nicholson playing Napoleon will be incredible.

BLDD: Do you expect to costume that?

MM: I'm hoping to. They sent me the scripts to see if it appeals to me.

BLDD: What are your most important concerns in designing clothes for women who work?

MM: I found that it was a totally different market than anything that we had been involved in, and the things that sold were the clothes that faded into the wall. Whenever I went beyond that we couldn't cut 5,000 units, which was the number we were cutting of a particular garment. The simpler the design was and the less design that was in it, the greater number of units we could cut.

BLDD: In many ways you yourself redefine the idea of the working woman. How do you manage it all? Where do you get the energy and the discipline?

MM: I have a lot of responsibilities. That's true. Running a factory is like being a mother to fifty people. Every day there is a problem. And every day you have to talk to people, whether they are in sales, production, or administration or the lawyers, accountants, assistant designers, or the design staff. They are, in a way, like a family to me. I feel very responsible for them. We've worked for a long time to achieve our present level. In fact, my assistant designer is probably my best friend. She's in the hospital tonight and I hope that she's going to be all right. When you have this kind of responsibility, your whole life is really in the factory, because you're there, either physically or on the telephone, from nine in the morning until five at night, dealing with various divisions or with the licensees. So the discipline comes from a fighting spirit that's in your blood. Of course, to begin with, New York gives you a fighting spirit. There's a great deal of competition in New York and it affects you. Maybe if I lived in a sleepy town, I might sleep all day. But New York isn't like that. You feel the incredible momentum and that's why I love it.

BLDD: In addition to all of your designs for clothing and jewelry, you design home furnishings. How do you apply those same distinctive designs to the needs of a mass audience? What is it that you do in home furnishings?

MM: We have a licensee with Martex for sheets, towels, bed coverings, and comforters, and we have upholstery and wallpaper.

BLDD: How do you shift your design priorities from the one woman who has a great deal of money, a very rarified lifestyle, to that anonymous mass audience who is going to spend a night or a week in a hotel using your bed linen?

MM: I don't shift. It's the same thread that runs through my work, the same fingerprint. However I think in couture, I give it to them in home furnishings.

BLDD: Does your interest in home furnishings stem from a desire for a more durable influence than fashion—which, in a way, is momentary—or is it a commitment to a more totally designed environment?

MM: I don't look at it like that because, for the most part, I never see these houses with my products in them except in photographs. I really consider it an extension of fabric design. We're painting beautiful fabrics and how they're used is up to the person who buys them. The most important thing to me is the beauty of the fabric.

BLDD: You've said that we should surround ourselves with everything that is beautiful and pleasing to the senses. That's a nice idea, but how do we accomplish that in today's overly-rushed and overly-expensive world?

MM: It requires a lot of research, a lot of imagination, and a very careful allocation of time. A good brain doesn't hurt. If it is your will, it is achievable. We are the masters of our destinies. I believe very strongly that we can achieve whatever we want.

BLDD: The fashion press tells us every season what is in and what is out, and it seems invariably that what's out before, is in now. With such abundant and ephemeral advice, to whom should we listen?

MM: Because I'm constantly on the road, I know how much information there is from films and television, newspapers and magazines. But I'm also

Mary McFadden, fall/winter, 1983

aware, that it doesn't affect the American woman that much. Perhaps only ½ to 1 percent of American women are effected. They are much more individualistic now than they were in the '60's, when the designer said do this or do that, and they did it like robots. The woman of the '70's and the '80's and the '90's has greater freedom. She starts to understand herself at a younger age. We're going through a body cult right now. I think that's a beautiful thing. Not that there haven't been such cults in all civilizations. Some fads continually recur and disappear, and they always fascinate me. I do not believe that the fashion press, with all the media that they use, has been as influential as I had hoped they would be. I think that the '90's is going to show a much greater change than the '80's in terms of the effectiveness of the press.

BLDD: And how will it affect what people will be wearing? Do you see more synthetic fabrics, more uniform dressing?

MM: There's no question that manmade fibers, whether they be polyester, rayon, or combinations, are much more durable than natural fibers and also much cheaper. The inroads being made in the development of manmade fibers, particularly in Japan, are very interesting to watch.

BLDD: You've already been the recipient of three Coty Awards, elected to the Hall of Fame, and enjoy worldwide distinction. You obviously have a very restless and curious mind. What next?

MM: We're going to get into the movie business eventually, by hook or by crook, and we're going to get onto Broadway. We almost did "The Brothers Karamazov," but it didn't work out. Dostoevsky is a very heavy man with rather dull ideas about God and life and death. He's basically interested in murder of every type, patricide, political murder and so forth. They're heavy concepts and people don't like things that are heavy. They want to be amused.

BLDD: You've been involved in many different professions. Is there any field that you haven't turned to, that if you had the time or the opportunity you would like to?

MM: Building a theatre would be fascinating. I've just designed some mobile gardens. I spent six months studying mobile gardens. I've always been fascinated with garden history and garden design. I studied every type, from Palladio to Hadrian to le Nôtre to Burle Marx, who I think is the greatest garden designer of the twentieth century. Russell Page is a classical designer because his gardens get better with age. Although I'm not fascinated with classical design in that sense. We worked six months on these mobile gardens. They're very small as mobile gardens go; some stretch up to 25 acres. This was basically a water garden, and it was so beautiful. It cost a million dollars to build. It's a very expensive proposition. I found out afterwards that it had a lot of defects. It was my entry into garden design. You have to start somewhere and then expand your sensibilities. I also became fascinated by the Mexican architect, Luis Barragan, and realized that he too had been influenced by mobile gardens, but had taken the concept into the 21st century. Now I'm re-thinking how I'm going to redesign that mobile garden some day.

BLDD: Did you ever expect your life would unfold the way it has?

MM: No. When I was young I expected I was going to be a scholar my whole life. I think God has blessed me with an incredible gift so that I've had a wonderful life.

BLDD: Which of all the things that you have done would you describe as reflecting that special gift?

MM: I don't know exactly what it is. For instance, in writing: I couldn't even speak when I was very young. I was totally inarticulate. I could make maybe one sentence at a time. I had to work hard just to learn how to speak because I was so shy. That was number one. And I suppose because I had to work so hard at that it turned out that I was able to create some beautiful writing.

BLDD: Do you always give that much effort to what you do?

MM: Yes. Otherwise it doesn't work. I don't think anything simply happens naturally. In the beginning, when I first started designing clothes, I think I was up every night, all night, sketching. I don't do that anymore. But I think the gift that God gave me is my sense of beauty, which is inside of me, and I can project that onto the various projects with which we work.

Mary McFadden, fall/winter, 1983

Albert and Pearl Nipon

Albert and Pearl Nipon have been collaborators in marriage, parenthood, and business for almost thirty years. Their Philadelphia-based firm is well known for the intricate detailing, classic proportions, and affordable prices of their clothing designs.

BLDD: How did the two of you first come together?

PN: He threw me in a pool.

AN: With all her clothes on.

PN: With all my clothes on!

BLDD: So you needed something new to wear?

PN: No. I fell in love. It was just like that.

BLDD: It was his strength, no doubt.

PN: It was his nerve.

BLDD: Why *did* you do that?

AN: Oh, she dared me. I guess I wanted to impress her. I sure did.

PN: I couldn't swim.

AN: But I threw her in the shallow end of the pool. I knew that.

PN: And my shoes floated away and my pearls came off and my falsies came out of my dress. I was really a sight.

BLDD: So where did you go from there?

PN: To the altar. Where else?

BLDD: How long after this liquid beginning did you come together?

AN: While she was in the water I asked, "Do you still want to go out with me tomorrow night?" She says, "Sure." And then, just a few weeks later in September, we were dancing—it's a true story—I asked, "What would you like for your birthday?" And she said, "An engagement ring." I figured I had a lot of time to get myself out of this situation, so I said, "O.K." But the next day she came back with a bag of diamonds and asked, "Which one?"

BLDD: Obviously you're a fellow who is very responsive to a dare, and obviously you're a very enterprising woman. How did you develop from the beginning a business collaboration and a marriage?

AN: Pearl was always in business. She left college at nineteen to start her own dress business, and it was very successful.

BLDD: What prompted it?

PN: Necessity. Necessity is possibly what starts most things. I started a boutique because I loved pretty clothes and wasn't able to afford them. The next best thing was to buy them and sell them, so I'd have a chance to own some, too. This was before our marriage. After we married, the next necessity became maternity clothes and that's when Albert and I started the business together. I became pregnant and developed the first one-piece maternity dress in the industry.

AN: Pearl made them for her own use and sold them to her customers on a custom-made basis through her retail shop. They were so successful that I left my job and started manufacturing clothing. The name of the company was Ma Mère.

BLDD: And what were you doing before?

AN: I was a graduate accountant and I went from accounting into sales with the Du Pont Company. My experience in colors started when I got transferred to the Paints and Finishes Division.

BLDD: Obviously that experience helped you as your career evolved.

AN: I think every step in my life has been a good step.

BLDD: You're a lucky fellow. What are the advantages of your unique partnership?

AN: We gained a great deal of respect for each other. That's the most important thing. Living together is not like working together all the time, for in that case you see each other in only one dimension, such as a wife and a mother. Pearl did that very well. She made a beautiful home and raised our family.

PN: That's because Albert would tell me how feminine it is to scrub floors and to wash dishes.

AN: I think it is.

PN: He thought they were the most feminine things a woman could do, and I did all of them.

AN: I do think being domestic is part of a woman's femininity. And Pearl did do it very well.

PN: I loved it! I used to scrub the floor with a toothbrush.

AN: Well, that just shows how compulsive she is in everything she does.

PN: It's amazing how quickly you learn that you don't have to scrub, how much time it wastes and how many better things there are to do.

BLDD: When you decided there were better things to do and the two of you went into this business enterprise, did you do the designing from the very beginning? Tell us about the nature of the collaboration: who does what?

AN: Pearl is completely responsible for the aesthetic, creative, design end of the business. I do the management, the production, the marketing concepts. But there's an overlap.

PN: I have my area, but I also interfere in his area. He lets me do what I want in mine. He says if I see two people having a conversation, I stop and listen, because I like to get involved in everything. He's very good-natured about it.

BLDD: There are obvious advantages to living and working in such close proximity. Are there any limitations?

AN: I don't think so. We get the best of both worlds. Living together is one dimension. Then by working together, we're able to gain a lot of respect for each other's talents and ability, and we can take the work home with us and discuss it at leisure. While we're working we don't have a lot of contact. She has her area and I have mine, and sometimes we won't see each other at all during the day except when we travel home at night, or at the dinner table. Then we can communicate. And that's very important, that private time to communicate. So many people don't have private time during their day's work. They're involved with meetings, with telephone calls and so forth. We're able to be more creative, and get insights into what the other is doing, and feed off each other's ideas and knowledge and creativity. It does give us another dimension.

BLDD: You have remained in Philadelphia, your original home—an unusual base for such a well-known national clothing design and manu-facturing company. What caused you to do that?

AN: The reasons are that Pearl and I both were born, bred, and educated in Philadelphia. Our families are there, and so we started our business there. Ma Mère, the parent company, started in Philadelphia and in it we had the nucleus of a very, very successful organization. Ma Mère was considered the design label of the maternity industry. With the people and organization we had with Ma Mère it was easy to make a transition into the design market.

PN: Very little fashion manufacturing is actually on Seventh Avenue. It can be done in South Carolina or upstate Pennsylvania. It can be done in Brooklyn or in the Bronx.

BLDD: But the showrooms and sales staffs are centered on Seventh Avenue.

PN: Exactly. What we have in Philadelphia is our factory and our business offices, but everything else is in New York.

BLDD: How much time do you spend in New York?

PN: A lot.

AN: We split our time.

PN: We're in between Philadelphia and New York. We have the best of both worlds.

BLDD: How do you get back and forth? What's a day like?

AN: We get up at about five o'clock in the morning, do some exercise, and make a 7 or 7:30 train to New York, so we can get there about 9 or 9:30.

BLDD: Do you always use the train?

AN: Yes. We enjoy that because, again, it affords us that private time. Pearl loves to read or just have that time to herself. Very often I'll go into the office very early, for half an hour or an hour, and go through my mail. I take an hour's worth of work with me on the train, and leave what I have to with my secretary.

PN: I will give you a perfect example of our coming and going. I was in Philadelphia yesterday and Albert was working in the New York show-room. He was still there at 7:30 and he said he was going to take the 8:30 train. I suggested that he stay over because there was no point in taking the 8:30 train, since we would be back on the 7:30 train again in the morning. So, he said, "I'll call you if I'm going to make the 8:30." I didn't hear from him, and assumed he didn't make it. At 12:30 he walked in the house. He had made the 8:30. It sat on the tracks for two-and-a-half hours.

BLDD: Where he designed the entire spring line?

AN: I did. I was lucky because I brought a lot of work with me, to keep me busy the entire three-and-a-half hours. So it wasn't intolerable.

BLDD: Does living in Philadelphia give you a more accurate view of what is going on in the rest of the country?

AN: As Pearl said, we have enough contact with New York and we get the best of both worlds. We're able to get out of the hustle-bustle of New York. If we lived in New York, we would live with our work constantly. In the evenings, when we stay over, we're with our customers or else we're in our showrooms working. Going back to Philadelphia gives us a change of pace and the ability to relax and communicate and get away from the business.

BLDD: Are there fashion precedents for the kind of association that the two of you have?

PN: Yes. As a matter of fact, some of the most successful houses have been couples. Anne Klein, for example. At first, it was Anne and Ben Klein.

AN: But that was before the company was known as Anne Klein.

PN: At first it was known as Junior Sophisticates. She worked with Ben. And then "Anne Klein" consisted of Anne and Ben Klein, and they worked together for many, many years. They even worked together after they were divorced. Then she went into business with her husband Chip Rubinstein though the company was still called Anne Klein. The Lazars worked together for Kimberly Knits for many, many years, very successfully. One of the points in the development of our business when we first started and needed financial help was the fact that we were a couple, and that he owns me as his designer.

AN: The creditors and factors in our industry are very strict. One of the reasons they gave me extra credit was the security of our husband-and-wife business. It's an intangible, but it's amazing how much creditors do take that into consideration.

BLDD: How do your approaches differ?

PN: I start every conversation with, "I disagree." Albert has a more positive approach. I play the devil's advocate. Albert comes right to the situation and handles it calmly. I need the excitement. I'm argumentative and I enjoy it, not because I have to win a battle, but because I think it turns everybody's juices on.

BLDD: You like the provocation?

PN: Yes.

BLDD: Who gets the last word?

AN: If you ask the people who work for us, they'll tell you we're a very democratic company. We are run by committee and Pearl's a committee of one!

BLDD: So now we know who decides who decides.

PN: That's not really true. They like to think that it's true. And it's not fair either. I was trained well—right from the beginning of our marriage I knew that Albert was to be the head and I was to be the neck, and I could turn the head any way I want. It works very well for us.

BLDD: Do you design everything that you wear?

PN: Yes.

BLDD: Do you ever wear anyone else's clothes?

PN: Only if I've lost my luggage while I'm travelling.

BLDD: Has that happened to you often?

PN: A couple of times. I don't really have the need to wear anybody else's clothes. We make everything.

BLDD: What *are* some of the things that you make?

PN: We do the Albert Nipon Collection, a collection of costumes, dresses, gowns and suits, and we make the Collectibles, a division of separates. We do the Boutique line, which is wonderful dresses for more of a price factor and then we do the Executive Dress and the Executive Blouse line. They are for the young executives.

BLDD: Are there things you could produce that might be very popular or acceptable commercially but just not the sort of thing that you would wear?

PN: No. I have to take pride in what we do. I have to feel comfortable with it. I don't feel the need to do everything for financial gain. It has to give us some pleasure, and we can do so many nice things. Why should I do something I don't like?

AN: That's true. Pearl puts her stamp on everything that goes in any collection, whether it's one of our own divisions or one of the divisions that we've licensed. Not only does she put her stamp on the design and the aesthetic end of it, she fits each design. If she doesn't personally fit every garment we produce, she'll look over the fitting to see that they've constructed the garment in proportion, the way she thinks it should be. She's unique in the amount of care she puts into our collections.

BLDD: Like most other well-known fashion designers, you do have licenses. Would you tell us about some of them?

PN: We have scarf, luggage, and home furnishings licensees and also table linens.

AN: In the last year we've signed up four new licensees: fragrance, home furnishings, table linens, luggage. And there's a lot more that we are negotiating. The thing that interests the licensee is how much we put into the creation of our line. We're very particular about those to whom we'll license our name. Our position as a licensor is unique. We have one of the largest designer fashion companies in the United States.

BLDD: How much assistance do you have?

PN: I have 72 people in our design area.

BLDD: Solely in design?

PN: Yes.

BLDD: What do they do?

PN: Sometimes I wonder! No. They're wonderful. I'm very fortunate because our design staff has been with us so long.

AN: The first employee I had twenty-eight years ago, the girl I hired to work for me to design the maternity collection, is still one of our designers. And my second and third designers are also still with us. We go back a long way.

PN: We have all the same people in our design room that we started with twenty-nine years ago. They do everything that a design room does. They're responsible for putting out all the collections.

AN: We have designers, assistants, pattern people, tailors, sample makers, cutters, sketchers.

BLDD: I've heard that the sense of family is something that's very important both in your Philadelphia operation and in your New York showroom and, in fact, that there are a number of members of your own family who are employed in your company. To begin with, how large is the company?

AN: We employ about six hundred people.

BLDD: How many Nipons are among that number?

AN: Well, every time we go to a meeting with one of our licensees or the fragrance people, they have to announce, "Here are Messrs. Nipon, Nipon, Nipon, Nipon and Nipon." Our two sons, and our daughter-in-law, and Pearl and myself, and we also have two of my brothers working for the company.

PN: And a sister-in-law.

AN: Oh, yes, we just added a sister-in-law. And it's a lot of fun. We're very comfortable with that kind of family relationship. Large companies for some reason frown on having husband-and-wife teams or families working within a business, particularly in the same department. But it's worked so well for Pearl and myself, we feel comfortable with it, that we have four other husband-and-wife couples working in the same department: our computer manager, one of our design teams, and one of our head shipping couples.

PN: I'm not sure whether we would have as good a marriage if we didn't work together. This is a very demanding business. We travel a great deal.

BLDD: Together?

AN: We've made a policy never to travel separately, at least on weekends. If I have to be someplace on a weekend, Pearl will be with me, but during the week I might be in one place and she in another so we can get double exposure.

PN: Considering we start out at five o'clock in the morning, and don't finish up 'til eight, nine, ten, eleven o'clock at night, if we didn't do this together, it would be a pretty lonely life for one of us.

BLDD: What time or culture or designer has influenced you most? Is there a particular period or designer to which you most respond?

PN: I think the person I responded to most was Claire McCardell.

BLDD: So many people mention her. Can you tell us about Claire McCardell and why she was such a significant influence?

PN: She was a genius. She was the only designer that I could say was truly American. Her clothes were totally individual. I don't know where her ideas came from because I never climbed inside her head, but they were all

her own ideas, she didn't take from anyplace else. Unfortunately, she wasn't around long enough for many people to have had the pleasure of knowing her. She died very young. She was brilliant.

BLDD: You say you don't know where an idea comes from or where design originates. How do you get your ideas?

PN: It's in the air. How does everybody any particular season come out with a short straight skirt?

BLDD: That's what we consumers would like to know: how do you all get the same idea, in the same color, in the same season?

PN: We all have color services—and we are given many choices. That selection starts a year before we're ready to start a collection. Many people come out with the same colors because they happen to be appealing. You come off of a muddy season and you go into a bright season. You come off of a bright season and you might go into a pale season. There is a cycle.

AN: It's also important to realize that most of the fashion fabrics come out of Europe. Every fashion designer in the world shops in the European market. So you get a feel from what's being shown. Since fashion and change are synonymous, you look for a change. Before we even show the collection to the retailer, who eventually will sell it to the consumer, Pearl's already tired of it. She has lived with the fabric, the colors and the prints for a year. Then for months she lives with the creation of the collection. By the time its finished, she finds it unexciting.

PN: By the time it's finished, I never want to look at another dress again. But then I get a new piece of fabric and it becomes exciting all over again.

BLDD: You've just said that fashion and change are synonymous. Perhaps then you can explain to us why we've been told, particularly in recent years that fashion is collectible.

AN: We categorize fashion in two ways, for our own market and our own company. Fashion is either trendy or classic. We consider ourselves classic. Trendy is for today only. Classic is for today and tomorrow. Our designs have a long life. Pearl has said many times that she doesn't design obsolescence into our clothes. Yet she has to create enough newness to give our customer a reason to buy another Nipon, to add to what she has. This has been one of our successes. The dresses we made, ten years ago, are still wearable today. We take it as a great compliment that women wear our dresses for many years and collect them. To a designer that is the ultimate compliment.

BLDD: It's also a compliment to their cleaners. How does one manage to take care of clothes to last that long nowadays? Any particular suggestions or advice?

AN: Somebody asked us, "Are your clothes washable?" And Pearl said, "Yes, once." It is a matter of caring, particularly today. People spend hundreds of dollars for their clothes, and they should have the sense to take care of them. Clothes are an investment, and if they are taken care of they prove to be a very, very worthwhile investment.

PN: Some people are just more careful. I have four children. When I gave away our oldest son's clothes, they were like new. I never could give away my middle son's clothes because they were like rags before he finished with them. It depends on how a person cares for his clothes. When you take something off you should hang it properly. Clothes should be properly pressed. You should wear the proper undergarments to protect your clothes. Cleaners can be a problem, but find one who is reliable—there are many good methods today they can use.

BLDD: You mentioned four children. Three of them are boys. It strikes me that it might have occurred to you in the course of those growing up years to design clothes not only for women, but for men. Is that something that you've considered?

AN: We were talking about it. Two of our sons are now in the business and they are very interested in doing a men's market. Our oldest son works closely with me. His talent and aptitude are for marketing and sales and production. Our youngest son, who works with Pearl, has an aptitude for designing. He's Pearl's clone, and our oldest son, Larry, is my clone.

BLDD: Is that the way they see it too?

AN: Oh, yes.

PN: Yes, they see it that way, too.

AN: They love working with each other. They have mutual respect for each

other's talent and ability which is very important. They've shown a lot of interest in men's clothes and we're talking to people about doing a men's line.

PN: I have always shied away from boy's clothes but perhaps we'll consider the idea now that our sons and Albert have this interest. I once saw little boys in grey Eton jackets and short grey flannel pants with kneesocks and an Eton shirt and a little Eton hat, and that's the way I sent our oldest son to school the first day. He came up and hit me. I knew then I could never send him to school like that again!

BLDD: I suspect that most people would identify Nipon clothes by what you call your signature—Nipon tucks—those rows of fine pin tucking that are one of the recurring themes of your fashions. What would Niponized men's clothes look like and would you be the designer of them?

AN: As a youngster, my first suit was a navy pinstripe or a shadow stripe or a grey flannel suit. Today I still wear shadow stripes and pinstripes and flannel suits. The fabrication in men's clothing is very difficult.

PN: But they're not tucked and pleated.

AN: We have our own theory about men's clothing.

BLDD: Are you going to be the designer of the men's line?

AN: As Pearl said, she gets involved in my area, and I get involved in hers. I have a feeling the most important thing in men's clothing is the fit and the look.

BLDD: How do you manage to do that with clothing "off the rack"?

AN: It's in the cut. Men look at the fabric, and feel the fabric. You buy an eye first. The fashion is the eye getting accustomed to fashion. We have our own ideas on fit.

BLDD: How do you manage to keep the price affordable with such attention to detailing and quality of workmanship?

AN: It's a constant struggle. It's done through mechanization. I think if you want a craftsman's job, you have to have craftsman's tools. We send our production staff to the machinery show in Cologne and to the shows here in the United States, and we're always buying the most modern machinery. We constantly train people in specialized operations. Specialization is very important. Most manufacturers send special operations out to contractors. There's one that does tucking, another that does pleating. There may be a contractor that does fagotting. We've been able to buy all those machines and to install our own pleating plant. We are very self-contained and don't depend on outside subcontractors for any of our specialization work. We've developed sections and people who are experts. So without using a middleman we do more specialization work, and better specialization work than anybody else.

BLDD: What's the price range of your clothes?

PN: Albert Nipon retails from about $250 to $600. The Boutique retails from about $180 to under $300. Collectibles is in the same price category as Albert Nipon. Executive Dress retails for $90 to $130. Nipon Blouse retails under $100, and mostly about $50-$60.

BLDD: Sales have been so widespread in legitimate and well-established department stores that recently it has been possible to buy clothes at close to wholesale prices even in season. Do you see this practice becoming a trend, and has it influenced your designs or the pricing of your own clothes?

AN: I think we've responded to the customer. The price is more of a factor than it has ever been before. There are many ingredients that make up the value of a dress—the design, the fabrication, the quality, and the price. Whereas they may have all been equal before, in the last year price has become most important. To answer your question about the retailers, I don't think that will become a practice. I believe it was a necessity of the times. With the economy what it was in '82, the stores were just responding to needs. They were having sales sooner than they ordinarily would have to turn over their inventories and bring in fresh goods. Automatically the value goes down.

BLDD: Don't you think the consumer has a new awareness of what is possible? Might that not cause restructuring of, or at least some change in, the pricing in the fashion industry.

AN: No. It won't change the pricing of the fashion industry. The designers who are most successful have always given value. Again, price is only one of the ingredients that make up value. The popular or licensed designers are long established. If you think about it, there is no Johnny-come-lately. They have all been well-established for ten years or more. They have a track record of good business ability and their product has total value. There will be a change with retailers, I think, in the sense that they're buying closer to the vest. In the early '80's people wanted to buy three or four months before they were going to use the product. It cost them 10 to 15% more just in investment money. Everybody's started to buy closer to their needs. And the retailer has responded that way. But as business and the economy come back to normal, which I see happening right now, we'll see the retailers getting back to the habit of having to get good fashion merchandise. They have to extend themselves, because we need lead time to make the merchandise: buy the fabric and put it into production. It is a matter of time. You can't cut corners and give the same quality. But what you see now is a result of the economy.

BLDD: You've won a great deal of applause from the fashion press, but your most enthusiastic reviews seem to come from your customers themselves. What do you think it is that you do, or you give them, that other designers don't?

PN: It's so pleasing to go to the stores and meet our customers. A very tall lady walked over to me and said, "Oh, you've saved my life. Nobody else's clothes fit me. You made clothes that were just right for a tall figure." And then this little tiny person walks over to me two minutes later and says, "Ah, you saved my life. You're the only designer that makes clothes for a little person." I think what we are able to do is fit just about any figure. I can't even explain why it happens or what it is about the construction, because I didn't realize our good fortune until I saw how many people we were fitting. But I think we give people a sense of security, that they can go out and find a pretty dress without having to do a great deal of alteration.

BLDD: Is that why you use so many elasticized waistbands?

PN: I like the elasticized waist because I find there's an expansion there all through the day. When you're twenty years old, everything fits, but when you're starting to get on, these are problems that you have to be aware of. Also I think it's important that a person feel comfortable, particularly in the waistline. Wouldn't it be awful to be all strangled in the waist? When I use the elastic, you don't know it's there. It just expands with you and feels good.

BLDD: For what age group are your clothes meant?

AN: Our audience is ageless. When we do shows, Pearl and I often go out to meet our customers in the stores, and I find we can sell the mother, the grandmother and the daughter all at one time. In fact, we have had many instances where we sold to three generations. We haven't had a show in which we couldn't satisfy a mother and a daughter.

BLDD: How important is it for you to travel the countryside and meet your customers? What do they tell you that you then translate into your own designs?

PN: It's very important and they tell us a lot. You can see what they're trying on in the dressing room, and how easy it is for them to get in and out of it. They might comment, "Oh, this is nice because I don't have to mess my hair," or "I can pull it up from the bottom" or "I like the idea that I have no waistline to contend with." You listen to all the comments. Then when you're going into your new season you know what was great and what didn't work too well.

AN: We learned you can't be in an ivory tower. When we create things, we imagine how they are going to work and make certain assumptions. But when we actually see the clothes in action on the customer, and the customer's reaction to them, it gives us another insight that we can translate into our next collection.

BLDD: One of the things that you've satisfied is the very widespread need for practical, good-looking clothing for the professional woman. You seem to have your own favorite solution.

PN: As a matter of fact, I'm going to be publishing a book on just that. It infuriates me when I hear about people who lecture graduating classes at universities and tell the women going into the professions how to prepare their wardrobe; telling them to buy a grey flannel skirt and a navy blue jacket and button-down shirts and put a scarf at their neck because, "Remember, you're competing in a man's world." You may be competing in a man's world, but why do you want to look like a man?

AN: It's not a man's world anymore.

PN: That's true.

AN: It's a business world today.

PN: You wouldn't see a man dressing like a woman. Why would a woman want to dress like a man? A woman should be feminine. She should be soft. Her clothes should have movement. Her wardrobe should be lacy and charming, not strict.

BLDD: And what are you going to call this book?

PN: Maybe *Pearl's Pearls*.

BLDD: And what do you tell them to wear?

PN: Nipon's. Lots of Nipon's.

BLDD: So many women today travel, both for business and pleasure. Has that affected your designs or perhaps the fabrics that you use?

AN: That's one of the saleability features of our clothes. The fabrication is serviceable and seasonless. We can use the same fabric twelve months of the year. The only way we bring a design into season is by color. It is important today because our customers—our business people or wives of professional people—who travel need clothes that are serviceable, travel well, pack well. This has been Pearl's talent. She's recognized, certainly in the United States, as one of the most talented fabricators in the women's design field.

PN: I would love to see cotton and wool become twelve month of the year fabrics. Consumers have not adjusted to the fact that cotton is not an intimation of spring or summer. Cotton can be made to feel like beautiful wool.

BLDD: Don't you think we were conditioned to believe that for so many years?

PN: You're absolutely right.

AN: Why weren't men conditioned that way? Wool, you know, is a twelve month a year fabric.

BLDD: Except there are lightweight wools and heavier wools.

PN: Exactly. When we show our spring collection in August, we start delivering it in October. And when they see the wool, they say, "Nope. Too late. We can't sell wool at that time of the year." I remember the wonderful wool spring suits, and the navy blue wool dresses with white collars, for spring.

AN: That you would sell right up until Eastertime.

PN: There are some weights of wool that you can wear twelve months of the year. They're lighter than silk. They feel beautiful. They travel beautifully.

BLDD: Don't many people dress that way today, as if there is one ongoing season—with a few special clothes for extremely cold and others for extremely warm weather?

AN: Some, but not a lot. You'd be surprised at the resistance retailers give us. They won't take a wool garment into the stores after October or November. Think about it. Winter doesn't start until December.

BLDD: You've told us about executive dressing. Now let's talk about that man or woman on the go. How do you "pack for success" —any tips or advice there? It would be helpful to know what you do.

AN: When I travel, I like to keep everything in one color. In other words, if I were to go away for a few days I might take black shoes and wear a grey or navy suit, and dark socks. And I could mix the ties that would go with it. I'd try to keep within a certain color range.

PN: I feel that you have to try to take as little as possible.

BLDD: How do you discipline yourself?

PN: I have had so much in my closet that I never knew what to wear. It became confusing. What I have started to do is keep less in my closet and wear what is there again and again. I try to travel with as little as I can possibly take.

AN: We have a regular travel pack for toilet articles always ready.

PN: I bring one home and one is packed for me to go.

BLDD: You are almost your own best model. Don't you find that somewhat of a burden?

PN: No, I like to get dressed. I love it. I love to put on pretty things.

BLDD: What colors do you think are especially flattering to almost anyone?

PN: Red, red, red. Red and black. I think red is a wonderful color. Everybody looks good in it.

BLDD: Are there any colors that almost all of us should avoid?

PN: No. I hear people say, "I can't wear green," or "I can't wear yellow." You can wear everything. It's how you accessorize it.

AN: It's the shade of that color that counts. There are so many shades of every color, that you can find a shade of any color that you could wear. As Pearl says, accessorize properly.

BLDD: You've mentioned the word feminine today several times, Pearl, and I'm not exactly certain what you mean when you use that word. What does it mean to you?

PN: "Feminine" is like a girl. How does the dictionary describe "feminine"?

AN: I think "feminine" is something that makes a woman look pretty.

PN: Pretty, soft, cuddly, attractive, alluring, sexy.

AN: "Feminine" is when a woman looks at herself in an Albert Nipon dress and she likes the way she looks and feels. The same people that are marketing the Albert Nipon fragrance also own two other designer fragrances. They did a national survey in the United States. They listed nineteen international and American designers, and asked which was the most recognized in the United States, and Calvin Klein won the vote—obviously from the proliferation of his jeans and other products. But then they asked, "Which designer do you buy?" And the most bought designer in the United States was Albert Nipon. They established a profile of all the different designers and the one thing that was consistent with Albert Nipon, the one thing for which we got more votes than any other designer in the world, was femininity. Women say they like our clothes and they feel good in them. Our clothes are functional, serviceable and they're feminine.

PN: Feminine is not masculine.

BLDD: And what is "masculine"?

PN: Albert.

BLDD: Now we see why your collaboration is such a success! Last year you went to The White House for a private consultation with Mrs. Reagan, who ordered, from what I read, six dresses. Were those dresses created for her specifically?

PN: No. We took the collection there and she picked six dresses from the collection. A couple of them were red. She also chose a white organdy gown that was so beautiful and so feminine. She wanted to wear it to the Sadat dinner that she was hosting. I decided to take the dress off the line so that she would be the only one to have it. I took it out of the collection, and I put it back a year later.

BLDD: Are there any other prominent figures that summon you to show off your line for them? Is that something that you do frequently?

PN: We've never taken our collection to any celebrity other than Nancy Reagan. That was really a command performance.

BLDD: How did that come about?

PN: I got a call from The White House and I took the next train. I didn't need much coaxing. I was delighted. They go through tremendous security before you get there. They investigated everyone that came with me. We had to file Social Security numbers for everybody, including the drivers that we sent down with the collections and the driver that was bringing us. It was an adventure.

BLDD: What did you learn about this country from that experience?

PN: I don't think it had anything to do with running the country. It was just a very exciting experience. The White House was beautiful and she did a fabulous job. It was very colorful and clean and bright and cheery, and she was very warm and friendly. She made us very comfortable. I had a good time. She was just like any other customer. And she knew exactly what to do with the clothes. She's a size 4 and our samples were 6's and 8's. She knew just how to move it around, put on a belt and hike it up, to see how it looked. She looked like she was born in the dress.

BLDD: Test marketing happens so often with many consumer products. Does it happen with fashion as well?

AN: No. We don't test market our product. I think we've established our credibility, and the collections that we produce are what the retailers buy. As long as our things keep selling the way they have, and we get the support of the retailer and the acceptance of the consumer, we are alright. As Pearl said earlier, we know how to constantly upgrade the product or bring it more into fashion. The stores rely on us for direction. There are

Albert Nipon, fall, 1983

Albert Nipon, fall, 1983

those in the industry that are called knockoff artists. They look to us for direction of what to make, and even what to copy.

BLDD: Does that mean that they adapt your clothes?

AN: They don't adapt. They copy.

BLDD: Does it flatter you?

PN: No, it annoys me.

AN: She thinks everybody should be creative, but, Pearl, there are people that are not creative.

PN: I just feel that if you're in an industry that demands fashion, that's what you should give. You should create your own identity.

AN: Honey, that's why we have our identity, because we have created an identity.

BLDD: You both obviously have very clear identities. In the thirty years that you have worked together, there must have been some areas of real disagreement. What's the most vivid recollection you have of that?

PN: Retirement. Albert never wants to retire.

BLDD: You don't either, do you?

AN: Well, she's changed her mind lately.

PN: I change my mind every week.

AN: When she's under the pressure of putting together the collection, she says: "This is the last collection."

BLDD: How often does she say that?

PN: Every collection!

AN: She threatens me.

PN: No, it's not said as a threat. It's desperation. It's a very emotional business and it takes a lot out of you.

BLDD: Is every collection like starting over? How much success do you have to have to be persuaded that it's going to happen again?

PN: It's always like starting over. You're only as good as your last line. Every season it's a new business, and the pressure is great. It is emotional. You see something come out of the design room and it's like one of your children. You have to develop it. You've created it.

AN: The retailers depend on us for saleable merchandise. They make great investments. They invest millions and millions of dollars in our product, which they in turn want to sell and make money on. So it's a great responsibility.

BLDD: Pearl retires every season to release the pressure. What do you do?

AN: I just thrive. I handle pressure well; to me it's a motivator. It drives me. And Pearl does, too. When pressure becomes stressful, then it's a problem. We don't let it become stressful—momentarily it might become stressful, but we know how to handle it.

PN: The pressure is a turn-on. Stress is painful. You can't have stress in our business. I'm working with many very talented people. Talented people are temperamental, and I have to deal with each person's temperament.

BLDD: How do you manage?

PN: I cry.

BLDD: How do *you* manage?

AN: Well, I handle it well.

BLDD: Is this gentle, placid fellow what Albert Nipon is always like?

PN: Yes, always.

BLDD: That's why you named the fragrance for him? I think Pearl would be a wonderful name for a perfume.

PN: The next one in the sequence is going to be "Albert Nipon's Pearl."

BLDD: In the years that you've been in business, how has the field changed?

PN: It's become tougher. There is not as much ingenuity as there used to be. Every designer used to have their identity. Today there's very little identity and that worries me.

AN: Those designers that have developed an identity probably are the most successful. And they have gone beyond fashion. Now we're into lifestyle and licensing and designing many products. We're into home furnishings, linen, luggage. We're recognized not only as fashion designers, we're putting fashion into a lifestyle. Now people want to read about designers' lifestyle and see how they live and what they do. That's the new trend of the last decade.

PN: They've made stars out of designers. I actually saw a lady faint when she was introduced to Albert.

BLDD: Perhaps she didn't have any breakfast.

PN: We were in the shop in Dallas, and Albert was doing a personal appearance, and one young woman did not realize that Albert was there. They said, "We'd like you to meet Albert Nipon." And she said, "Really," and swooned; she was out.

BLDD: Is that the effect you usually have on women?

AN: Not really.

BLDD: What would you recommend for those with more taste than funds, who wanted to start their wardrobe all over and had only $500 to spend? Where do you begin and what should you get?

PN: I think you should buy very little. Take that $500 and buy a dress that has a limitless season, one that is wearable twelve months of the year.

BLDD: What does it look like?

PN: It has to be a fabrication that is neither heavy nor sheer. A jacket that goes well with that dress can give it a totally different concept. The dress should have the kind of neckline that you can do a great deal with, with jewelry, scarves, bows, ties, or what-have-you. A coat is also very important. I think you just spent the $500!

BLDD: I think you spent more than that which means we'll have to get it wholesale.

PN: No. That means you buy the dress one year, the jacket the next, and the coat the third year. And always good shoes. That's extremely important, that the shoes are attractive, that a person is well-shod.

AN: We will look at a customer and at the way she's accessorized and know what kind of customer she is.

BLDD: What's the giveaway?

AN: Quality accessories. They do add or detract from what you wear.

BLDD: What women do you consider to be the role models of fashion?

AN: Nancy Reagan's done a lot for fashion. Her influence has been very positive. No First Lady since Jacqueline Kennedy, with the pillbox hat, has had as much effect on fashion as Nancy Reagan.

PN: I don't agree with that. I'm not sure that there is a role model today. You have a tremendous amount of individuality among people today. I can't think of anybody in fashion that has created an impact comparable to Marilyn Monroe's when she wore the very slinky dress with the fur boa and the spike heels. Then you had a look. But today, I can't think of anyone.

AN: Women wear everything. Women's wardrobes are not made up of only pantsuits. When we started, in 1972, you had a choice of pantsuits to wear when you opened your closet. There were no such things as dresses then. Then we started with separates, and dresses, and even jeans. For the women's lifestyle today, all those things are a necessary part of a wardrobe.

BLDD: Part of your success was based on making the dress popular once again. Now everything has come full cycle. If you open your closet next year, you might find one pantsuit and yet another pantsuit.

PN: Who says so?

BLDD: Yves St. Laurent seemed to say so.

PN: I'm not sure that I got that message from Yves St. Laurent or from anybody in particular. I think that pants are part of the wardrobe, though. A woman should have a variety. Pants are a part of a wardrobe, along with a skirt, and a dress.

AN: I don't think any one item is going to dominate women's fashions again. Women, as Pearl said, are very independent today, much more expressive. A professional woman needs her business clothes, her social clothes, her spectator clothes, her sport clothes, and her active wear.

BLDD: What are spectator clothes?

AN: The separates, sportswear, things like that. And then your active wear.

PN: Like the navy skirt with the blue jacket and the white shirt! You refer to what St. Laurent says. I do feel that he is well-received in the fashion world, and I think he is a fashion force.

BLDD: Is he the pre-eminent fashion force, as you see it?

PN: I don't think anybody is a pre-eminent force anymore; however at one time it was Paris and Italy that did all the forecasting for us. Today America has gained its own place in the fashion industry. Somebody once said to me, "What do you make?" And I said, "Give me an order." If pants are going to be the fashion of the day—though I don't think they are—we're going to follow the need of the consumer. I don't think that anybody can dictate to women. Women have shown that they don't want that. They don't want to be told where the hemline should be. They want to do what they want to do, and I think that's great.

AN: That's why we make three lengths.

BLDD: Did you ever expect your lives to unfold the way they have?

AN: Not really. I don't think we envisioned this. I don't think people do when they start out. We're very competitive, and I've always liked being a winner or leader, and tried to do whatever I did to the best of my ability, and to excel in it. But I never envisioned this.

PN: You know, when Reagan was acting, he didn't envision being President. It's the same thing. You start a business and work to make it successful, and then what is success? Everything is relative.

AN: It's a challenge to reach a certain plateau—and then you want to go on.

BLDD: Where do you want to go next?

AN: There's no end. I feel we've been lucky. I think the ultimate is to constantly improve the quality of one's life. And Pearl and I have been able to do that with our family and that is quite satisfying. We appreciate it. We do cherish it.

PN: Are you asking me where I want to go now? I want to go to the spa.

BLDD: But will you?

PN: Yes. After each collection I go to the spa for five days.

AN: At the end of this month we're starting the fragrance launch and will be traveling constantly for about six weeks. We're doing about fourteen cities, fourteen shows, and it's going to be the most tiring undertaking we've ever done.

BLDD: What do you do for relaxation?

PN: He chops wood.

AN: I work out. I like exercise.

BLDD: If you had to do it over again, what would you do differently?

AN: I don't think I'd do anything differently. I've been lucky. I can't think of much that I would have done over again.

BLDD: Pearl, you always have a new idea. What would you do otherwise?

PN: I really wasn't supposed to be in the fashion business. I wanted to be a lawyer. Maybe in my next life I'll be a lawyer. In this life I like what I'm doing.

BLDD: Why is the company called Albert Nipon?

PN: When you form a company, you don't think that the name is going to make the company a success. The company is going to make the name a success, and you don't even think about the name. Albert Nipon sounded just fine to me.

BLDD: But you're the one in the fashion business. How did he end up with his name on *your* company?

PN: I was raised that way. My father was king of our home. My father sat at the head of the table, he was served first. Everything was Daddy first. I was always raised with this thought, and I like it.

AN: There's another reason. Pearl was retired from the business for fourteen years, and came back to stimulate the design area in the maternity business in 1972. When we showed our first collection to Saks Fifth Avenue, Arnold Johnson, then president, asked, "What's the name of this company? Where have you been?" So, as I'd had a staff of designers working for me for eighteen years, I just said, "It's Albert Nipon." We do have to consider the people working for us. I made it known that it was a company, that it wasn't just myself. This all went through my mind in a split second, and I thought to myself, "If I put Pearl's name on the label at this time, it would create a lot of problems in the existing organization." They'd been working for me for eighteen years and Pearl was a newcomer. When she came back to direct the design room, after the first week she came in crying and said, "No way I'm going to let those people . . ." I said, "If you quit now, you'll never be able to work with them. Go back." That is the true story of why Albert Nipon is called Albert Nipon. It is a company, and Pearl, and myself, and our children, our brothers, we're all detached from it. I've always had one pet saying: "If you start believing your press, and you let your ego get in the way, you're going to be in a lot of trouble." So we all work hard, and the people in the company respect the amount of work that we do. Our management people tell me that the day they can't communicate with me or the day that we get too big—we are one of the largest designer companies in the United States—that they can't talk to me, then they don't want to work with us anymore. We are good role models for the rest of the people in the company. They don't mind working hard for us as long as we work with them. We lead them, we don't push them. And that's why we still have the same people with us after twenty-nine years.

Albert Nipon, fall, 1985

162

MP

Mollie Parnis

Mollie Parnis has long been known for her unerring sense of what the well-to-do want to wear, and for her commitment as a civic activist to making life more pleasant for all people—even those who may never own one of her designs.

BLDD: Why don't we start at the beginning? When did you start out in fashion?

MP: While I was a sophomore at Hunter College I got a job for the summer and liked it so much that I never went back to school. However, that is one thing I would never advise any young person to do. I'd always tell them to go back to school, because if I applied for a job today with my training, I probably wouldn't have a chance. The young people who I see now are graduates of Parsons or the Fashion Institute of Technology, or other good design schools, and they know so much more than I do that I'm embarrassed. Most young men and women who graduate from the Parsons School can make a dress. I can't, and it took me a long time to get over the fact that I was never going to learn either. It is something you must learn when you are very young.

BLDD: What was that first job?

MP: I waited on customers in a showroom of a blouse firm. From time to time they let me help the designer, and I would tell her to put a Peter Pan collar on a blouse instead of a jabot, or a jabot instead of a V-neck, or to shorten or lengthen the sleeve. By the time fall came I was so hooked, I never went back to school. I wound up being the designer for the firm.

BLDD: How long did that take?

MP: About a year. They opened another department and they let me design.

BLDD: How did blouses graduate to dresses?

MP: My next job was in a dress house, again as assistant designer, and helping in the showroom. I was fascinated by the designing, and wound up staying there for about three years, until I got married. Then my husband and I decided to go into business together—on less money than the price of almost any gadget in my current apartment! I think between us we had about $10,000, very little. You can imagine how small the firm was. We had one telephone. That was in 1940.

BLDD: What a year to go into business!

MP: Yes—it was the depths, with the war beginning. But by the end of that first year, we had grown. The first ten years we were so young and inexperienced. My husband had never been in the dress business, only in textiles, but he was a good businessman. We never had a year when we didn't make money; we made more and more and I thought that was the way it was supposed to be. We had a baby; we had a business; we kept growing. After about two years, we moved to 530 Seventh Avenue, where we still are.*

BLDD: Did you know what the Mollie Parnis look was going to be at that early stage in your career? Was there a design philosophy that started it all?

MP: No. Being a designer is being a personality. It's creating a look that you like, that your friends like, and that belongs in the life you know. In America, there are so many different life styles, and tastes, and different needs. That's why we need such a variety of clothes, and so many designers. I have never been a "trendy" designer, and today the trendy idea is dying out. No. I've never had trendy friends. I have worked all my life for everything I possess. Of course as time went on and we made a little more money, my tastes changed, but not drastically. I was very young when I moved to the apartment where I live now. That was 1943, and, it still looks more or less the same. So, I haven't changed very much. My business is in the same place where we moved two years after we started the firm. Of course, my possessions have changed, as have my interests, and because of that, the people I see most frequently. Just because you've known somebody a long time doesn't mean you must cling to them indefinitely—thinking "She must be my best friend because I went to school with her"—that's crazy! There's more to friendship than time.

BLDD: While we're talking about evolution, you said that your own interests have changed. How would you describe how they have evolved?

*Mrs. Parnis went out of business in January, 1985. Since then she has designed a collection called " Mollie Parnis At Home Clothes."

164

MP: My personal interests today are far removed from my business. I have a philanthropic family foundation today that takes a great deal of my time. I organized a project called the Mollie Parnis Dress Up Your Neighborhood program. I am on the Citizen's Committee for New York City. I'm intensely interested in politics. I'm a frustrated journalist, and my foundation sponsors a series of awards for young journalists.

BLDD: How did you first become so interested in politics?

MP: It was during the Truman-Eisenhower campaign. I had never been around anyone but Democrats and had never voted for anybody before Roosevelt. I thought that if a Republican was elected the sun wouldn't shine and that the world would change. I worked terribly hard for my party. So imagine my frustration when a few weeks after Eisenhower was nominated I found myself making Mrs. Eisenhower's clothes—I felt like a fifth columnist! I used to go up to Morningside Drive, to Columbia University where they lived before moving to the White House.

BLDD: Was it during the presidential campaign that you first started to make Mrs. Eisenhower's clothes?

MP: During the campaign, I worked for Stevenson. I'm sure my young son who was at Yale thought I had no integrity, if I could support Stevenson, and at the same time make clothes for Mrs. Eisenhower.

BLDD: How did you justify it?

MP: By not talking about it very much. They were much nicer to me than I was to them. The first time I went to The White House after President Eisenhower was elected, in February of '53, I got off the elevator in the Family Residence just as the President was going downstairs. I had intended to tell them I was a Democrat, because I didn't want somebody else to tell them, but I didn't mean to tell him the way I did. He stuck out his hand and said what he always would say to me, "Oh, Mollie, how nice of you to take time out of your busy schedule to come here and help Mamie." I said, "Hello, Mr. President, I'm a Democrat." And he looked at me and answered in a surprised voice, "So are millions of other Americans." He just assumed I was a Democrat for Eisenhower.

BLDD: Do you think it would have made a difference to him, or to her?

MP: No, I don't think she was terribly interested in politics. I think it would have made a difference to him, but he just assumed that since he was a nice guy everybody liked him. By the end, I did like him. I liked them both very much.

BLDD: What was most striking about your relationship with them?

MP: I think it was realizing that Presidents were human beings, with the same kind of problems as anyone else, only magnified.

BLDD: Tell us a little about Mrs. Eisenhower. Did she have any sense of fashion?

MP: No, she didn't. How could she have had? She had spent all her life on Army bases and bought her clothes from post exchanges. I had to work very hard to lead her away from that synthetic world into that which her position demanded. Pure silk and pure wool were the only answers to her social and travel schedule.

BLDD: How did she come to you in the first place?

MP: We had a mutual friend, Jock Lawrence, an aide to the General in the war. I had met General and Mrs. Eisenhower long before he was even considered as a candidate. I went to their house in Neuilly, outside of Paris, where the General made a barbecue for a big group of friends. When they came back to America, we continued to meet and she became both a client and a friend.

BLDD: After Mrs. Eisenhower, your next First Lady was Mrs. Johnson. How did that come about?

MP: I had met Lady Bird Johnson years before at Neiman-Marcus in Dallas when I showed my collection there. When she moved to The White House, her social secretary, Bess Abell, whom I had known in Washington, called me and asked if I'd talk with Mrs. Johnson about the clothes she would need. From that first visit we developed a very precious relationship. She's a very, very special lady and we are very good friends today. In fact, knowing President and Mrs. Johnson and their family has been the most exciting experience in my life.

BLDD: How well did you know President Johnson?

MP: Very well. He came to my apartment many times. I gave small dinners

for him, and sat and talked to him alone by the hour.

BLDD: Were you involved with politicians before that time, or was that your first taste of the high political life?

MP: I got to know many people at that time who excited my interest in world happenings, particularly important journalists. One of my friends, Carol, married Arthur Ochs Sulzberger, now the publisher of *The New York Times*. Through them I met many writers and policy makers who have become close friends: Mike Wallace, Betsy and Walter Cronkite. I knew Bill Moyers and Jack Valenti when they were aides to President Johnson, and they are still close friends.

BLDD: Were you present at anything that was particularly historic, or personal, or interesting when you were with the Johnsons?

MP: Probably the most exciting experience I had was in 1972 during a few days visit to the LBJ Ranch. Johnson was no longer President, and Senator McGovern and Sargent Shriver, the candidates, were coming down to have a talk about strategy. Incidentally, as much as I loved Mrs. Johnson, I was always much less formal with the President than with her. I kept saying to him, "I wish I could listen in. This is history in the making." He promised to tell me everything after they left. And he kept his word. I was sent in the helicopter that brought the two visitors out from Austin to lunch at the LBJ Library. When word came that they were on the way back I was there on the helicopter pad to take it back to the ranch. As I came in the house after their meeting the President called, "Mollie, come in here." He was resting in his bedroom after what must have been an intense session. I said, "Hurry up and tell me what they said and what you said." And, my God, he did! He told McGovern to stop complaining about the United States and our policies, and to give positive ideas. "Just say cut out the waste. Everybody's for cutting out the waste. Remind them that where else could a minister's son from South Dakota become a candidate for President of The United States." The very next day, Senator McGovern made a speech at New York University and said those very things!

BLDD: And how was that received?

MP: Very well. I cut out *The New York Times* report of the speech and sent it to President Johnson. I wrote, "You've turned out to be a good teacher, after all."

BLDD: After your close involvement with the Johnsons, how did you manage to design clothes for Mrs. Nixon, as well?

MP: Although I like Mrs. Nixon very much, I was never a personal friend of hers. Mrs. Nixon is a very introspective person. Whether you're introverted or extroverted, to be a President's wife is a great strain, so much is expected of you. I don't know Nancy Reagan as the First Lady, although I know the Reagans slightly through friends in California. No wife of a president has an easy time. Mrs. Johnson took to it because she loved politics, but she is unique.

BLDD: Did you meet President Nixon?

MP: Yes. President Nixon seems more outgoing than his wife. When he was campaigning we returned from California on the same plane. There was an empty seat next to me and he sat down and talked to me as if I were 100,000 voters.

BLDD: Did he persuade you?

MP: Well, no, he didn't.

BLDD: Of those three Presidents' wives that we talked about—Mrs. Eisenhower, Mrs. Johnson, Mrs. Nixon—did any of their husbands take an interest in fashion?

MP: President Johnson certainly did. Most people have the wrong impression of him. He was warm, kind, generous, a last-of-the-big-spenders type, a real Texan. He was easily hurt. He was easily pleased. He cared about the next fellow. Just before Christmas he would come to my office, with a list of about forty women—family and friends—he wanted to buy dresses for. He took time to do things that one wouldn't expect of him.

BLDD: Do you think current history treats him unjustly?

MP: Yes, because of Viet Nam. I was not for Viet Nam. He knew it, and so we never discussed it. That was one of the wonderful things about him; he respected opinions other than his own. If it hadn't been for Viet Nam, he would go down in history as one of the great Presidents. In fact, I think he

Mollie Parnis, spring, 1968

still will: because of civil rights, the Great Society, Medicare, and grants for education. He cared for people.

BLDD: In addition to overseeing your work at Mollie Parnis, Inc., you obviously care for people, too. You're known as a philanthropist, a collector and a cultural activist. How did you first become involved in philanthropy?

MP: My first full-fledged effort was the "Dress Up Your Neighborhood" campaign.

BLDD: Was Mrs. Johnson an influence on your interest in beautification?

MP: I had already become interested by 1967. I was in Jerusalem that summer. The six-day war had just ended and the mood was very happy. I knew the Mayor of Jerusalem, Teddy Kollek, and one day I said to him, "I'd like to do something for Jerusalem. I'd like to give the money to get these streets cleaned up." He said, "That's the most wonderful idea. We'll put the money in the bank. At 12% interest, we can give prizes to the schools who do the best job of it." The idea worked so well in Jerusalem that a couple of years later, when John Lindsay, was Mayor of New York, I told him about it. By that time I even had a name for the project—"Dress Up Your Neighborhood." Mayor Lindsay accepted right away, and we've been doing it every since. I wanted to get all the people in the under-privileged neighborhoods involved. New York is too big a job for school children to handle alone. I was given an office at City Hall and a staff. Eventually we combined with The Citizen's Committee for New York City. Now we give eighty prizes, half to neighborhood groups and half to school children's efforts. When my son Bob Livingston died in 1979 he left his estate to our family foundation. I established the Livingston Journalism awards in his memory and in admiration for journalism that we both shared. Three prizes of $5,000 each are awarded to young journalists under 35. The competition is conducted by the University of Michigan School of Journalism, a very good school. The prizes cover local, national and international reporting.

BLDD: Tell us how the winners are selected and what you hope to achieve through the awards.

MP: I want to encourage fine journalism in all areas of the field. Last year we had over four hundred applications. They were screened by a group invited by the Dean of the University of Michigan. Their selections of about twenty entries are then studied by the judges. They include Barbara Walters, David Brinkley, Mike Wallace, Richard Clurman and Charlotte Curtis.

BLDD: The aim of your "Dress Up Your Neighborhood Contest," is to encourage neighborhoods to clean up, do plantings, create pocket parks, and create play areas. Do you notice any striking developments?

MP: Last spring, we took a van up to The Bronx. And it was unbelievable— in a neighborhood where every other house is burnt out or abandoned— suddenly, you come on a little pocket park, where people are growing vegetables and flowers and have built benches. You'd be amazed at the things that they have done. An herb garden up in Harlem supplies fine restaurants and is beginning to show a profit.

BLDD: It seems for you, relaxing has always meant getting involved in a good cause, whether it's cleaning up a city or making certain that those who deserve distinction receive it. What has motivated you to make the environment and life itself more livable for other people?

MP: I don't know that I set out to do something for others. It was part of my own growth. I'm not a do-gooder at heart. I'm not even a workaholic, like many of my friends. When I leave the office at five-thirty or six o'clock, I really don't want to discuss my business. I'm interested in learning what's happening in the rest of the world. I really am a news freak.

BLDD: How do you feel the news itself affects fashion, as a personal and political statement, not merely body covering. How do your designs reflect our world in terms of color, designs, fabrics?

MP: Fashion of course is a reflection of life. The clothes we wear now contain elements of nostalgia, anxiety, rebellion, love, romance, fear, joy. That's what life is everyday. Inevitably we are attracted to clothes that display our own inner feelings. It has always been true. However, today because life is more complex, fashion is more complex. It is also more interesting, because people know more about themselves and express that identity.

BLDD: What changes in fashion and the fashion industry have you noted since you've started your career?

MP: At this point, the fashion industry is particularly fascinating because of the number of very young people working in it. They are a big influence, and one that the industry needed. The day is gone when a girl wanted to look like her mother. The mother is more apt to try to look like the daughter.

BLDD: It's been said that the essence of your work is a quiet elegance of design. Is that quiet quality something for which you deliberatively strive?

MP: No. I think the essence of a designer's work is the designer's own personality. I wouldn't know how to make a dress, say, for Diana Ross. I'm a big fan of hers. I love her records. I go to her openings, and I love to see her, but I wouldn't know how to make a dress for her. I wouldn't know how to make a dress for Cher. I make dresses for people who live the kind of life that I live and understand.

BLDD: So, in a sense, you are your own best model?

MP: I'd like to think my customers look better than I do in my designs.

BLDD: But you design primarily dresses that you would be comfortable wearing?

MP: Yes. I had my first big blow in business when I realized that I couldn't expect to wear everything I designed. I had to broaden my view, to understand that my clothes represent women who lead busy lives, who are, or whose husbands are, executives with the needs of that world. I've never met a woman who didn't want to be pretty, no matter how great a feminist she is. I understand that factor, and cater to it. Take a man like Bill Blass. He's an attractive, dynamic, cultivated single man. He's familiar with the world of luxury and power. Year after year, his designs look more and more like the people he knows. That's important today, much more than striving to design the merely "different." I hope my clothes also reflect the life I lead.

BLDD: How would *you* describe the clothes you make?

MP: Feminine. Easy to wear. Clothes you wear, not clothes that wear you. When a woman enters a room wearing one of those drop-dead dresses, people may remember the dress, but not who wore it. I never make clothes like that. And since we sell 10 million dollars worth of dresses each year, we must have a point. That's a lot of dresses.

BLDD: How many, exactly?

MP: Good Lord—I'm going to make a confession to you—I've never learned to read a balance sheet, and I've been in business all these years. I'm not really all that good at business. I've always had to depend on my husband or on an associate or an accountant. I just have an intuitive sense of when we're doing well and when we're not.

BLDD: Do you think you have an intuitive sense as a designer, as well?

MP: Yes, that's essential. First, you look at the fabric and then you think of the dinner last night, and the one last week, when all the women wore black. Stunning black dresses. Now, that says something: ladies feel like wearing black in the evening. On the other hand, I had spent two days making a personal appearance at Bergdorf Goodman, and I cannot tell you how many women asked, "Have you got a red dress? I feel like wearing a red dress."

BLDD: Are those the only two colors in demand?

MP: The two most important, certainly. Mrs. Reagan had something to do with it. She's attractive, with a wonderful figure and she loves bright red. She has made all women conscious of red, including myself.

BLDD: Did you get one?

MP: Not yet, but I will have one before the season is over. I didn't even have a new black dress this season.

BLDD: Do you acquire a lot of new clothes each season?

MP: I have lots of clothes, but never at the right time.

BLDD: Let's talk about the design of the Mollie Parnis Collection. You have described yourself as an editor, that you know what you want and that you know how to get the message across.

MP: Yes. I respect the people who develop the designs. I don't walk into the design room and say, "That's a terrible dress." Even if I thought so, I wouldn't say it, because, one, it would take the heart out of the person and, two, what would I have accomplished? But I might say: "Look, that collar's

Mollie Parnis, fall, 1977

too big, the sleeves are too wide. Take some of that fullness out," and by the time I'm finished, the dress is right.

BLDD: Are the designers who work for you men or women?

MP: One man and one woman.

BLDD: Is there any difference in how you can communicate to either of the two of them? I once heard that you said you could get your message over more easily to a man. Was that an accurate quotation?

MP: It may have been at the time. If they're talented, it doesn't really make a difference. As it is now, I get my message over easily.

BLDD: There are two divisions now—Mollie Parnis, Inc., and the Mollie Parnis Studio, which is less expensive and more for young career women. What, if anything, differentiates the look of the two divisions, and what do they share?

MP: They all have the Mollie Parnis feeling of easy elegance that is simple and yet luxurious, but the Studio clothes are less lavish in detail and are made of more basic fabrics.

BLDD: You mentioned that earlier in the week you appeared at a store with your collection. How important to your work as a designer is getting out there and meeting your customers—seeing what people are actually wearing?

MP: I cannot tell you how important. I don't do it as much as I should. I really only do it in New York City, or out-of-town if it's a charity or a big event or a lecture. I don't have time for tours, but I do as much as I can.

BLDD: What do you learn from all those visits?

MP: An immense amount. Take the average mother-of-the-bride. It will be one of the most important occasions of her life. Her dress must be right and you must help her choose it. It becomes a fascinating challenge.

BLDD: How should a mother-of-the-bride look?

MP: She certainly shouldn't outshine the bride, but she should look very special. One of the things I discovered in my trips is that today the average mother-of-the-bride is no more than 45 years old and wears a size 8. She's young, and she wants to look young.

BLDD: By the way, even though you don't do trendy clothes, do you pay much attention to those trends that trickle up from the street?

MP: Naturally. Life itself is a fashion influence. Clothes cannot be made in a vacuum, and if you lead an active, full life, its every aspect will contribute to the way you react as a designer.

BLDD: What have you learned lately from the street?

MP: Women were beginning to get tired of layers and want to snuggle into coats. And they didn't all want fur. That was a signal to me to include pretty cloth coats in our next collection.

BLDD: You've said that the more complicated everyday life becomes, the more selective women become in their choice of clothes.

MP: One of the things I've noticed is that thoughtful women are buying fewer but better clothes. I find that the more people consider what they are doing, the more careful they are about what they buy in every area. Possessions are bought to last.

BLDD: What makes a well-dressed woman well-dressed?

MP: Hair is well done, skin taken care of, makeup attractive and subtle. Pretty shoes, a good handbag. All of these things are important. A well-dressed woman knows herself and her life. I have a close friend who's a size 4. It doesn't matter what the current fashion is, she intends to show her wonderful figure. She works very hard for it. She has her own look, and she looks divine. On the other hand, I have a friend, who's tall, almost six feet. She has lovely shoulders and therefore likes strapless and one-shouldered dresses. It's that kind of selectivity which gives women a reputation for elegance.

BLDD: Your designs have long been associated with some of the leading women and first ladies of our country. What have you learned from dealing with such prominent shapers of public opinion?

MP: They're no different than you and I except that they have the courage of their convictions. When they're choosing clothes, their first questions are, is it becoming? and is it pretty? Whether it is trendy or all that different is not a consideration.

BLDD: Are you saying that creating clothes for the influential, the privileged, or the well-known is really no different than designing for your less well-known customers?

MP: That is what I'm saying. The privileged, have more money to spend, so they get better fabric and more detailed workmanship. Whether it's Norma Kamali who designs for the far-out, or Bill Blass who designs for sophisticates, or myself who designs for a wider range of women, we all do our best to express a certain way of life.

BLDD: Do you ever have a specific person in mind when you're designing clothes? So many of your friends are also your customers.

MP: When the designs are finished, I may say, "Doesn't that look like Nancy Kissinger" or "Doesn't that look like Anne Douglas?" or some other woman I know and admire.

BLDD: Have you ever been interested in designing clothes for men?

MP: No. But I'm not a very good example. I have never wanted to license my name on anything that I don't actually create myself. I figured out I can only eat three meals a day and wear one dress at a time, and I made enough money early enough to satisfy my urge to collect good paintings.

BLDD: How did you first become an art collector?

MP: I first became interested through my friendship with Enid and Ira Haupt. I learned a great deal from them. We often spent Saturday afternoons going to art galleries and they would point out things that were tremendously helpful to me.

BLDD: Does art still interest you?

MP: It's the one thing I really love and want. I'm not an art expert, though. Almost all my pictures have the same colors. Forms and colors attract me primarily, rather than technique. I'm very, very lucky to own one of the world's most important Matisses' but I did not know when I bought it that it would be considered that valuable. What I saw was its divine colors and the shapes on the canvas. Little by little, I redid my whole living room to set off this Matisse painting, "Asie." The original designer of my apartment was Billy Baldwin and I believe I was Billy's first real client. He was then with Ruby Ross Wood and she scared the hell out of me. I was young and timid about my taste. She would tell me what to do, but it wasn't always what I wanted. Billy came along as her assistant. One day, I said, "Billy, can't we work alone?" And he said, "But Mrs. Wood is . . ." and I said, "I know, but let's work alone." He helped me learn how to put things together. My son had wonderful taste, and a fine collection of pictures.

BLDD: Your life has never been dull. You not only have eclectic interests and eclectic friends, but you're practically as well-known as a hostess as you are as a designer. Has that helped inform your work?

MP: I think so. Knowing people like Henry Kissinger and Mike Wallace and other spectacularly well-informed people affects everything you do. It's like taking a graduate course.

BLDD: What makes for a good dinner party, do you think?

MP: The mix of people.

BLDD: And what's the ideal mix and the ideal number for you?

MP: My favorite dinner party is ten people at one round table. I like guests who are interested in what is happening in the world.

BLDD: How important is the food and service?

MP: Quite important, but I've been to parties in wonderful apartments with wonderful food, wonderful flowers and wonderful appointments, with a boring man on my right and another on my left. Food and service can't overcome boredom.

BLDD: What advice then would you give a hostess?

MP: Get lucky and know some interesting people. Seriously, I don't know that you can give advice. The people that I know and like receive ten invitations for every one that they accept. I'm very lucky that they come to my home.

BLDD: Why have so many people liked coming here for so long?

MP: They know they'll meet six or eight other people that are not going to bore them. I never ask anybody to dinner because I owe them something.

BLDD: How do you pay people back?

MP: If I go once and I know I'm not going to go back, I send them flowers and a note. If you work all day, you cannot fill up your evenings with people who don't really interest you. I don't want to go to cocktail parties, nor to great big events just because they are big.

BLDD: What's the best hour for dinner?

MP: In my house, people are asked to come at a quarter-to-eight. We sit down at eight-thirty promptly, and if they leave at eleven, they don't hurt my feelings at all.

BLDD: And Sunday nights?

MP: We are apt to have our first course upstairs to look at "60 Minutes." Dinner is served right after eight o'clock, and by ten-thirty everybody's gone. We have coffee at the table if we're having a good conversation and I don't want to spoil it.

BLDD: What aspect of your multi-faceted career have you enjoyed most?

MP: My friends. I've gone through several phases in my friendships. At one point we knew everybody in Hollywood. My husband loved California. After he died, I remained close to Anne and Kirk Douglas, and still see a lot of them. One of their children is my godchild.

BLDD: If you had it to do over again, what would you do otherwise?

MP: I think I'd probably have spent more time with my son while he was small. I think that's the only change I would make.

Opposite:
Mollie Parnis, spring, 1980

Below:
Mollie Parnis, spring, 1983

AS

Arnold Scaasi

Arnold Scaasi has been called New York's last custom designer. His beautifully tailored and dramatically designed clothes are presented two times a year to his small army of devoted customers.

BLDD: You were raised in Montreal, Canada, and in Melbourne, Australia, educated in Canada and in France. That's certainly not a typical background for a fashion designer. How has your eclectic background influenced your work?

AS: I've grown and traveled; I've picked up things along the way, and everything has helped shape what I do today. I grew up in Montreal and in Australia with a very fashionable aunt who was dressed by Schiaparelli and Chanel. Much of my background and feeling about clothes came from my Aunt Ida.

BLDD: Was Aunt Ida the person who particularly influenced you in your choice of career?

AS: At the beginning, yes. She *was* a fascinating woman. Because she traveled extensively, she was very knowledgeable, and always growing. That rubbed off on me.

BLDD: It's surprising to think of this very fashionable woman nearly thirty-five years ago in Australia. What did she do that was so dramatic and so impressed you? And what did she wear?

AS: It was her whole lifestyle. She lived in a wonderful house with a great garden. Her lifestyle was extremely elegant, something that I don't think exists today. I was very fortunate to have been part of it.

BLDD: Did you ever have any formal training as a designer?

AS: Yes, I had many years of formal training. I returned to Canada from Australia in my teens and went to a wonderful school called the Cotnoir Capponi School of Design. That was the beginning of my formal training before I went on to Paris, where I studied. Afterwards I worked at a house called Paquin, which was then a very stylish and well-known house of fashion.

BLDD: How did your apprenticeship with Paquin influence your design philosophy?

AS: I don't know exactly how one is influenced by what one goes through in life. Your eye sees things, and your mind works them out, and then finally they become your own style. Paquin dressed many celebrities. So I was probably influenced by the atmosphere of wonderful quality and beautiful fabrics, of a place with no limitations on how and what you designed. The search was always for something new.

BLDD: How important is that kind of formal apprenticeship to the career of a designer?

AS: It's the most important thing, the basis for any career. Afterwards you can go on and do your own thing. But if you don't have that basis, you may have to repeat and go back.

BLDD: Was that European training as important or more important than your early training on Seventh Avenue?

AS: It was the most important part of my life. First of all traveling gives you a feeling of what people in other countries do, and that there are people outside of your own little world. That was how I began to know what went on in the world and for whom I should be designing.

BLDD: How did you wend your way from Paris to New York?

AS: I arrived about 1953. My parents had come down to drive me back to Montreal, but I was offered a job here and I never went back.

BLDD: Did that happen as soon as you arrived?

AS: The next day. I went to meet Charles James, who was then a very well-known custom designer. He had heard of my background and immediately said, "Would you like to stay in New York and apprentice with me?" I said, "Absolutely." That was my dream. I was very lucky it happened right away, the second day I was in New York. I worked with Charles James for two-and-a-half years.

BLDD: And then decided it was time to go into your own business, a ready-to-wear business?

AS: I did decide it was time to leave Charles James and do something else. I was then going to go into a made-to-order business. When you are that young, you have lots of courage. Nothing can stand in your way. Only when you get older do you get more worried. I just decided that I wanted to do something on my own. I didn't do it immediately.

I worked on Seventh Avenue for a year or two before I finally opened my own business.

BLDD: When did you start calling yourself Scaasi?

AS: About twenty-five years ago.

BLDD: By the way, what *is* your name?

AS: Arnold Scaasi.

BLDD: What *was* your name?

AS: My name was Scaasi spelled backwards. I thought the name sounded great. I loved the way it sounded. From the day I changed it, I never thought of having another.

BLDD: Do you think your work would look otherwise if you were still called Arnold Isaacs?

AS: No, of course not.

BLDD: Did you feel a need for a more dramatic Western European-sounding name?

AS: I really don't know. My name was going to be used in an ad, and suddenly someone said, "Wouldn't it be terrific to use your name backwards, and you'd be known as Scaasi from then on." And I was.

BLDD: At one time your very successful ready-to-wear line was carried by over two hundred American stores. But you discontinued it when you decided to design couture clothes. What made you decide to devote yourself to a custom couture collection?

AS: I always designed couture clothes, even in the ready-to-wear. "Couture" means clothes that are better quality, better made, maybe more inventive and more expensive than non-couture clothes. At that time, I was doing so many things. I had eight or ten licensing agreements. I was doing a boutique collection four times a year, and the couture ready-to-wear four times a year. I did nothing but work. Suddenly in 1964 I decided that I was working too hard and not getting any fun out of life. So, I decided to stop everything and take a sabbatical. I went to Europe for a year. When I came back I thought, "Now, what do I really want to do that I love to do?" I went back to my first dream, making made-to-order clothes. I liked the idea of working directly with a customer, finding out what her life was about and what kind of clothes she needed. I liked filling a need in her life. It's proven to be a very successful and happy experience.

BLDD: Where did you get the backing to do that?

AS: I had made a great deal of money in the ready-to-wear business and in all the licensing. So I had the backing.

BLDD: Where did you get the money to go into business in the first place?

AS: I'd saved $2,000. In 1957, that's all you needed to make up some dresses and present them to the stores. Stores then were very open to new ideas and new people. Also the time was right for the kind of things I did.

BLDD: Where were you housed?

AS: In my apartment—a walkup on 58th Street and Lexington Avenue. We had a tailor and a seamstress, and for the first year of business everything was made there. Then we skyrocketed and did a lot of other things.

BLDD: You've described yourself as being totally visual. In fact, you are interested in the look of the total environment. How does that relate to your work as a fashion designer?

AS: Everything I see must be beautiful or have some feeling of beauty. I don't think it can be planned. It just happens. Everybody's eye is different.

BLDD: There is a relationship, I assume, between your work as a designer and your interest in art.

AS: Yes. When I choose a painting or a sculpture, it must be pleasing to my eye. Very often, it turns out that it is also a good piece of art, I guess because I have a good eye. The same thing happens in clothing. The proportion and the balance of a dress are very important to me. These aren't things you learn; they're something you know instinctively.

BLDD: How did you become a collector of works of art?

AS: I decided that if I was going to invest, I should invest in something that pleased my eye. My very first acquisition was interesting. It was a painting by Leonora Carrington which I bought in Mexico. She was married to Max Ernst and was an important surrealist. I just saw a new Dali museum in St. Petersburg, Florida, the Morse Museum. It's a great museum. They mention Leonora Carrington. Anyway, that was my first acquisition. I just liked it and had to have that painting.

BLDD: Do you still have it?

AS: Yes. I went on from there to Léger.

BLDD: How do you explain the shift in taste and in interest?

AS: I don't think you can explain why or how, but your taste changes and grows.

BLDD: Do you think yours has become emboldened?

AS: No. In fact it may have become more careful over the years. Every now and then you see something that you'd love and you don't know why, because maybe ten years ago you hated it. I have a great deal of orange in the new collection. It's a color I've always thought was unflattering to women and not right for clothing. Yet suddenly this season it is absolutely spectacular and looks right. I cannot tell you why. There is no explanation. I just saw some orange fabric in Paris and I thought, "That looks terrific."

BLDD: What works of art have you found most inspiring or influential?

AS: I'm not influenced by any artist. However I am inspired by Louise Nevelson, because she's a friend and I dress her. I love her feeling about clothes; she's very creative with them. We have a wonderful mesh because she finds that I'm very creative in making the right kind of clothes for her.

BLDD: That is a very open-minded and creative act on the part of a designer—to allow clients to have very independent ideas of their own. One assumes that Louise Nevelson is dressed both by Arnold Scaasi and by Louise Nevelson. It's very generous of you to let someone else alter your designs.

AS: They're not really altered, but clothing must be worn, and the wearer must be happy wearing it. That's the first rule. I have made a lot of clothes for people in the theatre and in films, and the most important thing is that the person be relaxed and easy in their clothing and that the clothes do something for them. I made a lot of clothes for Barbra Streisand and found her extraordinarily creative. There was a wonderful give-and-take, as there is with Nevelson and many other people, people who are not necessarily artists.

BLDD: How has Barbra Streisand adapted her tastes to your designs?

AS: Many years ago, we had a white faille wedding dress in the collection that had a hood and was very covered up. After she saw it, she called and asked if I would consider making the wedding dress in black. "Yes," I said, "I guess so, but it's a terrible color for a wedding." She said, "I'm not going to use it for a wedding. I want to use it as an evening coat. I think it would be terrific." Of course it was. Every time she had a hunch about something special, it was right for her. I saw that. Afterwards it is my job to make it right from a design point of view.

BLDD: Does she know a great deal about clothes?

AS: Oh, yes, she has a great feeling for them. It's an innate feeling, as is Nevelson's. She can take three outfits and put together one piece of each, and create a whole new look.

BLDD: How do you feel when Nevelson wears a collage outfit, a cross between a princess and a peasant—for instance a lavish beautifully-tailored, Scaasi brocade suit, with an ordinary denim workshirt worn underneath.

AS: I think it's great. That's what makes it hers, and it doesn't in any way play down what I've done. It wouldn't be possible without my having done the brocade suit. But what she does with it is terrific—it makes it even better.

BLDD: Are you ever inspired by color, or material, or place, or mood, or a client who isn't quite so well-known?

AS: Yes, all those things, depending on where I am.

BLDD: Are there any colors besides orange that you have always thought were not appropriate or not flattering for women?

AS: In the evening grey, dirty colors are very unflattering because you're mainly in artificial light. Up colors are more helpful.

BLDD: "Helpful" is a generous word.

AS: That's why we make clothes, to make people look attractive. To me up colors in the evening, bright colors, are more attractive.

BLDD: What is your favorite "up" color?

AS: Red and shocking pink mixed with purple or orange, all those colors together. I love that spectrum of pinks and reds and oranges.

BLDD: What are the most "helpful" colors for the day-time?

Arnold Scaasi, 1954

Arnold Scaasi, 1955

Overleaf:
Arnold Scaasi, 1958

AS: I don't know that there really are any helpful colors for the daytime. I guess blues are a good safe bet. Bright red. Red is great in the daytime, and can be helpful.

BLDD: You live in a very dramatic apartment, a spectacular duplex overlooking New York's Central Park. What about the relationship between fashion and interior design? Were you deeply involved in the design of that apartment?

AS: Very much so. In fact, I've decorated all of my residences myself. You begin an apartment or a residence by finding out what's there. As you have a body on which to build, you have four walls and you must decorate them. You do it with the same eye that you do anything else.

BLDD: Your other residence is a very elaborate Long Island house. What did you do there?

AS: Because the house was built in 1910 and had not been decorated since then, I did everything. There were walls and windows that I took out and new shapes and forms of walls that I put back in. But I always wanted to keep it a 1910 house. I don't think that you can totally change the feeling of a house or an apartment. But you can take what's there, and build on it. Everything I did in the Long Island house was meant to look and feel like it had been done during the first twenty years of its existence. Although the swimming pool has heating and all the conveniences, it is done out of red brick and looks like it was done in the 1920's.

BLDD: Does your philosophy about colors that are pleasing and make you feel comfortable relate to the way you design a house or apartment?

AS: I think so. Even though I've said there are no rules I do have one—you can use great color and very upbeat wallpapers and prints in rooms that you're not going to be in very long.

BLDD: Can we assume that you have a red-and-pink living room somewhere?

AS: No. You're in the living room a long time. But I do have a red and yellow hallway which you pass through. It's bright red and it has bright yellow doors.

BLDD: What colors were you able to use in the living room?

AS: Softer colors, that are not jarring. In a living room, where you may be for most of a dinner party, you want to have colors that are pleasant to be with. I like white. That's the basic, easy color. A wonderful background for people and art.

BLDD: Did you ever consider a career as an interior designer?

AS: Yes, I once did, but then I was told by my interior designer friends that I should stick with dress design. I asked why, and they said, "Because when you're designing a dress you only have one person to worry about— the woman for whom you are designing. But when you've decorated a room the wife of the couple may okay it, but then suddenly the husband might say, 'I hate it all' and you have to start all over again."

BLDD: Was that enough to persuade you?

AS: Absolutely.

BLDD: As a designer whose work is not subject to the whims of store buyers either, do you feel a greater sense of creative freedom now, than when you catered to a mass market?

AS: Yes, much more so. I went into made-to-order clothes because I wanted that freedom. I felt that I was being pushed by stores to do certain things that I really didn't like doing and didn't want to do.

BLDD: There must be some appealing aspects of a ready-to-wear line that is mass distributed.

AS: I don't know. I had it so long ago. I went through that ego trip and all the publicity and stuff, and I am very happy today doing what I love to do.

BLDD: Did you ever consider doing ready-to-wear again?

AS: One day I think of it seriously, then the next I see how pleased I am doing what I'm doing and I think no, that's silly.

BLDD: Do your ready-to-wear designer friends tell you, "You've got to be kidding, Arnold?"

AS: Everybody tells you you've got to be kidding about any business you want to go into.

BLDD: I can see how a designer could easily prefer the liberty of made-to-order and custom design and how a customer would like the results. But don't clients ever feel a bit uneasy about spending $4,000 to $8,000 for one single item of clothing?

AS: Not really. If you spend $4,000 for a dress that has been made for you, unless you gain or lose a great deal of weight, that dress will always fit you—it really is *your* dress. Then there are all the years that you wear it. I have many clients who wear a dress for two years, put it away for two years and then bring it out as a totally new dress. It does look like a new dress, and at the same time they have the joy of having something that was made for them that is really theirs, and looks wonderful on them. And it looks just as great on them the sixth year as it did the first. If you spend $4,000 for a dress and wear it for eight years, the cost is $500 a year. So, it depends how you look at it. Made-to-order clothes are very special and they are for very special people who understand about clothes. They are for a woman who would like to have a few great things in her wardrobe a season rather than many ordinary ones. The average upper middle class woman who buys clothes for weekends and parties and for just living in, probably spends as much as one of my clients. But she probably ends up with a lot of clothes that she won't want to wear the next season, either because they will be out of style or they don't fit her quite right, or because she is bored with them.

BLDD: Just what *does* one get for $4,000?

AS: You get everything that you want.

BLDD: Why does it cost so much?

AS: Labor is very expensive today. People who do these kind of clothes are very hard to find; they are like jewels. You nurture them, you take care of them. They're great artisans. Unfortunately, in America we don't care very much about quality, we keep pushing it aside.

BLDD: I thought there was a revival of interest in quality.

AS: There is. Since not very well made ready-to-wear clothes are also very expensive today, it doesn't matter if you have to spend a little bit more to get something that's really well made. Europe has always held on to the couture side of clothing, and there are still many couturiers in France and Italy. We don't have much of that in America. So the woman here who buys a made-to-order dress greatly appreciates quality.

BLDD: But, by any standard, $4,000 to even $6,500 is a lot of money. Will you give us some idea of the break-down of the costs? Everybody knows that hand labor is expensive, but how much does it cost exactly?

BLDD: Today a great seamstress gets paid between $350 to $400 a week. The fabric I use, which is exclusive to me, is made in France or Italy.

BLDD: Does all of your fabric come from Europe?

AS: Yes, because we don't find the quality, or the design quality, here. The people who make mass-produced fabric are not interested in doing something terribly special for only ten or fifteen yards of fabric. They want thousands of yards. And you can't make thousands of yards of hand-embroidered something-or-other or hand-screened prints. We might use a print that has thirty or forty colors in it. It's very difficult. You can't have that made in America.

BLDD: How much does that cost a yard?

AS: Anywhere from $150 to $200, and I might use five yards in a dress. So I'm already spending around $1,000. That doesn't include the lining, the trimmings, the belts, the fitting time. A woman may come in and have five or six fittings for a dress, and each time the dress is totally taken apart, reshaped for her, and put back together again. All this costs a great deal of money.

BLDD: How many days do you allot to make each garment?

AS: About two weeks.

BLDD: How many dresses of that sort can you make a year, let alone sell. How many customers generally buy them?

AS: We can make about 500 a year and we don't want to make more. At this time there are about a hundred customers a season, two seasons a year.

BLDD: Most designers show four and five collections. How did you manage to restrict your designs to two seasons?

AS: I don't think it's necessary to show more; it only confuses the customer. My women order their clothes twice a year—fall and winter clothes when it's about to become fall and winter, and summer and spring clothes at those times of year.

BLDD: Do you begin your work with a sketch, or by applying fabric to a mannequin, or by dealing with a live model? How does one of your designs evolve?

AS: I begin somewhere between the fabric and the sketch. Either the sketch comes first because I have an idea for a new shape or a different detail of some kind, or I'll see a fabric that is spectacular and then do a sketch with that in mind.

BLDD: How far in advance do you begin to work?

AS: About three months before we show the collection. The spring fabrics are bought in November in Europe and then they're shown sometime in February.

BLDD: How do you decide on a particular color or design or even skirt length for any particular season?

AS: Each designer decides according to his or her talent, and eye.

BLDD: How about color? How do all the designers decide one year it's black, another it's grey, another year burgundy?

AS: It's a feeling that you get. There must be a kind of hidden society that tells you.

BLDD: That's what I want to know about. Where and who is that hidden society?

AS: I really don't know. Why did all the impressionist artists suddenly paint impressionistically? Or how did pop art suddenly come into being?

BLDD: You not only have dress designers but shoe and bag designers, and hosiery designers, all of whom coordinate their colors.

AS: I think it all begins with a handful of people. When store and fabric people and designers go to the European collections, whatever they see may be what happens the following year.

BLDD: You often dress well-known women who have distinct ideas of their own about how to dress. Some of them are also public performers, whom you dress for their performances. How involved do they get in the design? Do they tell you how they'd like to look, or do you tell them how you think they should look?

AS: Designing made-to-order clothes is so different from designing any other clothing because you get so involved with the client. Yes, she does tell you how she wants to look, and then it's up to you to make her look that way. If you don't totally believe in it, then you try to explain to her what she should do differently. There is a lot of give-and-take. That's why the dress or the item of clothing is so special.

BLDD: For whom did you do that most recently?

AS: Joan Rivers.

BLDD: How do you envision Joan Rivers, a woman who, on the one hand, is a broad-based comedienne as a performer; and on the other hand, wears elegant clothes? How do you bring the two together?

AS: She wants to look very sophisticated, very New York. Since she feels comfortable in that kind of clothing and looks right in it, then it's very important that I make those kind of clothes for her.

BLDD: How much give-and-take is there between a client and yourself? Are there any rules that just simply cannot be broken?

AS: Absolutely, yes.

BLDD: What are your ground rules?

AS: A client may decide she wants to use a fabric in some way that is not possible. It may not drape or handle the way she thinks it will. It's then up to us to tell her.

BLDD: What's the most unusual request you've ever had.?

AS: I guess to make a nun's habit.

BLDD: And what did you design?

AS: It was interesting. The Mother Superior said, "You know, we are not like other women, so don't think of designing something for us like for other women." As we do with everyone who comes us, we found out what their needs were. For instance, the clothing did not have to be short. There was then a trend to shorten nuns' habits. I didn't understand that at all. I guess one of the great things I did was to suggest to them that the simplest underdressing was panty hose. They had never heard of panty hose. So I brought panty hose to the church. I don't mean to be irreverent about it.

BLDD: And what did you learn from the experience? What did the nuns bring to you?

AS: An idea I had never thought about before: that people of the church are different from most people. They have a completely different way of life and of thinking than ours.

BLDD: Did that awareness alter your designs for your usual clients?

AS: I don't think so. It's just another challenge, another way of doing things for another group of people.

BLDD: How about sharing some of the tricks of the trade? There must be all sorts of things that tone down a less attractive shape and make almost anyone's silhouette look more ideal. Will you share some of your camouflage secrets?

AS: If you have a large bosom, you should wear a low neck, because it automatically cuts the line—unless you like to emphasize a large bosom. But even if you like a large bosom, a low neckline will both show it off and help cut the expanse from the neck to the point of the bosom. If you're stout, you should wear darker colors because they make you look thinner. But we've also done all kinds of tricks like putting darker panels of fabric at the sides of a dress, which automatically slim down the silhouette. Sometimes women say, "I have very broad shoulders therefore, I don't want shoulder pads. I don't want my shoulders broadened." What they don't realize is that their shoulders might be an asset that they should exaggerate them not try to slim them down. When I first did clothes for Joan Crawford it was interesting to find that she really had those big shoulders.

BLDD: Those were not shoulder pads?

AS: Only for the shape. Adrian had no choice but to give her those shoulders. He just emphasized them.

BLDD: What was she like as a client?

AS: She was quite marvelous and very neat. She loved to hang up her clothes and put them away and straighten everything up herself.

BLDD: You don't get many clients like that, do you?

AS: No. They usually drop clothes on the floor and wait for the maid to pick them up. But she knew what her image was and what she wanted to portray: a sophisticated, glamorous movie star. A lot of sincerely glamorous movie stars now want to portray another image, sometimes of youth, of casualness about clothes. I make it look as if they decided what to wear on the spur of the moment.

BLDD: How have your customers changed in the twenty years that you've been in business?

AS: Years ago the made-to-order customer was thought to be a very wealthy older woman. Today, the same customer is much younger, often in her mid-40s. She may not be terribly rich, but her successful husband wants her to look that way. It is very common for men to want their wives to look a certain way, just as much as the women themselves want to look a certain way. For instance he really likes her to look like the wife of a young, affluent executive. And she doesn't want to wear what all of her friends are wearing.

BLDD: That sounds a bit like a pre–Women's Liberation Movement kind of description.

AS: I will not get into women's liberation. All the women that you and I know were liberated long before the movement ever came into being.

BLDD: Then why don't they themselves decide what they'd like to look like?

AS: They do. The women decide what they want to look like, but their husbands give them suggestions.

BLDD: How important is fantasy to fashion design?

AS: I think it's the most important element. Whenever I give a class in a school, I always say, "I don't care what you design, but make it as fantastic as you can." Because when a designer starts out, it's the only time he is not guided by rules. You can do whatever you want. The most important thing in creative fashion is fantasy and what you dream about.

BLDD: What have you been dreaming about?

AS: I ended this collection with a big dress of white tulle with silver stars all over it. We called it Cloud's Starry Night.

BLDD: You don't design runway clothes as do other designers. You seem to want real clothes that real people buy and wear. How do you make that happen?

AS: It has to do with my knowing how to make a dress. A lot of designers today really don't know how to. They don't know where to put the seams and the zipper, and how to open and close it and, they may not know how a dress moves. It might look great on a sketchpad, but then how does it all work out? That's why if you're going to be a good designer you need an enormous amount of training at the beginning.

BLDD: You use so much fur—you must know a great deal about it. Is it very difficult to work with?

AS: You have to think another way when you work with fur, but my father was a furrier, so I grew up with furs.

BLDD: How do you transfer design from cloth to fur?

AS: You scale it down. Because fur is thick, you work with it as if you were working with a thick fabric. The silhouette must be scaled down because two inches more will be added onto the width or the length.

BLDD: What furs do you prefer?

AS: I like things that move—the long-haired, fluffy furs, all the foxes and lynx and things like that. But I also love sable. It's not bad. I use a lot of it for trimmings.

BLDD: Do most of the furs come from Canada?

AS: No. A lot of them come from Russia.

BLDD: Fashion is more than just body covering, it reflects society's values. Fashion is also a personal and political statement. How do you think the clothes that you design reflect current trends?

AS: Although everyone talks about recession these days, I think there is a great deal of affluence in our country. What I do probably reflects that. The women I dress want to state their belief in quality. If you look at clothes in museums, such as the beautiful clothes from the turn of the century, you notice a great feeling for detail, for quality, for art. The people who made the handmade laces and embroideries and the people who dyed the fabrics were all considered artists. Sadly, we've lost a great deal of that in our time. Many of the women that I know and dress still feel it is a very important part of dressing.

BLDD: You dress artists and actresses and ladies that own racing stables. Is there something that they all share, however diverse their backgrounds?

AS: Yes. They're a very energetic group of women. If they're not working, I mean paid for work, then they are working on a special project. They are very philanthropic, very interested in giving and sharing. And they are interested in getting a great deal out of life. They're not senseless ladies, as one might think. They don't only care about clothes. But the clothing they wear mirrors the lives they lead.

BLDD: How influential is the opinion of the press, of magazines and newspaper fashion editors, in the design of your collections?

AS: Oh, not at all.

BLDD: How susceptible are you to their judgment or their appraisal, their criticism?

AS: You like to be judged and have your work appreciated. But I think if you do something that you really love and believe in, then, like any artist—and I really am not sure whether a designer is an artist or not—you don't let the press dictate to you. A painter doesn't say, "Well, I'm going to do it this way because it will please Barbaralee more or less." He just does it because it looks right to him.

BLDD: Who's the tougher critic, your individual clients, or the store buyer, or the press?

AS: Clients are the most difficult critics because they must wear the clothes and work them into their lifestyles. And probably the client's husband is the toughest of all.

BLDD: How do you know? Do you ever get any feedback?

AS: I get lots of it.

BLDD: From the husband or the client?

AS: From both. Very often the client will call and say, "My husband thought that was the most beautiful dress I'd ever worn and he was so excited about it and thrilled by it."

BLDD: Is this before, or after, he receives the bill?

AS: The bill has nothing to do with that.

BLDD: You lead the same kind of life as many of your clients. Do you think that your affinity for their affluent lifestyle helps you understand and meet their fashion needs?

AS: Absolutely. I go to many of the balls they go to. I go to many of the

Arnold Scaasi, 1959

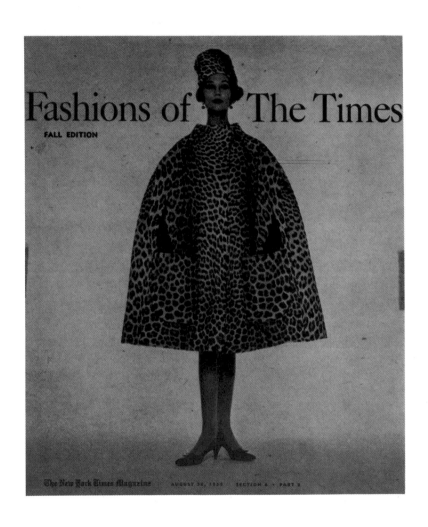

Fashions of The Times
FALL EDITION

The New York Times Magazine   AUGUST 30, 1959   SECTION 6 · PART 2

dinner parties they go to. And I go to Saratoga in the summer with my racing friends, and to Europe. I go wherever they are because they are my friends, and also because it gives me an understanding of how they live and what they need in their lives. The first question I'd ask if you came to me for clothing is "Where are you going to wear this dress? What will you be doing? When do you leave for Europe? When do you come back? How much time do you spend in what kind of a climate?"

BLDD: Is there anyone you wouldn't want to clothe?

AS: I can't think of one. There must be a lot, but I can't think of one now.

BLDD: Are there women who you think personify American beauty?

AS: "Beauty!"—that's a strange word. It's all in the eye of the beholder. But I do think there are many people who look wonderful. The first thing you notice when you walk into a room is how someone looks. That first impression before anyone says anything reflects what fundamentally a person is like. Jacqueline Kennedy is a marvelous example. She has always dressed very well, and shown her personality. And she's always dressed correctly for the occasion. If she's at her office, she has on a blouse and a skirt. If she's going for a walk, she has on a pair of trousers and a jacket, and, if she's at a dinner party or an opening, she has on the right kind of dinner dress. I think she personifies for our time what glamour and dressing well and showing your personality off to the best advantage is.

BLDD: The most widely photographed woman today is Princess Diana. What do you think about her public presence and how she looks?

AS: I've never thought about it. Isn't that terrible? I guess she's always been very well-dressed any time I've ever seen pictures of her. I think she does all right.

BLDD: How would you describe that rare quality referred to as "taste"?

AS: It's innate. I don't think you learn it. For example, I learned through many discussions with Barbra Streisand that she always loved things of quality. When she had very little money she purchased antique clothes because that way she could get quality inexpensively. She preferred to do that than to go buy a synthetic dress in a bargain store. That's what taste is all about.

BLDD: Can there by now be anything new in fashion design, or has it already all been done?

AS: It's always new, because proportions change. The broad-shouldered look is now popular but if you took out an old suit from 1944 with broad padded shoulders, you'd find that looked totally dated, because the proportion of clothes changes all the time. Also, the attitude of the person wearing them changes. In the Victorian era, women did walk as if they had a bustle on their behind. Today, if you put the same dress on a woman, she would walk totally differently.

BLDD: Are there any widely accepted styles today of which you particularly disapprove?

AS: Layers. I hate layers. I don't think women know what to do with them. I don't think anybody knows what to do with them. It's very unattractive to see a woman loaded down with lots of things on her. It adds a lot of extra bulk. Usually the woman who wears them is too short and too small, so she really looks dwarfed by all of the stuff. Then when they begin to get undressed, it's a mess. It's just everywhere, all these pieces moving around. It's terrible.

BLDD: What are your favorite things?

AS: Pretty women. Women that look pretty in pretty clothes, the clothes that I try to make.

BLDD: Which of your designs have been the most successful?

AS: Pretty clothes, things that are feminine. I never like to say what I think I have introduced, because sometimes I find someone else introduced it first.

BLDD: There are some things you've done that really are your signature— print dresses and coats that match, bubble tops, lavish ensembles with jackets and skirts.

AS: I did start things like that. I invented them because they were needed. The timing was right.

BLDD: Are there any of your designs that you think are less successful than others, that you're sorry that you ever did?

AS: Oh, yes. In every collection there are a handful of dresses that make you wonder why you ever designed them or how you ever let them out on the runway. They are then called discards because you immediately hide them in the closet. Usually you give them to a thrift shop. Sometimes you keep them and then five years later, you see them and think, "My God, that's really spectacular." It looks right at that moment. Sometimes you're ahead of yourself.

BLDD: If you had a retrospective of your work now, what would you emphasize? What would you want to have shown?

AS: I've always loved day clothes even though I'm better known for my evening clothes, for making women look glamorous in the evening. Five years ago I had a twenty year retrospective at Lincoln Center, and I was surprised that all the day clothes shown were really wonderful clothes that looked right today. I like the feeling of what I do in day clothes. And people are usually surprised by them.

BLDD: How would you describe the look of your day clothes?

AS: I always want a woman to look glamorous and outstanding. That's my fantasy of how women should look. But it is very difficult to transform that fantasy into a day outfit that doesn't make a woman look silly, and overdressed walking down the street. It's a great challenge. Someone once asked me, "How do you know when to stop draping or adding?" I think it's like a painter who stops putting the paint on the brush and on the canvas. He knows when the painting is finished. That's part of being a professional.

BLDD: How do one of your clients or the rest of us know when enough really is enough?

AS: There is no answer to that.

BLDD: Do you see lots of fashion victims walking around?

AS: Not as many as one would think. Strangely enough, walking on Fifth Avenue recently I was amazed whenever I saw a kind of fashion victim, or someone who looked strange. I realized that they all had put on something to liven up their costume. For instance, one woman wore a red velvet bus driver's cap. It had nothing to do with the rest of her outfit. But I realized afterwards she probably put it on to cheer herself up. That's fine, if it works for the wearer.

BLDD: It's been said that you were the first American designer to become involved in licensing. Is that true?

AS: Yes. I did the first licensing in 1957, which is a long time ago.

BLDD: What did you do?

AS: I did children's wear and men's ties and sweaters, and in 1958 I did the first Ben Kahn fur collections. Licensing really meant that you got credit for designing what designers always designed, but had never received credit for before.

BLDD: Is there a Scaasi scent?

AS: There's a Scaasi scent on the horizon, but it isn't perfect yet.

BLDD: A successful designer must look to the future. What are your fashion predictions?

AS: I don't think that the human race has changed its feeling about living or loving or working. So, I don't see why clothes should change. For example, if there was nuclear fall-out and we were all forced to wear identical protective suits, then sooner or later someone would decide to color theirs red just to show some individuality. I don't think individuality or the personality of the human race changes very much through the centuries. So I don't think clothing will undergo a complete change.

BLDD: What's been the greatest satisfaction of your career?

AS: Having the career. I love it; it's been very rewarding, very satisfying.

BLDD: Any great frustrations?

AS: As in every career, there have been some but that's all part of working. You overcome them.

BLDD: Do you feel that you've made any major sacrifices because of your career? Obviously, you felt that way twenty years ago, when you took a year off. But how do you feel now?

AS: I haven't made any more sacrifices. I'm so lucky to have been given the talent and the wherewithal to use it. I'm very happy with my life.

BLDD: If you had it to do over again, what would you do differently?

AS: I don't know that I'd do anything differently. I may not have worked so much in the beginning, but perhaps doing that made it possible for me to work less afterwards.

BLDD: Is it all still exciting for you?

AS: Very, yes. I always think before I go to Europe, "Oh my God, I have to look at another fifty collections of fabric. After looking at fifty times 200, how could you possibly find anything new?" And then you open up the suitcases and there are wonderful things, and suddenly something looks new to you.

BLDD: Is each collection like starting over?

AS: Always, yes. I'm just as nervous about it, until we begin to sell the clothes, as I was the first time.

BLDD: Even now you aren't certain of yourself and your audience?

AS: No. Never. No.

BLDD: What would do that for you?

AS: I don't think it's possible with my temperament. I was in Dallas the other day and I saw my friend Liza Minelli. She'd just done a show and she said, "Was it all right?" And I thought, "My God, after all the opening nights you've done, isn't it time that you knew?" But I don't think you ever know. Maybe that's part of your talent, that you're always striving for something better than what you did the last time and hoping that you'll stay on the same creative level. With clothing, it's different. You don't want to make the clothes look strange, but you want to make them look new. So you're working within a framework that doesn't allow much freedom, yet you want your clothes to be free and new-looking. So, it scares you to death until somebody finally buys that new dress you have just designed.

BLDD: Did you ever expect your life to unfold the way it has?

AS: I never planned any of it.

BLDD: What did you have in mind?

AS: To work as little as possible and to make as much money as possible, and to live as nicely as possible. It didn't work out that way but in a way it did. I planned to be a designer, but I had no idea that I would be a designer in New York and that after opening my first collection, I would be successful, and become a known name.

Arnold Scaasi, 1982

S

Shamask

Shamask draws on forms from the art and architecture of many cultures to create clothes that are both classic and the epitome of high fashion. Through his carefully composed shapes and uncluttered detail, he makes fashion a fine design art.

BLDD: There's something I've always wanted to ask you. Is Shamask your first or your last name?

RS: It's my last name. I think Ronaldus is rather a lot to say. Shamask is an abbreviation.

BLDD: Much has been said about the "architectural quality" of the clothes that you design. Why is it that most fashion critics use the term "architectural" to describe your clothes? What does that mean?

RS: I think what happened was that there was a fashion movement toward extreme femininity that became somewhat of a dead end, causing some to look toward contemporary art for inspiration, specifically the structured modernist movement. This gave the fashion world an opportunity to develop a vocabulary that would make it respectable in the world of design and art. It was logical to look in the direction of architecture, as architecture creates habitable structures and, of course, clothing is also in some ways a habitable structure, a very intimate habitable structure . . .

BLDD: But is it wearable?

RS: If the design is successful.

BLDD: How would you describe your work?

RS: It has to do with elimination rather than applied decoration. Decoration is something that can hide the structure, something that stylists often use incorrectly as a tool to camouflage mistakes and problems. When you reduce and eliminate, cut and proportion remain and, of course, the structural elements, the seams, are then conspicuous. These structural elements become the decorative part of the clothes, as well. I'm interested in design which employs logic and reasoning.

BLDD: Why don't you explain the logic and reasoning of this applied seam decoration on the dress I'm wearing. What led you to this form and shape?

RS: What you are wearing is a very simple structure. To honor the change of grain in the fabric, the lower seam forms a triangle which then dictates the placement of the pocket. If I should begin by pretending that the seams aren't there, or if I would say, "This dart is ugly, please don't look at it," then I would have failed completely in my attempt to create something that—to me—is beautiful. To conceal the seams is illogical. They are there because they *are* the garment, they *are* the design, the idea, the way in which a flat piece of fabric becomes dimensional, with a unique proportion or drape or silhouette. This involves both the art and science of design. If I attempted in the end to conceal this work, I would be defeating my purpose by camouflaging the essence of the design.

BLDD: You spent most of your childhood in Amsterdam before moving to Australia as a teenager. Why Australia, in the mid-1960's?

RS: My parents went there.

BLDD: That's the logical place for a fifteen-year-old to be: with his family. But why Australia? What led them there?

RS: It seems a long time after the war, but I think that had a lot to do with it. They wanted to go somewhere away from Europe. I don't know why they decided on Australia.

BLDD: What did you do in Australia? Did you know early on that you wanted to be a designer?

RS: From the time I was a child, I always designed and drew and painted.

BLDD: There you were in Australia and, as you have described it, very much in need of making your own way. What was your first job?

RS: The circumstances were such that I had to start working immediately. I don't really find that a bad thing, you know. My first job, because I did not speak English, was pushing a trolley in a department store. In the back of my mind, or course, I was a designer and an artist. There are people that can paint or write all day, every day, and still are not writers, nor painters. Someone like Marcel Duchamp can do something once every now and then and always be a great artist. It is not something which comes and goes. It has to do with a deep sense of discovery within yourself, an exploration of what you think you're about or what you want to do.

BLDD: Your first job in design, as I recall, was also in that department store. You left that trolley car behind in a hurry.

RS: Yes. I was doing window display, and that was the closest I could get to art at that time.

BLDD: How did you know what to do? What does a fifteen-year-old do in a department store window?

RS: I was *told* what to do! It was a good experience—a limiting one, but at the time it was good. It taught me something that set a precedent for the rest of my life.

BLDD: What lesson was that?

RS: I think there are two schools in life: one where you learn a technique and with that technique find something to do, and one where you find something you want to do, and then develop the technique to achieve it. I never had an opportunity to study first.

BLDD: What do you mean when you say "never?"

RS: It means that I didn't have the time just to study, not without also doing. But by understanding the end result, I already had an advantage, and could get there, discovering the tools along the way. By understanding the end result you are striving for you have an advantage over people that might, from the beginning, have the tools and technique but are still looking where to go. I would think that would be a very frustrating predicament.

When I was about twenty I left Australia for England. A friend of mine was doing fashion illustrations in London and making a lot of money. I thought that was a great idea. I had never done any illustration, but I put some drawings together, and got jobs at *The Observer* and *The Times* in London, doing fashion illustrations.

BLDD: How did you manage to get those jobs?

RS: I asked them the same question. I said, "Why me?" They had applications from about forty people a month from colleges and schools, but the reason they said they chose me over the others was because somehow I managed to convey the essence of the garment that I was illustrating. I was fortunate. From there I got involved in different areas of design and different forms of art. After all, technique is not in itself the whole of a design, its purpose or vision. Once the vision is clear, there is not much difference between designing a window and designing a chair and designing a concert or a symphony, and designing a garment.

BLDD: Do you really believe that?

RS: It's simple. It's logical. I think the true vocabulary of architecture and painting and music is the same. Of course, the difference lies in your focus, in where you place your attention. When you take a photograph, your attention is to light, and in clothes, to gravity. I never understood gravity until I designed clothes. When people say, "You've only been designing clothes for four years," I add that it's been over twenty years now that I've been a designer.

BLDD: Did you go to London intent on becoming a fashion designer?

RS: No, because I was never really interested in fashion. I intended to be a painter and sculptor. Of course, clothing is a movable sculpture. It's somebody wearing something with a certain shape and a certain color, and moving through space. And it's three-dimensional, and you can walk around the wearer or they can walk around you. This evokes discussion on the difference between cubism and futurism.

BLDD: And where do you place yourself on that spectrum?

RS: I think a combination of both. If you stand still and I walk around you, I might consider the experience to be cubist, because I see you from different angles. If, on the other hand, I remain stationary and you move around me very quickly, I think that maybe my experience could be considered futurist.

BLDD: Why don't you tell us how you finally wended your way from England to the United States and why you came here?

RS: Actually I never really had any desire to come to the United States. The opportunity came about when a multimedia arts company that was sponsored by the New York State Council on the Arts in Buffalo, N. Y. tried to create a cultural center. People like Lukas Foss were there, Allen Ginsberg, Leslie Fiedler, and a lot of other people. It was in the late '60's when I went up there. I was asked to be the artist-in-residence.

BLDD: How did this cultural center in Buffalo, New York, locate you, coming from Amsterdam to Australia to London, to become the multimedia

artist-in-residence for a dance company at a state university? Perhaps you could tie all those pieces together for us.

RS: The people heading the company were Christine Lawson, who came from the Martha Graham School, and her husband, Graham Smith, with the Royal Ballet in London, who was Australian. I had met him in Australia. From time to time I would do sets for amateur opera companies, or other theater productions, and I ended up doing something for the ballet company in Australia. So we kept in touch, they followed what I was doing and I followed what they were doing. It seemed appropriate to go into theater because I very much enjoy the opportunity for total design. As I said, I believe that one kind of design overlaps with another and, therefore, the rules are often the same, and you should be capable of going from one medium to another. They also believed that. So they asked me if I would come to the United States and work on something in Buffalo. It was an exciting learning experience, but very depressing, because due in part to the weather, Buffalo is not a very cheerful place.

BLDD: Did you ever study any of the disciplines you've mentioned in a formal or organized way?

RS: No. I never had time. Obviously I would have liked to learn techniques. It certainly helps. It's very important. It's nice to know how to mix paints when you want to be a painter or to know how to sew or to draft up plans. But I don't think it's essential. If you really understand the purpose of your input, your energy, and what it's going to lead to, then you can find a means.

BLDD: Do you think your work would be different if you had some formal training and education?

RS: Probably. I probably would take fewer risks. I might question less, because I might already feel I know the answers. And the questioning, of course, sets up a whole stream of thought-provoking possibilities, because once you start questioning, it can lead you to all sorts of results that you might otherwise not experience. If you take things for granted, which you do when you have knowledge—of course wisdom is something else—but when you have knowledge, it's concrete information which you don't really feel you have to question. In my case I didn't know, so I had to question.

BLDD: In Buffalo, you were designing costumes and sets and posters for the stage and dance. You referred to them as illusions. What does that mean?

RS: Clothes, of course, I see as a valid, important form of design. I would not have started designing clothes if I hadn't thought that they could also be accepted as art, as valid design. In the theater, we were dealing with illusions, and I was not then interested in the structure. I was not interested in the cut of a costume. I was interested in creating an impression. It's therefore a very different state of mind, because it fulfilled a different need and was going toward a different end result.

BLDD: Were the designs that you created mostly for dance?

RS: No, they were also for film, drama, music. At the beginning, people in Buffalo were doing Robert Wilson–type presentations. The opera, the concert, was done not only from a sound point of view, but from a static dynamic point of view.

BLDD: Won't you describe for a moment what that kind of presentation is like?

RS: An opera is a marriage of arts, it's singing, it's music, it's acting and dancing, it's the costumes and it's the sets. It's very easy for one of these disciplines to take precedence over the others, and quite often in traditional opera the singing was the important art form while the choreography, the sets and costumes were horrible dug-up things. Or if they weren't, they were designed to give an impression of the mood.

BLDD: So what was your innovation?

RS: Well, to begin with, I felt, like Bob Wilson, that if you present a production that involves more than one medium, all of it should be equally good. For Mr. Wilson, who put on an opera called "Einstein on the Beach," the visual aesthetics were very exciting, equally as beautiful as Philip Glass's music, and that provided me with an insight into how all the arts could be a marriage within a performance.

BLDD: It also provided you with a role model for the presentation of your own fashions, currently your fashion shows are different from almost every

Shamask, spring/summer, 1981

other designer's. There's no disco beat at your shows. Why don't you describe your own theatre—what you present at your fashion shows? What's the mood, what's the tempo, what does it look like and what does it sound like? What is the marriage of fashion and the other arts that you create?

RS: It goes back to the very first fashion show that I did. It was a very small collection of fifteen pieces, and it was done in a showroom, and if you have fifteen pieces and six models, you'd better have people walk slowly, very slowly, so that it lasts longer! However, it worked for me, because it gave people the opportunity to see every seam, every detail. In fact, it demanded it. I believe that if you remove applied decoration and remove anything like jewelry, and have no bouffant hair-dos, people can indeed become beautiful sculptures. I like the thought of presenting them as a living mobile. And I choreographed it in such a way that although nothing happened it was exciting. It was not about the action, but about balance and proportion—like the clothes. You had to focus, and you had to learn to think and learn to see. If you realize that the fashion press and the buyers spend two weeks in Milan, two weeks in Paris, and then England, and they come here for two weeks, they see a lot of people and a lot of theatre and a lot of drama, all condensed into a short space of time. They're absolutely bombarded by it. I allow people to become bored. Once people are bored, of course, their defenses are down. And when their defenses are down, it is easier to look and really see. And when you start seeing, you notice what I'm trying to do. That was the purpose of the slow-walking models, the richer choreography. Through the mobile I was creating, I wanted people to see structure and to see my kind of detailing. If you present something that's conspicuous, like I said, with camouflage, it's much harder to ask people to notice something subtle, that has to be pointed out. It has both its pros and cons, of course. In doing a slow fashion show, I was able to make people aware of it.

BLDD: It sounds, though, like the very opposite of costume design. Of necessity, nothing can be truly subtle in a costume for the stage. How did you translate that experience to your current one?

RS: I think there are very many forms of theater, and in some subtle ways life is a theater. It's a ceremony. And clothes are ceremonial. Theatre is considered dramatic, but when you look to the Kabuki or the Noh Theatre in Japan, it is an exercise in subtleties. So it depends on what point of view you take. I learned a lot from the Noh Theatre and I'm sure Mr. Bob Wilson did, too. There's an ability to create an excitement and drama *not* by excess. In fact, it becomes poetry. But their sense of poetry is different than ours, as we embellish and they take away.

BLDD: That may be the key to your own sense of fashion design: reduction rather than embellishment. Is that a fair description?

RS: Absolutely. I am often asked if I've ever been to Japan. Unfortunately, I haven't, but in a recent lecture that I gave, I showed a slide of Piet Mondrian, my countryman, that overlapped, was almost identical, with a slide of a detail of the Katsura Palace, that was built in the sixteenth century in Kyoto. These two structures—one a building and one a painting—came from totally different parts of the world and yet they had something in common. A complex simplicity was used to convey a message or a mood in an elegant manner, and to create a structure for living. It was an attitude that they had in common.

BLDD: You not only left school at the age of fifteen, you left home, as well. To what role model did you look? Who, or what, gave you the notion to work the way you do?

RS: It wasn't people, it was discontent that inspired me to look and to question and to find out if there would be a better way. Certain abstract end results were more important as role models for me than people.

BLDD: You once said that you were raised to believe that nothing was possible, and now you are a triumph of optimism and success. Whatever sustained you in this young life of yours to dare to try?

RS: As I said, I was discontented, and yes, in Holland I was taught that nothing was possible. The society was intimidating. You were restricted. In Australia everything was possible. The reason, I think, is that Holland, like any European country, has an obligation to history, and history, of course, can be very intimidating. Australia, like America, has a history that's very short, so the obligations are not felt as much. Australia really taught me that everything is possible.

BLDD: I hope America confirmed that view.

RS: Somewhere along the road, there's a balance between the views of Europe and America and Australia.

BLDD: How and when did you come from Buffalo to New York City?

RS: I moved to New York, permanently, in 1972. While I was in Buffalo, I would do anything to get here. I came to New York City every other weekend, I think.

BLDD: How did you manage that? How could you afford to do that?

RS: I would fly, go by bus, hitchhike, whatever was possible. In 1972, I decided that I really should be in New York. When I first got here I thought, "Well, I was successful in Buffalo. Now all I have to do is sit back and opportunities will arise and I will find work." Of course that didn't happen.

BLDD: What did you intend to do when you came here?

RS: I did not know. Maybe that was one of the problems.

BLDD: Well, there you were, waiting for opportunity to knock—and it didn't. What did you do?

RS: I took any kind of work that was offered to me. In other words, I would do interior architecture or fabric design, I would design sweaters, I would design folding screens, or a bathtub.

BLDD: How did you get these jobs?

RS: People knew what I was doing, and once you have one job, it leads to others. Then I had a private client who after I had designed a house interior, requested that I design a fur coat, which I did. And after she had a fur coat, she needed a dress to go with it.

BLDD: What was the fur coat like?

RS: It was chinchilla and knit. I never really liked chinchilla very much, but it was a request of my client, and I believe that, when you have a framework for your work, although you might not like it, you can turn it into an asset. I did not really like chinchilla. However, I thought it would be a very exciting challenge to make it work. I designed a coat that was a combination of both knit and fur. It was done in such a way that the end result was like a puzzle. And when it was brought together, at Maximillian furriers, Madame Potok put it together with me. That was my first involvement in clothes. I saw Mr. Charles James' clothes and I realized again that fashion could be an important form of design and not necessarily have anything to do with trends or fads, and that interested me. And I thought I would like to do that.

BLDD: So that when you first came to New York, you did not have the intention of being a fashion designer?

RS: No. I had no idea what I was going to do. I thought I might paint or sculpt or something like that.

BLDD: That's a lingering thought with you. Does the idea still persist?

RS: To a certain extent, except I'm having such a good time.

BLDD: You said the coat design led to a dress. What did you do then?

RS: I did a muslin collection of about fifteen to twenty pieces. I presented the collection to some press and buyers. Noni Moore was the fashion editor of *Mademoiselle* at the time—and a very good friend of mine—so she came to look at it.

BLDD: You've described a collage of activities from the design of interiors to the design of fabrics. When you finally decided to go into business on your own, how did you go about it?

RS: When you're involved in a project there are many ways of going about it, and opportunity can come in many forms, in many ways. I felt that I wanted to be in business with somebody I could relate to, in a relationship which would give me enough control as well as communication and respect for the other person. I wanted to create a working vehicle that would make it easy to get the end results necessary, in order to make a success. So, I tried to find people that would finance me, and many opportunities were available. I think the key is to find the right relationship and the right organization, whatever that means.

BLDD: You found a partner, sometime in the late 1970's, along about 1979. Can you tell us a little bit about that arrangement? Who does what, and who decides?

RS: It's a little complicated because we both do everything. My partner is Murray Moss and we are both concerned with every aspect of the company. He's as involved in design as I am in the business part of the company.

BLDD: Did he come to the company with a business background? Is that why you selected him as a partner?

RS: No. I'm not quite sure if I really selected him as much as he selected me. It was sort of an affinity. Murray was not interested in fashion. He was interested in design. We had that in common—we could be making chairs or cutlery. It just happened to be clothes.

BLDD: Why don't you tell us about the shop and showroom that this odd couple—odd for fashion, that is—opened on upper Madison Avenue in New York City? What does it look like, and who designed it?

RS: I designed it, and I designed it with a purpose. It had to be a shop/showroom and it had to exemplify the reasoning in my approach to fashion. It is in an old building, like a brownstone, and it's also unique in that it is on the top of a two-story building. I found that it had two skylights, and eight windows all around. I wanted to create a background that enhanced the clothes I was about to design. The place already had a point of view. It had charm. It had certain pleasing proportions. All I really had to do was elaborate on them, take advantage of them. I did this, and the end result is very minimal, but at the same time exciting, because of its detailing. There was one window on the south side and seven windows on the east side. The lines of the window created a grid pattern, which I then translated into a parquet floor. That pattern dictated the placement of the dressing room, the mirror, and other structures. So suddenly there was harmony in the shop. You don't necessarily know why there's harmony when you see it, but it is well calculated. It also shows one principle of design, that any form of art should look as if it just happened. You should never see the problems and the struggles involved. I hoped that this environment would give a pleasing background for the clothes.

BLDD: You referred before to your interest in Japanese design, and we talked about your minimalist, non-embellished approach to your work. I've often wondered if the kimono was a particular source of inspiration to you.

RS: I think it's probably a source of inspiration to most people who are interested in design, architecture, or art, because it is unique in being a one-size-fits-all garment. It is an absolutely perfect design as it allows flexibility for height and different sizes. It's fascinating to see the amount of variations that are possible within one pared-down design. There are different moods, different attitudes, that can be conveyed through the same design. So yes, it's a very educational garment.

BLDD: You've lived in many places, done many things. I wonder, because of all the time that you spent out of this country, if you consider yourself an American designer.

RS: I consider myself a designer. I think America or Europe doesn't count very much as far as a label is concerned. It used to. It was very important to be known to be either French, Italian, Japanese or American, so that the designs could be marketed as such. Now there are ways of designing that do not necessarily reflect the country of origin. The public is aware of it and so are the stores. So therefore, Gianfranco Ferré, from Milan, or Armani, or Issey Miyake, or myself could be found in the same area in the store.

BLDD: Do you find your clothes particularly sympathetic with those designers? What is the common thread that binds your work to that of Miyake and Ferré and Armani?

RS: I believe Miyake's designs are based on function and logic. They look beautiful because they are perceived as perfect designs. The better garments clearly magnify the thought, hence design, behind the structural choices by the designer. I think that's probably what we have in common. He has different values and different techniques, and so does Gianfranco Ferré, but that's what is overriding. We're all searching and finding a reason for something. I keep trying to find the difference between design, and styling. I keep talking about art and truth. To elaborate on that a little bit, the Oxford Dictionary explains high art as truth with beauty as a by-product, and low art as beauty with truth as a by-product. Of course, styling is something that has neither of those attributes. Style just aims to please. Any form of art caresses the senses. I am in awe of someone like the Mexican architect Luis Barragan, or the Spanish painter Zurbaran, because that is precisely what they set out to do, and they are successful at it.

BLDD: Do you think that this country produces stylists or designers?

RS: With exceptions, probably stylists. I'm not putting down the stylists. I think it's a whole industry. I don't know much about it, but I know, for instance, that someone like Calvin Klein is brilliant at it, and I admire him for it. It's an area that's very large, it's the biggest part of our industry. He's exceptional because he is very good. That area is more attractive to people than designing because it is more accessible.

BLDD: And who are the exceptions to the stylists that you made reference to? Who would you call a designer, yourself excluded, of course?

RS: I'm sure there are a lot of designers who are never exposed or accepted, who are doing it without getting recognition or funds. I find it very, very hard to name anybody in the United States.

BLDD: On an international level?

RS: Certainly, as I said before, Miyake, Ferré, and probably Armani. I haven't quite decided on that yet.

BLDD: And no one French?

RS: I think Yves St. Laurent, of course.

BLDD: Is he a designer or a stylist?

RS: Probably both. I think he made a great marriage between those two elements. He also is capable of creating a marriage between the commercialism of the industry and the idealism of art and beauty. He's an exception.

BLDD: Sometimes I think about the perfection of your clothes in terms of their design and their execution, and, as you become more celebrated and your clothes more sought-after, I wonder how *you* will be able to make the marriage between design and commercialism? Is that something that you consider? Does such a prospect please you or trouble you?

RS: I think it's going to be easier. When you design a coat and can only produce five copies of it because you have one tailor in the workroom, every coat probably looks different. When you make five hundred of one item it means that you have to create a technique and a discipline to make sure that all of them are the same. It's no longer open to the interpretation and consistency of the tailor. It is an end result created through a different art, other techniques. And so the end results are better. No emotions are involved. It has to be done almost automatically. Another element is that when you produce more of something, you can sell it for less money and reach more people, and therefore get more pleasure out of it.

BLDD: Is that something you'd like to do?

RS: Very much so. If you deliberately set out to make a cheaper product, it doesn't necessarily have to be "cheaper" in the end result, "cheaper" in the sense that it's badly made. It just means a different thing, a whole different approach that is equally as valid. I find it an exciting challenge.

BLDD: In spite of the fact that you had some difficulty in naming a French designer, it's commonly agreed, at least historically, that the French have produced first-rate designers. Why do you think that's the case?

RS: The French have a love for anything that is frivolous, and fashion, of course, is, and was, considered a frivolous form of art. They made it into an important form, and that's why the French have become so important.

BLDD: Without any formal education in fashion, you've managed to create a very unusual design technique. Tell us about the innovative method that you've developed.

RS: Because I did not know anything about fashion, I asked a close friend of mine, the designer Betsey Johnson, "What do you do?" And she said, "To design and make clothes is like baking a cake. First you buy all the ingredients." She said, "Buy your pins and your muslin." When you have these things, the question is then what do you do? I had absolutely no idea, so I tried to use the means that I had from the past. I knew how to do a blueprint and I knew how to do drawings to scale. At first I thought, "Well, what I'll do is hire the best pattern maker that is available." Of course, they're all already employed and very highly paid and traditionally trained. So in frustration I used the same method that I'd used for architecture to draw clothes. I would do life-sized blueprints, which were very rigid, with every detail in them like maps. That's all very well, and helps you to see what you want to attempt. But it's only a beginning, because when you work on the real fabric, or in muslin, you have to become totally spontaneous and allow the fabric to dictate to you what *it* wants to do. What

you do on the flat or in a drawing does not necessarily work in the fabric. If it does, it's affected by the differences between fabrics. Therefore, it's almost a two-tiered system. One aspect to draw in large scale and detail what you set out to do, and the other is to be totally spontaneous and improvise with the fabric.

BLDD: How do you use the blueprint?

RS: I translate it into muslin. I work from it. It gives me information. A drawing is only good in the way that it holds information. So a drawing becomes unnecessary when you have that information in the muslin. The muslin will give you more information than the drawing can because it's three-dimensional. You can walk around it and you can see it inside-out. Then the drawing becomes insignificant.

BLDD: Will you tell us something about the spiral seam which you seem to have invented, and that you use on so many of your designs?

RS: A spiral seam was based on the peel of an orange or lemon. I wanted to design a coat that, at first glance, was a basic shape that was pleasing and flattering. However, I also wanted to place the seams in such a way that they fall around the body in a beautiful manner, and that they became decorative. A side seam and an underarm seam and a shoulder seam, is a good solution to a problem. It's the most obvious one and it's the one that's used all the time. What I wanted to do was to find another way of constructing and come to the same end result, and allow that seam to become a completely decorative aspect. In fact, to become the design itself. So, I made a muslin that just had side seams and shoulder seams, and with a pencil I wound around the body, and then I tried to make it flat. Of course, it doesn't always work. In this case, after several trials it worked. The sleeve would fall forward—the lemon peel would wind forward on this arm and wind backwards on that arm and somehow met in the middle.

BLDD: Was that a good idea?

RS: It was a bad idea, because after I had the basic coat, which had side seams, and even though it hemmed beautifully and was perfectly balanced, when I started cutting it up and playing with grains, it became unbalanced. So, I had to make several attempts. In the end I thought, "Well, if the cut and proportion is what I'm about, and if the seams *are* decorative, I don't want to have to talk about it. It would be very nice for people to find out for themselves." So we inserted a contrasting color into the seams, so that you could see this spiral going about the body. We called the open seams "shimmer" seams, and they are very subtle, which I found was necessary. I didn't want it to be conspicuous. It became an important cut only because it embodied the reasoning and the logic behind a lot of my designs. It also creates mystery. Everyone who would have the coat would know that something special is going on. It's a little bit like having a black Japanese box—and knowing that inside is a lacquer scene in gold that's very special. Of course, there's no reason to have the seam doing what it does except that it is a different way of creating a structure. It's a different way of seeing truth and, of course, it's unexpected. And anything unexpected creates emotion.

BLDD: Obviously you are a very thoughtful fellow, and the design of clothing is for you a vehicle to do many other things. In fact, you've said that you only spend 5% of your time designing. Would you tell us what you do the other 95% of the time?

RS: Worry. I have a very small company and when you have very few people involved in a company you end up doing a lot of things yourself. Even if you do have a large staff, you still have to oversee and manage. I am involved in the marketing, the advertising, the promotion, the production. Production, for instance, takes a long time. After the garment is finished, we start from scratch. We start all over again draping it and developing it on a so-called "perfect" size 8 model. That's time-consuming. Also, there is choosing fabrics, traveling. It's important to go to places where the clothes are sold in order to reach the public and communicate and learn what their lifestyle is and what the social structure is.

BLDD: One of the things I imagine you don't spend a great deal of time on is the selection of color. You only use a few. Why have you decided to restrict your palette?

RS: I seem to always use primary colors.

BLDD: But not all the primary colors.

RS: Some are more flattering than others: red, black, white, blue. When you have a small collection there's only so much that you can do. I use basic fabrics that have very little personality, that allow the design to speak for itself. Therefore, prints are very difficult for me. All I really need in order to bring the garment to completion is a fabric that is basic and that has a color that is flattering, and I think you can find that in primary colors. People like the Mexican architect I talked about, Luis Barragan, have shown repeatedly that primary colors can be very, very exciting. He has been an inspiration in that regard. Sometimes I would like to use other colors, but I think the design would probably have to change to balance that.

BLDD: What other colors would you use?

RS: Grey. I'm being facetious. I would use colors that are subtle mixtures. In order to do that, I think the designs would have to be more subtle also.

BLDD: Are you considering altering the designs?

RS: No, it's not that. With my discipline and technique a lot of variations are possible, and what I'm doing now is just one area, one part of it. I look forward to using the technique and finding other things to do with it.

BLDD: You said that you travel around the country to get a better idea of what your customers are like and what their lifestyles are like. Are there regional differences in taste? Do your clothes sell as well, for example, in Des Moines and Dallas as they do in New York or in Newport?

RS: I think taste is affected to a certain extent by your surroundings and climate. What we wear here in New York has to do with the way we live, and with the weather. In Dallas, of course, it's very different. People don't walk. They take cars. They never behave as a New Yorker would.

BLDD: Are you talking now about taste or good taste?

RS: I'm talking about taste, I think. Good taste is relative.

BLDD: What is good taste, while we're on the subject?

RS: I think there's even good taste in kitsch.

BLDD: That's a familiar view, but how do you justify it?

RS: I can't, but I believe there has to be. Of course taste is extremely personal.

BLDD: What's good taste to *you?*

RS: Good taste is based on harmony, on knowing what to do under certain circumstances, not to offend the senses. That's good taste.

BLDD: Have you ever considered the possibility of designing clothes for men?

RS: Oh, yes. At first I never really thought that I would like the idea, but now I think it could be very, very exciting.

BLDD: Are you planning such a line now?

RS: Not at the moment, but the possibility is there. One of the reasons that I'd like to design menswear is that when I design women's clothes I can only do it from an intellectual and aesthetic point of view. When I design men's clothes, I should be able to do it also from an emotional point of view, because when you put on a garment you're affected by it emotionally. And, of course, designing women's clothes is very difficult for me, in that sense.

BLDD: Do you think you or any other male designers can bring anything special to designing clothes for women? Is there a special insight you think that you have?

RS: Maybe subconsciously. I don't know. I have an uncluttered attitude that I think may be more conducive to menswear. It seems that way.

BLDD: You talk a great deal about aesthetics, so it's little wonder that in the short time that you have been a designer you have already been the subject of a museum retrospective. You have been included in a museum exhibition at the Massachusetts Institute of Technology, an exhibition on "Intimate Architecture," which referred, of course, to contemporary clothing design, and another one which was a retrospective of your brief career. Did you ever expect your work to receive the kind of attention that it has?

RS: I didn't really think about it. To succeed it was necessary, of course, to get attention. One of the reasons my designs did get attention was that there's nothing more shocking than simplicity. If you go to a cocktail party and everybody's wearing Roccoco, the best way to stand out is to wear something very simple. I think there's so much Roccoco around that I became conspicuous by doing very little.

BLDD: That very little has caused a great reaction in the press. In fact, criticism about your work appears nearly as frequently in design and art journals as in the fashion press. What do you think this says about the current state of fashion vis-à-vis the other arts?

RS: I think fashion goes through many, many changes, and, through history, of course, many artists get involved in fashion. People like Popova, one of the Russian constructivists, would design clothes because they felt that the only true function of art was designing for the masses. It was always accepted as a form of art, and then it moved away and the Bauhaus picked up on it. On the other hand, it's frowned upon as an important art. Now people are interested in making investments in clothes because of the economy. It would be very nice if you could not only make an investment in a house or a set of cutlery, but also in clothes, that your wardrobe would not be a waste of money but, in fact, an investment of your money.

BLDD: Is fashion an art or a business or something else entirely?

RS: As with most forms of art, it's both. It's a marriage between business and art. A philharmonic orchestra cannot perform unless it's a business and, of course, fashion is more conspicuous as a business.

BLDD: Did you ever expect your life to unfold the way it has?

RS: Yes and no. Yes, because I care about designing. I am a very visual person. And so in that way I knew I would be doing *something*. I did not know I would be doing *this*. It's probably the last thing that I thought I would be doing.

PT

Pauline Trigère

For nearly forty years, Pauline Trigère has been known as Seventh Avenue's designer and tailor *par excellence.* Her dress and coat designs, both functional and elegant, are intended for years of use.

BLDD: As a child, you spent a lot of time in your father's shop in Paris. Did observing his work affect your choice of career?

PT: Actually not. In Paris we had the factory and the apartment in the same building. When I came back from school my work was to pick up pins on the floor. So I did that, but actually, I wanted to be a surgeon. Not just a doctor, a surgeon. And Papa said, "Absolutely not! My daughter is not going to play with cadavers!" So I'm cutting dresses instead.

BLDD: What was *his* line of work?

PT: My father was a tailor, my mother was a dressmaker. So I really breathed the work. Sometimes it amuses and fascinates me that I am considered a critic or a teacher at Parsons, or at the Fashion Institute of Technology. I had no schooling for what I do now. My schooling was something I got entirely on my own. All my mistakes were my own, and they still are. It was a very hard learning process. Here we have fabulous schools where everybody learns something. I didn't have that. Instead I watched my mother cutting my dresses and my father cutting my coats. So I guess that was in my blood.

BLDD: You've said that you can still remember, and still sketch, the very first dress that you designed.

PT: Well, I can sketch nothing, if you really want to know the truth, because I'm not a sketcher. But I could make a little sketch of the very first dress I made for myself when I was thirteen years old. My mother got me the pieces of fabric and I cut it and I even sewed it. Now I hate to sew and don't want to take a needle in my hands. I cut more readily. I don't sketch. I only make little drawings at the concert or at the theatre. They really are like a notebook or like shorthand for a secretary. I put them on a piece of paper in a taxi when I go to work, and those little sketches are a reminder like notes you make at night of the telephone calls you have to do in the morning. It's a way of telling myself what I have to do. But I can't make a sketch that means anything to anyone else. I cut directly on the live model.

BLDD: What did that first dress look like?

PT: It was a plaid taffeta in red, blue, and green with little pleats at the bottom, and three little organdy collars. I was practically as tall as I am now, and fatter. I went to my first dance in that.

BLDD: At that time did you harbor any notion of becoming a fashion designer?

PT: No. I didn't. I really wanted to be a surgeon. And then when my father said no, I said, "Fine, I'm going to go on the stage." Well, that didn't succeed either. I couldn't sing. Maybe I could act a little.

BLDD: I suspect you could.

PT: Maybe. Anyway, I act all day long now for all the people that work with me.

BLDD: Have you ever regretted that you have not had any formal training as a designer?

PT: No, I don't think so. I've always said that I would have liked to have one week, one month, or even an hour working with Balenciaga or with Madame Lanvin. I regret I didn't have that kind of learning, seeing what people do on the spot. I'm a very visual person. For instance, when I cook, which is quite often—I have a collection of cookbooks—I read the recipe and then I close the book and do what I want. I am completely, absolutely incapable of using exactly the specified amount of salt and pepper. I read and I do what I want. But I'm perfectly capable of reproducing a dish my way. The same thing is true in my work. I regret not sketching. If I had been a sketcher, I would make sketches and give them to my slaves and they would come back with something. Since I don't do that, I have to cut the fabric directly myself, and that's a tremendous amount of work.

BLDD: How do you think your designs would have been affected if you had had the kind of apprenticeship that you refer to?

PT: I don't think it would have affected me, because what I've got within me is still with me, respect for extremely good quality. I'm not a frilly person. I don't think that I would have done clothes other than those I do now. I would probably have had an easier time starting. When I came to America I was a little housewife, with two small children, and a husband who really didn't want his wife to work. He didn't like the competition. That's why I am not married to him anymore. He was a European husband, I suppose. And America fascinated me the first time I put my foot in New York City on the 6th of January, 1937.

BLDD: Under what circumstances did you leave Paris and come to New York?

PT: There was a little man named "Hitler" on the horizon. That was the only reason I left my home. We had a wonderful life. My education, everything, was French. I was born in Paris, right in the Place Pigalle. There was no reason for me to leave except my husband's vision. We all thank him for that. We came here en route to Chile, with no money, intending to stay for six weeks, and here I am nearly fifty years later!

BLDD: What did you decide to do once you arrived, and what made you stay once you were here?

PT: We took the double decker bus from 57th Street all the way down to 34th Street. And we walked. It was very, very cold. To see New York we nearly froze to death—my brother, my husband and I. We did both sides of Fifth Avenue: Russeks, B. Altman, all of those stores. Everything was terribly expensive. Then I came to Saks Fifth Avenue, which was like it is today except the displays were even higher than they are now, and on that freezing cold day, what do I see? Naked ladies with bathing suits and a big "sun" in the back. I said, "These people are crazy, or I am." I didn't know about Florida. I didn't know there was what we call a resort collection. I said to myself, "This is fascinating." Then we walked to 57th Street and here was Stein & Blaine, Patrick Hermann, Tappé, Henri Bendel. I was overcome! We went to Detroit to see some family we had there, before going to Chile. After that I said, "I'm not going; I'm staying right here." And I did.

BLDD: And how did you begin this business, as a housewife with two children? What was that first workroom like?

PT: I began as an assistant to Travis Benton at Hattie Carnegie. It was a tough job. I had never assisted anybody. I like to be the boss. I have had that in my blood since I was little. I worked with this man who gave me sketches of trains and floating panels. I had to find a way to make those clothes. I made the muslin. I learned a lot, because I had to do it. Miss Carnegie, with whom I eventually became good friends, used to say that she could not understand a woman designer. She never believed in them. She liked men designers. She had many. She had Jean Louis, Travis Benton, and, of course, the great Norman Norell, and she had Bruno. There were no women designers with Hattie Carnegie. And that was the reason I didn't work with her. I left December, 1941, after Pearl Harbor. Hattie Carnegie said she was closing everything. After making $65 a week, I was in the street with no job. It wasn't much money, but it *was* $65 a week.

So there was nothing to do. I went to see two or three friends of mine. They lent me some pieces of fabric. And I made eleven dresses.

BLDD: Where did this all take place?

PT: In the workroom of Hattie Carnegie, who by that time decided she was also closing that little office. It was a small workroom at 18 East 56th Street. I said, "Miss Carnegie, since you're closing everything. Would you please let me use the back room? I'll pay the rent." She agreed. I paid her $50 a month, half of the rent. I stayed there January and February, and in March, 1942, somebody came into the place I was occupying and asked, "Who is Pauline?" I said, "I am." He told me, "We're closing so you have to just pack up."

So I took over this little office of Hattie Carnegie, and had to pay double the rent. You know what it is to pay $50 and then all of a sudden you pay double? But I took over the lease, and that's how I started.

BLDD: Among other things there was heat and fuel rationing.

PT: There was no janitor and everybody disappeared because it was wartime. And there were no pins, nothing. At five o'clock they stopped the heat. I remember wrapping my feet in newspaper to keep warm. And *I* cut my first hundred dresses. It's fun to remember.

Anyway, I worked late, and we got somebody to come at night to help me. They worked on Seventh Avenue until five o'clock, and then from six to eight they worked with me. Also Saturdays and Sundays. Today nobody wants to work. Then I worked very hard and very long hours.

BLDD: What gave you the strength and the drive to go on?

PT: I had to eat. It was as simple as that. It wasn't a drive to become a great designer. I didn't know my capacity. But I had two small children and a mother, and we all had to eat. I had to produce something to pay the rent. Today, the students that I have in classes, only want to design. I suppose they want to go to La Grenouille for lunch or "21" for dinner and have their name in the papers. It wasn't like that for me at all. Everybody asks "Why did you do it?" Because I had to eat, and drink, too, a little bit. My brother and I really started the Trigère House in 1942. We moved from 56th Street to 57th Street, to a much, much bigger place. It was tough going, but here I am, so I guess it was all right.

BLDD: I notice that there are three turtles on your shoulder and at least one crawling up your leg. When and how did you come to choose the turtle as the Trigère signature?

PT: Actually it's not a Trigère signature. I had a friend in 1945 who was in the jewelry business, and he said, "Why don't you design something that will look impressive and doesn't require too much gold so that we can sell a thousand?" So I doodled, and I have the proof of it—it's now in the safe and going to go to the museum—this big turtle here, without the diamonds. We made this turtle, and it was all right, so we cast it, and then we made the baby and the baby's friend with the diamonds. We had the three turtles. In those days the turtle was selling for $39.95 in gold.

In 1949, I got my first Coty Award. My brother, who was then my partner, gave me a Fabergé turtle. He brought me a little Fabergé sapphire turtle with diamonds, so then I had four turtles. Two years later I got another award, so he gave me another turtle by Fabergé. So I had five. That year, in '51 or '52, I was looking for a house in the country that I could afford. I saw a house with a muddy pond with snakes and mosquitoes and everything, but on the rock in the middle of that pond were three turtles sunning themselves. I said to my brother, "If I buy that house I'm going to call it *La Tortue*, which means "turtle" in French. I bought the house, and the mail used to be addressed to Madame La Tortue. Today I've got 972 turtles. The turtles become a *scary* thing.

BLDD: What has the turtle come to symbolize for you?

PT: In Japan and in China the turtle is a god-like animal. First of all, the shell of a turtle has thirteen divisions. My scarves all have thirteen divisions. In France, when a boy courts a girl, he sends her a charm with a number 13 on it. Here, the number 13 is bad because of the "Last Supper," and you can't invite 13 people for dinner, and things like this. But in the Orient the turtle is revered. It signifies longevity, sturdiness, happiness. When I went to Japan I bought all kinds of things with turtles. They have embroidered turtles on pillows to carry the baby to the grandparents. It's like the good fairy, that brings the baby happiness, sturdiness, and the rest.

BLDD: Your son, Jean Pierre Radley, is now your business partner. He is president of the company.

PT: He made me chairman of the board.

BLDD: What does that mean?

PT: I don't know. It's exactly the same setup as before but I made him president, so I had to become somebody.

BLDD: How does that mother/son collaboration work out?

PT: It's difficult, from every point of view. We love each other very much, but I'm terrible and so is he. It's all right.

BLDD: But other than the obvious, there must be some special benefits, and some special limitations, of such an unusual business partnership.

PT: It's really not a partnership. I am sole owner of my business. Jean Pierre is president of the company, but he's also an employee. Right now I don't think that I want any partner. But he runs the company. He runs the offices, does the finances and the paperwork. I know a little bit about it, but I don't bother with that. I guess if there was someone other than my son in that position, I might have a little more patience, and he with me, too.

BLDD: In 1942 you established the Trigère firm, and by 1945 the name was already becoming quite well known in the New York fashion world. How did that happen so quickly? To what do you attribute the immediate success of the designs you began to produce?

PT: I believed in what I was doing, and made a certain type of clothes. I

Pauline Trigère, fall, 1954

wasn't doing what everybody else did. I made a very classical, tailored, well-cut dress or coat. We still do. That enormous museum collection proves the longevity of Trigère. I made clothes of quality. I only trusted my good sense. I didn't want to be Miss Carnegie, nor Miss somebody else. I just wanted to do clothes I believed in. It proved to be the right direction. I always say that you are only as good as the next collection, never the last. Your customers come back for what they trust. Buyers don't come to Trigère to buy frills and ruffles. We don't do those. The customer comes to Trigère in search of what I do. We experiment with an awful lot of cuts. In my long career we've done big coats, small coats, fitted coats, reversible coats. I think that I know what works. I also think I have a certain advantage: I wear the clothes, I travel a lot, I'm not particularly careful. The clothes must perform for me. I have to be at ease with what I wear, and I think that the customer immediately feels the same way. I don't like to be cramped into anything. Even the bustle, every tight or strapless dress that I used to wear ten years ago has to let me dance. I shouldn't be worried that something will fall out. Wearing clothes has taught me a great deal.
BLDD: How did you get your clothes worn, or your name known, in those very first years?
PT: We had no money. My brother simply put the few dresses that we made in suitcases. There were no planes, no flying. We couldn't even afford the train to Chicago. So it meant going by bus first to Nan Duskin, in Philadelphia, and Hany Blum in Chicago, as well as to Polly in New York, and opening the suitcase in front of those buyers who were looking for something different. Taking out the dresses—we didn't even put them on hangers. Today, how can you ship without hangers? And one customer led to the other. My brother did that from New York to Philadelphia, to Detroit, to Chicago, to Cleveland, probably to Los Angeles, and back again. They just came back for more. I had to learn what a size 12 meant. I had to learn what a size 14 meant. I had none of that knowledge. I learned, and nobody did it for me, my dear. I did it.
BLDD: What was life like then on Seventh Avenue?
PT: It was horrible. I was on 57th Street, and changed location there twice. In 1952, the same year I bought my house, I moved to Seventh Avenue. In the beginning I thought I would never settle on Seventh Avenue.
BLDD: What did it symbolize to you?
PT: There was no fine restaurant. But it was a crazy attitude because Seventh Avenue is where it really happens. I love it today. But in those days it was beyond my imagination to even take the bus or subway to 40th Street. We couldn't afford the rent there until the loft that we now occupy became available. I told my brother that we couldn't afford to move. We couldn't even afford the dollar for the taxi. But we went, and I looked, and I said, "That's what I want." When I told Polly, one of my first customers on 58th Street, I was going to move, she said, "Don't do that. Go see my sister. She's the foremost horoscope reader. She's terrific. She only costs $25." I said, "Don't be ridiculous. I can't afford it." She said, "Go, you pay later." I went and saw this lady who read my chart and said, "You can't move, you can't do anything. It's going to be so black." I said, "Well, suppose I do it." Then she said, "You will know the difficulties that you will encounter, so you will be better prepared, and good luck to you."
BLDD: How close to the truth was she?
PT: Oh, very close. She told me that the first year we couldn't pay the rent. Please! We couldn't pay the telephone! It was awful.
BLDD: What made the business turn around? What made it come to life?
PT: I went to see Mr. Louis Adler, the landlord, when we couldn't pay the rent. He was in the blouse business years ago, and also responsible for 550 Seventh Avenue. I said, "Mr. Adler, I'm at your mercy; I can't pay the rent." He said, "So? For six months you don't pay the rent. Go and work." I was so overcome. We had two contractors who made a few suits for me on Seventh Avenue. One of their representatives, Louis Levine, said,, "Listen, you haven't paid the contractors." I said, "I know. We have no money." He said, "Go to the bank and they'll lend you some money." I said, "Just like that? We have a bank, Manufacturer's Trust Company on 57th." We were so intelligent, we had been on Seventh Avenue and 40th Street almost six months, and we still had our account at the bank on 57th Street.

He said, "Well, there is a bank just opened on the corner, and they are looking for customers." I said, "I don't understand that. A bank is looking . . ?" "Yes, the Chemical Bank on 39th Street and Seventh Avenue. I'll talk to the man." So he did and Mr. O'Hara came. He's been retired for many years, but he still sends me notes for my birthday and for Christmas. He came to see me—my brother was somewhere on a trip—and he looked at the place. It was freshly painted. He asked to see a statement. I said, "I was told not to give it to you because it's a very bad one." He says, "May I see it anyway?" So he did and then called me back and said, "Come and see us."
I will never forget the day; it was the 15th of August, 1952, and hot as blazes. I was dressed up in a little woolen dress and high heels. It was very hot when you cross the street. I thought I was never going to get across. They asked me all kinds of questions and I started to cry. The president of the bank said, "How much do you think you need to carry on?" I said, "I don't know—$40,000?" He says, "Oh, no, my dear, you couldn't do it for $40,000. You need at least $75,000 to start going. I said, "Really?" "Yes. We'll give you $65,000." That's the way it turned around. It was an extraordinary experience because they had trust in me. I was terribly sincere. Whatever I couldn't say, I didn't. They asked me a question, and I said I don't know. I didn't try to impress them with something that I knew I couldn't produce. So, they trusted me and it was truly enormous luck for me, to have the confidence of those two men at the Chemical Bank, who are still our bank today. Today they call me when we don't borrow enough. They say, "What's the matter, you don't want our money?" It took a long time.
BLDD: I suspect there are very few things that you do in an ordinary way. In fact, even your working day is described as completely unorthodox. What makes it so?
PT: I have no system, really. I am at the head of a business which I think has a very good name, but it's still a very small business. If I don't like the fit of a garment, I go into the factory and I correct it. If five pieces of goods arrive from Europe with a defect, I know about it. I wish I didn't have to. If a worker has a toothache and doesn't come in, I know about it. If somebody is having a baby, I know about it. It's not a big enough business for me to be completely detached. I plan to come in the morning and start my day quietly, nicely, and I arrive and—oops—something happens and I say I shouldn't have gotten up today. That happened yesterday. It was a terrible day.
BLDD: Was today a better day?
PT: It *was* a better day! Tomorrow is another day, like Vivien Leigh said. The only thing that I resent is the fact that at a certain date I have to produce a collection, and I have to have it finished. That, to me, is the worst. I don't like deadlines. But we have to have them. They come five times a year. But I will never be ready and I don't know how to be ready ahead of time. You start the collection with all the best intentions, with all the things that you want to do, you start a dress and maybe it's going to be good, maybe it's going to be bad, but you don't know. You think you're on the right track. So you make six dresses or six coats. But then they are no good. You start again. When all of a sudden something happens and everybody smiles and says, "That's it," then we go on and do more stuff.
BLDD: What's the design process like at Trigère? Do you have a hand in every aspect of design?
PT: Oh, yes. Otherwise it wouldn't be Trigère. My assistant and righthand person for so many years, Lucie Porges, and I do it together. But still, I can be wrong. Sometimes I like something that is not going to sell. You never know until it goes into the showroom and the buyer puts the seal of approval to it.
BLDD: One thing that you do know is which clothes really work. As you said before, they have to be "Pauline-proof" in order for you to understand them. You are known for your own sense of style in dressing. In fact, it's often been said that you epitomize the Trigère look.
PT: Well, that's nice. I hope so.
BLDD: How would you describe that look?
PT: That's a difficult question. You know, though I'm wearing red today, I also wear a lot of black. After a long experience I know what's good for me. I know what's going to be good if I'm traveling, for instance. Either I'm

going to have a very long V-neck or very high neck. I can remove a scarf at the neck and go out for cocktails.

BLDD: How do you define style?

PT: Style is something that you do yourself. Fashion is something people try to impose on you. Fashion is what the magazines print, or the newspapers try to say, and what women try to copy or capture. Style is something completely individual, something that's *you*. It's an old scarf, an old pin, an old coiffure. It's something that you have tried to develop. It's very hard to describe. Most women don't have it.

BLDD: How do you learn it?

PT: I have a little theory. If you go out at night for cocktails or whatever you do, and you have a good time, it may be because of your makeup, your coiffure. I ask everybody who says, "Oh, it was fabulous last night," what did you wear? Look at yourself. Did you have a blue dress, or a red dress, and was it fine? Don't try to fight it next week when you go buy another one. Buy the same type of dress. It's a very difficult thing. But it can be learned.

Also, I think that you should trust a salesperson. Try to go to the same store. The American woman is very difficult. For instance, in New York, a customer might go from 34th Street and up Fifth Avenue, shopping at all the stores. That may be a good way of doing it if you have a lot of time. But if you don't, I think it is very important to develop a rapport with a salesgirl, who can tell you, "No, Mrs. Smith, don't wear this. I have it in blue."

BLDD: What do you consider your greatest strength as a designer?

PT: I think we make intelligent clothes that are wearable. We don't make clothes to be photographed, or to look funny. We make clothes that make a woman comfortable, pretty.

BLDD: What is the price range of your clothes?

PT: We're not going to discuss that. It's like Channel 13—public television—telling you that if you send $35 it only costs you ten cents a day to belong to Channel 13. I would say the same thing about Trigère clothes: you're going to pay a thousand dollars for a dress and wear it for five years. Divided by so many days, it costs fifty cents a day. Quality merchandise is always much cheaper in the end. I pity people who haven't got much money. I always pity women who have to buy an inexpensive pair of shoes for their baby. It's like buying a piece of paper shoes. If you can afford better quality, I am sure that the money is well spent. We do respect the customer. If you don't like the style, that's fine. It's my problem, not yours. But the quality of the fabric, the lining, the way it's made, is the best I can give. That's what we offer at Trigère.

BLDD: What fabrics do you like to work with?

PT: All kinds of fabrics. If I want to drape something that I'm not sure about, I take leftover yardage. I drape with that. But, preferably, I take the fabric and cut directly. I need the girl's reflection in the mirror. I work here and the mirror is there, and I look at her in the mirror. I need the quiet of the evenings to do that, because the telephone may be a wonderful instrument but it's also the enemy of the people. During the day I'm on the phone a lot, but at night from five to seven I can design. It may not always come to life, but I can do four or five dresses in about a week. I cut and pin one-half of a garment, and then I give the rest to an assistant. Sometimes it comes back and I say, "Why in hell did I do that one?" I don't remember. It happens.

BLDD: What's most important to you in choosing a fabric and where do you go for the fabrics that you use ?

PT: I would say that eighty to ninety per cent of the fabrics that we buy are imported from France, Italy, England, Spain, Switzerland. I go to France at least once a year to look. But our suppliers are delighted to come and see us. So we see the collections one after the other. Sometimes they are boring. Sometimes people come with five cases, and when you see them coming you say, "Oh, my goodness, I'm going to be here for three hours." We make a selection and then I look at them on my stage. I am there with the model in the lights, and I see what the fabric does. Then we begin to buy. The amazing thing when Lucie and I buy is that when we buy a red or a blue, and maybe a print, all of a sudden as we work with them and eliminate, and the collection ends up all purple or all red or all blue. From one collection to the other, something different happens.

So, the people who come to us with fabrics are responsible for the

beginning of the collection. What makes the fabric important to me is the quality. It's got to be drapable, it's got to be something that I can touch with my fingers. I'm very tactile. I must feel it, and if it does something to my hands, I'll drape it. If it doesn't, I put it on the floor.

BLDD: You've been called the top coat designer in the industry. What is it about designing a coat that continues to intrigue and inspire you?

PT: It doesn't intrigue or inspire me. I just love to make coats. Right now I'm making a lot of coats for Abe Schrader. It's a fabulous line at fantastic prices. They retail from $350 to $600, and it's fantastic. So I make more coats now that I did before.

BLDD: What's important to look for in selecting a coat that will last, as well as look good?

PT: If you buy a Trigère coat, it will last. It lasts because we use good quality fabric and the best lining we can have for the price. The style is a different thing. Now what are you going to do with your coat? Are you going to wear that one coat when you're going on the subway in the morning and at lunch and at dinner? Then wear the coat in black. Or wear the coat in red and try to make your wardrobe again. Are you buying a coat to go over your blue dress of last year? It's a very tough question. But at the price of the Schrader line you can buy three coats.

BLDD: You say that your major concern is creating clothes not for magazines or photographers—not funny clothes, you called them—but designing clothes that wear well and clothes that sell. How do you make decisions as to what will sell?

PT: We don't make the decision. We try. When we start the collection we go in many directions: a fitted dress, a full dress, a jersey. We don't know. All of a sudden something happens that lets us know we know we are on the right track. We have a little rehearsal in the showroom with the sales people, and then they look and say, "Got no sleeves," or "It's too fitted." "That's not going to do." "This is too much." "That's going to be too expensive." But all of a sudden there is something everybody likes. Hallelujah! So we say this is what we should do again, and we do a little more of the same thing. We never know. And even when the collection is edited and we show 125 to 130 pieces the day of the show, we may produce only 90. Because the final factor is not only the buyer who is in our showroom, it's the consumer. The clothes have to sell in the stores. They cannot just be something in my head that's going to be on a hanger in a closet. Clothes have to be worn to mean something. When we ship we like to know that something is very good and is going to be reordered.

BLDD: What does sell best?

PT: That's an impossible question. You see, suppose you have a dress with beads that is priced at $2,500—we do, and we sell them—when we have sold twelve or twenty-five, it's a lot. If you have a less expensive woolen dress and don't sell 300 or 400, that's a disaster. But at Trigère we really don't cut that many garments. You won't see what we do coming and going. On the other hand, if Mr. Schrader doesn't have an order for 500 of one coat, it's out. We cut twenty or fifty garments one at a time. There is a difference in the marketing process of these things.

BLDD: Isn't it something of a paradox, if an old story, that the industry of designing clothes for women is generally populated by men?

PT: It may have been true here years ago, but not in France. The women here didn't have the courage, I suppose, to go and ask. I didn't ask; the money came to me. Maybe there is something that frightens a woman starting her own business. But we're changing all that. I never had to suffer because I was a woman. But I think many women wanted to mind their babies, their husband, their lovers. It takes enormous stamina to have a career and also something at home. I don't think it's easy for anyone. Nor is it easy for a man to come home at night and hear of his wife's problems. Nothing is easy. When you have children, a husband, a home and also the responsibility, it's tough. But women do it more and more.

BLDD: Did you ever consider designing clothes for men?

PT: I'd have to be asked but, I guess so. Why not?

BLDD: Many of your clients are well-known, celebrated, and distinguished. Does your relationship with these clients, ranging from Nancy Kissinger to Alice Tully, affect the designs themselves?

PT: No, no, no. No, because you see, we are not in the couture *per se* like in

France. For instance, let's take Nancy Kissinger or Mrs. Hugh Carey or Polly Bergen, all those women who are in the public eye. They come and see the collection and then they say, "Listen, Pauline, I want that dress. I don't want it in red, I want it in blue. And make the neck a little lower." That we will do. But we don't go and create something special for someone. It takes too much time, and is very costly. Anybody who tells you that they do, forget it, it's not true. But the couturier in France used to have that exchange—a man like Balenciaga, a woman like Lanvin, and probably it's true of St. Laurent, too. When you have someone like Zizi Jeanmaire, the dancer married to Roland Petit, she would say, "Yves, I would like to have this like this." It's wonderful for the designer. I get that interchange and feeling of doing something for my clients when I go on the road. When I do that, the collection is already made, naturally, but then I see a dress on a short little woman or a very tall person, and it teaches me an enormous lot.

BLDD: Is that one of the reasons that you go on the road? Is it part of your own education?

PT: It's not one of the reasons but it is a fantastic education. The rapport I might have with Mrs. So-and-so in Cleveland, or in Dallas, or in Houston, is tremendous for me, to see how she reacts to my clothing. Actually, we don't really work in a completely closed box, because as the clothes are being designed we see them on models. But it's fun to see them really worn.

BLDD: How do you feel when you come into a crowded room in a city where you've never been, and suddenly you see one, four, eight Trigères?

PT: I feel very good. Recently I went to Columbus, Ohio, and there were three women out of 200 at lunch who wore Trigères. One wore a coat that was fifteen year old, another in a suit said, "Look, I'm still wearing it." Maybe I would have been happier if they had bought one yesterday, but I was very glad to see them still wearing the clothes and happy with them.

BLDD: What American woman or women would you say have had the most impact on the course of American fashion during the last decade?

PT: Mrs. Onassis. When Jacqueline Kennedy was this young, attractive woman interested in clothes—she wasn't fancy—I think it was the first time that someone so high up was an example. Mrs. Roosevelt was fantastic, but you couldn't call her a stylish woman. Nor was Mrs. Truman. So Jackie Kennedy was the first First Lady people could look up to and emulate. And, of course, now we have Nancy Reagan. She's very thin and dresses a lot, and I think that's terrific. We don't have the Queen of England and maybe that's just as well.'

BLDD: We've talked about comfort and about style and about taste. What about glamour? How do you define that?

PT: Glamour is your makeup, your hair, your allure, your entrance into a room, or the way you carry yourself. You might wear a fifteen-year-old dress. You either have it or you don't.

BLDD: Can you learn that?

PT: When I first went to the opening night of the opera, when it was across from where I now have my office, at 40th Street and Seventh Avenue, it was glamorous. People dressed. Today, unfortunately, people don't care. They go to the theatre in jeans. There's nothing wrong with jeans or sweaters—they are fabulous. But I don't think they are right when you go to the theatre. You don't have to wear satin or even a bow tie, but I bemoan the fact that there are no first nights anymore where women look glamorous. When I go to a restaurant in Paris, there is no glamour there, either. The première is one thing that I would like to re-establish. At a première, it would be black ties, and everybody dressed up. I'd love that.

BLDD: With which of your designs have you been most pleased? Is there a special favorite among your designs?

PT: You can't have a favorite because fashion is fickle. If you were really in love with one design, you would probably stop working altogether. Fashion has to move and go on—sometimes in better directions, sometimes worse. But I am pleased when I do something that I will put in the museum, and say, "Well, this is something that I will look at with great pleasure ten years from now, if I'm still around."

BLDD: You recently were asked what you really wanted to be, and even though we know that you have a high sense of humor and that there's always an edge to what you say, your reply was that you wanted to be a courtesan.

200

It's an unusual aspiration, especially in this last fifth of the 20th century. What did you really mean?

PT: I didn't really mean that. I meant that I would have liked to be pampered. Isn't a courtesan pampered? Yes, she's taken care of. But I never was. Maybe that was in my mind. Being a courtesan is someone to whom people give things. I would have my wolfhound, my vodka, my carriage at the door, something like that. It was a dream. Like everybody else, I can always dream.

BLDD: Some years ago you went to France to receive a highly coveted award from the Mayor of Paris, La Medaille de Vermeil, that was awarded to you for a lifetime of achievement.

PT: It came from the city where I was born. A marvelous event for me. And I really was thrilled. It doesn't come that easy. I got the silver medal of the City of Paris in 1972. And in 1982, they gave me the highest decoration of the city. It's not the Legion D'Honneur, it's La Medaille de Vermeil de la Ville de Paris. It's a big medal, and I'm going to put a frame on it and wear it. What I wear now is part of the one that I got ten years ago—it's the "coat of arms" of the city of Paris. It was given to me at the Hotel de Ville, one of the most beautiful buildings in Paris. It is a fantastic, beautiful 1900 monument. It was lovely. It was presented by Mayor Chirac. And they gave us French champagne and French petits fours. It was beautiful.

BLDD: It's good to see the honor go where it is so deserved. But after all this time here, do you still think of yourself as being French?

PT: *No.* I think, accent and all, I'm terribly American, and I wouldn't live any other place but New York. This is my love, my life. This country has been given to me—well, I selected it—and I love it. I couldn't live in France anymore. I love to go there, I love to see my friends, I love to go to new restaurants and things like that, but it's another life and you cannot redo your life again and again. When we came here it was traumatic and very difficult. The children were small. They hated the milk, which was superb. I knew no English. None! Now I do the best I can with the accent. In France I hear beautiful French being spoken, and I can't do it anymore. But I don't like the French habit of turning off the electricity when they go out of the room. That's not for me anymore.

BLDD: What has been the greatest satisfaction in the course of your career?

PT: I was born the little girl of a tailor and a dressmaker. I didn't know anything. Now it's a great achievement and a great pleasure for me to go places and to be recognized, I like that. It came through an enormous amount of work. I have fabulous friends in all walks of life—in the arts, in the theatre, in the restaurant business. I'm very proud of my friends and the achievement that came to me because of my work. It didn't come because I courted those people. They come to my house, I go to them, and that's an enormous satisfaction. I came from nowhere, and being a little somebody today is wonderful.

BLDD: What's been the greatest frustration of your work?

PT: Not to be able to achieve what I want to get done in a day. That's the frustration of the everyday. It's also frustrating when there is a full moon and everybody including me has a temper. I would like to do more entertaining at my two homes but it's difficult to work late at night and then to start cooking or arranging the flowers. But I do my share of entertaining.

BLDD: You seem to have the time to do a great deal. And in a time when many designers' signatures can be found on anything from home furnishings to tableware to sheets, what are the products that bear the Trigère touch, the Trigère name?

PT: I have probably been too difficult with licensing. Many of my competitors have fabulous licensing and make an awful lot of money with it. But when I started with the license business, and the product came to me, I didn't like it, so there was friction immediately. Instead of going on, I said forget it. You have to be somewhat relaxed about the product you're going to get with your name. When I do the Trigère coat for Schrader, they're absolutely impeccable. And we do sports clothes now, and furs. We do a few ties. We don't do too much because it takes an awful lot of my time. I suppose I don't know how to delegate things. This is one of my great problems. If I could, I would tell people to go and do it. But I don't, so it's all on my head, and I'd rather go home and read a book.

BLDD: What haven't you done yet that you would someday like to try?

PT: I haven't been on Mt. Everest yet. I would like to go to the theatre more. I would like to travel more than I do. I would like to do my immediate future project which will happen in the next few weeks, I hope—my perennial garden, which is now in my head. I know nothing about perennial flowers, just as I knew nothing about flowers when I started gardening. This is my immediate project and I hope I'm going to succeed.

BLDD: What are you going to do?

PT: I have a garden that I've worked at a long time now. It's rather interesting and pretty. Not an English garden, because I don't think English flowers go as well in Connecticut as they do in London or in Sussex. I am buying every book I can and I'm looking at every color and size of the flowers. Suppose they come to thirty inches, sometimes they come thirty-six inches. That's the surprise. The fun will be to do it myself. The gardeners will help. But I'm going to decide where I'm going to have the delphinium, where the daisies will go, and I hope it is going to be all right.

BLDD: You said that one of your dreams is to build a house from scratch, and I guess you have it planned almost down to the square foot.

PT: Yes. It's a dream. But it's not going to happen because my little house is now 180 years old, and I'm just adding to it. The frustration and the aggravation is too much for me. The modern house that I want will never be built, unless I find somebody who buys me the land and gives me the money to build it. Then I'll do it. It won't happen. I love my house and I love the garden, and it's a big enough project for me. But I can tell you that if I build a house from scratch it would have two entrances: a front and a back and it will be a huge room with a kitchen in one corner, the living room and the dining room, and then, all around on a balcony, three bedrooms. Just one square thing. Very practical, very neat.

BLDD: Did you ever expect your life to unfold the way it has?

PT: I never even thought about it. I was never going to make my living as a designer. When I think of the things that I haven't done, for instance, spend a lot of time with my granddaughter. That's a joy that I would like to have for many years to come. I hope she's going to have fun with me because I'm having fun with her. I have only one and she's cute and pretty.

BLDD: Do you dress her?

PT: We did. But right now she's too difficult. My daughter-in-law is more difficult, unless she buys the clothes. We did some coats for her. She grows too fast. So I dress her doll. I think I am permitted to do that. She has the best Trigère-dressed doll in America. It would be fun to make special clothes for Karen, but it would be too costly. If I made a dress for Karen, the labor alone would cost $200. Now we buy three for that price, or more.

BLDD: If you had your life to do over again, is there anything that you would have done otherwise?

PT: I would have married a rich man.

BLDD: It's not too late for that!

PT: Oh, yes, it is. I'm too difficult. Much too difficult. I wish I was not so volatile, not so temperamental. Maybe I could make an effort and be different. But if I had to do my life all over again, what would I do? I just don't know. A bad day for me is when I say, "Gee, we haven't one good dress. There isn't one skirt, one sleeve that I like." But if one day I see something I think is a good dress, I'm very happy. Fundamentally I'm a happy person. I tell jokes in the middle of my greatest rage. At the end of the day if I feel that I've done something that may be fruitful for the firm, I'm happy.

Now why, w-h-y, is a thing that I tell people never to ask, because if you ask why, you're never going to get the right answer. Things happen, that's all.

PHOTOGRAPHY CREDITS

Richard Avedon: p. 196
Malcolm Batey: p. 29
Peter Davidian: pp. 145, 146
Edgar De Evia: p. 174 (top)
Jack Deutsch: pp. 14, 40, 42, 43, 44, 45
Michael Doster: p. 120
Sandi Fellman: pp. 104, 106–107
Peter Fink: p. 181
Charley Gerli: pp. 110, 112, 113, 115, 116
Jesse Gerstein: pp. 16, 60, 63, 64, 65, 66, 67
Loren Hammer: pp. 55, 56
Hiro: p. 178
Harlan Kayden: pp. 18, 25, 80, 82, 85, 87, 88, 89, 149, 150, 151, 186, 187
Cookie Kincaid: p. 190
Robert Kirk: p. 163
Erica Lennard: pp. 17, 74, 75, 76, 77
Gideon Lewin: pp. 26, 51, 53, 54, 57, 155, 156, 159, 160, 200, 202–203
Butch Martin: pp. 20–21
Mary McCulley: p. 27
Gordon Munro: pp. 48, 182, 183
Helen O'Hagen, Saks Fifth Avenue: p. 13
Stanley Papich: pp. 92, 95, 96, 97
Denis Petoe: p. 135 (home furnishings), 140–141
Ken Probst: pp. 28, 192–193
Richard Ruttledge: pp. 174 (bottom), 176
Saks Fifth Avenue: pp. 32, 35, 36, 37
Susan Schacter: pp. 100–101 (copyright 1985)
Pierre Schermann: pp. 23, 123, 125, 127, 128, 129
Sing Si Schwartz: pp. 22, 111, 117
Bruce Weber: pp. 24, 135 (fashion), 138, 139